Marked in Your Flesh

Marked in Your Flesh

Circumcision from Ancient Judea to Modern America

LEONARD B. GLICK

OXFORD
UNIVERSITY PRESS

2005

OXFORD
UNIVERSITY PRESS

Oxford University Press, Inc., publishes works that further
Oxford University's objective of excellence
in research, scholarship, and education.

Oxford   New York
Auckland   Cape Town   Dar es Salaam   Hong Kong   Karachi
Kuala Lumpur   Madrid   Melbourne   Mexico City   Nairobi
New Delhi   Shanghai   Taipei   Toronto

With offices in
Argentina   Austria   Brazil   Chile   Czech Republic   France   Greece
Guatemala   Hungary   Italy   Japan   Poland   Portugal   Singapore
South Korea   Switzerland   Thailand   Turkey   Ukraine   Vietnam

Copyright © 2005 by Oxford University Press, Inc.

Published by Oxford University Press, Inc.
198 Madison Avenue, New York, New York 10016

www.oup.com

Oxford is a registered trademark of Oxford University Press

Library of Congress Cataloging-in-Publication Data
Glick, Leonard B.
Marked in your flesh : circumcision from ancient Judea to modern America / Leonard B. Glick.
    p. cm.
Includes bibliographical references and index.
ISBN-13 978-0-19-531594-3

1. Circumcision—Religious aspects—Judaism.   2. Circumcision—History.   3. Judaism—
History—Medieval and early modern period, 425–1789   4. Judaism—Relations—Christianity.
5. Jewish physicians—Germany—History.   6. Medicine—United States—History.
7. Medicine—England—History.   I. Title.
BM705.G57 2005
296.4'422—dc22   2004020069

Printed in the United States of America
on acid-free paper

For Marilyn Fayre Milos

Preface

Several years ago, when I told Jewish family and friends that I was writing a book on circumcision, some responded with a mixture of puzzlement and rejection. What was there to write about? It was a simple snip that made the penis cleaner and prevented all kinds of diseases, even cancer. A few reacted with anger. Why would I want to stir up trouble over such a time-honored ceremony, they wanted to know. Wasn't a *bris* one of the most sacred Jewish customs? And wouldn't criticizing circumcision play into the hands of anti-semites?

Not everyone reacted along those lines, though. Others were not only interested but even eager to learn more; they admitted that they had always wondered why Jews had to perform such a disturbing ceremony. Yes, circumcision was supposed to ensure Jewish survival—but how, and why?

Although I'd like to claim that I had long asked such questions myself, the truth is that I had not. Until a few years ago, I took circumcision more or less for granted, like nearly everyone else. I never thought of it as an attractive practice, and although to the best of my recollection I have attended two ritual circumcisions, I tried not to see the surgery or even to think about it. I should add here that although my professional career has been as a cultural anthropologist and college professor, I have a medical degree and completed a general internship, in the course of which (again to the best of my recollection) I myself performed one circumcision.

To speak on an even more personal level, our own three sons were circumcised—not ritually but in hospitals soon after birth.

I accepted this without a second (or even a first) thought, assuming that it was not only medically advisable but appropriate for Jewish boys. Later, because their mother is not Jewish, all three underwent a ritual circumcision as part of a conversion. We took them to a Jewish urologist, who donned a skullcap, recited appropriate liturgy, and drew a few drops of blood from each juvenile foreskin remnant.

Those sons are now mature men. Had I known at their births what I know now, they would never have been circumcised. But as it happened, I did not begin serious study of circumcision until a few years ago, and only after becoming immersed in the research did I realize that my subliminal sense of unease was wholly justified. To my surprise, I learned that the United States is the only country in the world where well over half of all male infants are circumcised for nonreligious, supposedly medical reasons. Soon I came to understand much more: that the procedure has no medical value standing up to an elementary cost-benefit analysis; that removal of the foreskin destroys extremely sensitive genital tissue and diminishes normal sexual experience for both men and women; and that arbitrary reductive surgery on a nonconsenting person of *any* age violates that persons's fundamental right to physical integrity. With regard to Jewish circumcision in particular, I realized that the practice is rooted in anachronistic sexist ideology and, finally, that removing infant foreskins neither promotes anyone's later commitment to Judaism nor contributes to the enhancement of Jewish life in America.

Once I began to understand this, I felt that if I wrote honestly and forthrightly about what I had learned, most readers, Jewish or Gentile, would grant me a fair hearing and would decide for themselves whether they found my interpretations and conclusions credible. I've since come to realize that this may not be so; that, judging from what has already been published on this subject, I might be subjected to misrepresentation by some—physicians, rabbis, mohels, even scholars—with investment in seeing this practice continue. I accept that prospect (not with pleasure, to be sure) as the price one may pay for challenging an entrenched custom.

On the other side, though, are those treasured friends and colleagues with whom I share mutual support and enlightening exchange on matters historical, medical, legal, ethical, and practical. I belong to several organizations dedicated to ending all forms of genital injury to male and female children throughout the world. In this company, I think of myself as a scholarly activist, contributing my particular knowledge and perspective to the ongoing effort to educate people on why circumcision should be unacceptable in a society supportive of fundamental human rights. Since colleagues in these organizations have contributed immensely to my knowledge and sense of personal commitment, I want to cite and thank them here. First is the National Organization of Circumcision Information Resource Centers (NOCIRC), now a widely respected international organization, founded and directed by

Marilyn Fayre Milos; the book's dedication is a token of my admiration, affection, and gratitude. Thanks to the work of George Hill, NOCIRC maintains a website, CIRP.org, that is second to none as a source of thorough, dependable information on every aspect of the circumcision controversy; I recommend it to readers who want to learn far more than I can compress into these pages. Second is Doctors Opposing Circumcision (D.O.C.), founded and directed by Dr. George C. Denniston, a public health physician who has worked patiently to educate physicians and the public, not only on medical topics but also on the ethical issue raised when physicians perform circumcisions after having pledged to "first, do no harm." Finally, there is Attorneys for the Rights of the Child (ARC), founded and directed by J. Steven Svoboda, who has authored and coauthored some of the most thorough and penetrating articles on all aspects of circumcision, with particular insight into legal and ethical questions connected with nonessential surgery performed on nonconsenting persons. Among others to whom I owe special appreciation are Dan Bollinger, Norm Cohen, Rio Cruz, Amber Craig, Rob Darby, Paul Fleiss, John Geisheker, Ron Goldman, Frederick M. Hodges, David Llewellyn, Van Lewis, Martin Novoa, Hugh O'Donnell, Mark Reiss, Steve Scott, Jim Snyder, Dan Strandjord, Robert Van Howe, Hugh Young, and Avshalom Zoossmann-Diskin. Frederick Hodges, Rob Darby, Steven Svoboda, and Marilyn Milos provided invaluable critical readings of parts of the manuscript. I thank also my many other activist colleagues; all have contributed in various ways to my education.

I owe thanks to many others who have contributed their special skills and knowledge. John Koster, Anne Spier-Mazor, and Neil Zagorin provided essential translation assistance. Members of the Hampshire College Library staff—Stephanie W. Brown, Gai Carpenter, Susan Dayall, Christine Ingraham, Isaac Lipfert, Kelly Phelan, Dan Schnurr, Helaine Selin, Serena Smith, and Bonnie Vigeland—were always there to answer innumerable requests for assistance and for interlibrary loans. Noah Glick shepherded us through the maze of manuscript preparation. Matthew Bauer, Gail Glick, and Marian Glick-Bauer alerted me to the latest news and brought me up to date on popular culture. Stuart Jaffee and Sylvia Jaffee graciously answered questions from a friend who was outspokenly on the other side of the circumcision debate. Lester Mazor, Bob Meagher, and Barbara Yngvesson, Hampshire College faculty colleagues, offered vital support and advice. The college provides an exceptionally open intellectual environment where cross-disciplinary exploration and creative critical thinking are cultivated.

I thank also the many scholars whose work has provided essential foundations for my own. I must emphasize, though, that all interpretations and conclusions are mine alone, and that no one whose work I cite necessarily accepts or endorses anything I say; indeed, as yet most of them know nothing of this book.

I owe special thanks to my editors at Oxford University Press—Cynthia Read, Theo Calderara, and Linda Donnelly—for their generous support and guidance, and for their expressions of confidence in me and my work. Evaluative comments by two anonymous readers were just what I needed: incisive but supportive. At an earlier stage, Susan Rabiner offered encouragement and advice on how to present my work to potential publishers.

Nansi S. Glick has contributed so much to this entire project that routine acknowledgment will not do. Her editorial acumen and shrewd judgment on writing style and authorial voice; her insight into weaknesses in logic, explanation, and organization; her willingness to read chapters again, and again, and yet again; her crucial practical assistance; and her faith in me and in this book—all extended far beyond anything represented in customary expressions of appreciation for spousal support. Once more, and still inadequately, Nansi, thank you.

Although I am totally committed to a particular position in the circumcision controversy, I trust that readers will not find the book unduly polemical, and that those who stay with me will be prepared to explore all claims, counterclaims, and opinions for themselves, and to reach their own conclusions. With that end in mind, I quote or paraphrase rather freely and extensively, perhaps more than is usual in most histories, because I believe that we learn best about controversial issues when those on both sides speak for themselves. It's true, of course, that all quotation and paraphrase involves selection—highlighting some statements or phrases, choosing to omit others. Readers who want to know more about quoted texts may consult the references in the notes and bibliography.

Credits

Quotations from Jeremiah J. Berman, "Trend in Jewish Religious Observance," used by permission of the American Jewish Historical Society, New York, N.Y., and Newton, Mass.

Quotations from Alexander Pope, *Prose Works*, Vol. 1, used by permission of Blackwell Publishing Ltd.

Quotations from Maimonides, *The Guide of the Perplexed*, S. Pines, ed., and L. A. Hoffman, *Covenant of Blood*, used by permission of the University of Chicago Press.

Quotations from Gerald N. Weiss and Elaine B. Weiss, "A Perspective on Controversies over Neonatal Circumcision," used by permission of Westminster Publications, Inc.

Quotations from James Shapiro, *Shakespeare and the Jews*, used by permission of Columbia University Press.

Quotations from Roy S. Wolper, "Circumcision as Polemic in the Jew Bill of 1753: The Cutter Cut?" Copyright © 1982, the College of William and Mary, all rights reserved, used by permission of Duke University Press.

Quotations from Marc Saperstein, *Decoding the Rabbis*, Harvard University Press, Copyright © 1980 by the President and Fellows of Harvard College. Used by permission of Harvard University Press.

Quotations from *JPS Hebrew English Tanakh*, Copyright © 1999, The Jewish Publication Society, and David M. Gitlitz, *Secrecy and Deceit*, © 1996, The Jewish Publication Society, used by permission of the Jewish Publication Society.

Quotations from Elliot R. Wolfson, "Circumcision and the Divine Name," used by permission of the *Jewish Quarterly Review*.

Quotations from Leonard B. Glick, "Jewish Circumcision: An Enigma in Historical Perspective" and "Something Less than Joyful: Jewish Americans and the Circumcision Dilemma," used by permission of Kluwer Academic Publishers.

Quotations from Peter Abelard, *Dialogue of a Philosopher with a Jew and a Christian* (trans. Pierre J. Payer), used by permission of the Pontifical Institute of Medieval Studies.

Quotations from Elliot R. Wolfson, "Re/membering the Covenant: Memory, Forgetfulness, and the Construction of History in the *Zohar*." In *Jewish History and Jewish Memory*, ed. Elisheva Carlebach et al., pp. 214–46, Copyright © Brandeis University Press, reprinted by permission of Brandeis University Press/University Press of New England.

Quotations from Roy S. Wolper, *Pieces on the Jew Bill*, used by permission of the UCLA William Andrews Clark Memorial Library.

Quotations from Jacob Neusner, *The Mishnah*, used by permission of Yale University Press.

Quotations from www.circumstitions.com used by permission of Hugh Young.

Contents

Marked in Your Flesh

Prologue

Questioning Circumcision

"Nothing Could Have Prepared Me"

Marilyn Fayre Milos was a nursing student when she saw a circumcision for the first time. She was the mother of three sons, all circumcised with her consent. "My doctor had told me the surgery was a necessary health measure," she said later, "that it didn't hurt, and that it only took a moment to perform—like cutting the umbilical cord." That had left her unprepared for what she witnessed on a fateful day in 1979:

> We students filed into the newborn nursery to find a baby strapped spread-eagle to a plastic board on a countertop across the room. He was struggling against his restraints—tugging, whimpering, and then crying helplessly. No one was tending the infant, but when I asked my instructor if I could comfort him, she said, "Wait till the doctor gets here." ... When he did arrive, I immediately asked the doctor if I could help the baby. He told me to put my finger in the baby's mouth; I did, and the baby sucked. I stroked his little head and spoke softly to him. He began to relax and was momentarily quiet.
>
> The silence was soon broken by a piercing scream—the baby's reaction to having his foreskin pinched and crushed as the doctor attached the clamp to his penis. The shriek intensified when the doctor inserted an instrument between

the foreskin and the glans . . . tearing the two structures apart. . . . The baby started shaking his head back and forth—the only part of his body free to move—as the doctor used another clamp to crush the foreskin lengthwise, which he then cut. . . . The baby began to gasp and choke, breathless from his shrill continuous screams. . . . I found my own sobs difficult to contain. How much longer could this go on?

During the next stage of the surgery, the doctor crushed the foreskin against the circumcision instrument and then, finally, amputated it. The baby was limp, exhausted, spent.

I had not been prepared, nothing could have prepared me, for this experience. To see a part of this baby's penis being cut off— without an anesthetic—was devastating. But even more shocking was the doctor's comment, barely audible several octaves below the piercing screams of the baby, "There's no medical reason for doing this." I couldn't believe my ears, my knees became weak, and I felt sick to my stomach. . . .

What had I allowed my own babies to endure? and why? The course of my life was changed on that day in 1979.[1]

Working thereafter as a nurse on an obstetrical service, Milos campaigned against circumcision with nurses and parents until 1985, when the hospital administration dismissed her for insubordination. Soon thereafter, she founded NOCIRC, the National Organization of Circumcision Information Resource Centers, now an international organization dedicated to ending genital cutting of male and female children worldwide. In 1990 she was honored by the California Nurses Association for her "unwavering commitment to righting a wrong."[2]

Should we be surprised that a nursing student was shocked to witness an everyday procedure in American hospitals? Like most Americans, Milos had thought of male infant circumcision as a simple "snip," a minor operation involving removal of a bit of "extra skin." She learned that the reality is quite different. For one thing, despite its name, the foreskin (or prepuce, the ana-tomical term) is not just ordinary skin and it is certainly not extra. In fact, it is highly sensitive, delicate genital tissue, richly endowed with nerves, and protective of the glans. But equally important, the surgery is not so simple; it's an extensive *reductive* procedure—and, whether the "patient" later approves or not, the result is irreversible.

In 1980, about 85 percent of American boys were circumcised soon after birth, and although the rate has been falling since then, even now it is near 60 percent. The United States is almost unique in this regard; the over-whelming majority of males in Europe, Asia, Latin America, and most of Africa are genitally intact. England, Canada, Australia, and New Zealand—the Anglophone nations—practiced infant circumcision for a time, but during the past several decades their rates have steadily dropped, mostly down to single digits. In short, when it comes to circumcising baby boys in the millions, America is very nearly alone in the world.

How It's Done Elsewhere

Circumcision is still widely practiced by Middle Eastern, North African, and Southeast Asian Muslims, who interpret it as an Islamic ceremony (though circumcision is never mentioned in the Koran).[3] The practice is also prevalent among diverse African peoples, everywhere from Senegal to Uganda to Madagascar.[4] But there are crucial differences between our version of circumcision and theirs. In African and Islamic societies circumcisions are not perceived as medical; moreover, it is nearly always *boys* or *youths* who are circumcised, not infants. Compared to our version of the surgery, theirs may be relatively simple: The operators—not physicians but community elders, or, in some cases, itinerant specialists—pull protruding foreskin tissue forward and excise that part with a single cut, leaving the remainder intact. (In a few African societies, however, the surgery is more extensive, involving substantial removal of foreskin tissue.[5]) Initiation ceremonies, most often involving a group of boys and youths, sometimes extend over days. Circumcision is the featured event, and, in sharp contrast to what is unwillingly "learned" by our circumcised infants, the cultural significance of the experience is conveyed unforgettably to the initiates. In some African societies, young girls also undergo reductive genital surgery, sometimes so extreme as to obliterate their external genitalia. This is justified with explanations similar to those offered for male circumcision: It makes the child "cleaner," properly prepared to enter adult society, and eligible in due course for marriage and sexual life.[6]

A few Pacific peoples also practice various forms of male genital cutting—as usual, of boys or youths, not infants. A remarkable example in the Pacific region is subincision, practiced by native ("aboriginal") Australians. This involves slitting open the ventral (under) surface of the penis into the urethra; later the wound may be reopened and extended to cause renewed bloodletting—almost certainly the most dramatic of all male genital mutilations.[7] Studying other cultures, learning how they explain their practices, may shed some light on our own; but in the final analysis our questions must focus on how and why we came to circumcise so many infants in our particular manner.

Like Father, Like Son: Circumcision in the United States

As I've noted, other versions of circumcision bear little resemblance to circumcision in America; in addition to being surgically more radical than most, our practice differs definitively because we circumcise *babies*. But though in world perspective American circumcision may seem almost unique, it is not without precedent: Jewish ritual circumcision also involves removal of the entire foreskin, and Jews too circumcise infants, traditionally on the eighth day of life.

The first stage of a ritual circumcision—the initial cut—is called by the Hebrew term *milah*. The Hebrew word for "covenant," in the Sephardic pronunciation now used in Israel, is *brit*—hence the term *brit milah*, "covenant of circumcision." (I'll explain the significance of "covenant" in the first chapter.) But the Ashkenazic pronunciation, used over the centuries by European Jews outside Spain and Portugal, is *bris*—the term still familiar to Jewish Americans, as in "They're having the *bris* tomorrow." Most Jews know the term *bris*, but few realize that it means "covenant" rather than circumcision, and even fewer know to what covenant it refers. The second stage, a later addition to the original *milah* procedure, involves tearing the adhering mucous membrane and removing all foreskin to the base of the glans (the corona), so that the glans is completely and permanently exposed. This is called *peri'ah*, a Hebrew word signifying "opening."[8] Nowadays a few rigorously Orthodox *mohels* (ritual circumcisers) continue to perform the traditional third stage of the procedure, *metsitsah* ("sucking"): They complete the operation by sucking on the bleeding infant penis. Although this was (and is) claimed to reduce bleeding, the origin and initial significance of the practice are unclear. In a modified version (introduced when it was realized that some mohels were transmitting tuberculosis and syphilis by oral contact with freshly wounded penises) mohels suck blood through a glass tube, avoiding direct mouth contact with the penis. Some spit the blood into a cup of wine, then apply a few drops to the infant's lips. Very few contemporary Jewish Americans even know about *peri'ah* and *metsitsah*; the great majority have only the most limited understanding of the ritual procedure.

A Jewish ritual circumcision requires recitation of appropriate liturgy, but the *surgical result* is indistinguishable from that imposed daily on thousands of infants, Gentile and Jewish, in hospitals throughout this country. I emphasize this because the fact is that large numbers, very possibly the majority, of Jewish infants are now circumcised in hospitals—simply because their parents do not know, or do not care, that in Jewish religious law the surgery by itself has no validity.

How did it happen that the United States, one of the world's most medically and scientifically advanced nations, largely Christian, adopted a non-therapeutic surgical procedure long viewed as a strictly Jewish religious custom? Until fairly recently Christians not only rejected but often vilified circumcision; from Paul's time onward they interpreted the practice as prime evidence that Judaism was so fixated on irrelevant physical concerns that spiritual life was beyond reach. In the Christian view the only appropriate rite of initiation for infants, male and female, is baptism. Gentile Americans haven't really abandoned this doctrine, since most now think of circumcision as simply a medical procedure. Nevertheless, throughout the centuries, Christians everywhere, from theologians to ordinary folk, had denounced circumcision as not only worthless but disgusting. How, then, did this practice come to enjoy such widespread acceptance in the United States?

Asked why they approve of circumcision, most American parents say that a circumcised penis is "cleaner" or "healthier." Some have heard it said that circumcision protects against various diseases in later life; a few mention cervical cancer in women partners. Many focus on cosmetic justifications, saying that they want their son to feel "comfortable" among other boys in locker rooms, or that a boy should "look like" his father.[9] (The last is puzzling. Male readers might ask themselves how often, if ever, they gazed at a father's genitals with foreskins in mind. It seems more likely that fathers want their sons to resemble *them*, since they are the ones who see the child's genitals, not the reverse.) A few Christian fundamentalists, apparently more familiar with Genesis than with Paul's letters, explain that circumcision is "in the Bible." Presumably most Gentile Americans have at least some notion of the connection between circumcision and Judaism, but that seems of little or no concern.[10]

Judging from how seldom Americans, Jewish and Gentile, even think about circumcision at all, the entire subject is of little concern. Very few have a clear idea of what the surgery entails, or of the function and purpose of the tissue being removed. Many agree to the procedure by signing a consent form in the hospital (often presented to the mother shortly before or after delivery), naturally assuming that if they're asked to consent to surgery, it must be medically advisable. Most parents probably expect that their obstetrician or pediatrician will perform the procedure, which is sometimes the case; but many circumcisions are performed by resident physicians in training, or even by interns with little or no experience with this or any other surgery. Not only are parents unaware of the extent of the surgery, but few know that it is often performed *without anesthesia*; they consent because circumcision is a familiar custom, the accepted norm.[11]

This kind of thinking—minimal knowledge, disinclination to inquire deeply—applies equally to Jewish ritual circumcisions. What most Jews do know, however, as the popular writer Anita Diamant acknowledges, is that a *bris* is "something less than joyful."[12] That's an understatement. In contrast to the convenient obscurity of hospital circumcision, at a *bris* there is no way to hide or disguise the physical actuality of the procedure; the surgery is performed at home, and everyone hears the baby's cries of protest. Mohels may try to lighten the adult experience and relieve adult discomfort with religious homilies and cheerful patter; but although guests attend that part of the performance, most disappear into another room before the operation begins. At Orthodox circumcisions men and even boys are expected to remain as witnesses; but non-Orthodox men are more likely to scurry off with nervous expressions and perhaps feeble attempts at humor.

Neither Jews nor Gentiles know much if anything about circumcision rates in this country as compared with others. Some still think of circumcision as a distinctively Jewish practice; others view it as a modern American medical procedure. Jewish parents who choose hospital circumcision either don't realize or don't care that many more Gentile infants are being circumcised in the same place and in the same way. Jews almost never question how circumcision can define their ethnic individuality in a country where tens of millions of Gentile males have genitals indistinguishable from the Jewish version—and where an unknown but possibly substantial number of Jewish boys and men have *not* been circumcised. Moreover, although a circumcision without ritual accompaniment has no religious legitimacy, most contemporary Jewish parents neither understand this nor care. They consent, with few or no questions, to having their baby boys circumcised shortly after birth, just as do so many other Americans, and with the very same medical or cosmetic justifications. If this somehow helps to "make the boy Jewish" and satisfies the grandparents, fine.[13]

But there are questions worth pondering, particularly on the Jewish side. What exactly *is* the religious significance of circumcision? What is meant by saying that it initiates male (but *only* male) infants into Abraham's covenant? How can a newborn child know that he's being initiated into *anything*? Finally, perhaps the most obvious question of all: Why, when so many Jewish Americans have abandoned every bedrock traditional practice—daily (male) synagogue attendance and donning of phylacteries (*tefillin*), Sabbath observance, kosher diet, fasting on Yom Kippur, Passover dietary regulations, postmenstrual immersion in ritual baths for women, *even the prohibition against intermarriage*—why do most still believe that they must have their infant sons circumcised? According to the *Encyclopaedia Judaica* (published in 1971), "its observance is often the sole remaining token of affinity with Judaism, even after intermarriage, when the Jewish parent insists on the circumcision of the sons."[14] Not only do most Jews, even those barely engaged with Jewish concerns, take circumcision for granted, but many—especially but by no means entirely those in the older generation—respond with surprise and puzzlement to any suggestion that the practice might be reconsidered. Why does this single custom have such an uncanny hold among Jewish Americans, even the religiously indifferent?

Parents who opt for a ritual circumcision may well have more immediate questions. Aside from the obvious physical concerns—is it safe? what about pain? are complications possible?—they might wonder about the rite itself. Why only boys? Why the penis? Why must there be visible bloodshed? And since circumcision surely can have no religious meaning for an infant, what is supposed to be its meaning for the parents and other adult witnesses?

There is only one answer to what is *supposed* to be the meaning of a ritual circumcision: It initiates the newborn male child into a covenant established between God and Abraham, as recorded in the seventeenth chapter of Genesis. There God tells Abraham that he will make him "exceedingly fertile" and will deliver to him and his descendants "all the land of Canaan," provided that he circumcise himself and promise that all his male descendants will be circumcised on the eighth day of life. Are contemporary Jewish American parents aware of Genesis 17 and its significance? On questions of this kind no one has conducted systematic research; but I'm certain that, aside from the small percentage (well below 10 percent) who are committed to strict orthodoxy, very few even know the story of Abraham's covenant. Jews expect boys to be circumcised, simply as a time-honored ethnic custom divorced from historical or theological context. Like nearly everyone else—and quite correctly—they realize that in essence this is a surgical procedure. That's why many consent to hospital circumcision and never even consider engaging a mohel for a ritual event at home.

The practice of circumcision in American hospitals has not gone unchallenged. Opponents insist that no one has the right to alter a normal, healthy body without the explicit, informed consent of the person involved. They define circumcision as a human rights issue, arguing that our well-grounded refusal to sanction female genital cutting should be extended to males, and identifying the essential question as not whether one form of genital alteration is worse than another but whether *any* form is acceptable in an enlightened society.

But despite the efforts of opponents to focus on *hospital* circumcisions, to frame their challenges in medical and ethical terms, and to address all American parents and physicians, many Jews misinterpret any critique of circumcision as thinly disguised antisemitism.[15] Since for religiously observant Jews circumcision is a divine command, specific to Jews as a people, they dismiss out of hand any call to discontinue the practice; arguments about whether circumcision is medically justifiable or ethically acceptable are irrelevant to those who believe that they are fulfilling the explicit instructions of the Creator. But even secular Jews may believe that no one, Jewish or Gentile, should raise objections of any kind—because somehow circumcision is a Jewish personal possession, time-honored and beyond critical examination.

By now it will be apparent that this entire story is rich with paradox. We find millions of Gentile American infants being circumcised, mostly for ostensible medical benefits, but occasionally also because their Christian fundamentalist parents believe that they are following a biblical mandate—which, if the story be believed, was delivered to the original ancestor of the Jews. We find most Jews agreeing to circumcision for their sons, not to renew Abraham's covenant but because they, like their Gentile counterparts, assume that the procedure is medically beneficial and cosmetically preferable. Indifferent to the meaning and purpose of ritual circumcision, they choose hospital circumcision for their sons—who join the far larger number of Gentile babies circumcised in exactly the same manner. Feminists and others concerned about women's rights condemn female "circumcision" *in other parts of the world* as sexist cruelty with no rightful place in any society. But most ignore male infant circumcision here at home—or, even more remarkably, refuse to oppose the practice, in the belief that attention to one will somehow diminish or distract from efforts to end the other. Jews seldom wonder why girls are legitimately Jewish without surgery, while boys must be "made" Jewish by such an inherently disturbing procedure.[16]

Finally, what are we to make of the near-taboo against even discussing circumcision, let alone questioning it? What should we conclude from the coarse jokes, the ridicule of unaltered penises in television sitcoms, the language of avoidance evident in otherwise cheerful books on Jewish parenting? What does this semisubterranean evidence tell us about how most Americans, Gentile and Jewish alike, really feel about circumcision? Despite all that has been written and said over the years, we still do not fully understand why the practice took such firm hold in this country and why it has endured with such remarkable tenacity.[17]

An Overview

In this book I address two sets of questions—never completely separate, and increasingly linked as we move toward the present. The first set has to do with Jewish circumcision. How did this practice become a definitive feature of Judaism? By "definitive" I mean that for many people circumcision is the most obvious characteristic of Jews (Jewish *men*, of course), the *physical* characteristic (although seldom seen!) that supposedly distinguishes them from everyone else. Even now, despite the millions of circumcised Gentiles, many Americans still think of circumcision as a Jewish practice.[18] What did it mean originally, and does it still retain that meaning now? How has being circumcised influenced Jewish men's self-perception, and how have others perceived (or imagined) them and their mysterious rite? Have all Jews accepted circumcision without question, or have some challenged or even rejected the practice?

For answers we have to reach far into the past, beginning with ancient Judea and gradually working our way forward, right up to our own time. Appreciating the uncanny power of circumcision in the Jewish and Christian imagination requires that we explore some rather arcane topics—biblical and rabbinic texts, Christian theology, medieval Jewish mysticism, fantasies about ritual murder, and more. I trust that those who follow the narrative will recognize connections among what may at first seem to be disparate topics.

Some readers may wonder why I pay so much attention to Jews and Jewish circumcision. The answer is that until the late nineteenth century no one else in Europe or America regularly practiced infant circumcision. In Europe, as we'll see, Jewish and Christian imagery were so precisely opposite—Jews treasuring the practice as proof that they were the Lord's chosen people, Christians citing it as proof that Jews were too fixated on physical concerns to have any hope of salvation—that resolution or accommodation were impossible. Nevertheless—and here is one of the most remarkable paradoxes in a story replete with paradox—nineteenth- and twentieth-century British and American physicians rushed to adopt circumcision as an almost miraculous therapeutic and preventive operation, often supporting their claims with reference to the ostensible superior health and longevity of Jews: obviously attributable, they felt certain, to the one Jewish custom known to everyone.

Which brings us to the second set of questions: How and why did a Jewish ritual operation, rejected and vilified for nearly two millennia, come to be widely accepted as a routine postnatal procedure in American hospitals? What exactly were the connections in physicians' minds between what Jews had been doing for all those centuries and what they, the physicians, now began to imitate? And they did imitate. Circumcisions in American hospitals have no ritual accompaniment, of course, and surgical techniques vary to some extent, as do those of mohels; but—and this is a crucial *but*—the end result is the same. In short, although I intend this book to be read as a contribution to our understanding of *American* circumcision, I can accomplish that only by first according extensive attention to *Jewish* circumcision.

We turn, then, to the first question: What is Jewish about circumcision?

I

"This Is My Covenant"

Circumcision in the World of Temple Judaism

We thank You for the covenant sealed in our flesh.[1]

Abraham's Covenant

"I Am El Shaddai"

We begin with the biblical text on which everything depends: chapter 17 of Genesis. There the Lord appears before a ninety-nine-year-old man named Abram. "I am El Shaddai," he announces. "Walk in My ways and be blameless. I will establish My covenant between Me and you, and I will make you exceedingly numerous."[2] Abram, overwhelmed, falls to the ground. El Shaddai, now called God, continues:

> As for Me, this is My covenant with you: You shall be the father of a multitude of nations. And you shall no longer be called Abram, but your name shall be Abraham, for I make you the father of a multitude of nations. I will make you exceedingly fertile, and make nations of you; and kings shall come forth from you. I will maintain My covenant between Me and you, and your offspring to come, as an everlasting covenant throughout the ages, to be God to you and to your offspring to come. I assign the land you sojourn in to you and your offspring to come, all the land of Canaan, as an everlasting holding. I will be their God.[3]

Now, almost as though it were an afterthought, and without explanation, the Lord adds that the covenant comes at a price:

> Such shall be the covenant between Me and you and your offspring to follow which you shall keep: every male among you shall be circumcised. You shall circumcise the flesh of your foreskin, and that shall be the sign of the covenant between Me and you. And throughout the generations every male among you shall be circumcised at the age of eight days.

Even slaves must be circumcised, he adds, and Abraham must see to it that the order is obeyed forever: "Thus shall My covenant be marked in your flesh as an everlasting pact. And if any male who is uncircumcised fails to circumcise the flesh of his foreskin, that person shall be cut off from his kin; he has broken My covenant."

Abraham's wife, aged eighty-nine and childless, is also due for a name change and a miraculous promise: "As for your wife Sarai, you shall not call her Sarai, but her name shall be Sarah ["Princess"]. I will bless her; indeed, I will give you a son by her. I will bless her so that she shall give rise to nations; rulers of peoples shall issue from her."

Abraham finds all this hard to believe. He collapses again, but this time with laughter, as he says (to himself): "Can a child be born to a man a hundred years old, or can Sarah bear a child at ninety?" But God declares that Sarah will indeed bear a son, to be called Isaac (yitschaq, "he laughs"), and it is he who will inherit the covenant. Abraham's first-born son, Ishmael, son of Sarah's servant Hagar, will also be father to "a great nation." Isaac alone, though, will carry the covenant for himself and his descendants. Having delivered his message, the Lord disappears. The old man dutifully circumcises himself at once, then circumcises the thirteen-year-old Ishmael and all other males in his household.[4]

This chapter is the first of only two biblical passages in which the Lord declares infant circumcision to be a ritual requirement for the descendants of Abraham. (We'll examine the second, a single verse in Leviticus, shortly.) But there we have it. Remove Genesis 17, and infant circumcision all but disappears.

We need to know more about Abraham's covenant. First, though, it is important to recognize a fundamental point. Modern biblical scholarship adopts a historical perspective, suspending the traditional belief that God communicated, or transmitted, the Torah (the "Five Books of Moses," first part of the "Old Testament") to Moses on Mount Sinai. I begin, therefore, with the premise that, whether or not the Torah was divinely inspired, it is a human composition, created during specific historical times. For more than a century now, a host of scholars, Jewish and Christian, have studied the Torah with critical historical methods that have yielded a great deal of insight into when, how, and why the various parts of the Five Books were composed. We want to know what their research can tell us about the place of infant circumcision in Judaism, and about how Genesis 17 fits into the picture. Who composed it? When? And why did the author or authors select male infant circumcision as "the sign of the covenant"?

One point now seems certain: no single individual wrote the Torah. Biblical scholars have shown that the Five Books consist of a number of texts, composed over several centuries by authors with distinctive mentalities and styles, and eventually assembled sometime shortly after 500 BCE. Most scholars recognize four texts, labeled J, E, D, and P. The earliest, J, stands for Jahwist— that is, the text in which *Jahweh* (or *Yahweh*, "Jehovah") appears as the deity; in E he is often called *Elohim* (literally, "gods"). These two, probably composed during the tenth and ninth centuries BCE, include parts of what are now Genesis, Exodus, and Numbers. The text called D, constituting most of Deuteronomy, was composed in the seventh century by religious reformers intent on eliminating polytheistic worship of local deities and creating a religion devoted exclusively to Yahweh. They succeeded, but only gradually; regional cult worship probably persisted in rural areas well into the sixth century. Eventually, thanks to the determination of the reformers and their descendants, Yahweh triumphed over all other regional deities to become the sole and supreme god of the Judeans. Deuteronomy documents the advent of this new monotheism.

Finally, P was the work of the priestly class that emerged into prominence in the late sixth century, after the return from Babylonian exile. Also a composite text, it includes nearly all of Leviticus and much of Genesis (including chapter 17), Exodus, and Numbers. All the various texts were combined into a single Torah in the fifth century BCE by an unknown author or authors known as *Redactor*.[5]

Genesis 17 is part of P—*the last text to be composed* but *the first to mention circumcision*. Who were its authors, and why would they have included a narrative in which God commands infant circumcision? As I mentioned, these men were priests, members of the elite class who assumed virtually complete social authority in the newly reconstituted Judean society that arose after the Babylonian exile. Recall that in 586 BCE the Babylonians conquered Judea, destroyed the Jerusalem Temple, and exiled to Babylon priests and other members of the social elite. The prophets of danger and doom, particularly Jeremiah and Ezekiel, had proved correct: Yahweh had punished the Judeans for worshiping other gods. National salvation now required nothing less than exclusive allegiance to one god, Yahweh, and unwavering dedication to his service. Sixty years later the Persian king, Cyrus, conquered Babylon and permitted the return to Palestine of those Judeans who wanted to do so. Some did not; they remained in Babylonia as the nucleus of what would become a major community of the "Diaspora." But many returned to the homeland;

and prominent among them were religious purists who, convinced that exile had been punishment for backsliding, were now determined to revitalize Judean society and religion under their own priestly direction.

The responsibility was theirs alone; the monarchy had ended, never to be restored, and political leadership was possible only within the limits permitted by the Persians. This determined cohort of religious leaders constituted themselves as priests of the new dispensation. By 516 BCE they had rebuilt a Second Temple and had undertaken creation of a rigorously organized society, centering on Temple rituals, so as to maintain Judean identity and individuality in the midst of neighboring peoples with competitive religious beliefs and practices.

A Rite of Initiation

It was in this reconstituted society that male infant circumcision became a religiously mandated requirement, sanctioned by the single key text, Genesis 17. (We might note that this was some thirteen centuries after Abraham's putative lifetime.) Like a number of their neighbors, the ancient Israelites had practiced circumcision, but not as a *mandatory rite* and probably seldom on *infants*; nor did they associate it with the idea of covenant.[6]

The Bible itself confirms this conclusion. The essential features of the Genesis 17 narrative, complete with the Lord's covenant and his two definitive promises (prodigious reproductive success and a lavish land grant), appear first in Genesis 15, an earlier J text—but with one crucial difference: *there is no mention of circumcision*. Here is the narrative in its earlier, Genesis 15, version: The "word of the Lord" comes to Abram "in a vision." "Fear not, Abram," he says, "I am a shield to you; your reward shall be very great." Abram asks what he can receive, since he is fated to die childless, and his steward will be his only heir. Not so, says the Lord: "your very own issue shall be your heir." Then he delivers a prophecy and extravagant promises: Abram will have offspring as numerous as the stars; his descendants will be "enslaved and oppressed" for four hundred years, but then "they shall go free with great wealth" and will be endowed with a huge expanse of land, from the Nile to the Euphrates. To seal this covenant the only requirement is that Abram offer several sacrificial animals—a heifer, goat, ram, dove, and one other bird—the first four of which he cuts in two (the traditional way of establishing a covenant or treaty).[7] Here we find no mention of circumcision, no change of name, no mention of Isaac or Ishmael. The two major promises—reproductive success and land grant—are there, but confirmed only with the customary practice for establishing a covenant. (Note, though, that *something* must be cut.)

Returning now to the Judean priests: Having eliminated local cult centers dedicated to deities other than Yahweh, they centralized worship at their new Temple in Jerusalem in which they, and they alone, could conduct sacrifices;

moreover, only they, and they alone, could officiate as intermediaries between Yahweh and transgressors against the newly instituted social and ritual regulations. Absolution was possible only for a petitioner who brought the proper sacrificial offerings to the Temple and accepted the intercession of a priest. The list of misdeeds, particularly as set out in Leviticus, was long enough to keep anyone vigilant. Of highest importance and ever-present in the new texts was the distinction between pure and impure: that which was proper and admissible versus that which contaminated and polluted. And many regulations had to do with sexuality. As we'll see, a father's obedience to the commandment to circumcise signified his commitment to rigorous standards of sexual purity.

It was these priests, then, with their ambitions and concerns, who introduced infant circumcision as the rite of initiation into their male-centered society. And it was they who, without removing the original covenant text in Genesis 15, rewrote it as Genesis 17 to legitimate the new rite. But why did they choose circumcision—and why infants? Why not something more like bar mitzvah (a much later creation), that would mark a boy's passage into manhood at a time when he could understand, at least in an elementary way, his new rights and responsibilities, and could consciously and intentionally commit himself to playing his appropriate role in the society? Why "initiate" a newborn, who can consent to nothing, and can express unwillingness to participate only by screaming?

The Meaning of Ritual Circumcision

Be Fruitful and Without Blemish

In return for Abraham's agreeing to obey the mandate on circumcision, the Lord declared that he would become "exceedingly fertile," father to "a multitude of nations," and would receive land to match: "all the land of Canaan, as an everlasting possession." Such promises, concerned with progeny and property, can hardly be called "spiritual" in the modern religious sense; rather, they're characteristic of the material benefits bestowed by traditional deities in return for sacrificial offerings. At its most elementary, the covenant message of Genesis 17 is straightforward: cut your sons' penises and you'll be abundantly rewarded.

But why did the priests decide on *infant foreskins* as the sacrifice, rather than, say, another part of the body? And why did they not choose boys or older youths, or even sacrifice of one of the animals that sufficed on other occasions, as in the Genesis 15 narrative? No one can say for certain why the choice fell specifically on infants; perhaps it was because a newborn child is unable to effectively protest or resist. That question aside, it can certainly be said that male progeny were men's most precious possessions. In the penises of infant sons resided a father's dearest aspirations: for grandsons, great-grandsons, patrilineal continuity.

Furthermore, since patrilineal ancestry was the essential precondition for membership in the priestly class, it made sense that the same should hold true for all members of Judean society. The goal, shared by priests and ordinary men alike, was to maintain an ethnically exclusive patriarchy, dedicated to worship of Yahweh, and committed to sexual and marital restrictions to prevent reproductive contamination. What better way to accomplish this than by requiring that every male child be indelibly marked at birth? And who better qualified to place that mark than the child's own father? The original circumcision rite, as the priests devised it, required that the father himself be the operator—that in the presence of other males he perform on his newborn son a form of ritual surgery that was well understood to bear the risk not only of mutilating the infant but even of causing his death. In a very real sense, then, it was the *father*, not the infant, who was initiated; it was *he*, not his son, who was declaring loyalty and submission to the new social order.[8]

As for the choice of the penis, comparative anthropological research confirms what anyone might guess: first, that ritual cutting of immature penises has much to do with beliefs about potency, paternity, and procreation; second, that removing part of those penises is a sacrificial act, intended to ensure future rewards—in the form of potency, paternity, and procreation. Carol Delaney, author of a study of the near-sacrifice of Isaac (Genesis 22), points out that the Abraham narratives express a belief, or theory, about parentage: specifically, that men "beget" children by planting generative "seed" in wombs; hence, while mothers merely "bear" children, fathers create and own them. The entire Book of Genesis, she remarks, "is preoccupied with the interrelated notions of seed, paternity, and patriliny: who begat whom.... Men's procreative ability is defined in terms of potency—the power to bring things into being." This is why the "sign of God's covenant with Abraham, circumcision, was carved on the organ felt to be the fountain of generativity, the vehicle for the transmission of seed."[9]

Howard Eilberg-Schwartz (a rabbi and anthropologist) has shown that for ancient Judeans the trimmed penis was a symbol not only of patrilineal social organization but of male reproductive prowess and male social supremacy.[10] He points out that in verse 11 of Genesis 17 ("that shall be the sign of the covenant"), circumcision is called *ot*, which may be translated as either "sign" or "symbol." No great imagination is required to understand why the circumcised penis was an ideal symbol of the Lord's covenant, and of everything that the priests intended to promote with their new rite of initiation: male reproductive success, continuity in the male line, male-defined ethnic identity and exclusiveness, acknowledgment of patrilineally legitimated priestly authority.

Eilberg-Schwartz shows also that for ancient Israelites "fruitfulness" was more than mere metaphor; they knew about fruit trees from firsthand experience with figs, dates, olives, and other trees. Juvenile trees have to be pruned for several years if they are to bear fruitfully thereafter. In line with the common experience of the time, the creators of the P text described the fruit of immature trees as "foreskins" and the trees themselves as "uncircumcised." Hence, he says, circumcising the penis "is analogous to pruning fruit trees. Both acts involve cutting away unwanted growth from a stem or trunk and the purpose of both cuttings is similar. Circumcision...is a symbolic cut that ensures human fertility."[11]

Lest this sound far-fetched, a representative passage shows that the authors of the P text thought exactly in these terms. In Leviticus 19 the Lord (who, in this book especially, seems to have attended to just about every feature of life) provides instructions for proper management of fruit trees:

> When you enter the land and plant any tree for food, you shall regard its fruit as its foreskin. Three years it shall be uncircumcised for you, not to be eaten. In the fourth year all the fruit shall be set aside for jubilation before the Lord; and only in the fifth year may you use its fruit—that its yield to you may be increased.[12]

Eilberg-Schwartz concludes that in the minds of the priestly authors Jewish male infants literally required trimming to become fruitful: "One might say that when Israelites circumcise their male children, they are pruning the fruit trees of God."[13]

We recall that Genesis 15 (the earlier text, on covenant without circumcision) and Genesis 17 both include a requirement that something be cut—animals in the first instance, infant penises in the second. The usual translations of verse 18 in Genesis 15 say that "the Lord made a covenant with Abram." A more literal translation, however, would be "the Lord cut a covenant [karat...brit] with Abram." The anthropologist Erich Isaac has shown that the biblical term for covenant-making is likrot brit, "to cut a covenant." He remarks that "it would seem highly probable that 'cutting' was a covenant rite by which treaties between equals as well as vassal obligations were confirmed." This obviously suggests that, whatever its other possible meanings, the connection between covenant and circumcision may have derived from the requirement that a covenant be confirmed by cutting.[14]

Lawrence A. Hoffman has shown that foreskins carry still more meaning. We recall that when El Shaddai first appears to the elderly Abram, he says, "Walk in My ways and be blameless." The word translated here as "blameless," tamim, also means perfectly formed, without physical blemish; and in fact that's the usual meaning in the Torah. For example, in Leviticus we find sacrificial animals repeatedly required to be tamim: "a male without blemish" (Lev. 1:3 and 1:10); "two male lambs without blemish, one ewe lamb in its first year without blemish" (Lev. 14:10). The meaning, says Hoffman, can be extended to signify physically entire or complete (in the sense of being without any deficiency). He proposes as an alternative translation, "Walk before me *in a state of physical completion.*" And that, he says, "is P's official theology in a nutshell: Israelite men must be circumcised to be physically complete, and thus to carry the covenant." Abram's problem, lack of a legitimate heir, "requires for its solution that he complete his own body by paring away his foreskin and then appearing before God *tamim,* 'whole.' "[15]

"She Shall Be Unclean"

As for why infants had to be eight days old, we need to examine another P text, this one from Leviticus. Aside from Genesis 17, there is only one other explicit Torah reference to circumcision as a requirement for male infants. In Leviticus 12, following a chapter on animals forbidden as food, the Lord tells Moses to instruct the Israelites on the status of women after childbirth:

> When a woman at childbirth bears a male, she shall be unclean seven
> days; she shall be unclean as at the time of her menstrual infirmity.
> On the eighth day the flesh of his foreskin shall be circumcised.
> She shall remain in a state of blood purification for thirty-three days;
> she shall not touch any consecrated thing, nor enter the sanctuary
> until her period of purification is completed. If she bears a female she
> shall be unclean two weeks as during her menstruation, and she
> shall remain in a state of blood purification for sixty-six days.[16]

Why is a mandate for male infant circumcision found here—the only location aside from Genesis 17? The answer, as we'll have other occasions to see, is that this set of regulations has to do with two kinds of blood: female blood, the quintessential pollutant, and male blood, the supreme sacred substance.

Like people everywhere, the authors of the P text recognized blood as the essence of life—not just in the literal physical sense but as the carrier or embodiment of the soul. To a lesser degree this was felt to be true even for animals. Reading parts of the Torah, particularly Leviticus, one is struck with the emphasis on blood in Temple rituals. The priests slaughtered animals of every kind, splashing their blood on altars and even smearing it on themselves. Shedding animal blood atoned for every sort of sin and transgression; it transformed the impure into the pure, the profane into the sacred, the guilty into the forgiven: "For the life of the flesh is in the blood," the Lord tells Moses, "and I have assigned it to you for making expiation for your lives upon the altar; it is the blood, as life, that effects expiation."[17] In a P text inserted into Exodus, the Lord provides instructions for consecrating priests with ram's blood:

> Slaughter the ram, and take some of its blood and put it on the ridge
> [lobe] of Aaron's right ear and on the ridges of his sons' right ears,

and on the thumbs of their right hands, and on the big toes of their
right feet; and dash the rest of the blood against every side of the
altar round about. Take some of the blood that is on the altar and some
of the anointing oil and sprinkle [it] upon Aaron and his vestments,
and also upon his sons and his sons' vestments. Thus shall he and his
vestments be holy, as well as his sons and his sons' vestments.[18]

But this was animal blood. In sharp contrast, blood shed by women,
during menstruation and in the course of childbirth, had precisely the opposite kind of power. Although I have to speculate here, we can assume that
the authors of the P text (and indeed of the other texts as well), having little
understanding of menstruation, must have thought of menstrual blood as
blood like any other—part of a woman's essential being, the carrier of her
soul-substance. The same would have held for blood shed during childbirth.
But female blood could never consecrate or expiate; to the contrary, it was the
epitome of impurity and contamination.[19] Menstrual blood, shed mysteri-
ously each month for no evident purpose (and from a polluting source), must
have been considered a contaminant simply because its uncanny quality challenged the social order. Taboos and avoidance connected with menstruation
are so common in other cultures that this in itself would not be worth much
attention.[20] But viewing the blood of *childbirth* as a pollutant is much less
common. It seems clear that the authors of Leviticus were repelled not only by
menstrual blood but by *all* female genital blood.[21]

I suggested earlier that Judean circumcision was actually a rite of submission for fathers, not for their uncomprehending infant sons. But of course
it is the child whose penis is cut. Now we approach an explanation for why he
must be circumcised on the eighth day of life. For the first seven days he is in a
state of impurity because he has been in such intimate contact with his
mother's body and blood. (We learn in the same chapter 12 of Leviticus that the
mother herself was treated much as though she had sinned. She was required
to undergo a period of purification, after which she brought to the Temple a
lamb as a "burnt offering" and a pigeon as a "sin offering," both sacrificed "to
make expiation on her behalf." She was then "clean from her flow of blood.")
On the eighth day, when the child has been free of contact with female blood
for a full week, he is in a ritually neutral state and eligible for the first time for
initiation into the world of males. Thus the infant—the hope of his father's
patrilineage, promise of future reproduction and continuity—is retrieved, or
redeemed, as it were, from the ill effects of contact with his mother's blood.

We see now that the ultimate meaning of circumcision resides not just in
foreskin removal but in shedding of blood.[22] Phrasing the matter in the
starkest terms, whereas female blood contaminates, male blood sanctifies;
while the shedding of female blood calls for purification, the shedding of male
blood is an act of consecration.

Writing on the status of women in ancient Judaism, Léonie J. Archer cites recent theories about women as the gender associated with "nature" and men with "culture." The implicit idea here, she says, is that while women "merely conducted the animal-like repetitive tasks of carrying on the reproduction of the human race, men, by one supreme symbolic act, imposed themselves upon nature and enacted a cultural rebirth." The blood shed at circumcision, she continues, "served as a symbolic surrogate for the blood of childbirth, and because it was shed voluntarily and in a controlled manner, it transcended the bounds of nature and the passive blood flow of the mother at delivery and during the preparatory cycle for pregnancy, menstruation." Moreover, the child's blood, like that of animal sacrifices, "could also be viewed as cleansing the boy of his mother's blood and acting as a rite of separation, differentiating him from the female, and allying him with the male community." She adds that this also explains why only men can perform the operation.[23]

"You Shall Give It to Me"

So much emphasis on shedding blood raises yet another question: Since circumcision is a kind of sacrifice, or a representation of sacrifice, might it have been instituted as a substitution or replacement for child sacrifice? Although that may sound not only unpleasant but unlikely, the fact is that child sacrifice was widely practiced in ancient Canaan, and there is no good reason to assume that the Israelites differed in this regard from their neighbors.

The Hebrew Scriptures provide two kinds of evidence. First, a passage in Exodus (22:28–29) has Yahweh speaking quite plainly on the matter, clearly linking treatment of first-born sons with that of first-born calves and sheep: "You shall give me the first-born among your sons. You shall do the same with your cattle and your flocks: seven days it shall remain with its mother; on the eighth day you shall give it to Me."[24] In his study of the subject, Jon D. Levenson shows that, despite the expectable efforts of interpreters to find other meanings here, "give" means just what it says.[25] The reference to "eighth day" hardly requires comment.

This is not the only suggestive passage, though. In two other chapters in Exodus (13:1–2, 11–15; 34:19–20) we find the Lord demanding that first-born sons, along with various first-born animals, be "redeemed." And, of course, the redemption theme appears in the most familiar of all child sacrifice tales, the near-sacrifice of Isaac (Genesis 22, the *aqedah*, "binding"). That event has also been interpreted away, the argument being that since an angel provided a ram as a last-minute substitute, the Lord never required child sacrifice. But, as Levenson remarks, it would be "strange to condemn child sacrifice through a narrative in which a father is richly rewarded for his willingness to carry out that very practice."[26]

We have even more explicit evidence. The Scriptures include repeated references to worship of other gods, particularly the most fearful and repulsive of all, Molech, the god to whom infants and small children were sacrificed. Molech was a Canaanite underworld deity whose sacrificial site was at Topheth ("oven," or "furnace"), in the Valley of Hinnom, near Jerusalem.[27] Levenson suggests that the Molech cult may be connected with the biblical law that first-born sons must be ritually redeemed from service in the Temple, but he acknowledges that the evidence is unclear. He shows that eventually the Israelites adopted a number of "substitution rituals" possibly replacing literal sacrifice of first-born sons: the paschal lamb (whose blood redeemed Israelite children while those of the Egyptians were slaughtered); Levitical service in the Temple (i.e., as assistants to the priests); monetary ransoms; and vows to become "Nazirites," men who committed themselves to especially restrictive regulations.[28]

But how about circumcision? Is there reason to suppose that this too became a "substitution ritual" symbolizing (and recalling) child sacrifice? One text, says Levenson, "among the most obscure and the most disquieting in the Torah," tells of Moses' wife, Zipporah, circumcising one of their sons as a redemptive sacrifice—but on her husband's behalf, not the child's. This mysterious episode, which appears in chapter 4 of Exodus, takes place when Moses, his wife Zipporah, and their young sons are journeying to Egypt. The Lord had commanded Moses to return to Egypt for the confrontation with Pharaoh and the ensuing divine punishments on the Egyptians. Suddenly, inserted into the text without preamble or explanation, we find a circumcision narrative:

> At a night encampment on the way, the Lord encountered him and sought to kill him. So Zipporah took a flint and cut off her son's foreskin, and touched his legs with it, saying, "You are truly a bridegroom of blood to me!" And when He let him alone, she added, "A bridegroom of blood because of the circumcision."[29]

This peculiar tale may be explainable when we recall that Yahweh must be regularly appeased with the blood of sacrificial animals. Zipporah might have sacrificed a lamb had she had one available; instead, she chose what was nearer to hand: her son's foreskin. When she bloodied Moses' "legs" (a biblical euphemism for penis) with the severed foreskin, the Lord's wrath subsided. Her final comment would have expressed lighthearted relief: She had made Moses her "bridegroom" again by recalling the blood of marital consummation.[30]

But whatever the explanation, Levenson argues that one thing is "reasonably clear": "the blood of circumcision saves Moses from YHWH's [Yahweh's] sudden attempt to kill him.... Moses lives because Zipporah has circumcised the boy." He concludes that the evidence suggests that "the impulse to sacrifice the first-born son remained potent long after the literal practice had become odious and fallen into desuetude."[31] In short, sacrifice of foreskin symbolized and substituted for sacrifice of child.

Finally on this subject: Child sacrifice probably disappeared from Israelite religion, once and for all, during the sixth century BCE: the very time when the priestly class—authors of the P text, redactors of the Torah, creators of the equivalence between circumcision and covenant—were establishing their theocracy. Thus, in the book of the prophet Jeremiah, active in the years just before and after 600 BCE, we find Yahweh not only condemning child sacrifice but denying that he had ever favored such a practice:

> For the people of Judah have done what displeases Me—declares the Lord. They have set up their abominations in the House which is called by My name, and they have defiled it. And they have built the shrines of Topheth in the Valley of Ben-hinnom to burn their sons and daughters in fire—which I never commmanded, which never came to My mind.[32]

Although child sacrifice may never have come to the mind of Yahweh, there can be no doubt that it had come to the mind of the prophet. Considering all the evidence, it seems quite possible that infant circumcision originated as a substitute for such sacrifice.

Bride-Price and Bridegroom

Two tales about *adult* circumcision both have to do with marriage and massacre. In one, those who submit willingly to circumcision, hoping for marriage, end up slaughtered; in the other, the recipients of the operation have already died in battle. The victims in both narratives are aliens whom Israelites overcome. Here, in plain contrast to the idea of infant circumcision as acceptance and incorporation, circumcision of alien adults is portrayed unambiguously as an act of aggression and exclusion: those who do the circumcising dominate, humiliate, and destroy those whom they circumcise.

Chapter 34 of Genesis (a J text) is a grim tale of revenge. The principal actors are Jacob and his daughter Dinah, a Hivite man named Shechem, son of the chief Hamor, and two of Dinah's brothers, Simeon and Levi.[33] When Dinah visits the Hivites, Shechem falls in love with her, seduces (or rapes) her, then speaks to her "tenderly" and asks his father to obtain her as his wife. "Intermarry with us," Hamor tells Jacob and his sons, "give your daughters to us, and take our daughters for yourselves. You will dwell among us, and the land will be open before you; settle, move about, and acquire holdings in it." Shechem adds words of his own: "Do me this favor, and I will pay whatever you tell me. Ask of me a bride price ever so high, as well as gifts, and I will pay what you tell me; only give me the maiden for a wife." But Dinah's brothers, furious that their sister has been dishonored, play along only in order to draw the Hivites into a trap. "We cannot do this thing," they tell Hamor and Shechem, "to give our sister to a man who is uncircumcised, for that is a disgrace among us. Only on this condition will we agree with you: that you will become like us in that every male among you is circumcised. Then we will give our daughters to you and take your daughters to ourselves; and we will dwell among you and become as one kindred." The two Hivite men, thoroughly deceived, return home and urge every man there to accept circumcision, which they do. The reward follows:

> On the third day, when they were in pain, Simeon and Levi, two
> of Jacob's sons, brothers of Dinah, took each his sword, came upon
> the city unmolested, and slew all the males. They put Hamor and
> his son Shechem to the sword, took Dinah out of Shechem's house,
> and went away. The other sons of Jacob came upon the slain and
> plundered the town, because their sister had been defiled. They
> seized their flocks and herds and asses, all that was inside the town
> and outside; all their wealth, all their children, and their wives, all
> that was in the houses, they took as captives and booty.[34]

As Eilberg-Schwartz observes, Dinah's brothers punish the Hivites "by getting them to injure their own genitals. The rape has been reversed."[35]

Foreskins make a surprising appearance as bride-price in the story of David's courtship of Saul's daughter, Michal. Saul, already fearing the younger man as a potential challenger, decides to use Michal as a "snare for him, so that the Philistines may kill him." David, self-described as "a poor man of no consequence," is reluctant even to suggest that he might marry the king's daughter. But Saul sends a courier with a reassuring message: "Say this to David: 'The king desires no other bride-price than the foreskins of a hundred Philistines, as vengeance on the king's enemies.'" Saul hopes that David will die in battle, of course, but instead the young hero doubles the price and pays: "Before the time had expired, David went out with his men and killed two hundred Philistines; David brought their foreskins and they were counted out for the king, that he might become the king's son-in-law." Saul has to agree to the marriage, but he becomes "David's enemy ever after."[36]

Here again, circumcision of enemies is symbolically contrasted with marriage and sexual fulfillment. By mutilating the genitals of Philistine corpses, David asserts his dominance over them, and affirms his own virility by symbolically appropriating theirs. The foreskins become bride-price; he becomes bridegroom.

Zipporah's rescuing Moses by circumcising their son is also a tale of dominance and conquest; in this case it is the Lord who dominates and Moses who is conquered.[37] Moses, who is emerging as the earthly representative of a powerful male deity, must be humbled—must acknowledge that it is Yahweh, not himself, who is all-powerful. Thus, comments Eilberg-Schwartz, "God's attack on Moses is in part an attack on his masculinity. This is why circumcision appeases God. The blood of circumcision is a symbolic acknowledgment that a man's masculinity belongs to God. Submitting to God and surrendering one's masculinity amounts [sic] to the same thing."[38]

Whatever we make of this mysterious episode, it seems clear that in all three narratives we again have evidence that the deepest significance of circumcision resides not in abstract spiritual realms but in the basic facts of social life: sexuality and masculinity, power and weakness, dominance and submission.

"This Is the Reason"

Thanks to the research of scholars like Hoffman, Eilberg-Schwartz, Archer, and Levenson, we can explain ancient Judean circumcision with some assurance. But judging from the evidence provided by biblical texts, those living at that time neither wondered about circumcision nor tried to explain it; they simply accepted it. Among the best illustrations of that is the last biblical tale I'll examine—another with puzzling elements; it appears in the Book of Joshua, a text composed around 600 BCE. When, in their approach to the Promised Land, the Israelites are camped near Jericho, the Lord delivers a mysterious order for a "second circumcision." Precisely what this means isn't clear; we're told only that many of the younger men, having been born during "the desert wanderings," had not been circumcised, but we don't learn why that was so. Nor is it clear why the operation would constitute a "second circumcision." In any event, the time has arrived, and the Lord instructs Joshua:

> "Make flint knives and proceed with a second circumcision of the Israelites." So Joshua had flint knives made, and the Israelites were circumcised at Gibeath-haaraloth ["the Hill of Foreskins"]. This is the reason why Joshua had the circumcision performed: All the people who had come out of Egypt, all the males of military age, had died during the desert wanderings after leaving Egypt. Now, whereas all the people who came out of Egypt had been circumcised, none of the people born after the exodus, during the desert wanderings, had been circumcised.
>
> For the Israelites had traveled in the wilderness forty years, until the entire nation—the men of military age who had left Egypt—had perished; because they had not obeyed the Lord, and the Lord had sworn never to let them see the land which the Lord had sworn to their fathers to assign to us, a land flowing with milk and honey. But He had raised up their sons in their stead; and it was these that

Joshua circumcised, for they were uncircumcised, not having been circumcised on the way. After the circumcising of the whole nation was completed, they remained where they were, in the camp, until they recovered. And the Lord said to Joshua, "Today I have rolled away from you the disgrace of Egypt."[39]

Since the text says that the men had not been circumcised, the reference to a "second circumcision" is puzzling. But the Lord, in his usual manner, provides no explanations, only instructions. Men must be circumcised because they hadn't been circumcised earlier. Nancy Jay, author of an illuminating cross-cultural study of sacrifice, comments as follows on this scene:

> Verse 4 begins: "And this is the reason why Joshua circumcised them: . . . ," and you think, reading it, that you are about to be given a *real* understanding. But the "reason why" is peculiarly disappointing: "for they were uncircumcised." (You see? The means *are* the ends.) . . . Of course, what is explained is not why Joshua circumcised them in the sense we had hoped for, but why he did it then and there and not at some other time and place. Why he should circumcise them in the first place is not considered to need explanation.[40]

For the time being we leave it at that: Israelite men circumcised because the Lord, creator of heaven and earth, said that they must.

"He's Circumcised and He Snores": Jews in the Greco-Roman World

For about two hundred years after the return from Babylonian exile (late sixth to late fourth centuries BCE), the Judeans lived in a semiautonomous state, locally administered as a minor outpost of the Persian empire, with considerable authority vested in the Temple priesthood. Their territory, known then as Yehud, was a tiny piece of land, some twenty-five miles long and thirty-two wide; the only center of any size was Jerusalem, with about 125,000 inhabitants. Despite the inclination of historians to place the Judeans on center stage, we should recognize that Judean territory was a social and political backwater—distinctive, to be sure, in its religious culture, but of very little interest to anyone beyond its borders. The historian Elias Bickerman characterizes Judea as a "Lilliputian territory" and Jerusalem as "the obscure abode of an insignificant tribe."[41]

With the Hebrew monarchy gone forever and local administrators little more than agents of the imperial Persian dynasty, those to whom Judeans looked for social and political as well as religious guidance were the priests, and the institution that provided a visible focus for their sense of collective identity was the Temple. Their conceptual environment was a small, culturally conservative society with limited horizons. So there is little reason to wonder why Judean fathers would have accepted the obligation to perform infant circumcision. After all, it was a divine mandate, upheld by priests whose word was law for everyday life.

But following the conquests of the Macedonian king, Alexander the Great, in the fourth century BCE, the fragmented eastern Mediterranean world changed dramatically. During his brief lifetime (356–323 BCE) Alexander overwhelmed the Persians and their empire, subduing lands as far east as India and as far west as Egypt, where he founded the great city of Alexandria (soon to become the home of a major Jewish community). The ultimate product of these events, lasting centuries beyond Alexander's time, was a "globalized" cultural area, extending throughout the eastern Mediterranean and beyond, profoundly transformed by adherence to the customs, standards, and values of the Greek heritage. This Hellenistic civilization endured for several centuries until it was gradually absorbed by the Romans.

Alexander annexed all of Palestine in 333 BCE. After his death, two rival Greek monarchies, the Ptolemies of Egypt and the Seleucids of Syria, fought over the terrritory. For a century Palestine, including Judea, was under the rule of the Ptolemies, but in 200 BCE the Seleucids under Antiochus III expelled the Egyptians and gained dominion over the entire region. Though Judea remained a self-governing district, ruled by a council of "elders" and priests led by the High Priest, the ultimate authorities were the Seleucids.[42]

Seleucid rule was benign for a time. But according to two apocryphal texts, 1 Maccabees and 2 Maccabees, the situation deteriorated in 167 BCE, when the Seleucid king Antiochus IV Epiphanes, a determined Hellenizer, forcibly entered Jerusalem, plundered and defiled the Temple, and instituted widespread repressive measures. Now, in addition to prohibitions on Sabbath observance and other Jewish religious practices, Antiochus is said to have demanded that the Jews "leave their sons uncircumcised" and "to make themselves abominable by everything unclean and profane." Punishment for violations is described as severe: "they put to death the women who had their children circumcised, and their families and those who circumcised them; and they hung the infants from their mothers' necks." Again, "two women were brought in for having circumcised their children. These women they publicly paraded about the city, with their babies hung at their breasts, then hurled them down headlong from the wall." It was events of this kind that were said to have precipitated the Maccabean revolt that led in 164 BCE to creation of an independent Judean nation. One caveat, though: 1 and 2 Maccabees were composed as political propaganda supporting the Maccabees in their conflict with Judean "Hellenists" who favored accommodation to Greek rule and a more liberal stance toward Hellenistic cultural influence.

So although it seems likely that circumcision did come under some form of criticism or restriction, the details are open to question, and the motives and policies of Antiochus IV were more complex than these texts suggest.[43]

The widely held belief that the Jewish Diaspora began after the destruction of the Temple in 70 CE is incorrect. Long before then, as early as the fourth century BCE, emigrants from Judea, seeking economic opportunities superior to those of their isolated environment, and responding to the relative ease of movement in the Hellenistic world, began forming communities in many towns in the Mediterranean region.[44] They settled in significant numbers in Egypt, Syria, Mesopotamia, North Africa, Greece, Italy, and various towns and cities in Asia Minor. By the first century CE there were probably at least three or four million Jews in the Roman Empire, the great majority living not in Judea but in cities and towns throughout the Mediterranean world and beyond—"in diverse and ever changing social contexts," says the historian John Barclay, "ranging in status from the impoverished field-hand to the millionaire imperial favorite."[45]

Like everyone in the Roman Empire, Jews had been influenced by Hellenistic cultural values, some to the point of near-complete assimilation. In a way, Hellenism resembled the qualities we associate with modernity: cross-cultural communication, wide-ranging commerce, cosmopolitanism.[46] This kind of cultural environment—universalist in style and taste, tolerant of diversity, suspicious of claims to special or superior status—contrasted with the inherently particularist and exclusivist Jewish way of life. Barclay comments on the generally overlooked role of circumcision in reinforcing Jewish separatism and avoidance of intermarriage:

One of the most important functions of circumcision was in identifying with whom a Jewess may have sexual intercourse.... It fulfilled this function by making it taboo for Jewish women to receive from an uncircumcised man what Philo calls "alien seed."...Jewish girls were taught to shudder at the thought of a sexual encounter with an uncircumcised man.[47]

The historian Mary Smallwood observes that ethnic particularism was characteristic of Jews during the Roman period. Their definitive trait, she says, was "ability to preserve [their] national identity, even after generations of residence among Gentiles, and to resist assimilation." This was generally as true for Jews living in Diaspora communities as for those in Judea. Despite their speaking Greek, she continues, "the Jews of the Diaspora remained aloof, and their refusal to compromise one jot or tittle of their religion, either by abandoning or modifying their own practices, or by making courteous concessions to paganism, turned them into closely-knit, exclusive groups." Such behavior "bred the unpopularity" that led to anti-Jewish sentiment:

The Jew was a figure of amusement, contempt, or hatred to the
Gentiles among whom he lived. His abstinence from pork was ridiculed, and his insistence on circumcision either ridiculed or scorned
as a barbarity; and at a time when pagan religions were tending
towards syncretism, his denial of the existence of his neighbors'
deities set him apart as old-fashioned and obstinate.[48]

Despite occasional difficulties with Jewish separatism, the Roman authorities accepted Jews and their religion as peculiar but essentially harmless.
Although they rebelled on occasion, most Jews were inclined to accommodate
to foreign rule, and that was enough to suit the Romans.[49] Moreover, as Shaye
J. D. Cohen points out, some Hellenized Gentiles were strongly attracted to
elements of Judaism, observing Sabbath and holiday rituals, and attending
synagogues. Although these individuals "venerated in one form or another
the God of the Jews," they did not consider themselves Jews and were not
considered such by others. Moreover, there were limits: "One Jewish practice
they studiously avoided was circumcision."[50]

By the first century CE, Roman authors were writing about Jewish circumcision as a perverse custom, fit only for disparagement and ridicule.[51] The
historian Strabo, in his *Geographica*, composed early in the first century, describes the "successors" of Moses as having acted righteously for a time; but
eventually, he says, "superstitious" and "tyrannical" priests gained control
and the culture took a downward turn: "From superstition arose abstentions
from foods, such as are customary even now, and circumcisions and excisions and similar usages."[52] The first-century historian Tacitus also describes
Jewish culture in hostile language, citing circumcision as one of the "perverse, filthy" (*sinistra foeda*) practices characteristic of Judaism.[53]

Circumcision appears occasionally in Roman satires, always with reference to Jews, and always with negative connotations. In a satirical epigram by
Martial, we learn of a comic singer whose penis was encased in a sheath large
enough for all the other actors together. But one day, during exercises in a
public arena, the sheath slipped off, and everyone saw that the poor guy
(*misero*) was circumcised (*verpus erat*). The term *verpus* means a circumcised
man; but, as the historian Peter Schäfer explains, a *verpa* is an erect penis with
an exposed glans—obviously an obscene display, implying that Jews are
lustful and eager for intercourse, including the homosexual variety.

The last point comes out clearly in another of Martial's epigrams, addressed to a rival Jewish poet, whom he addresses repeatedly as *verpe poeta*.
You're jealous of my success, he says; you make up poems based on mine.
Not only that, but you seduce my boy (*pedicas puerum*), then deny it. The term
verpe appears four times in this eight-line diatribe.[54] The *Satyricon* of Petronius, also from the first century CE, includes a remark with similar homosexual connotation. A man boasts that his clever, multitalented slave has only

two defects, without which he'd be the perfect possession: "He's circumcised [*recutitus*] and he snores."[55]

"Lawless Men": Rejecting the Mark of the Covenant

Although Jews in the Roman Empire knew that others considered circumcision barbarous, most Jewish fathers acceded to what they believed was a divine mandate. But some, particularly those living far from Judea, rejected the practice, refusing to have their infant sons circumcised, and in some cases trying to stretch their own foreskins into a restored form. Foreskin stretching (called "uncircumcision," or *epispasm*) appears to have been a common practice among Hellenized Jewish men, from at least as early as the second century BCE. Key features of Hellenistic culture were athletic exercises in gymnasia and athletic performances in public arenas, where men appeared in the nude. A penis sheathed in an intact foreskin was an acceptable sight, but a circumcised penis was another matter entirely. As the medical historian Frederick M. Hodges has shown, the ancient Greeks and their Hellenistic successors considered the "ideal prepuce" to be long, tapered, and "well-proportioned." Removing it was mutilation.[56] The circumcised penis, with its exposed glans, perceived as a vulgar imitation of erection, simply would not do for public display.

Jewish men who wanted to attend public baths or gymnasia knew that the sight of their genitals would inspire laughter and ridicule. So it was inevitable that some, eager for acceptance in the larger social world, gave themselves a presentable appearance by pulling the remaining foreskin forward as far as possible, and keeping it under enough tension to encourage permanent stretching toward its original length. Using a fibular pin or a cord, they pierced the front of the remaining foreskin, drew it forward, and fixed it in place; sometimes they would attach a weight to maintain tension. Over time the foreskin stretched and restored at least some of the appearance of an intact organ. (Jewish circumcision at this time still involved only partial foreskin removal; later, as we'll see, the rabbis mandated *peri'ah*—complete foreskin ablation—specifically to prevent stretching.) But abandoning circumcision did not necessarily mean abandoning Jewish identity; although some men "quietly faded into the surrounding culture," others rejected circumcision but remained Jewish.[57]

Understandably, Jewish writers refer to this subject mostly by innuendo; we do have several reports, though, on events during the second century BCE. I Maccabees remarks on Jews who succumbed to the enticements of Hellenism: "they built a gymnasium in Jerusalem, according to Gentile custom, and removed the marks of circumcision, and abandoned the holy covenant."[58]

A wrathful condemnation of all backsliders appears in the Book of Jubilees (one of the Pseudepigrapha, anonymous postbiblical books with apocalyptic messages), probably composed in the second century BCE. The author, a zealot, denounces men who not only refused to circumcise their sons but also desecrated their own "members":

> And now I announce unto thee that the children of Israel will not keep true to this ordinance, and they will not circumcise their sons according to all this law ... and all of them, sons of Beliar [Belial, the Devil], will leave their sons uncircumcised as they were born. And there will be great wrath from the Lord against the children of Israel, because they have forsaken His covenant and turned aside from His word, and provoked and blasphemed, inasmuch as they do not observe the ordinance of this law; for they have treated their members [i.e., penises] like the Gentiles, so that they may be removed and rooted out of the land.[59]

Refusal to circumcise infant sons, stretching their own foreskins: these, then, were the options for Jewish men who rejected the sign of the covenant. But it seems clear that most chose the easier path: acceptance of circumcision for themselves and their sons. In any event, in the minds of everyone else in the Hellenistic world, circumcision was a definitive Jewish custom, even *the* definitive Jewish custom; part of the trio including dietary regulations and Sabbath observance—but, for obvious reasons, in a class by itself.[60]

"Excessive and Superfluous Pleasure": Philo of Alexandria

Little in the way of written defense of circumcision has survived from this period, with one major exception: the work of the philosopher Philo of Alexandria, active in the early decades of the first century CE. Living in a major center of Diaspora life, where many Jews embraced Hellenistic culture, Philo received a Greek classical education and learned to develop arguments in the manner of Greek philosophers. What he knew about Judaism came not from traditional rabbinic instruction but from attendance at a synagogue; he wrote in Greek and may not even have known Hebrew. Nevertheless, his most often cited work consisted of interpretations of the Torah (which he probably read in the Greek translation, the Septuagint). Since his books were "apologies" for Judaism, intended as much for Gentile as for Jewish readers, Philo sought rational explanations for Jewish customs, hoping to vindicate Judaism as a civilized religion.

To appreciate the hold of circumcision on the Jewish mind, he said, one had to search beyond the literal act for the symbolic meaning that was its true justification.[61] He proposed four "principal reasons" for continuing the practice: First, it protects against the "severe and incurable malady of the prepuce called anthrax or carbuncle." This may be a reference to the ulcer (chancre) of primary syphilis (although we know now that circumcision does not protect against sexually transmitted diseases). Second, it "promotes the cleanliness of the whole body as befits the consecrated order" (that is, *spiritual* cleanliness of priests, but perhaps referring covertly to all Jewish males—"consecrated" by Abraham's covenant, hence cleansed in the spiritual sense). Third, it "assimilates the circumcised member to the heart"—a reference to the prophet Jeremiah's call for "circumcision of the heart." But the "fourth and most vital reason" is that circumcision promotes fertility: "for we are told that it causes the semen to travel aright without being scattered or dropped into the folds of the foreskin, and therefore the circumcised nations appear to be the most prolific and populous."[62]

These are the literal explanations. Now Philo adds that he considers circumcision "to be a symbol of two things most necessary to our well-being":

> One is the excision of pleasures which bewitch the mind. For since among the love-lures of pleasure the palm is held by the mating of man and woman, the legislators thought good to dock the organ which ministers to such intercourse, thus making circumcision the figure of the excision of excessive and superfluous pleasure, not only of one pleasure but of all the other pleasures signified by one, and that the most imperious.

The second reason is "that a man should know himself and banish from the soul the grievous malady of conceit" among those who are so proud of their ability to beget children that they forget "the Cause of all that comes into being."[63]

But why circumcise only males? In a volume entitled *Questions and Answers on Genesis*, Philo's answer is that "the male has more pleasure in, and desire for, mating than does the female, and he is more ready for it. Therefore He rightly leaves out the female, and suppresses the undue [literally, superfluous] impulses of the male by the sign of circumcision. [So] it was proper that his pride should be checked by the sign of circumcision."[64] Thus, Jewish men progressed from literal means—diminished penis—to true spiritual goals: diminished pleasure, diminished pride. Philo may have been first to publicly recognize what we now know to be the case: that circumcision does indeed decrease sexual sensation.

2

"Great Is Circumcision"

Christian Condemnation, Jewish Veneration

> Look out for the dogs, look out for the evil-workers,
> look out for those who mutilate the flesh. For we
> are the true circumcision, who worship God in spirit,
> and glory in Christ Jesus, and put no confidence
> in the flesh.[1]

> He who separates himself from circumcision is
> like one separated from the Holy One, blessed be He.[2]

We are "the true circumcision" who "put no confidence in the flesh." I begin this chapter by explaining the meaning of that statement by the apostle Paul, to emphasize how central the *idea* of circumcision became in the division between Christianity and Judaism. I'll try to show why, in the long history of the Jewish-Christian encounter, the question of the meaning of circumcision has always been central to the difference between Christianity and its "parent" religion. First we'll look at this from the Christian side. Then we'll see what the rabbis meant by saying that a man who rejected circumcision "separated" himself from the Lord.

"O Foolish Galatians!" The Challenge from Christianity

The very first Christians—Paul and the other apostles, all Jews—were missionaries to their own people, setting out to convert fellow Jews to a new doctrine: faith in the sacrificial death and miraculous resurrection of Jesus, whom they had recognized as the long-awaited

Jewish Messiah. His sacrifice, they declared, had freed Jews from the Law: the ritual precepts that defined them as a *people* apart from all others. Instead, they were now opened to *individual* salvation and the prospect of eternal life in the Spirit. The destruction of the Temple in 70 CE confirmed for the missionaries that their destiny was to lead the Jewish people into a new way of life, centering not on Temple rituals but on faith and spirituality. But soon they came up against harsh reality: most Jews were not only indifferent to their message but sometimes actively hostile and even violent. After all, it made no sense that the Messiah, whom traditional Jews imagined as a warrior king, descendant of the mighty David, had accepted his fate passively and died such an ignominious death. That he had risen from the tomb was of course a matter of faith that could be readily dismissed.

In fact, those who did respond enthusiastically to the new message were most often "Gentiles," members of neighboring ethnic groups with no experience of Torah Judaism. Admission of Gentiles into the fellowship was possible only for those who understood that they were entering a particular *Jewish* community, the disciples of Jesus. For the earliest Christians, the heart of the matter was a single question: Did the death and resurrection of Jesus herald the birth of a completely new religion; or was that religion actually a renewed and revitalized form of Judaism? Because if, as most believed, the latter was the case—if the new religion was still Judaism—then anyone who wanted to join the new fellowship must either be a Jew or must first convert to Judaism. And if an aspiring convert was a man, did it not follow that he must first submit to circumcision? Nearly all of the earliest Christian missionaries—the apostles—believed that they remained Jews, and that anyone who joined them must also either be or become a Jew.

But there was one dissenter: Paul, the most brilliant of the group, and ultimately the most influential. Paul realized that insistence on conversion to Judaism had to be abandoned, if for no other reason than the obstacle posed by its most daunting requirement. Better than any of his fellow missionaries he understood why the old religion could not serve as a gateway to the new: Traditional Judaism was the religion of a single people, set apart by adherence to a Law requiring ethnic separation confirmed by physical practices—"external" signs, "matters of the flesh": circumcision, dietary taboos, animal sacrifices, regulations and prohibitions of every sort. But the whole point of the new message, as he saw it, was that the death and resurrection of Jesus had rendered all this obsolete and meaningless; what mattered now was not the "flesh" but spiritual rebirth and renewal. And if Gentile men were to be admitted into the movement in the large numbers that now appeared possible, it was obvious that circumcision—by far the most formidable single barrier—had to be abandoned. So Paul took a stand, unpopular with his colleagues, that would eventually become definitive. By around 45 CE he was recruiting converts throughout the eastern Mediterranean, describing himself as a "missionary to the Gentiles." He welcomed everyone. Physical and ethnic characteristics were of absolutely no import; all that mattered was belief in Jesus as Messiah. He asked little or nothing in the way of obedience to Jewish ritual regulations; above all, he did not expect men to accept circumcision.

Matters came to a head sometime around 48 or 50, when Paul came to Jerusalem for a tense conference with James (brother of Jesus), Peter, and other apostles who still insisted that conversion meant becoming a Jew first, and only then becoming a Christian Jew. (The usual term is Jewish Christian, but Christian Jew better describes what they had in mind.) Inevitably the debate focused on circumcision. The most complete description of the conference, chapter 5 of Acts, is not as clear as one would like—perhaps reflecting the uncertainty of the chronicler (probably Luke, author of one of the Gospels). It appears that James and Peter were immovable on what had become the central question; but eventually they agreed that Paul might proceed with his mission to the Gentiles, but should instruct them only "to abstain from the pollutions of idols and from unchastity and from what is strangled and from blood."[3] They remained unwilling, however, to concede full membership to anyone who had not undergone a complete conversion to Judaism. In short, James, Peter, and the others still understood their religion to be a revitalized version of Judaism, available only to members of the Jewish ethnic community or others who converted in the traditional manner.

Paul seems to have accepted these restrictions provisionally—but only provisionally, since as he saw the matter, the position of his opponents involved a fundamental contradiction. Either an initiate remained mired in "fleshly" concerns or he did not; either he found meaning in outmoded regulations, or he had transcended such trivia and progressed to genuine spiritual renewal. If the latter, the condition of his genitals, circumcised or not, meant nothing whatever. The same principle applied, of course, to the laws regarding kosher diet. James and his faction shared fellowship meals (their central ritual activity) only with full-fledged converts to Judaism. Paul regarded this restriction as just another kind of material concern having nothing to do with the essential redemptive message.

Paul's most outspoken statement on "flesh" versus "spirit" appears in his letter to a new Christian community in Galatia (a region in Asia Minor, modern Turkey), composed around 52 CE. Apparently the Galatians had agreed to be circumcised. Paul was furious:

> O foolish Galatians! Who has bewitched you, before whose eyes Jesus Christ was publicly portrayed as crucified? Let me ask you only this: Did you receive the Spirit by works of the law, or by hearing with faith? Are you so foolish? Having begun with the Spirit, are you now ending with the flesh? . . . Christ redeemed us from the curse of the law, having become a curse for us . . . that in Christ Jesus the blessing

of Abraham might come upon the Gentiles, that we might receive the promise of the Spirit through faith.[4]

The "blessing of Abraham" was of course the covenant promised in Genesis 17, but now with circumcision eliminated and the promise of reproductive prowess transformed into reception of the "Spirit through faith." Lest these untutored souls miss the point, he went on to repeat the message in even plainer language:

> Now I, Paul, say to you that if you receive circumcision, Christ will be of no advantage to you. I testify again to every man who receives circumcision that he is bound to keep the whole law. You are severed from Christ, you who would be justified by the law; you have fallen away from grace.... For in Christ Jesus neither circumcision nor uncircumcision is of any avail, but faith working through love.[5]

In short, either you became a Jew and accepted the entire Jewish Law as binding, or you became a follower of Jesus, understanding that the Law had been transcended and nullified. Paul concluded his letter with a dramatic contrast: "For neither circumcision counts for anything, nor uncircumcision, but a new creation. Peace and mercy be upon all who walk by this rule, upon the Israel of God. Henceforth let no man trouble me; for I bear on my body the marks of Jesus."[6]

The marks of circumcision, the marks of Jesus: what could have been clearer? Paul seems to be warning opponents who might "trouble" him that he is invincible because he has chosen the correct path and bears the only marks that matter. He identifies his Gentile congregation (and himself) as part of the new Israel, an Israel sanctified in the spirit rather than the flesh. The significance of this challenge can hardly be overestimated. Paul had taken it upon himself, in the face not of conventional Jewish opposition but resistance from his closest colleagues, to reject a practice that had become definitive for (male) Jewish identity. He was proclaiming that his was truly a new religion.

Paul's final and perhaps most penetrating statement on this theme appears in his letter to the congregation at Rome, composed about 57 CE. There must have been uncertainty in the Roman group regarding circumcision, and probably the connection with Judaism, since Paul obviously felt compelled to address these questions again. But the tone here is quite different from that in the letter to the Galatians, and in fact the argument is different. Here we find Paul speaking as a Jew on what he considered to be a fundamental *Jewish* question: If circumcision is indeed spiritually worthless, should it even remain part of Judaism? This letter, milder than the earlier one in tone, more deliberate, develops a subtle argument addressing the nature of Jewish identity: "the real Jew," he says, must be spiritually fulfilled, and the "true circumcision" has nothing to do with genitals. First he contrasts Jews who obey the Law of traditional Judaism with those who do not; but then he declares that the traditional path ("written code") is worthless in any event. The only thing that matters, he insists once again, is inner spiritual renewal. Preoccupation with that which is "external and physical" leads only to spiritual poverty:

> Circumcision indeed is of value if you obey the law; but if you break the law, your circumcision becomes uncircumcision. So, if a man who is uncircumcised keeps the precepts of the law, will not his uncircumcision be regarded as circumcision? Then those who are physically uncircumcised but keep the law will condemn you who have the written code and circumcision but break the law. For he is not a real Jew who is one outwardly, nor is true circumcision something external and physical. He is a Jew who is one inwardly, and real circumcision is a matter of the heart, spiritual and not literal. His praise is not from men but from God.[7]

Paul knew about circumcised hearts from the Torah and the prophet Jeremiah. In chapter 10 of Deuteronomy, Moses enjoins the Israelites to love the Lord and obey his commandments. He chose you as his people, Moses reminds them, but to ensure his continuing love you must "[c]ircumcise therefore the foreskin of your heart, and be no longer stubborn."[8] Jeremiah, writing around 600 BCE, adopted the same image: "Circumcise yourselves to the Lord, remove the foreskin of your hearts."[9] Later in the same text, the Lord (speaking through the prophet) declares that the time is coming "when I will punish all those who are circumcised but yet uncircumcised—Egypt, Judah, Edom, the sons of Ammon, Moab, and all who dwell in the desert...for all these nations are uncircumcised, and all the house of Israel is uncircumcised in heart."[10] Since "heart" signified what we mean by soul or spirit, we see Paul's call for circumcision "of the heart" as employing the Judaic tradition—Hebrew scriptural imagery—to serve his radical new vision.[11]

Eventually Paul triumphed, of course, not because his opponents conceded the point but because the demographics were all in his favor. As it became evident that few Jews were accepting the message of salvation through Christ, and as Gentiles from throughout the Mediterranean region flocked into the new religion in ever-increasing numbers, it became less and less feasible to insist on genital alteration or dietary restrictions. Circumcision of the heart carried the day.

"To Mark You Off for the Suffering": Justin's Dialogue

Paul's contrast between "flesh" and "spirit," often expressed as contrast between literal and allegorical understanding, became the dominant theme in

Christian polemics against Judaism down to our own time. By the second century, Christian theologians were composing sermons and tracts in the mode called *adversus Iudaeos*, "In Opposition to the Jews." One of the first was *Dialogue with Trypho*, a second-century fictional debate between a Christian first-person narrator and his inept Jewish adversary. The author was Justin, later sainted and called Justin Martyr, one of the early Fathers of the Church. Born about 100 into a non-Christian family in Samaria, Justin studied philosophy for a time, then converted and moved to Rome, where he died as a martyr in 165. His *Dialogue* is an elaborate defense of the new religion, supported by copious citations from the Hebrew Scriptures, all aimed at demonstrating to the benighted Trypho that Jesus was truly the promised Messiah, and that his sacrificial death had brought release from the Law's ritual requirements, including circumcision. His favorite form of argument demonstrates that everything in the Torah and in Judaism is a "type"—that is, a prefigured, or preliminary, representation, in literal or material form, of what was destined ultimately to reveal its true spiritual form in Christianity. For example, to cite an image that remains central to Christian self-representation, the paschal lamb sacrificed at Passover "was truly a type of Christ, with whose Blood the believers, in proportion to the strength of their faith, anoint their homes, that is, themselves"; and "the lamb, while being roasted, resembles the figure of the cross, for one spit transfixes it horizontally from the lower parts up to the head, and another pierces it across the back, and holds up its forelegs"; and so on, until the bewildered Trypho concludes that almost nothing of the old faith really means what he thought it meant.[12]

As for circumcision, Trypho learns that it "is not essential for all men, but only for you Jews, to mark you off for the suffering you now so deservedly endure." So whereas the Jews supposed that circumcision identified them as bearers of the Lord's covenant, in fact it singled them out for his wrath! Lest Trypho be slow (as usual) to get the point, the narrator rubs it in with a favorite argument:

> For if, as you claim, circumcision had been necessary for salvation,
> God would not have created Adam uncircumcised; nor would He
> have looked with favor upon the sacrifice of the uncircumcised
> Abel, nor would He have been pleased with the uncircumcised
> Enoch.... Noah, the uncircumcised father of our race, was safe with
> his children in the ark.[13]

Justin was probably the first in a long line of Christian authors to contend that those who still cling to circumcision fail to understand that it was intended to be temporary, and that its only remaining significance is as a mark of their disgraceful refusal to accept their own Messiah.

"As Though Fastening Them in a Chain": John Chrysostom on Circumcision

In the late fourth century in Antioch, the brilliant orator called John "Chrysostom," "the golden-mouthed," delivered a set of sermons entitled *Homilies on Genesis*. John did not like Jews. He is remembered in the annals of *adversus Iudaeos* literature for the series of passionate *Sermons against the Jews* delivered to his Antioch congregation in 386–87, warning them against associating with Jews or, worse, participating in any of their ritual celebrations.[14] In his discourses on Genesis John of course had something to say about circumcision. God demanded the practice, he explained, because he knew that Abraham's descendants would be untrustworthy. Thus, as though he were "putting a bit in their mouths," he ordained circumcision as a way of "curbing their unrestrained urges":

> You see, since he was aware of their lustful tendencies in not practicing restraint, even though it had been drummed into them countless times to refrain from their irrational impulses, he gave them a perpetual reminder with this sign of circumcision, as though fastening them in a chain, and set limits and rules to prevent their overstepping the mark instead of staying within their own people and having no association with those other peoples.[15]

Thus a divine blessing and covenant became mouth-bit and chain for a willful, unruly people. The time when such safeguards were necessary had long passed, John continued, because Christian salvation was now attainable for everyone. But unfortunately, "the ungrateful and unresponsive Jews … insist on keeping circumcision and betray their juvenile attitude." What value, he asked, do they find in this practice? "I mean, getting rid of skin contributes nothing to freedom of spirit, does it?" Of course the Jews understood none of this; "still seated in darkness, and despite the sun of justice shining and spreading its rays of light in every direction, they are still attached to the light of a lantern; and, despite the age for solid food, they are still dependent on milk." But we Christians, John concluded, remembering Paul's lessons on spiritual circumcision, have "put off the sins of the flesh and put on clean apparel."[16] Although expressed in some of the most imaginative language in the history of anti-Jewish polemics, John's message repeated Paul's: circumcision, like all other requirements of the old Law, is nothing more than an obstacle on the path to spiritual rebirth.

"The Filthy Jewish Mark": Combating Jewish Proselytism

From the second century onward, Roman imperial legislation regarding Jews devoted far more attention to Jewish proselytism than to any other question—at first for political, not religious, reasons.[17] Despite the small size of what the Romans now called Palestine, the increasing propensity of the Jews to rebel led the emperors to note any indication that Jews were trying to recruit new members to their ranks. So long as Jews kept to themselves and did not seek converts, the Romans were indifferent to Jewish religious practices. But conversion to Judaism signified loyalty not only to an alien religion but to the Judean political state, and this the emperors found unacceptable.[18] And since circumcision confirmed conversion, it was logical that legislation would focus on this practice.

In the Roman view, moreover, circumcision bordered on castration. An edict issued by the second-century emperor Antoninus Pius permitted Jews to circumcise their own sons but no one else; violators would "suffer the punishment of a castrator" (castrantis poena): death and confiscation of property.[19] Late in the third century, the Roman jurist Paul repeated the admonition: Jews were permitted to circumcise only their own boys. Anyone else who submitted voluntarily to circumcision "in accordance with the Jewish custom," and especially those who performed such operations, would be "exiled perpetually to an island and their property confiscated"; the operator would be executed. Jews who circumcised "purchased slaves of another nation" would also be banished or executed.[20]

Opposition to Jewish proselytism became even more intense after the fourth-century conversion to Christianity of Emperor Constantine I and the Christianization of the empire that followed. In 335, Constantine issued another law prohibiting circumcision of slaves, Christian or otherwise; if this was discovered, the slave was to be freed.[21] (Since Jewish law required that male slaves working in the home be circumcised and converted, this obviously placed Jewish slave owners in a legal bind.) Shortly thereafter, in 339, Constantine's son and successor, Constantine II, issued an even more punitive edict, indicating that with the widening influence of Christianity, Judaism was now perceived as such a serious threat that Jews were unconditionally prohibited from slave ownership. Slaves purchased by Jews were to be transferred immediately to the imperial authorities. Circumcision of a non-Jewish slave became the ultimate transgression, punishable by death.[22]

It would appear that, despite the severity of the threatened punishments, Jews continued to purchase even Christian slaves and to circumcise and convert them. In 384, a law issued jointly by several coemperors did not refer directly to circumcision but forbade that Christian slaves be "contaminated" by subjection to Jewish ritual practices. The punishment, in addition to removal of the slaves, was to be "suitable and appropriate"—presumably, death and confiscation of property, as ordered in earlier legislation.[23]

In 415, Gamaliel VI, the last "patriarch" of the Palestine Jewish community to be recognized by the Roman authorities, was formally censured and demoted, probably because he had protested too vigorously against oppressive measures. The coemperors Honorius and Theodosius II issued an edict announcing Gamaliel's loss of privileges and specifying restrictions on his future actions. He was to have no judicial authority in disputes between Christians, or between Christians and Jews. Christian slaves in his jurisdiction were to be delivered to the Church. Moreover, if he or any other Jew were to attempt "to pollute a Christian or a man of any sect, freeborn or slave, with the Jewish mark," he was to be "subjected to the severity of the laws" (presumably execution).[24]

Finally, in 417 the same coemperors issued another law with somewhat surprising provisions. Here they accepted Jewish ownership of Christian slaves, saying explicitly what was and was not permitted. A Jew could neither purchase Christian slaves nor receive them as gifts, but he could retain those he already owned or received as an inheritance—with one key provision: that he did not "unite them, either unwilling or willing, with the pollution of his own sect [caeno propriae sectae confundat]." As usual, the punishment for converting a slave would be confiscation of property and execution.[25]

Review of legislation issued in the early medieval centuries, by secular authorities as well as bishops' councils, reveals a very similar picture. Jews were generally granted limited rights to hold slaves, sometimes including Christian slaves, but they were not to convert them, and, most particularly, not to circumcise them.[26] The language of the legislation, Roman and later, with its references to filth and pollution, says all we need to know about the image of circumcision in the Roman and Christian mind.

The Rabbinic Jewish Response

Were Jews aware of what others thought of circumcision? Did they compose specific rebuttals to Christian arguments; or did they perhaps react only indirectly, by defending the practice with arguments of their own? In fact, although Jewish texts composed during the early centuries of the Christian era seldom refer directly to Christian arguments, they speak often of the virtues of circumcision. It seems likely that the rabbis who created these texts were well aware of what the other side was saying, and knew that, in a world in which Christianity was becoming more influential every day, their controversial custom needed defending. So in a sense we have to read between the lines and assume that when rabbis extolled circumcision they were also responding defiantly to the Christian critique.[27]

Although everyone now associates the term *rabbi* with Judaism, few may understand that rabbis became sole leaders of the Jewish community only after they replaced Temple priests. The priestly class that rose to power in the fifth century BCE retained most of its authority until 70 CE, when, in response to Jewish rebellion, the Romans occupied Jerusalem, destroyed the Temple, and instituted strict control over the region. That ended the priestly era. The country was no longer even called Judea, for the Romans renamed it Palestine (i.e., land of the Philistines).

Priestly Judaism was a sacrificial religion, appropriate to a settled agricultural economy. Ordinary people brought animals and crops to the Temple for sacrifices conducted by priests, either as communal offerings or offerings by individuals seeking absolution for sins and transgressions. This way of life persisted for more than five hundred years, through the Hellenistic period and into the era of Roman rule. But, as I've noted, by the second century BCE large numbers of Jews had left Judea and settled throughout the eastern Mediterranean, particularly in such urban centers as Alexandria, Damascus, and Antioch. Since these emigrants could attend sacrificial rituals in Jerusalem seldom, if ever, they developed their own version of Judaism, centering on synagogues, where they met for everything from communal prayer and Torah study to family celebrations and casual socializing. Men rose to leadership in these communities not through patrilineal descent, and obviously not through claims to priestly authority, but because their fellow Jews recognized and respected their learning and wisdom. It was these men who were called rabbis: "masters" or "teachers."

By the first century CE the term *rabbi*, used as a form of respectful address to teachers and learned men, had also entered the vocabulary of Jews still living in Judea, and in the second century, when the Temple—and, with it, priestly authority—had disappeared forever, rabbis assumed social and spiritual leadership. From that time on we speak of rabbinic Judaism, the form that has lasted (with modifications) to the present time. Historians of Judaism call the second to sixth centuries the rabbinic period, because it was during this time that the rabbis reinterpreted traditional Judaism, creating what was in effect a radically reconstituted religion designed to meet the needs of a restructured and widely dispersed society. The ultimate product of their intellectual labor was a set of texts—called Mishnah, Talmud, and Midrash—so influential that they compete with the Torah and the prophetic writings as core documents of Judaism. Originating in centuries of oral commentary on the Hebrew Scriptures ("Old Testament"), these texts evolved as extensive interpretation and complex new legislation covering every imaginable facet of social, political, and religious life.

Circumcision came in for rabbinic attention, of course, with momentous consequences for future generations. As I mentioned, Hellenized Jewish men sometimes used stretching techniques to restore the appearance of an intact foreskin. For obvious reasons this was anathema to the rabbis: tantamount to rejection of Judaism and defiance of rabbinic authority. At some point in the late first or early second centuries, they instituted a radical addition to the traditional circumcision technique. Until then, a circumcision (*milah*) had only required severing the frontal part of the foreskin; in the infant penis this is loose tissue that is not attached to the delicate mucosal lining of the glans. Now there was to be a second procedure, called *peri'ah* ("opening" or "uncovering"): grasping the remaining foreskin and underlying mucosal tissue, forcibly separating this from the glans (using sharpened thumbnails), and tearing it away. Failure to remove all "shreds" of foreskin tissue, the rabbis ruled, rendered the circumcision invalid.[28] Probably at about the same time they added yet a third mandatory procedure: *metsitsah* ("sucking"), sucking blood from the wound—perhaps in response to the abundant blood flow caused by *peri'ah*.

Oral Torah: Mishnah and Talmud

The rabbis wrote not factual history but exegesis, or commentary, in the mode of their time, bringing social legislation to life by embellishing it with the products of their collective creative imagination. But although we do not read rabbinic texts as *history*, we can interpret them *historically*, approaching them the way anthropologists have studied myths and legends collected among nonliterate people: asking what their narratives tell us about attitudes to circumcision during the early rabbinic centuries. Although these range over five or six centuries and represent the thoughts of many generations, we'll recognize a shared style of discourse. Pulling items from their full context, as I must do, can be misleading—may make them seem more significant, more central in the world of their authors, than they really were. I think it can be safely said, though, that the rabbis thought often about circumcision, even worried about how to defend it against hostile criticism from Christians.

The texts we're about to examine are all part of what is known as "oral Torah," a corpus of writings created by rabbis in dialogue with one another, that came to be accorded status paralleling—in a sense even exceeding—that of the Torah. Despite their age (dating back some 1,500 to 1,800 years), and however exotic they may sound to us, we should keep in mind that these texts are the bedrock of traditional Judaism, still studied faithfully by Orthodox Jewish students and scholars around the world. They are called "oral" because they came, actually or ostensibly, from the mouths of known individuals and had been transmitted by memory before being written down.

The initial task of the rabbis was to codify and interpret legal precepts, originating in the Torah and enlarged through centuries of oral discourse, to make them accessible as cultural guides. Their first major accomplishment was an elaborate behavioral code, the Mishnah (from the Hebrew *shanah*, to repeat—hence that which had been orally repeated and memorized). The Mishnah, completed around 200 CE, is an organized summary of every precept on social, economic, and ritual behavior that for centuries had been discussed, argued, and interpreted. It contains six main divisions, called orders, each made up of a number of tractates, which are further divided into chapters and sections. The six orders are so broad and familiar (e.g., "Agriculture,"

"Holy Things") as not to require citation. A passage is cited by tractate, chapter, and section; thus "Ned. 3.11" means "tractate Nedarim ("Vows"), chapter 3, section 11." But the Mishnah is not as dry as that sounds. It conveys a sense of an ongoing conversation or discussion among a group of rabbis, each adding or interjecting commentary as he sees fit. Although organized by its division into the named orders and tractates, within each chapter the discussion meanders along, pursuing a theme for a time, then following remarks that lead in new directions, in much the way a conversation among a group of friends or colleagues might proceed. It has the dynamic quality of legal or philosophical argument, yet shaped by a distinctively Judaic brand of mental gymnastics, endowing it with a unique character.[29]

To provide some idea of how the Mishnah combines precepts and commentary, I'll discuss two key passages on circumcision. The first appears in order Moed ("Festivals"), tractate Shabbat ("Sabbath"). The tractate has already presented seventeen chapters of prescribed Sabbath and festival behavior when, in the final section of chapter 18 (Shab. 18.3), we read:

> They do not deliver the young of cattle on the festival, but they help out. And they do deliver the young of a woman on the Sabbath. They call a midwife for her from a distant place, and they violate the Sabbath on her [the woman in childbirth's] account. And they tie the umbilical cord. R. Yose says, "Also: They cut it. And all things required for circumcision do they perform on the Sabbath."[30]

Here mention of delivering cattle leads to human childbirth; then talk of umbilical cords leads Rabbi Yose to note cutting the cord, then to comment on another kind of cutting that is also permitted on the Sabbath (despite comprehensive regulations against any other form of work on that day). That single remark generates so much attention that the rabbis go on to devote all of chapter 19 to circumcision, partly as connected with Sabbath regulations, partly not. Here is a section from that chapter:

> 19.2 They do prepare all that is needed for circumcision on the Sabbath: they (1) cut [the mark of circumcision], (2) tear, (3) suck [out the wound]. And they put on it a poultice and cumin. If one did not pound it on the eve of the Sabbath, he chews it in his teeth and puts it on. If one did not mix wine and oil on the eve of the Sabbath, let this be put on by itself and that by itself. And they do not make a bandage in the first instance. But they wrap a rag around [the wound of the circumcision]. If one did not prepare [the necessary rag] on the eve of the Sabbath, he wraps [the rag] around his finger and brings it, and even from a different courtyard.[31]

Here the rabbis specify the three stages (all of which would be defined as prohibited Sabbath "work" in other circumstances) of what had come to be the required form of circumcision: *milah*, *peri'ah*, and *metsitsah*. This is the first text specifying *peri'ah* as an absolute requirement. The same chapter is where we first find mention of the warning that leaving even "shreds" of foreskin renders the procedure "invalid."[32]

Next they remark on various actions accompanying the procedure, all of which would be ordinarily prohibited on the Sabbath. Presumably the bandage would have been soaked in a wine-and-oil mixture; but since mixing the two on the Sabbath was prohibited work, they had to be applied separately. The instructions on chewing the cumin poultice and applying a rag as a makeshift bandage may require no comment, other than to point out the likelihood that some infants contracted serious infections. That also applies to sucking blood from the wound, mentioned in the Talmud as a way of *preventing* infection—and still practiced by some Orthodox mohels despite its well-documented dangers.[33]

The final passage explains that, although making a bandage on the Sabbath is prohibited, because this would not count as essential work, someone may procure a rag for the purpose, may even carry it a distance (but wrapped around a finger, to offset the *appearance* of carrying, another prohibited act). In short, although Sabbath observance is an inviolable divine command, circumcision trumps even Sabbath.

So far we've seen straightforward instructions—a sort of "how-to" manual. Much of the Mishnah is in that style, but not all. Here, for example, is one of the most remarkable sequences in rabbinic literature. An arcane discussion, centering on whether the term "uncircumcised" is to be interpreted literally or as a reference only to Gentiles, leads to these comments:

> R. Eliezer b. Azariah says, "The foreskin is disgusting, for evil men are shamed by reference to it" . . . R. Ishmael says, "Great is circumcision, for thirteen covenants are made thereby." R. Yose says, "Great is circumcision, since it overrides the prohibitions of the Sabbath, which is subject to strict rules." R. Joshua b. Qorha says, "Great is circumcision, for it was not suspended even for a moment for the sake of Moses, the righteous" . . . Rabbi says, "Great is circumcision, for, despite all the commandments which Abraham our father carried out, he was called complete and whole only when he had circumcised himself as it is said, *Walk before me and be perfect* (Gen. 17:1)."
> "Another matter: Great is circumcision, for if it were not for that, the Holy One, blessed be he, would not have created the world, since it says, *Thus says the Lord: But for my covenant day and night, I should not have set forth the ordinances of heaven and earth* (Jer. 33:25)."[34]

Here, following a remark on which all could agree (that "the foreskin is disgusting"), one rabbi after another produces additional proof of the greatness of circumcision. The first recalls that the word "covenant" appears thirteen times in Genesis 17. The reference to Moses recalls the Zipporah narrative, which is usually interpreted to mean that Yahweh demanded immediate circumcision of Moses' son. We remember from the beginning of Genesis 17 that Abraham had to become *tamim*, meaning perfect or unblemished. The torrent of praise culminates in a striking finale, by an anonymous contributor: had it not been for circumcision ("covenant") the Lord would not have bothered to create the world!

The Mishnah was completed shortly after 200 CE. But the rabbis were only beginning. They continued to discuss every line of their "Oral Torah," along with the original written texts, and over the next several centuries they created an even more extensive and elaborate document, the Talmud (from the word for learn). The Talmud did not supersede the Mishnah; it incorporated the Mishnah intact and greatly enlarged on it, with explanations attached as additional discussion. So we can think of Talmud as Mishnah plus extensive added commentary. Talmudic commentary is even more elaborate and imaginative than that of the Mishnah. Although the Talmud certainly includes a full share of legalistic discourse, it is rich with creative additions of every kind: retold or reworked myths and legends, narratives, anecdotes, fanciful word-play, surprising digressions, all in the service of ever-deeper understanding of foundational texts.[35]

Let's return to the Mishnah text featuring praise for the greatness of circumcision. The Talmud picks up on that discussion with a rabbi's observation that all of Moses' commendable deeds were not enough to excuse him when he failed to circumcise his son. The rabbis imagine that God was punishing Moses for attending to travel details (for his journey to Egypt) rather than circumcising the child at the proper time. Next, two rabbis speculate on why Moses was neglectful, and on whether in fact it was Satan (not the Lord) who sought to kill Moses.

Another rabbi joins the discussion: When Moses neglected the duty of circumcision, Af and Chemah "swallowed him up," leaving only his legs exposed. Both *af* and *chemah* mean "anger" or "rage." These personifications of divine emotion, he says, swallowed Moses down to the legs—that is, as far as the groin, to show Zipporah that this area in the child's body demanded immediate attention. Then a commentator returns to the "Great is circumcision" theme with one new gloss and repetition of two that we've heard before: the familiar reference to becoming "perfect," and the observation that circumcision is so "great" that without it Creation itself would have been pointless. "Great is circumcision," he adds, for despite Abraham's devotion to his religious duties, he became "perfect" only after his circumcision. Moreover, comments another, circumcision is so great that it outweighs in importance all other Torah precepts. Another proposes that were it not for circumcision, neither heaven nor earth would endure (a variant on the theme of God's reluctance to create a world in which penises remained intact).[36]

The Talmud follows the Mishnah fairly closely here, adding still more words of praise for circumcision, offering yet another warning that men ignore it at their peril. We may wonder why this commentary repeats almost verbatim so much of what is already found in the Mishnah text. I think this was a way of emphasizing its importance. The rabbis seem to say that we can never be reminded too often of the greatness of circumcision.

The rabbis knew of course that some infants died after being circumcised. Twice in the Talmud we find instructions on how to proceed if a previous son or sons have died as a result of the operation. The first, in tractate Shabbat, comes in the form of paired narratives (possibly a single narrative retold with slight variation) by a Rabbi Nathan, who recounts his response to this situation. In each case he was asked to rule on circumcision for a child whose three siblings had died after the operation. In one case, he says, the child's complexion was too reddish, while the second was green (probably a reference to infant jaundice). He told the first mother to wait until the child's blood was "absorbed," and the second to wait until her child attained "his full blood." Both mothers waited, then had the babies circumcised. Both survived, and both boys were named Nathan in his honor.[37] The second text, in tractate Yebamot ("Levirate Marriages"), follows a discussion of whether a divorced woman may marry again; the rule is that she may marry a second husband but not a third. This reminds the participants of rulings on circumcision: One rabbi had ordered that when two of a woman's infants have died following circumcision, the third should be spared. Another was less lenient: circumcise the third, he ruled, but not the fourth.[38]

Midrash: Rabbinic Commentary after the Talmud

Rabbinic commentary did not end with the Mishnah and Talmud; rabbis went on discussing every text they inherited, from Torah onward, creating a wealth of new texts, known collectively as Midrash, meaning interpretation or exegesis. These followed the style of discourse in the Mishnah and Talmud, adding new twists to old themes. Here I'll discuss some memorable comments on circumcision found in four Midrash texts: *Genesis Rabbah* (literally "Great Genesis"), interpretations of passages in Genesis; *Exodus Rabbah*, for Exodus; *The Fathers According to Rabbi Nathan*, on a single Mishnah tractate, called "Fathers"; and *Pirkei de Rabbi Eliezer* ("Chapters of Rabbi Eliezer").

Two chapters in *Genesis Rabbah* follow the text of Genesis 17, verse by verse, more or less in order. They're an excellent example of how the rabbis improvised, beginning with a familiar biblical text and wandering as far afield as their imaginations carried them. The discussion begins with a comment that just as figs at first ripen one at a time, then become so abundant that they're harvested in baskets, similarly the Israelites became ever more "fruitful" after Abraham's circumcision. Moreover, just as the only inedible part of a fig is the stalk, so it was with Abraham: God declared that his single "blemish" was his foreskin. Remove that, said the Lord, and you will be *tamim*, perfect.

Then the rabbis imagine Abraham himself addressing a pointed question to God (already familiar to us from Christian polemic): "If circumcision is so precious, why was it not given to Adam?" The Lord offers a cryptic reply: Let it be sufficient, he says, that we two are in the world. If you won't accept circumcision for yourself, it will be enough that the world has existed until now, and it will be enough that circumcision has been neglected until now. Now Abraham (surrogate for the rabbis themselves) poses the very question that was central for Paul and the early Christians: How about prospective converts: Will they agree to being circumcised? This draws a dismissive reply: Let it suffice that I'm your God and your protector—and not for you alone, either, because I am the God and protector of the world.[39] The plain message here was that there can be no compromise. Knowing full well that circumcision repelled Gentiles, including prospective converts, the rabbis (rejecting Paul's argument) held fast to the doctrine that circumcision belongs to Abraham and his true heirs; if others reject it, so much the worse for them.

Now the discourse turns to the meaning of *tamim*. A rabbi tells a story about a woman whom the king commanded to pass before him for inspection. She did so, pale with fright, thinking, what if he finds me flawed? The king declared that she was perfect but for a single small defect: the nail on her little finger was too long. Shorten that, he instructed her, and you'll have no defect. And that is what God told Abraham: Remove the one blemish on your body and you will be perfect.[40] Fingernails and foreskins: pare them down and they'll pass muster before any king, human or divine.

Commentary follows on all sorts of questions: Why circumcise the foreskin and not, say, the ear or the mouth? Why did Abraham fall on his face when he heard the message about covenant and circumcision? Why was circumcision required for the territorial grant? Further along, the rabbis ask what exactly creates the circumcised Jewish male: Is it foreskin removal or shedding of blood? The discussion revolves around the opinions of two major rabbinic schools. Their points of disagreement are inconclusive—thus all the more interesting to the discussants. First we're told that the two disagree about the need to draw blood from a new convert who has already been circumcised; but one rabbi says the only question is whether blood must be drawn from an infant born without a foreskin if the eighth day is a Sabbath, or whether this can be postponed for a day. Since the child has no foreskin, is it still necessary to draw blood on the Sabbath? The rabbis can't agree on the Sabbath question, but they do agree that circumcision requires bloodshed.[41]

The discussion continues, lighting on details of the Genesis 17 narrative. Then the rabbis reach the verse saying that Abraham circumcised Ishmael and all the other males, including slaves, in his household:

R. Aibu said: When Abraham circumcised those that were born in his house, he set up a hillock of foreskins; the sun shone upon them and they putrefied, and their odor ascended to the Lord like sweet incense. God then said: "When My children lapse into sinful ways, I will remember that odor in their favor and be filled with compassion for them."[42]

Aibu may have drawn the image from the tale of Joshua's circumcising Israelite men at the "Hill of Foreskins" (Joshua 5:2–8), but the sweet odor rising to heaven was his own contribution.

"More Unclean Than All Unclean Things"

The mark of circumcision is so powerful, the rabbis tell us, that it protects Jews from the very fires of hell. We learn in *Exodus Rabbah* that "no Israelite who is circumcised will go down to Gehinnom." But circumcision will not be sufficient to redeem Jewish "heretics":

To stop the heretics and the wicked ones of Israel saying [i.e., who say]: "We will not descend to Gehinnom because we are circumcised," what doth the Holy One, blessed be He, do? He sends an angel who stretches their foreskin and then they descend to Gehinnom.... When the Gehinnom sees their hanging foreskins, she opens her mouth and devours them.[43]

Here an angel, ordinarily a benign figure, becomes an avenger of the Lord; and Gehinnom (or Gehenna), the hellish furnace to which condemned souls are consigned, is visualized as a monstrous female with a gaping mouth—an image I haven't encountered elsewhere.

The rabbis imagined God as a circumcised male.[44] In *The Fathers According to Rabbi Nathan* we learn that since God created man in his own image, Adam was born circumcised. (This disposes of the question of why Adam was created with a foreskin—he wasn't!) And not only Adam. The same passage tells us that many other biblical heroes were born "circumcised," each claim supported by a biblical text. Job is described as perfect or flawless (*tam*) in the first verse of his book.[45] The same applies to Noah, Jacob, and Joseph, each called *tam* or *tamim*. Moses too was born without a foreskin, since we read in Exodus 2:2 that his mother recognized him as an especially "fine" (*tov*) infant. What did she see that made this child more beautiful than others? "Only that he was born circumcised." (This may have been introduced to explain the fact that the Torah says nothing about Moses being circumcised. The remark by the pharaoh's daughter, in Exodus 2:6, "This must be a Hebrew child," was a logical supposition, since, acccording to the narrative, her father had ordered that male Hebrew infants be thrown into the Nile.)

Other biblical texts inform us that Balaam ("although wicked"), Samuel, David, Jeremiah, and Zerubbabel (the last heir to the Israelite monarchy, said to have encouraged the building of the Second Temple) were all born with the sign of the covenant already inscribed on their bodies.[46]

Foreskins come in for specially heavy invective in the *Chapters of Rabbi Eliezer*. This volume is attributed to an early second-century rabbi, but parts were composed later, probably as late as the eighth century. A commentary on Genesis 17 declares that the foreskin "is more unclean than all unclean things...a blemish above all blemishes." A man who "separates himself from circumcision" has separated from God. Only the worst of men would do this, of course; Esau, for example, though circumcised, "despised the covenant of circumcision just as he despised the birthright."[47]

We learn why Abraham circumcised every male in his household, even slaves (who were not parties to the covenant):

> Because of purity, so that they should not defile their masters with their food and with their drink, for whosoever eateth with an uncircumcised person is as though he were eating flesh of abomination. All who bathe with the uncircumcised are as though they bathed with carrion, and all who touch an uncircumcised person are as though they touched the dead, for in their lifetime they are like (the) dead; and in their death they are like the carrion of the beast, and their prayer does not come before the Holy One, blessed be He, as it is said, "The dead praise not the Lord" (Psalm 115:17). But Israel who are circumcised, their prayer comes before the Holy One, blessed be He, like a sweet savor.[48]

So circumcision had now come to mean far more than covenant. The rabbis declared that being circumcised was virtually equivalent to being a living human being, and that an intact man was like a corpse. In their minds, retention of this part of the male body had become a symbol of death-like corruption, ample justification for consignment to hell.[49] We might note the irony: in contrast to the usual beliefs about contamination from women's bodies, here are expressions of loathing for male bodies that have not been surgically purified.

"In Your Blood Live"

We need to consider more fully rabbinic discussion of a key element of circumcision: shedding of blood. As Lawrence Hoffman remarks, one cannot read rabbinic texts on circumcision without encountering references to blood. The rabbis, he says, developed "a new conception of the Jewish compact with God. Gone is the agricultural imagery; gone, too, is the fertility concern.... Instead, we get the rabbinic notion of salvation, symbolized by the blood of circumcision, which saves." And midrashic texts are our best source for insight into what circumcision meant in the rabbinic mind.[50]

We return to the *Chapters of Rabbi Eliezer*. According to the Genesis 17 narrative, Abraham obeyed the Lord's mandate by circumcising himself on "that very day." And because a passage in Leviticus (23:28) uses the same phrase to refer to Yom Kippur (the Day of Atonement), Abraham's auto-circumcision must have occurred on that day.[51] This leads to a discourse on blood as atonement: "Every year the Holy One, blessed be He, sees the blood of our father Abraham's circumcision, and He forgives all the sins of Israel. . . . In that place where Abraham was circumcised and his blood remained, there the altar was built."[52] The authors imagine that the Temple was constructed at the site of Abraham's circumcision, hence that his blood lay at the base of the sacrificial altar. By connecting the Genesis narrative with instructions for the conduct of animal sacrifices, the rabbis added new meaning to Abraham's circumcision: not only did it ensure abundant progeny and land for his descendants, but, like all sacrifices, it also atoned for their sins.

Another passage develops further the connection between circumcision blood and redemption. The discussion has moved to the exodus from Egypt. The pharaoh, declares the author, had forbidden the Israelites to practice circumcision. But now they were free:

> And on the day when the children of Israel went forth from Egypt, all the people were circumcised, both young and old, as it is said, "For all the people that came out were circumcised" (Josh. 5:5). The Israelites took the blood of the covenant of circumcision, and they put (it) upon the lintel of their houses, and when the Holy One, blessed be He, passed over to plague the Egyptians, He saw the blood of the covenant of circumcision upon the lintel of their houses and the blood of the Paschal lamb. He was filled with compassion on Israel, as it is said, "And when I passed by thee, and saw thee weltering in thy (twofold) blood, I said unto thee, In thy (twofold) blood, live; yea, I said unto thee, In thy (twofold) blood, live" (Ezek. 16:6). "In thy blood" is not written here, but in "thy (twofold) blood," with [two bloods], the blood of the covenant of circumcision and the blood of the Paschal lamb.[53]

This is not the easiest rabbinic text to understand, but it is packed with meaning. The term "twofold," placed in parentheses by the translator, explains that the Lord saw two kinds of blood, that of lambs and circumcisions. In the narrative cited from Ezekiel (which has no direct connection with circumcision), the Lord scolds the Israelites for "abominations" and reminds them of their obligations to him. He portrays Israel metaphorically as a helpless female infant that was "left lying, rejected, in the open field," until the Lord, seeing her "wallowing" in her own blood, rescued her and raised her to womanhood. I'll return to this in the next chapter, since, despite its explicit reference to a female infant, the passage was incorporated into the ritual circumcision liturgy. Here we need note only that, although the Ezekiel text says nothing about circumcision, the rabbis included it because of the vivid *blood* imagery, particularly the repeated phrase about living in one's blood. By invoking the doubled phrase they linked two kinds of sacrificial blood, the blood shed at circumcision and that of the paschal lamb. The Israelites, so went the new interpretation, smeared *both kinds of blood* on their door lintels as a message to the Lord: We've sacrificed to you properly—foreskins and lambs—and displayed for your approval blood from both; now slaughter Egyptian boys, not ours! In short, it is not just foreskin removal that redeems; it is *genital blood*.

As we reflect on these texts, with their almost obsessive need to justify infant circumcision, it seems that the rabbis themselves realized that they had inherited a challenging task. They must have felt compelled to defend circumcision—not only against the formidable Christian critique but probably also against ordinary Jewish men who questioned the practice. Otherwise, why all the effort to prove that circumcision is so precious to God, so glorious a practice, that he created the world on its behalf? Whatever we choose to make of these explanations and interpretations, one thing seems certain: the authors were struggling with a difficult commandment.

3

"Offering Incense to Heaven"

Jewish Circumcision in Medieval
and Early Modern Europe

> The opening of circumcision results in an opening up to
> God, a receptivity, which enables one to stand in God's
> presence and to behold the Glory.[1]

> Whoever nullifies the covenant of our ancestor Abraham and
> retains his foreskin or stretches it, even if he possesses
> knowledge of the Torah and practices good deeds, has no
> portion in the World to Come.[2]

> Copulation is difficult for the true *zaddik* [righteous man].
> Not only does he have no desire for it at all, but he experiences
> real suffering in the act, suffering which is like that which the
> infant undergoes when he is circumcised.[3]

Often one hears people speak of "Jewish traditions" or "traditional
Jewish culture." Very little of what they have in mind, though—and
this includes ritual circumcision—even vaguely resembles the culture
of ancient Judea; virtually all contemporary Jewish American customs and practices originated in Europe. Jews have lived in Europe
for a very long time—some sixteen hundred years. Already by the
early fourth century the Roman emperor Constantine the Great issued an edict granting the town councilors of Cologne the right to
nominate Jews for council membership, and there are numerous
references to Jewish life in Gaul thereafter. During the reigns of
Charlemagne (786–814) and his Frankish successors, Jews were
established participants in the economic life of the empire; and

despite onerous discrimination and persecution from the eleventh century onward, they endured in tightly knit communities, non-Christians in the
world of Christendom.[4]

Throughout the long period extending to the beginning of the nineteenth
century, circumcision remained entrenched as an indispensable rite of male
initiation, not only into Judaism in the formal religious sense but into the
Jewish community—the only community in which a Jew could survive as a
socially recognized person. The circumcision rite—that is, the ritualized liturgy and practices accompanying the surgery—evolved in Europe into the
form still maintained by Orthodox Jews today. Jews also introduced folk
customs endowing circumcision with a singular aura.

In one sense nothing changed from the time of the ancient rabbis to the
early nineteenth century: Jews not only held on to circumcision but elevated it
to a position of supreme significance—not surprising, perhaps, for a people
trying to survive as a tiny minority in an often hostile world. I'll turn to the
Sephardic Jews of Spain and Portugal for two especially striking illustrations
of how passionately European Jews everywhere were determined to retain
their most mysterious practice, the one that outsiders most reviled.

But there were critical Jewish voices—not necessarily opposed to the
practice but more insightful than those who praised and defended it without
reservations. Here I'll discuss the commentary of two of the most profound
thinkers of the entire period: Maimonides, the twelfth-century physician-
philosopher whose interpretation of circumcision differed remarkably from
those of his rabbinic predecessors; and Spinoza, the seventeenth-century
philosopher whose observations on circumcision have often been misinterpreted as favorable when in fact they were not.

"Delivered from the Pit": The Rite of Circumcision

Circumcision was instituted by priests as a religious practice in the fifth
century BCE; but the circumcision rite—a dramatic performance, as it were, in
which an infant is circumcised in a ritually ordered manner, with a prescribed
liturgy—was created by rabbis long afterward. The core elements were probably in place by the second or third century, though relatively minor additions
and modifications were instituted as late as the medieval period. We can
already anticipate the essential message: that the infant is sanctified and redeemed by the shedding of his blood, a sacrificial act confirming his admission into a cohort of similarly sanctified males.[5]

The rite, as still conducted by Orthodox mohels (though not others), has
three sections: an introduction, a two-act core involving the actual surgery,
and a brief conclusion. What calls for our particular attention is the core
section, during which the infant is circumcised and the mohel intones the

recitations that reveal most clearly the original meaning of what is happening: "a ritualization of male status within Judaism." This part was the earliest to be instituted; the introduction and conclusion were added in the medieval period.[6]

I'll describe the entire rite in detail, combining interpretations from Hoffman's *Covenant of Blood* with my own comments. (I have placed reference numbers immediately following sections of the liturgy to be analyzed.)

As the infant appears in the room, the assembled witnesses (traditionally all men) welcome him with "Blessed is he who comes." The mohel takes the infant and recites a brief invocation recalling the opening verse of Genesis 17: "[T]he Holy One, Blessed be He, said to Abraham, our father, 'Walk in my ways and be perfect.'" [1]

Then he recites lines from Numbers 25 that might lead anyone to ask how they relate to circumcision:

> The Lord spoke to Moses, saying, "Phinehas, son of Eleazar son of Aaron the priest, has turned back My wrath from the Israelites by displaying among them his passion for Me, so that I did not wipe out the Israelite people in my passion. Say, therefore, I grant him My pact of friendship" [or "My covenant of peace"].[7] [2]

The mohel then places the child on the knees of a man, called the *sandek*, who will hold him during the circumcision. The sandek is usually a grandfather, or other close relative or family friend. Next to his chair is another, called "the chair of Elijah." The mohel says, "This is the chair of Elijah the prophet, remembered for good." The mohel and the child's father declare that they are "ready and willing" to perform the commandment. [3]

As the mohel circumcises the infant, or immediately thereafter, the father blesses the Lord, "who has commanded us to bring him into the covenant of Abraham, our father." The witnesses proclaim: "As he has entered the covenant, so may he enter Torah, marriage [literally, the wedding canopy], and good deeds." The mohel then blesses a cup of wine and delivers the following invocation:

> Blessed art Thou, Lord, our God, King of the universe, who sanctified the beloved one from the womb, and placed Your statute in his flesh, and sealed his descendants with the sign of the holy covenant. Therefore, as reward for this, O Living God, our Portion and our Rock, may You command that the beloved of our flesh be delivered from the pit, for the sake of His covenant that He has placed in our flesh. Blessed art thou, Lord, who creates [literally, *cuts*] the covenant. [4]

Then he places a drop or two of wine on the infant's lips and recites a prayer announcing the child's name and calling yet again, in more explicit language, for his deliverance or salvation:

Our God and God of our fathers, preserve [or sustain] this child for
his father and mother, and let his name in Israel be [name], son
of [father's name]. May the father rejoice in the issue from his loins,
and may the mother receive happiness from the fruit of her womb,
as it is written: "When I passed by you and saw you wallowing in
your blood, I said to you, 'Live in spite of your blood.' Yea, I said to
you, 'Live in spite of your blood' [more precisely, 'In your blood,
live']."[8] [5]

This prayer continues with reference to the covenant and to the circumcision of Isaac, and concludes with another call for the child to enter Torah
study, marriage, and good deeds. Then the mohel recites a second prayer on
the theme of redemption through sacrifice. I quote only the first line: "Master
of the universe, may it be Your will to regard and accept this as though I had
offered him before Your glorious throne."[9] [6]

He follows this with a prayer asking that the "tender child" be granted
"complete healing," and that his father be deemed worthy of raising him to
Torah, marriage, and good deeds. Everyone says, "Amen." The rite ends with
a standard concluding prayer, *Alenu*, declaring acceptance of God's will that
the people of Israel should differ from all others. Then the group adjourns for
a festive meal, and the child is returned to his mother.

Interpreting the Liturgy

I've described a traditional Jewish circumcision rite, as instituted by rabbis
from the second century CE into the medieval period. This is not what one
hears at circumcisions performed by most American mohels nowadays. But
here I explain the meaning and intent of the traditional rite, as practiced for
centuries in Europe and elsewhere, and as still conducted by Orthodox mohels. (Bracketed numbers refer to the corresponding numbers in the liturgy
quoted in the previous section.)

[1] The liturgy begins by repeating the first verse of Genesis 17 ("Walk
before me and be perfect"), recalling the idea that the foreskin is an imperfection that must be removed to make the male body *tamim*, flawless or
perfectly formed.

[2] The story of Phinehas is in Numbers 25. While the Israelites were
encamped in Moabite territory during their journey into Canaan, Israelite
men "profaned themselves by whoring with the Moabite women" and sac-
rificing to the local Moabite deity. An infuriated Yahweh imposed a plague on
the entire community and commanded Moses to have the leading transgressors impaled. But before Moses could carry out the executions, Aaron's
grandson Phinehas entered a tent where a high-ranking Israelite man was
copulating with an equally high-ranking Midianite (not Moabite) woman and
drove a spear through them both. This deed so gratified Yahweh that he

relented and ended the plague (although twenty-four thousand had already died). The liturgy's quoted passage on turning back wrath follows.[10]

The traditional explanation is that Phinehas was rewarded for risking his life "to avenge the desecration of God's name." Yahweh not only approved Phinehas's action but even mandated that his descendants should become priests. Phinehas, explains one commentator, "felt utter abhorrence" when he witnessed the "brazen desecration" of the "mark of circumcision"—and that justified the double murder.[11] Note that the "desecration" was not worship of an alien deity, since Phinehas's deed had nothing to do with that; the "desecration" was insertion of a circumcised penis into forbidden territory. The rule was (and is) that any intercourse with a non-Israelite woman, or any adulterous intercourse, violates the sanctity of the consecrated organ.[12] Thus the tale of Phinehas found a featured place in the circumcision liturgy as a warning against all forms of sexual misbehavior.

[3] By the fifteenth century women had been eliminated almost entirely as participants in the circumcision rite. Until then, it had been customary for the child's mother to hold him in her lap during the operation, but around 1400 a prominent rabbi in Germany ruled that the mother was to have no role whatever. Instead, another woman, called *ba'alat brit* (literally, "mistress of the covenant"), was to deliver the child to the door and hand him over to a male counterpart, the *ba'al brit* ("master of the covenant"), who now held the child, and at the conclusion of the rite drank the wine. At about the same time, the term *sandek*, which had been current in southern Italy and the Mediterranean region for several centuries, moved northward and replaced *ba'al brit*.[13] What mattered, though, was not terminology but social reality. The male sandek had not only replaced the mother as bearer of the infant but had been elevated (at least in some minds) to a position of striking significance: his knees, on which the infant lay, were "likened to an altar, as if he were offering incense to heaven." A sixteenth-century rabbinic ruling said that a sandek takes precedence over a mohel in synagogue honors (in the order of being called to the reading of the Torah)—and thus of course no woman could serve as sandek, since that would constitute "brazenness."[14]

Earlier, around the seventh or eighth century, a new custom had been introduced into the Ashkenazic (western European) circumcision ritual: placed to the right of the sandek's chair was another chair, richly carved and upholstered, for the prophet Elijah. He was also accorded a separate cup of wine. The chair appears first in the liturgy as "seat of honor" (*moshav kavod*) in the midrashic text that I cited earlier, *Chapters of Rabbi Eliezer*: "people should have a seat of honor for the Messenger of the Covenant; for Elijah, may he be remembered for good, is called the Messenger of the Covenant."[15]

Elijah's symbolic presence at the rite is customarily explained either by this reference, by calling him the "Herald of the Messiah," or by describing him as a "protector" of children. But there is good reason to conclude that in this context he is not such a benign figure. In chapters 18 and 19 of 1 Kings we learn that when Elijah defeated and slaughtered the "prophets of Baal," the furious Jezebel threatened to kill him in retaliation. Elijah fled for his life and, following a journey of forty days and forty nights (sustained by a single meal of bread and water), he arrived at Horeb. The Lord appeared and asked, "Why are you here, Elijah?" He replied, "I am moved by zeal for the Lord, the God of Hosts, for the Israelites have forsaken Your covenant, torn down Your altars, and put Your prophets to the sword. I alone am left, and they are out to take my life." The Lord assures Elijah that only seven thousand Israelites— "every knee that has not knelt to Baal and every mouth that has not kissed him"—will survive his wrath.

The crime of the wayward Israelites was having "forsaken" the Lord's covenant by worshiping the Canaanite god Baal. The biblical reference is to the covenant at Sinai, but in the circumcision liturgy this word recalls Abraham's earlier covenant. Here the rabbis interpreted "covenant" to refer not only to the agreement sealed by Abraham's circumcision; the "covenant" *was* his circumcision, and every circumcision thereafter. So the message is clear: any violation of the "covenant"—most particularly, misusing the organ embodying the "covenant"—is a grievous sin. Elijah, like Phinehas, was an agent of the Lord's vengeance who punished sinful men with death. Both appear in the liturgy as warnings against sexual misconduct and disrespect for sacred doctrine.[16]

[4] Hoffman explains that the "beloved one," in whose "flesh" God set the original "statute," is Abraham, "the model for all Jewish fathers." But the "beloved of our flesh" [i.e., of *our* flesh] is the infant. He notes that the "pit" means She'ol, the underworld where the dead live an eternal featureless existence (although it seems equally likely that the reference is to the pit of Gehinnom). The prayer asks that the infant be delivered from death as a reward for the offering of his foreskin—sacrifice of part of a precious organ as substitute for the entire child.[17] By the second century child sacrifice belonged to the distant past, but the prayer shows that the idea of sacrificial redemption endured.

[5] Immediately after reciting the passage referring to "wallowing" in blood, the mohel dips his finger into a cup of wine and places a drop on the infant's lips. The usual explanation for this today is that the wine soothes and distracts the child, but there is more to it than that. The blood imagery is drawn from chapter 16 of Ezekiel; I mentioned this passage earlier, but now I'll examine it in more detail. The Lord, speaking through the prophet, castigates the Israelites for practicing "abominations" and reminds them of their debt to him. Employing graphic metaphor, he recalls that they were a desperate people, whom he likens to an abandoned female infant "from the land of the Canaanites," child of an Amorite father and a Hittite mother:

As for your birth, when you were born your navel cord was not cut,
and you were not bathed in water to smooth you; you were not
rubbed with salt, nor were you swaddled. No one pitied you enough
to do any one of these things for you out of compassion for you;
on the day you were born, you were left lying, rejected, in the open
field. When I passed by you and saw you wallowing in your blood,
I said to you: "Live in spite of your blood." Yea, I said to you: "Live in
spite of your blood." I let you grow like the plants of the field; and
you continued to grow up until you attained to womanhood, until
your breasts became firm and your hair sprouted. You were still
naked and bare when I passed by you [again] and saw that your time
for love had arrived. So I spread My robe over you and covered
your nakedness, and I entered into a covenant with you by
oath—declares the Lord God; thus you became Mine.[18]

In biblical times, unwanted infants, especially illegitimate female infants,
were abandoned to die from exposure and starvation. Here we read of such an
infant (a metaphor for the Israelites) who is rescued and reared to maturity,
then "entered" into a covenant. But had the rabbis just been seeking the word
"covenant" in a biblical text, they might have considered a number of more
appropriate choices. What drew them to these verses was the mention of *blood*
along with covenant. The Jewish Publication Society translation of the key
sentence, "Live in spite of your blood," reverses (and disguises) the literal
Hebrew meaning: "In your blood, live." The rabbis included the passage in
the circumcision liturgy to indicate that the blood shed in circumcision is
redemptive; it brings the infant nothing less than the reward of life.

Ordinarily the blessing over wine is recited by those who intend to drink
it, but in this case it is only the infant who "drinks" when the mohel places a
drop or two of wine on his lips. Why do the adults not drink the wine? Here is
Hoffman's explanation: "It was not meant to be consumed *as wine* at all, but
was instead reserved as an oral transfusion of wine *as blood* for the child. In a
nutshell, blood escapes the system; wine as blood enters it." He suggests that
the rabbis may have been reluctant to acknowledge the association of wine
with blood for two reasons: rival symbolism in the Christian Mass, originating
in the story of the Last Supper, and medieval accusations that Jews required
the blood of Christian boys for healing circumcision wounds.[19] (I'll discuss
these accusations later.)

[6] Finally, the prayer offering the child before the Lord's "glorious
throne" is further confirmation that circumcision is interpretable as a sacrificial offering by the infant's father, in the hope and expectation that the child
will be redeemed into life. A part has been sacrificed to preserve the rest.

To recapitulate, in a ritual circumcision the child's father offers his son's
foreskin as a bloody sacrifice, perhaps as a replacement for what may once have

been sacrifice of the entire child. He declares acknowledgment of paternity, readiness to submit the child to a perilous procedure, avowal of sexual restraint in his and the child's future, and intention to raise him as a conforming member of the male-centered collective. In effect, he represses his own reluctance and dread, surrendering himself and his son to the will of the male elders.[20]

To "Him," Not "Her": Synagogue Circumcisions and Exclusion of Women

Until about the ninth century, circumcision was a private affair (as it is now), conducted at home in the presence of friends and relatives. The infant's mother played an integral role: she held him in her lap during the operation, drank some of the wine (supposedly to promote her recovery from childbirth), and heard prayers recited on her behalf. But sometime during the early medieval period the rite was moved to the synagogue and became a featured event of the prayer service. And with that shift in location and significance the presence of the mother or any woman became problematic.[21] Although women were ordinarily excluded from participation in synagogue services, for several centuries mothers appear to have retained their traditional role, even in the synagogue. But in the thirteenth century rabbinic authorities issued resolute objections to any and all female participation in, or even presence at, synagogue circumcisions. Here is a representative statement by Meir ben Barukh of Rothenburg, the leader of thirteenth-century German Jewry, as cited by his student Samson ben Tsadok:

> I am not at all in favor of the technically permissible custom that one finds in most places: namely, that a woman sits in the synagogue among the men, and they circumcise the baby in her lap. Even if the *mohel* is her husband, or her father or her son, it is not appropriate to allow a beautifully dressed-up woman to be among the men and right there in the presence of God.

Meir noted that women had been excluded from the Temple courtyard because "they were afraid that the young priests would compete for her." Moreover, the command in Genesis 17 was to "him," not "her." That being the case, "how could it possibly be that they circumcise children on their mothers' laps, thus snatching away the commandment from the men. Anyone who gets the opportunity to prevent such goings-on should do so." And a pious man who sees a baby being circumcised in its mother's lap, added Samson, "is obliged to walk out of the synagogue, lest he give the false impression of aiding and abetting sinners."[22]

By about 1400 the only woman participating in the rite was the *ba'alat brit*, "mistress of the covenant," who carried the infant to the synagogue door and delivered him to her far more important male counterpart, the sandek. But men conducting a circumcision were careful to avoid anything beyond strictly limited contact with women. A fifteenth-century compilation of customs advised that a man should not go to the mother's room to fetch the infant, because "it is the custom of the women to grab the coat of the one taking the baby to the *mitzvah* [commandment]"; and since women should not mix with the men, "clearly a man should also not be among the women, since one who tries to stay away from them as much as possible should be praised."[23]

"Watch Nights" and Blood Rites

Over time, European Jews introduced other practices associated with circumcision. The night preceding the rite became known as Watch Night, or Vigil Night (German and Yiddish, *Wachnacht*; Italian, *Veglia*), when friends and relatives gathered at the parental home, perhaps originally to protect the infant and his mother from malevolent demons. Watch Night seems to have evolved from beliefs about demonic danger to the infant and mother in their time of weakness.[24] In Jewish popular culture, circumcision was said to empower the child so that evil spirits could no longer harm him. The hours just prior to the rite were the most dangerous, when the spirits might make a final effort to secure a victim. Obviously, then, it was unwise to leave mother and child alone. Instead, friends and relatives gathered at the home for raucous celebrations at which customary restraints were abandoned. Women and men ate, drank, sang, gambled, and even danced together, having a good time while performing a good deed in the bargain: ensuring that the house was so well lit and filled with noisy festivities that no demon could hope to make an entrance.

Eventually however, the rabbis stepped in, declaring that, although keeping watch was indeed meritorious, drinking, dancing, and reveling definitely were not. They urged that the only guests be pious men who would study and pray throughout the night, maintaining the vigil as a sacred undertaking. But evidence from various places suggests that some guests upheld the festive tradition, even while nearby elders recited sacred texts. In time, beliefs about guarding infants against vicious demons may have faded from memory, but the merrymaking lived on.

Several new practices placed special emphasis on bloodshed. After performing *metsitsah*, sucking blood from the circumcised penis, the mohel would spit some blood into the cup of wine from which he would place drops on the child's lips. He wiped blood from his hands and mouth onto a cloth, which was laid across the entrance to the synagogue. Some blood would be dripped into a cup and emptied before the Torah ark.[25]

Traditionally the infant lay on a linen cloth during the operation. Following the rite, the bloodstained cloth was turned over to the mother and women relatives, who tore it into strips to be sewn together to form a single long binder. This was then embroidered or painted with suitable messages and images: the child's name, date of birth, and zodiac sign; the standard hope that he live a life of "Torah, marriage, and good deeds"; and a wealth of elaborate designs representing the stages of life, as well as figures of exotic plants and animals. When the child was about two or three years old, he was taken to the synagogue to present the binder as his personal gift. At the end of that day's Torah reading, the scroll was fastened with the new binder, and the child was lifted by his father to hold one of the wooden spindles as the Torah was displayed before the congregation. The binder remained on the scroll until the next reading and might be used again when the boy read from the Torah during his bar mitzvah.[26]

Weakened Organs: Maimonides and Isaac ben Yedaiah

"In as Quiet a State as Possible": Guiding the Perplexed

The first half of the twelfth century was the culmination of the "golden era" of Sephardic Jewish life in Spain (brought to an end after 1147, first by an invasion of the Almohades, fundamentalist Muslims from Morocco, later by the Christian "Reconquest"). The outstanding representative of the Jewish cultural efflorescence was destined to achieve his reputation not in Spain, however, but in Egypt. Moses ben Maimon, better known by the Greek version of his name, Moses Maimonides, was born in Córdoba in 1135 but spent most of his life in a town near Cairo, where his family settled after fleeing the new fundamentalist regime. There he established his reputation as a physician, community leader, and, above all, as "the outstanding representative of Jewish rationalism for all time"—a philosopher who introduced a radically new form of discourse into Jewish religious commentary.[27]

The work for which Maimonides is most admired is *Guide of the Perplexed*, completed in Arabic in 1190 and translated soon thereafter into Hebrew (*Moreh Nebukhim*). Maimonides interpreted traditional Jewish belief and practice in a rational manner, resolving apparent contradictions between biblical texts and standards of logic derived from Aristotelian philosophy. The book was addressed not to ordinary readers but to the author's "select contemporaries," rabbinic scholars who had also been exposed to classical philosophy and science, and "might be floundering in the apparent inconsistencies between the two traditions"—hence its title.[28] Maimonides' comments on circumcision echo in part those of the Hellenistic philosopher Philo, but with deeper insight. In fact, the *Guide* departs so thoroughly from anything advanced by Maimonides' predecessors that we recognize an entirely new perspective, in some respects strikingly modern.

Near the end of his book, following a discussion of forbidden forms of sexual intercourse and prohibitions against interbreeding of two species, Maimonides turns to circumcision:

[W]ith regard to circumcision, one of the reasons for it is, in my opinion, the wish to bring about a decrease in sexual intercourse and a weakening of the organ in question, so that this activity be diminished and the organ be in as quiet a state as possible. It has been thought that circumcision perfects what is defective congenitally.... How can natural things be defective so that they need to be perfected from outside, all the more because we know how useful the foreskin is for that member? In fact this commandment has not been prescribed with a view to perfecting what is defective congenitally, but to perfecting what is defective morally. The bodily pain caused to that member is the real purpose of circumcision. None of the activities necessary for the preservation of the individual is harmed thereby, nor is procreation rendered impossible, but violent concupiscence and lust that goes beyond what is needed are diminished. The fact that circumcision weakens the faculty of sexual excitement and sometimes perhaps diminishes the pleasure is indubitable. For if at birth this member has been made to bleed and has had its covering taken away from it, it must indubitably be weakened. The Sages, may their memory be blessed, have explicitly stated: "It is hard for a woman with whom an uncircumcised man has had sexual intercourse to separate from him." In my opinion, this is the strongest of the reasons for circumcision.[29]

Note how radically Maimonides reverses the standard rabbinic argument on removing the foreskin to become "complete" or "perfect." He grants the possibility of "moral" perfection but is under no illusions about the physical damage.[30] Moreover, he not only acknowledges the painfulness of the operation but even calls it the "real purpose." Whether or not he was correct about impaired sexual capacity as the principal *reason* for circumcision, he recognized this as the principal *result*. We recall that Genesis 17 promised outstanding reproductive success as a reward for circumcision; that message seems not to have impressed this philosopher.

Although he has said nothing yet about the idea of covenant, Maimonides turns now to "another very important meaning": ethnic unity as a function of shared religious beliefs. Here he employs the term "covenant," but with a subtle change in emphasis that significantly alters its biblical meaning:

[A]ll people professing this opinion—that is, those who believe in the unity of God—should have a bodily sign uniting them so that one who does not belong to them should not be able to claim that he was one of them, while being a stranger.... Now a man does not perform this act upon himself or upon a son of his unless it be in consequence of a genuine belief. For it is not like an incision in the leg or a burn in the arm, but is a very, very hard thing. It is also well known what degree of mutual love and mutual help exists between people who all bear the same sign, which forms for them a sort of covenant and alliance. Circumcision is a covenant made by Abraham our Father with a view to the belief in the unity of God. Thus everyone who is circumcised joins Abraham's covenant. This covenant imposes the obligation to believe in the unity of God.... This also is a strong reason, as strong as the first, which may be adduced to account for circumcision; perhaps it is even stronger than the first.[31]

Here the radical departure from traditional rabbinic thought may not be apparent until we think carefully about what is being said. The covenant, as Maimonides understands it, is not between God and Abraham, or God and the Israelites; it is an "alliance" among living *men*, members of an ethnic group who are united by shared loyalty to a religious principle. This explanation for circumcision—perhaps even stronger than the first, he suggests—is not theological but *sociological*. He is saying that men branded by such a "very, very hard thing" are forever bonded.[32]

Finally, Maimonides proposes three reasons why the operation is performed on infants rather than on mature persons with understanding:

The first is that if the child were let alone until he grew up, he would sometimes not perform it. The second is that a child does not suffer as much pain as a grown-up man because his membrane is still soft and his imagination weak; for a grown-up man would regard the thing, which he would imagine before it occurred, as terrible and hard. The third is that the parents of a child that is just born take lightly matters concerning it, for up to that time the imaginative form that compels the parents to love it is not yet consolidated.... Consequently if it were left uncircumcised for two or three years, this would necessitate the abandonment of circumcision because of the father's love and affection for it. At the time of its birth, on the other hand, this imaginative form is very weak, especially as far as concerns the father upon whom this commandment is imposed.[33]

With regard to the modern tenor of this twelfth-century philosopher's mode of thought, these comments speak for themselves. Even the belief that infants experience less pain and trauma than adults, although now known to be incorrect, is still widely held.

In summary, aside from his reference to the Genesis 17 myth—offered almost as an aside and reinterpreted at that—Maimonides' commentary on circumcision presents arguments that might well be persuasive, if not necessarily appealing, to those seeking rational explanations for ritual practices. One wonders whether, with regard to this particular practice, "perplexed" readers have found his observations reassuring.[34]

*"Performing His Task Quickly": Isaac ben Yedaiah
on Gentile and Jewish Lovers*

If Maimonides departed radically from the usual style of rabbinic commentary, what are we to say about one of his followers, Isaac ben Yedaiah? A talmudic scholar who lived in southern France in the latter half of the thirteenth century, Isaac was a follower of Maimonides who was especially attracted to creative midrashic texts and nonlegalistic passages in the Talmud. His works aimed to demonstrate that beneath the surface of imaginative rabbinic commentaries lay important spiritual truths and guidance for appropriate everyday behavior.

Isaac was largely ignored until 1980, when Marc Saperstein published a detailed study of some of his writings. These show Isaac to have been deeply misogynous but obsessed with sexuality and thoughts of libidinous men and women. "Throughout his commentaries," says Saperstein, "he protests that discourse about the physical beauty of a woman, erotic desire, and sexual activity is by its very nature tedious, irreverent, useless, and shameful, drawing the speaker and listener into the power of sin and diverting the intellect from achieving knowledge of God."[35] Be that as it may, Isaac had a great deal to say about sexually excitable women and male erotic desire. His observations on circumcision surely stand alone for their musings on the difference between circumcised and intact penises. One of the operation's most useful results, he argues, is repression of sexual energy. Jewish men, sexually subdued and readily controlled by their wives, don't stray into mischief: If a man desires other women, "his wife will guard him, and his craving for the forbidden woman will disappear, because his foreskin has been removed from him, and the power of his member has been diminished, so that he has no strength to lie with many lewd women." Not so for Gentile men; equipped with foreskins and sexually vigorous, they are always in search of adventure: "his one wife is not able to restrain him from the other women he pursues, compelled by his nature; he does not fear to fulfill the desire of his hungering impulse."[36]

Women who have had an opportunity to make comparisons, he continues, know quite well the difference between circumcised and intact lovers. But it's all for the best, since Jewish men don't waste time and energy trying to satisfy women sexually:

> [An attractive woman] will court the man who is uncircumcised in
> the flesh and lie against his breast with great passion, for he thrusts
> inside her a long time because of the foreskin, which is a barrier
> against ejaculation in intercourse. Thus she feels pleasure and
> reaches an orgasm first. When an uncircumcised man sleeps with
> her and then resolves to return to his home, she brazenly grasps him,
> holding on to his genitals, and says to him, "Come back, make love to

me." This is because of the pleasure that she finds in intercourse with him, from the sinews of his testicles—sinew of iron—and from his ejaculation—that of a horse—which he shoots like an arrow into her womb. They are united without separating, and he makes love twice and three times in one night, yet the appetite is not filled.

And so he acts with her night after night. The sexual activity emaciates him of his bodily fat, and afflicts his flesh, and he devotes his brain entirely to women, an evil thing. His heart dies within him; between her legs he sinks and falls. He is unable to see the light of the King's face, because the eyes of his intellect are plastered over by women so that they cannot now see light.

But when a circumcised man desires the beauty of a woman, and cleaves to his wife, or to another woman comely in appearance, he will find himself performing his task quickly, emitting his seed as soon as he inserts the crown. . . . He has an orgasm first; he does not hold back his strength. As soon as he begins intercourse with her, he immediately comes to a climax.

She has no pleasure from him . . . and it would be better for her if he had not known her and not drawn near to her, for he arouses her passion to no avail, and she remains in a state of desire for her husband, ashamed and confounded, while the seed is still in her "reservoir." She does not have an orgasm once a year, except on rare occasions, because of the great heat and the fire burning within her. Thus he who says "I am the Lord's" will not empty his brain because of his wife or the wife of his friend.[37]

Maimonides understood that the foreskin is a highly sensitive source of sexual pleasure, and he seems to have viewed with ambivalence the "indubitable" fact that circumcision "sometimes perhaps diminishes the pleasure." Isaac expressed himself more forthrightly. He believed that the foreskin was a "barrier against ejaculation" and that circumcised men climaxed quickly during intercourse. But, as he saw it, far from being an argument against circumcision, this was a point in its favor. Sexuality was not intended for pleasure; it was an obstacle to be overcome. Isaac claimed that Jewish men were able to complete the "task" of procreation speedily and efficiently, without having to engage in prolonged sexual encounters that could only distract them from concentrating on spiritual pursuits. As Saperstein remarks, although Isaac demonstrated "an understanding of female sexuality that is impressive," he appears to disparage women's sexual satisfaction. In his view, while a frustrated woman was no concern, a fulfilled woman posed the most dreadful danger: that a man might fail to achieve eternal life because he tried to satisfy excessive sexual demands.[38] What mattered about women, of course, was not their sexual desires but their wombs; their personal concerns were of no consequence. Likewise for men: since the sole purpose of sexuality was procreation, the sooner one completed the task of impregnation, the better.

Revealing the Concealed: Circumcision in the Jewish Mystical Imagination

Kabbalah: Path to the Divine Presence

In a series of brilliantly revolutionary publications, Gershom Scholem (1897–1982) revealed a tradition of Jewish mysticism that began at least as far back as the first century BCE, appeared in various forms thereafter, and continues into our own time as Hasidism. As I've mentioned, rabbinic writing was by no means confined to strictly legalistic matters; it ranged widely into all kinds of imaginative narrative, allegory, and so on. Scholem's achievement was to show that over the centuries there were men who, although rooted in the rabbinic world, had aspired to a form of transcendental religious experience enabling them to achieve communion with the God of the Torah. The mystics who carried this practice to a climax called their creations *kabbalah*, meaning insight or understanding that has been "received," suggesting that they viewed themselves as adventurers within the rabbinic tradition, seeking to reveal spiritual mysteries hidden along familiar paths.

The ultimate experience for Jewish mystics, as for mystics everywhere, was personal apprehension of the Divine Presence. Although their imaginations often carried them well beyond the usual realms of interpretation, mystics continued the fundamental rabbinic practice: exegetic glossing of texts. They departed from conventional practice in that through their own versions of exegesis—penetrating, esoteric—they sought to reveal what they conceived to be the Torah's most deeply hidden secrets, beholding that which others could not even imagine.

In an introductory chapter on "general characteristics of Jewish mysticism," Scholem observes that, in contrast to other traditions, Jewish mysticism is a wholly "masculine doctrine, made for men and by men." This appears "to be connected with an inherent tendency to lay stress on the demonic nature of woman and the feminine element of the cosmos."[39] In contrast, Jewish men, by virtue of carrying in their "flesh" the sign of the covenant, could aspire to achieve transcendent spiritual experience.

The foremost text in the Jewish mystical canon is the Zohar—*Sefer ha-Zohar*, "Book of Radiance," or "Book of Splendor"—composed in Castile in the late thirteenth century, by a group of mystics led by Moses de León. The central doctrine in the Zohar is that God contains, or incorporates, ten emanations radiating from the innermost recesses of the Divine Being, the *Ein-Sof*, "Without End." The Ein-Sof—the "root of all roots," the "cause of causes"—is utterly concealed, beyond human apprehension or comprehension. But with lengthy preparation and dedication the mystic can achieve vision of the emanations. They are "the outer layers" of the Ein-Sof—"like the rays of the sun in relationship to the sun itself."[40]

Each emanation has its own name or names and its association with a particular aspect of the Divine Being. The first three—"Crown," "Wisdom," and "Intelligence"—are imagined as emanating from the divine head. Others are linked to other parts of the body: "Mercy," with the right arm; "Judgment," with the left; and so on. The lowest two are *Yesod*, "Foundation," the circumcised phallus; and *Shekhinah*, "Divine Presence," or "Queen." Shekhinah, imagined as the specifically feminine aspect of the Divine Being, is the gateway into the upper realms.[41]

The Zohar and other mystical texts speak about circumcision with unparalleled imagery, reaching well beyond what we've encountered in Talmud and Midrash. Since the men who composed the Zohar—medieval Jewish mystics living in late thirteenth-century Spain—obviously differed radically from us in psychological disposition and cognitive orientation, many of their ideas and images may seem bizarre. But the fact is that within their own social and cultural world the authors of the Zohar and other mystical texts were respected for their creative ability; their work is still read with admiration, and contemporary Jewish writers of a mystical bent still draw on their ideas and images. (This is not to suggest, though, that mystical interpretations of circumcision or any other practice will or should appeal to the rational mind.)

Emerging from the Foreskin: Circumcision
and Mystical Vision in the Zohar

The early rabbis had already advanced a claim for circumcision that became central to arguments in the Zohar. A commentator in *Genesis Rabbah* remarked on the significance of chapter 19 of the Book of Job, where we read: "But I know that my Vindicator lives; In the end He will testify on earth— This, after my skin will have been peeled off. But I would behold God while still in my flesh [literally, from within my flesh], I myself, not another, would behold Him."[42] Overlooking the obvious contrast between the living and the dead, the rabbis interpreted the passage to mean that only by peeling away *foreskin* "flesh" (*basar*) is a living man enabled to behold the Lord. Conclusion: only a circumcised man can achieve genuine communion with the Divine Presence. The historian of religion Elliot R. Wolfson explains:

> Circumcision is not simply one good deed amongst many in consequence of which the person merits seeing God. It is precisely and exclusively by means of circumcision that one can see God, for this act removes that potential barrier—symbolized by the cutting of the

foreskin—separating human and divine. Circumcision is the vestibule or portal through which one must pass if one is to have a visionary experience of God. The opening of circumcision results in an opening up to God, a receptivity, that enables one to stand in God's presence and to behold the glory.[43]

Rabbinic Midrash, then, had already expressed a connection between circumcision and vision of God. But *absolute* vision, enabling union and communion—the ultimate goal of mystical Judaism—receives much more elaborate exegesis in the Zohar. There the imagery takes on sexual meanings rooted in conceptions of the Shekhinah as the feminine emanation of God through which the mystic hopes to achieve union. Such consummation is attainable, of course, only for a man who has been properly prepared: "One who is uncircumcised cannot see God (or the *Shekhinah*), for seeing involves some sort of intimate contact, touching, immediacy, and only one who is circumcised can have such an experience."[44]

Another Zohar text expands on this theme with grandiose phallic imagery: "Come and see: when Abraham was circumcised he emerged from the foreskin and entered the holy covenant and was crowned in the holy crown, and entered the foundation upon which the world stands."[45] The "holy covenant" and the "holy crown" are images of the Shekhinah; the "foundation" is the Yesod. The foreskin symbolizes the realm of "demonic powers" from which one must emerge to enter the holy realm. Visionary experience is therefore "dependent on transference from the demonic to the sefirotic [mystical] worlds"—possible only when the phallus is no longer "encased in the demonic shell."[46]

It seems reasonable to interpret this as saying that "release" from fully expressive sexuality enables one to achieve vision of God—that apprehension of the divine realm can be anticipated only by men who are physically diminished; ultimate self-fulfillment requires partial sacrifice of sexual capacity. Another way of thinking about this: diminishing the ultimate *physical* experience prepares the way for the ultimate *mystical* experience. Moreover, while the corona of the intact penis is visible only with an erection, the circumcised penis reveals the object of mystical vision in the flaccid state, without the base physicality of sexual arousal.

Entering the holy covenant, initially accomplished through circumcision, is equivalent to entering the Shekhinah, the feminine emanation of the Divine Being. In the final analysis, says Wolfson, to behold the Shekhinah is to gaze upon "the exposed corona of the phallus. . . . [O]n the one hand, it is the task of the female to conceal the male organ; but on the other, when the male organ protrudes," one beholds the female aspect (the "crown") of the "androgynous phallus"—precisely the part that is first "revealed" by the rite of circumcision.[47]

Inscribing the Holy Name: Yod, Seal of the Covenant

The tenth letter of the Hebrew alphabet is *yod* (י), transcribed in English as either *y* or *i*. *Yod* is the last of the three Hebrew letters in Shaddai (sh-d-i, שדי), the name by which God first announced himself to Abram in Genesis 17. ("I am El Shaddai. Walk in my ways and be blameless.") This mysterious name, occurring only occasionally in the Scriptures and never fully identified as to origin, seems to have fascinated the rabbis who created Midrash, especially because of its appearance in the key chapter on covenant and circumcision. They were attracted to the letter *yod*, which they imagined as a representation of the exposed glans—hence as the sign, or "seal," of the covenant inscribed on the circumcised phallus. A midrashic text explains that because the Lord "seals" his name, Shaddai, on the bodies of circumcised men, they enter the Garden of Eden after their deaths: "He placed the *shin* in the nose, the *dalet* in the hand, and the *yod* on the [place of] circumcision. Therefore, when a Jew dies there is an appointed angel in the Garden of Eden, who receives every circumcised Jew and brings him into the Garden of Eden." The letter that stands foremost here, the one that ensures divine protection for the circumcised Jewish male, is *yod*.[48] By the twelfth and thirteenth centuries, European Jewish mystics, envisioning yet more esoteric realms, elevated the *yod* to new heights of significance. Beginning among mystics of the Rhineland known as Hasidei Ashkenaz (the "Pious of Germany"), later among the kabbalists of Spain who created the Zohar, the *yod* gained special recognition as not only the final letter of Shaddai but also the first letter of the most secret name of God, the Tetragrammaton: YHWH (יהוה). Circumcision was thus the ultimate inscription: being circumcised meant being *imprinted* with the name of the Lord.

But it was not only that the seal of ritual circumcision enabled a man to behold the Divine Presence; his "opened" penis was literally the path to revelation. In the Zohar, the letter *yod* became identified with *Yesod* (יסוד), "Foundation," the ninth emanation, which corresponds to the divine phallus. By revealing a man's *yod* (the corona of the glans), circumcision also reveals the *yod* in the realm of emanations: that is, Yesod. In this sense the circumcised phallus is both source and location of vision. A fulfilled mystic is able to view the Divine Presence *because of*, and *from*, the sign of the covenant imprinted on his body.[49]

Secrets

The mystics viewed Torah study as itself the pathway to vision. Exegesis led to revelation: disclosure of "secret" meanings by "opening" the text—achievable, of course, only by men who had themselves been "opened" and "revealed." A key text here appears in Psalm 25: "The secret of the Lord is for those who fear Him; to them He makes known His covenant." The Zohar explains:

[T]he Holy One, blessed be He, has not given the upper secret of the Torah except to those who fear sin. To those who do fear sin the upper secret of Torah is disclosed. And what is the upper secret of the Torah? I would say, it is the sign of the holy covenant, which is called the secret of the Lord, the holy covenant.[50]

The Lord's "upper secret" is circumcision, which is at the same time the pathway to the innermost secrets, or "mysteries," of the Torah. The very term *sod*, "secret," is contained in Yesod. He who is uncircumcised is closed to revealed knowledge: he cannot "open the text" (decipher its secrets), and therefore cannot approach the Divine Presence.[51]

Discussing the work of another prominent thirteenth-century mystic, Abraham Abulafia, Wolfson points out that circumcision is "the secret that God reveals to those who fear him, because it is the foundation of the mystical knowledge of the divine name, a knowledge that results in the union of the individual and God." But "the secret is not simply a theological concept that is too difficult for the ignorant to comprehend. Rather, the name itself is the secret to which the kabbalist is conjoined in ecstatic union, which is experienced as an erotic bonding predicated on the death of the body, and particularly the *weakening of the sexual drive*." As Abulafia and other mystics understood circumcision, the "rationale for cutting the foreskin is to subjugate the body, or more specifically the sexual urge, and this is necessary so that one's intellect will be fully actualized."[52] Mystics thus radically transformed Abraham's covenant, with its promises of collective reproductive prowess and land ownership, into an intensely individualized—but dematerialized—relationship with the Divine.

In kabbalist thought, Torah, name of God, and circumcised phallus were essentially identical—manifestations of a single ineffable mystery. The letters of the Hebrew alphabet, the elemental components of the Torah, were envisioned as a visible representation of the Divine Being; while the immediately visible object, the Torah scroll, was the "divine edifice," hewn from God's name.[53] And the circumcised phallus, having been inscribed with God's name, could itself be envisioned as a sacred text. So insertion of a Jewish penis in forbidden places was an immense sacrilege: betrayal of the Divine Name:

One must not lie in the name of the Holy One, blessed be He. And what is this name? The covenant of circumcision, the sign of the holy covenant, for the one who lies with respect to this covenant lies with respect to the name of the Holy One, blessed be He.... And in what does the lie consist? He should not enter this covenant in the other domain.

The "other domain," is of course the body of a non-Jewish woman. Moreover, declares a related text,

> He who lies with respect to the sign of the holy covenant which is
> inscribed on him is as if he had lied with respect to the name of
> the King, for the name of the King is inscribed in man.... In what
> does the lie consist here? He spread out his hands to the other power
> and lies with respect to [the place of] this covenant.... for he who
> guards this covenant is as if he was guarding the entire Torah.
> And he who lies with respect to it is as if he had lied with respect to
> the entire Torah.[54]

Here the imagined non-Jewish woman is the "other power." The same prohibition applied to adultery, and for the same reason: "For the one [who
commits adultery] lies with respect to the name of the Holy One, blessed be
He, which is inscribed in man.... And the one who lies with respect to that
lies with respect to the King."[55]

In short, confining sexuality to marriage with a Jewish wife guards the
sanctity of the inscribed phallus—and that in turn means nothing less than
ensuring the sanctity of the entire Torah.

Although most Gentiles are conceived to be the categorical and un-
touchable Other, the bodies of those few who are destined to convert to Judaism bear their own special secret: a Jewish soul, temporarily trapped in a
contaminated Gentile body, waiting to be released into a mantle of cleanliness. In one of his books Moses de León described this process of purification
and liberation—the convert imagined, of course, as a male:

> You must know that the uncircumcised nations have no soul except
> from the side of impurity, for they are immersed in the foreskin, and
> on account of this their spirits are impure.... When they remove
> from themselves this filth, which is the foreskin, their impurity de-
> parts from them.... Thus the convert is called the righteous con-
> vert... and this is the secret of the covenant and the eternal life.[56]

"The Place in Which There Is No Forgetfulness":
Circumcision and Historical Memory

The Zohar was composed in the late thirteenth century, a time when the
Christian "reconquest" of Spain from Muslim rule was virtually complete.
Like so much in the Ashkenazic tradition, this Sephardic text reflected the
encounter with Christianity: an encounter characterized by inevitable assimilation of elements of Christian culture but also by intense hostility and
conscious distancing. Thus, as might be expected, the Zohar portrays Christianity as the cause of Jewish suffering and the source of endless attempts to
seduce Jews "onto the path of heresy and licentiousness." Christians are "the
embodiment of demonic impurity in the world"; they are the living Edomites,
descendants of wicked Esau, impure like menstruous women—and equally

seductive, for their efforts to convert Jews are like the wiles of a menstruating woman who encourages an unwitting man to have intercourse with her.[57]

The Zohar portrays the struggle with Christianity "in overtly erotic terms." We've seen praise of the circumcised phallus as the rabbinic response to Paul's insistence on the uselessness of circumcision. The Zohar goes further by *reversing* Paul's argument: The "spiritual circumcision of baptism" cannot supersede physical circumcision; rather, "literal circumcision of the flesh" unites body and spirit, by inscribing the body with a physically visible but consummately spiritual "sign." Hence Abraham, not Jesus, was "the Word" that became human: "In the final analysis, circumcision (*milah*) is the true incarnation of the divine word (*millah*) in the flesh," and it was Abraham who was the true manifestation of God's creative power.[58]

The mystics supported this startling twist with a wealth of creatively interpreted texts. For example, combining verses from the Song of Songs with references to Adam, then gliding into the appearance of the Lord to Abraham at the beginning of Genesis 18, there is the following:

> "The song of the turtledove is heard in the land," this is the word of the Holy One.... When Adam came into being, everything existed. After Adam sinned, everything departed from the world and the earth was cursed ... [but] when Abraham came to the world, immediately "the blossoms appeared in the land." ... "The time of pruning has come" [refers to] the time that the Holy One, blessed be He, told him to circumcise himself, for the time had come when the covenant should be found in Abraham and he circumcised himself. Then this verse was fulfilled in him, the world was established, and the word of the Holy One, blessed be He, was revealed through him, as it is written, "The Lord appeared to him."[59]

So whereas Adam's sinful behavior caused desolation, Abraham's circumcision (*milah*) restored the word (*millah*) of God and renewed fertility in the world. Thus, contrary to Paul's claim, "circumcision of the flesh" never lost its preeminent role in revelation and redemption.[60]

The circumcised phallus was further envisioned as the embodiment of historical memory. In the earliest kabbalistic text, the *Sefer ha-Bahir* ("Book of the Brightness"), the author asks: Why does one passage on Sabbath observance (Exodus 20:8) say *Remember* the Sabbath, while another (Deuteronomy 5:12) says *Keep* the Sabbath? The answer: "remember" (*zakhor*) is for the male (*zakhar*), while "keep" (*shamor*) is for his bride. The mystics noted the equation between memory and maleness and interpreted it to allude to the "secret" emanation, Yesod, representing the circumcised phallus: "everything is the mystery of the masculine. The secret of the holy name, YHW [sic], is inscribed there, and [that which is] below needs to be sanctified, and it is sanctified through *zakhor*, for from that it takes all holiness and all blessings."[61]

Thus the Zohar links the circumcised phallus with collective Jewish memory, rendering history meaningful, and affirming that the identity of the individual (male) Jew is indelibly bound with the "sign" embedded in his flesh. Just as circumcision differentiates between male and female, it also signifies the difference between Jews, bonded to particularized, embodied ethnic memory, and adherents of the pan-ethnic universalized religion, Christianity. Moreover, in a dramatic reversal of the familiar stereotypes, the circumcised Jew becomes the embodiment of divine masculinity, while the Christian is identified with emasculated, "feminine" reticence or withdrawal (exemplified in monastic celibacy).[62] Circumcision was often associated in the Christian mind with castration and feminization; in the symbolism of the Zohar it represents the precise opposite!

"Transcendental Transitional Significance": The Meaning of Circumcision for Returning Converts

Sephardic Jews—those in Spain and Portugal—lived in a cultural environment much different from that of the Ashkenazic Jews in Germany, France, and other parts of western Europe. The difference lay, of course, in the dominant religions of the two regions: Islam and Christianity. Jews were relatively well tolerated in the Islamic territories; many prospered and a few achieved high public office. Moreover, the two cultures developed in tandem, to such an extent that one historian has characterized the relationship as a "Judaeo-Islamic tradition."[63] But the thirteenth-century Christian "reconquest" of Spain radically altered the status of the Jewish population, and in time Jews were faced with the choice of either converting or going into exile. Converts who continued to practice infant circumcision could face disastrous consequences.

Some converts and their descendants eventually made their way out of the Iberian peninsula into other parts of Europe, the Balkans, and the Americas. Most decided to "return" to Judaism and to join communities established by exiled predecessors. For men, willingness to be circumcised was the key to reentry into the Jewish world. Here I want to discuss briefly the meaning of circumcision for these men and for those who insisted that they undergo the ritual surgery. The intensity of their focus on circumcision, as the indispensable demonstration of intent to renounce the past and "become a Jew" again, emphasizes the remarkable significance in the Jewish mind of this single ritual act.

By the mid–thirteenth century, only the southernmost parts of Spain remained under Muslim control, and even there such towns as Seville and Córdoba were in Christian hands. For a time the Jewish population got along well, in fact achieving enough social and economic prominence to generate

Christian resentment. Monarchs, recognizing their usefulness, usually took their side against hostile clergy, and this protected them for a time. But by the late fourteenth century, hostility rooted in bitter religious antagonism as well as economic competition led to a series of murderous riots that signaled the end of comfortable existence for the Jews of Spain. Following a vicious assault on the Jewish quarter of Seville in 1391, mobs attacked Jews in a number of cities, confronting them with the choice between conversion and death. It has been estimated that within a year the Jewish population, numbering some three hundred thousand when all this began, had been thoroughly decimated: about one-third had been murdered and another third forcibly converted; the rest had gone into hiding or had fled into Muslim territory. By 1415 another fifty thousand had converted, either voluntarily or under compulsion.[64] By the fifteenth century, the number of Spanish Conversos—converts and their descendants—far outnumbered those still openly professing Judaism.[65]

Although most Conversos came to accept their conversion and became fully practicing Catholics (with what degree of inner conviction we can only speculate), some few—definitely a minority—secretly tried to remain loyal to their Jewish heritage. In 1478 the ruling monarchs, Ferdinand and Isabella, instituted the Spanish Inquisition, aimed not at the remaining Jews—about whom there was nothing to "inquire"—but at Conversos accused of being Crypto-Jews: insincere converts who had "relapsed" into Judaism. How many of these supposed heretics had actually "Judaized" (engaged in Jewish practices) is open to question; it seems likely that some were guilty only of arousing the malice of "Old Christians" who wanted them out of the way for personal or economic reasons.[66]

As is well known, the remnant of openly professing Jews was expelled in 1492. The Edict of Expulsion, issued that year by Ferdinand and Isabella, charged Jews with trying "by whatever ways and means possible" to seduce decent Christians away from the Catholic faith and to "attract and pervert them to their [Jewish] injurious belief and opinion, instructing them in their ceremonies and observances of the Law." Among the specific charges was "trying to circumcise them and their children."[67] Since it seems highly unlikely that Jews would have approached ordinary Christians with attempts at circumcision and conversion, the people identified here as targets were almost certainly Conversos.

Some Jews moved into Portugal, hoping to settle there. But in 1497 the Portuguese king ordered that all Jews in his realm be immediately converted. Many Spanish and Portuguese Jews fled to the more friendly lands of the Ottoman Empire and to welcoming countries in Europe (most notably Holland), where they established new communities. For Jews who had recently converted to Christianity under duress, emigration was also an attractive option, and over the years those who managed to leave often reidentified as Jews in order to join established Sephardic Jewish communities abroad. Many ultimately migrated to the Balkans, Italy, France, and Holland, as well as to "New Spain" (present-day Mexico, adjacent parts of Central America, and the southwestern United States), Brazil, and the islands of the Caribbean.

There has always been disagreement on the question of whether Spanish and Portuguese Conversos and their descendants became sincere Catholics, or whether some Crypto-Jews continued practicing Judaism to the best of their ability while remaining outwardly Catholic. Though probably most converts did become faithful Catholics, there is evidence that a small minority hung on to the memory of their Jewish past. After the fifteenth century, Conversos and their descendants in Spain and Portugal, as well as those who emigrated to Spanish or Portuguese colonies in the Americas (particularly New Spain and Brazil), lived in rigorously Catholic societies in which there was always the threat of arrest by Inquisition authorities. Though it appears that Conversos and their descendants tended to live among other "New Christians" and to marry among themselves, even limited and carefully hidden adherence to Jewish practices constituted a risk that few were prepared to undertake. More-over, while some might manage to fast on Yom Kippur or to privately recite a few vaguely recalled prayers, circumcision at any age permanently and danger-ously marked a boy or man as a "Judaizer." The cost of such a decisive step, not only for the individual but for his family and perhaps even other associates, could be life imprisonment or burning at the stake.[68]

Nevertheless, a few risked it. Converso infants, like all others in Spain and Portugal, were baptized soon after birth. But in the privacy of their homes a few parents scrubbed the baptismal chrism from the child's forehead and had him circumcised. Some even held celebratory parties attended by family and friends. As time went on, though, Converso men began to marry "Old Chris-tian" women, who surely would have protested any suggestion that their sons be circumcised. Very occasionally, a rabbi or mohel ventured a clandestine visit to Spain to perform circumcisions, but the danger was obviously so great that this could not have happened often. Eventually circumcision disappeared along with other vestiges of Jewish practice, and Conversos blended into the general population.[69]

For male Conversos or Crypto-Jews who emigrated to lands outside the Spanish and Portuguese domains, the first requirement for readmission into the Jewish community was circumcision. Their earnest commitment to this demonstration of intent to become wholly Jewish can hardly be over-emphasized. The historian Yosef Hayim Yerushalmi, writing on Conversos in Venice, remarks that nowhere else in Jewish literature does one find "so great an emphasis on the rite, or such glowing praise of it," as in the writings of former Conversos.[70] Most communities viewed this single act as the defini-tive portal of entry into full acceptance as a Jew and full participation in com-munal life. Even though some men recoiled at the prospect, most underwent the operation as soon as they could. Those who resisted were subjected to such coercive pressure that few could hold out indefinitely.

A seventeenth-century Converso, originally named Cristóbal Méndez, who had emigrated to Venice and accepted Judaism, made the unfortunate mistake of returning to Spain to rescue relatives. He was apprehended and placed on trial by the Inquisition, and in the course of his interrogation (no doubt accompanied by torture or at least threat of torture) he described his experience in the Jewish community of Venice. He was uneasy about undergoing circumcision, he claimed, but agreed to it under pressure from his uncle and a rabbi. The operator, an elderly merchant, performed a ritually complete circumcision. The pain was so great, Méndez recalled, that he was barely aware of the benedictions. Following the operation he received a prayer-shawl (*tallit*), phylacteries (*tefillin*), and a prayer book. After a recovery period lasting nearly three weeks, he attended the synagogue and was called up to the open ark to recite the traditional blessing for deliverance from peril. He had become a Jew.[71]

Exiled Spanish and Portuguese Jews were settling in Amsterdam by about 1500, but it was not until late in the sixteenth century that Conversos arrived and began applying for admission as "returning" Jews. By the mid-seventeenth century a substantial part of the community consisted of former Conversos. The principal historian of the Amsterdam Conversos remarks that circumcision was "a particularly crucial rite of passage—not merely an act of compliance with Jewish law, but a ritual replete with powerful symbolic meanings." In the minds of Conversos, she continues, "circumcision took on a transcendental transitional significance, perhaps akin to that of a Christian sacrament." Nevertheless, some men did their best to avoid the painful experience, hoping to gain acceptance into the community even though they might be denied participation in ritual practices.[72]

But Converso men seeking to join the Amsterdam Jewish community could not escape circumcision. In 1620 one Amsterdam congregation ruled that men "who had not undergone circumcision by the upcoming sabbath prior to Rosh Hashanah would not be permitted to enter the synagogue, and that newcomers would be given two months to be circumcised." Two years later a man who refused circumcision for himself and his sons was excommunicated. Men known to have Old Christian female ancestors in the maternal line (e.g., a maternal grandmother) were technically non-Jewish and could be denied basic privileges, including right to burial in the Jewish cemetery, until they had undergone ritual immersion as well as circumcision. At least two, who had perhaps died soon after arrival, were circumcised after death, then granted burial. Rabbis in London and in Italian cities also issued rulings banning uncircumcised men from synagogue attendance and denying burial rights in Jewish cemeteries.[73]

A Portuguese Converso, grandly named Estevan de Ares de Fonseca, traveled widely in Europe for a number of years before authorities of the Spanish

Inquisition arrested him for "Judaizing." In the course of his trial in 1635, he provided a detailed autobiographical confession that included a description of his experience as a newcomer to Amsterdam. Like all such confessions, this has to be read critically, but it does suggest the centrality of circumcision for Conversos and their Jewish hosts. The Jews of Amsterdam welcomed him, he reported, "with great celebration and rejoicing, telling him that it was the Lord's miracle that someone who had been living blindly in the Christian law should by undreamed-of means become a Jew." But from then on it was downhill:

> And then they began to try to make him a Jew. They wanted to circumcise him, saying that even if it were by force and against his will they were going to circumcise him. . . . And when they saw that this witness did not want to be circumcised nor become a Jew, they placed him in the company of a rabbi . . . so that he could persuade him to follow it. And when he had been with him for six months and they finally saw that they could not convince him, they excommunicated him in the synagogues, so that no Jew would speak to or with him. And when he had been some days . . . without anyone speaking to him nor helping him, finally he consented to be circumcised. And they circumcised him and gave him the name David.[74]

At this distance it is impossible to know for certain how Converso men felt about the prospect of circumcision. Did most welcome it as the time-honored badge of entry into Judaism and the Jewish community, or did they dread the agonizing experience, accepting it only because they had no choice? I suppose the truth lies somewhere in between. No man could have welcomed the prospect of painful genital surgery, but most agreed to it because the rewards were substantial. As for why the rabbis consistently refused any compromise on this matter, the answer seems to be that circumcision had always been recognized as the ultimate demonstration of an aspiring convert's readiness to accept the full burden of the Law. To have given way even partly on this principle would have meant opening the door to confusion about who was Jewish and who was not. As a seventeenth-century rabbinic court ruled in Livorno, Italy, permitting uncircumcised men to handle ritual objects "would result in ruin, for they would put off entering the Covenant of Abraham if they saw that although uncircumcised they are denied nothing. . . . Such an unacceptable situation will not develop if an explicit distinction is made."[75] Of course, also "ruined" would have been the rabbis' claim to absolute authority.

"No One People Is Chosen": Spinoza on Circumcision and Jewish "Election"

Perhaps the most frequently misinterpreted passage in the history of Jewish thought on circumcision appears in the *Theological-Political Treatise* of Baruch

(Benedict) de Spinoza, the seventeenth-century pioneer of the Enlightenment and founder of modern liberal political philosophy.[76] A descendant of Conversos who had settled in Amsterdam, Spinoza was formally excommunicated from the Jewish community of that city as punishment for his views, which were condemned as heresy.[77] Judged by the criteria of Orthodoxy he was indeed a heretic, since he challenged the worth of Orthodox Judaism as the path to what he envisioned as genuine liberation and emancipation. Like Enlightenment philosophers who followed in the next century, Spinoza anticipated "the gradual and steady substitution of reason for superstition and science for religion." He saw himself "as engaged in a life and death struggle with the adherents of religion or orthodoxy."[78] As I'll try to show, his remarks on circumcision invite quotation out of context, making them seem to say precisely the opposite of what he intended.

At the end of the third chapter of the *Treatise* Spinoza addressed the question of whether the "election of the Jews" (their possession of God's particular favor and protection) was "everlasting" (*aeternam*), no matter what their political condition, or whether it was simply provisional and "concerned only with their political independence"—that is, necessary only while they were an autonomous nation. He argued that the latter was the case—"that God did not choose the Jews for ever," but only for as long as they required his special attention. By this he meant that divine favor was bestowed on the Israelites solely for their *political* welfare, not because they were morally or spiritually superior to anyone else. Hence, he concluded, "the Jews of today have absolutely nothing to which they can lay more claim than the rest of mankind."[79]

Regarding the survival of Jews as a distinct people—often cited as proof of their permanent "chosen" status—Spinoza recognized nothing miraculous. To the contrary, he argued that this was because "they have incurred universal hatred by cutting themselves off completely from all other peoples; and not only by practicing a form of worship opposed to that of the rest, but also by preserving the mark of circumcision with such devoutness [*religiosissime*]."[80] Since Spinoza's political ideology centered on mutual social acceptance, he rejected practices expressing particularism and self-aggrandizement. But he was not advocating Jewish "disappearance"; rather, he looked forward to integration of modernized Jews into a community of enlightened European peoples. Then came the comment that is often misinterpreted by quotation out of context:

> The mark of circumcision is also, I think, of great importance in this
> connection; so much so that in my view it alone will preserve the
> Jewish people for all time; indeed, did not the principles of their
> religion make them effeminate,[81] I should be quite convinced
> that some day when opportunity arises—so mutable are human
> affairs—they will establish their state once more, and that God will
> choose them afresh. . . . In conclusion, if anyone wishes to defend the

view that the Jews were chosen by God for ever, either because of
the mark of circumcision or for some other reason, I shall not oppose
him, as long as he admits that insofar as this election—whether
temporary or everlasting—is peculiar to the Jews alone it is concerned
only with their political organization and worldly prosperity . . . and
agrees that in respect of understanding and true virtue no people is
distinguished from another, and consequently that in these respects
no one people is chosen by God in preference to another.[82]

The opening words of the first sentence of this passage (to the second
semicolon) are often quoted alone (and in part), ostensibly demonstrating that
even the rationalist Spinoza acknowledged the value of circumcision as a
singularly dependable preserver of Jewish identity.[83] This is true only in the
sense that he viewed circumcision as serving to preserve precisely the version
of identity that he adamantly *rejected*. But careful reading of the entire passage
in the context of what preceded it shows that he disavowed the idea of an
eternal covenant signified by circumcision, arguing rather that continued Jewish dedication to anachronistic beliefs and practices, particularly those promoting self-segregation, was a defensive reaction to the enforced isolation of
Jews in European society. As the intellectual historian Steven B. Smith has
explained, Spinoza—"the prototype of the emancipated secular Jew," committed to "renunciation of Jewish particularity"—envisioned Jewish liberation
from both the confinement of Orthodox Judaism and Gentile oppression. His
vision of Jewish survival in the future meant not survival through "chosen
people" ideology but through creation of a Jewish "democratic-republican
state" established on "purely secular or rational principles."[84] The passage
might obviously be taken as a proto-Zionist declaration, but only in a strictly
secular sense, since Spinoza envisioned no place for "belief in the divine
revelation of the Torah and the expectation of redemption."[85] It was most
assuredly *not* an endorsement of ritual circumcision.

"Performing a Great Service": Circumcision in New Spain

Many Conversos migrated to Mexico and adjacent Spanish colonial territories
during the sixteenth century; in Mexico City by midcentury there may have
been up to three hundred in a total population of some twelve hundred
colonists.[86] By the early seventeenth century, the Inquisition was operating in
Mexico, prosecuting Conversos accused of "relapsing" into Judaism. The
record of one of these trials included a description (almost surely elicited
under duress) of a circumcision ostensibly performed by the accused on his
son sometime around 1640:

> One afternoon, around five o'clock, . . . his wife and mother-in-law
> locking the door ordered the boy to take off his pants, and they told

him to be quiet...and they held him tightly on their laps. He came like a rabbi, with his head covered and with a little knife or another sharp little tool. He knelt down in front of the boy, and with full devotion and turning his eyes and thoughts to heaven, as one who was performing a great service for the God of Israel, he took the genital member of his son and, holding it in his left hand, with the little knife or tool he cut it full across, in the part between the foreskin and the glans. He wrapped the member in some bandages, and put his son to bed for several days, giving him light food and pastries and sweets to eat. And some nights they lit a wax candle in his room from the time of evening prayer until dawn. Two days after he got up from bed, his wife washed the boy with hot water, from his knees down, and dressed him in a clean shirt.[87]

Although it appears that absence of circumcision was no protection in Inquisition trials, its presence was obviously paramount evidence of crypto-Judaism. In order to offset this prospect, some men and boys received a longitudinal incision in the foreskin as a symbolic substitute for the usual operation.[88] Not all, though, were so cautious. Occasionally an intrepid individual followed Abraham's lead and circumcised himself. Luis de Carvajal (1566–96), a Converso who became governor of New Spain, only to be executed at age thirty as a Judaizer, reported in his personal memoir that he circumcised himself, probably at about eighteen. His biographer says that Luis was "thunderstruck" when he read about Abraham's circumcision in Genesis 17 and "reached the verse that warns against the neglect of the commandment of circumcision—the one threatening that the violator would be "cut off from his people." He determined to "remedy his flaw" at once:

Without even taking the time to close the Bible, he jumped up from his seat, found a pair of shears, and as quickly as his legs could carry him, ran down to a tree by the bank of the Pánuco River to perform the sacred rite upon himself. Though the operation was painful and clumsily executed, Luis's anxieties turned to felicity once he had fulfilled the divine precept. Thereafter he always believed that the circumcision provided a powerful restraint to his lust.[89]

A few years later, de Carvajal's elder brother performed the same operation on himself, using a barber's razor, but was seriously wounded. His suffering was somewhat relieved, remarked Luis, by knowing that it "furnished him with no small merit to counterweigh his past sins."[90]

In his final testament, composed just before he was burned at the stake, Luis defied the Inquisition by affirming his fundamental beliefs: the unity of God, the imminence of the messianic age, and the central importance of the "sacrament of circumcision."[91]

4

"The Height of Foulness"

*Circumcision in European Religious
and Popular Culture*

> At first glance, it seems amazing that God chose such a
> bloody or even so ridiculous a sign. Indeed, why not rather
> ordain that the ear or lip or the digits of either hand be
> circumcised...? To be sure, God could have so ordained,
> had he wished; but this sign pleased him.[1]

During the early medieval centuries—from the fifth to the
eleventh—the Jewish population of western and central Europe was
small but for the most part fairly secure. Nearly all European Jews
lived in market towns, often near cathedrals or monasteries, where
they had little contact with the rural majority of the population. They
were more familiar to court personnel and the higher clergy, because
only people of that kind could afford the imported luxury items
that Jewish merchants typically offered for sale. Useful to the elite,
but for others mainly out of sight and out of mind, Jewish communities survived and even prospered. But by the eleventh century
their situation began to deteriorate—not as a result of their own
actions but because of profound changes in European society. During
the eleventh and twelfth centuries Christian Europe experienced
rapid commercial, technical, and intellectual advancement, setting
the stage for the brilliant cultural achievements of the thirteenth
century. Towns grew, Christians entered commerce in large
numbers, and young men left the countryside to try their luck in the
newly emerging economy. But for Jews none of this was good news;
competition increased, especially in local trade, where Jews had
never specialized, and ambitious Christians resented the relatively

privileged status of wealthy Jewish merchants. Eventually there were moves to force Jews out of the working economy and relegate them to the despised status of moneylenders.

Adding to their problems was the steadily increasing role of the Church in public affairs. By the close of the eleventh century, medieval Europe had become *Christianitas*, Christendom—a society that transcended regional and ethnic boundaries, united by a sense of shared identity surpassing what we ordinarily understand by the term "religion." To be European was to be a member of Christendom, with a Christian soul and a Christian destiny. "Christian" now meant person.

One people, however, stood apart: those who denied the redemptive message of the Crucifixion, clinging instead to what was perceived as an outmoded religion in which they seemed eternally trapped. Until the eleventh century, popular attitudes toward Jews and Judaism were more or less neutral. But from then on, hardening economic competition and steadily increasing Church hegemony led to outright hostility and frequent outbursts of violence. Although circumcision was certainly not the only practice defining Jewish difference, a case can be made that in the Christian mind—and perhaps in the Jewish as well—it stood out above all others.

The Christian Critique

"That Member Sanctified to the Lord": Peter Abelard's Dialogue

Medieval Christian theologians made a point of arguing that circumcision expressed, physically and symbolically, the impossibility of Jewish integration into the world of Christendom. The outstanding philosopher-theologian of the twelfth century was Peter Abelard (1079–1142), most often remembered now for his passionate love affair with Heloise, but in his day a controversial intellectual whose writings led eventually to his condemnation for heresy. There was nothing heretical, though, in his comments on circumcision. Among his last works was an unfinished treatise entitled *Dialogue of a Philosopher with a Jew and a Christian*, composed sometime after 1136. Although the characters are fictional, the philosopher obviously speaks for Abelard. Medieval philosophers aimed to demonstrate that Christian truths accorded with the dictates of reason—that rational thought and criticism sustained the principles of Christian faith. Congruent with this, Abelard's argument is that whereas Judaism is incompatible with reason, Christianity and rational philosophy comfortably coexist.[2]

Since the treatise is concerned with the relation between rational philosophy and revealed religion, the Jew and the Christian converse only with the philosopher, never with one another. Abelard begins with the Jew—and that is where we'll remain, since in this intentionally unequal contest the dialogue with the Christian serves only to confirm the predetermined defeat of the Jew. Although it would be going too far to say that circumcision predominates in the discussion, it plays a prominent role.[3] Following Paul and others, Abelard views circumcision as cardinal evidence of the Jewish failure to recognize the superiority of spiritual over material concerns. Throughout the conversation the philosopher is on the offensive, and although the Jew is occasionally permitted to score on a provisional point, he is reduced for the most part to a hopeless defensive strategy. Almost from the start he admits that being a Jew is burdensome:

> The amount of difficulty which the precepts of the Law involve is not unknown to anyone who considers it, so that we are afflicted as intolerably by the yoke of the Law as by the oppression of men. Who would not abhor or fear to receive the very sacrament of our circumcision, whether out of shame or because of the pain? What part of the human body is as tender as the one on which the Law inflicts that wound, and does so on small infants too?[4]

Now the philosopher extends a familiar argument: not only were Abraham's uncircumcised predecessors—Noah and the rest—blessed by the Lord, but even Abraham himself was already "justified by faith" before he was ordered to circumcise himself. It was his willingness to sacrifice Isaac, not his acceptance of circumcision, that earned the Lord's final blessing and the promise of triumphant reproduction. Moreover, if the phrase in Genesis 17 about being "cut off" really refers (metaphorically) to "damnation of the soul," the mutilation is even more irrational: it would even bar entry into "the kingdom of heaven to infants who die before the eighth day but who had not yet done any evil to merit damnation."[5] What, therefore, asks the philosopher, do you people gain from your circumcision and other misguided practices? Only "earthly" rewards—sheep, crops, and so on; whereas the "greatest benefits"—spiritual blessings—never come your way.[6]

Finally it becomes the Jew's turn to reply as well as he can to this "whole series of objections which are difficult to keep track of." Even if we were to concede that salvation was possible through natural law alone, he says—"that is, without circumcision or the other carnal prescriptions of the written Law"—this wouldn't mean that the Law had become superfluous. It still plays an essential role in our lives as in those of Abraham's early descendants: it is "like a wall" between us and the pagan world, which was God's intention. Since people are especially united by marriage and shared meals, the Lord commanded food restrictions and, above all, circumcision to ensure that we would remain apart:

> For the sign of circumcision seems so abhorrent to the Gentiles that if we were to seek their women, the women would in no way give

their consent, believing that the truncating of this member is the height of foulness, and detesting the divine sign of holiness as an idolatry. Or even if they were to offer us their consent in this, we would shrink in horror from associating that member with the foulness of unbelieving women—that member sanctified to the Lord precisely through that sign by which we enter into a covenant with him alone.[7]

Now the Jew, resourceful and inventive (as he must be if he is to be convincingly refuted), develops his argument on circumcision and separation from another angle: just as the effects of the operation are permanent and indelible, so is the covenant between God and the descendants of Abraham rendered indelible by the sanctification of Jewish male genitals. Moreover (adding a non sequitur of sorts), the Christian call for circumcision of the heart is also fulfilled:

[H]e instituted circumcision as a fitting sign of the covenant between himself and us, so that those who are conceived through that member which is specially consecrated after obediently receiving circumcision, are also admonished to sanctify themselves to the Lord through the very instrument of their conception. In this way they are circumcised interiorly in the heart from vices, just as already they were outwardly circumcised in the flesh.[8]

Finally, he offers a pair of arguments that we encountered in rabbinic texts, on agricultural pruning and sexual continence, each with a few creative twists: Just as grapevines require pruning to bear good fruit, so "the cutting away of the foreskin signifies the care of the divine husbandry towards us by which God made a beginning of our cultivation." Moreover, since Adam shared in the primal sin in the Garden of Eden, it is fitting that men share the punishment by suffering in precisely the appropriate place.[9] A valiant effort, but of course to no avail: the Jew is predestined to be dismissed as an anachronism when the philosopher and the Christian find their moral and ethical precepts to be entirely in accord.

The arguments of the philosopher and his Jewish antagonist in this "dialogue"—both invented by Abelard, of course—epitomize the Christian-Jewish debate on circumcision. The claim that Jews are deficient in philosophical capacity is Abelard's way of affirming Paul's argument that preoccupation with matters of the "flesh" ("earthly" concerns) is fatal to the spiritual life. The Jewish antagonist, confined largely to unconvincing arguments about the need for genital circumcision as a complement to circumcision of the heart, serves simply as a foil, a rhetorical device for demonstrating once again the truth of Christianity.[10]

"The Diminishing of Fleshly Concupiscence": Thomas Aquinas on Circumcision and Baptism

Saint Thomas Aquinas's *Summa Theologiae*, composed between 1267 and 1273, is considered the supreme achievement of scholastic Christian philosophy. One section concerns circumcision. Perhaps its most remarkable feature is that Thomas mentions Jews only in passing, and without polemical intent—the reason being that Jewish beliefs and practices were irrelevant to understanding the significance of circumcision for Christians. The Jews' fundamental deficiency was their inability—or their refusal—to understand that everything in their Scriptures (the "Old Testament") symbolically announced ("prefigured") the salvation that would become possible through faith in Christ. Their insistence on retaining the old ritual observances simply reaffirmed their spiritual blindness. The only meaningful question was how an Old Testament command should be interpreted in the light of Christian revelation.[11]

What Thomas wanted to know about circumcision, therefore, was the meaning or significance *for Christians* of God's command to Abraham. His essential question was the relation not between circumcision and *covenant* but between circumcision and *baptism*. He begins with a tentative answer: "Circumcision resembled baptism in regard to its spiritual effect. For just as circumcision removed a piece of skin, so baptism strips a man of his carnal behavior." But resemblance is not equivalence. Circumcision "prepared" for baptism, nothing more; it was only "a profession of faith" in the salvation that would later become available through baptism, not in itself an agent of salvation. Moreover, since "from the sin of the first man on, no one could ever be saved except through faith in the passion of Christ," circumcision should have been instituted not for Abraham but for Adam—"as a remedy for original sin which is contracted from the father and not the mother." The all-important difference between the two sacraments resolved, therefore, into when they had been instituted: whereas circumcision conferred "grace" only as a "sign of faith" in what was forthcoming, baptism acted "by the power of the sacrament itself."

Furthermore, circumcision was never truly appropriate (*conveniens*) as "a profession of faith," since "faith is rooted in man's cognitive faculties"; therefore, "the sign of circumcision should have been given to the head rather than to the organ of generation." Why, then, did God, whose wisdom is infinite, choose that organ? Thomas proposed three reasons: First, circumcision was "a sign of that faith by which Abraham believed that Christ would be born of his seed." Second, circumcision "was a remedy for original sin which is transmitted through the act of generation." Finally, God ordered the practice for "the diminishing of fleshly concupiscence which thrives principally in those organs because of the intensity of venereal pleasure."[12]

Note how completely Thomas eliminated the idea of covenant—and with it, the particularity and specificity of Judaism. Most remarkably, he seems to have followed Maimonides, focusing on the obvious connection between circumcision and sexuality with references to "carnal behavior," "original sin," and "fleshly concupiscence." His only mention of the Genesis 17 narrative comes when he portrays the first circumcision as a sign not of the covenant but of Abraham's faith that Jesus would be among his descendants. By interpreting circumcision as solely a preparatory experience, an expression of faith in the prospect of future salvation through Christ, Thomas universalized the sign of Abraham's very particular covenant while relegating it to a position strictly subordinate to baptism. Following Paul's lead, he granted its provisional appropriateness for men who had lived before Christ, as a temporary, but ultimately worthless, step toward the true salvation achievable only through baptism.

"A Clumsy, Stupid, Foolish Lie": Luther on Circumcision and Boasting

In 1523, Martin Luther, responding to charges that he had denied the virginity of Mary, published a treatise entitled *That Jesus Christ Was Born a Jew*. In the course of confirming his orthodoxy regarding Mary, he devoted considerable attention to the question of how Christians should treat Jesus's brethren, the Jews, particularly with the hope of their eventual conversion in mind. Insulting and vilifying Jews, as was the practice among many clergy, he declared, would certainly not encourage them to accept Christianity: "They have dealt with the Jews as if they were dogs rather than human beings; they have done little else than deride them and seize their property." If we want to make real progress in conversion efforts, he concluded,

> we must be guided in our dealings with them not by papal law but by the law of Christian love. We must receive them cordially, and permit them to trade and work with us, that they may have occasion and opportunity to associate with us, hear our Christian teaching, and witness our Christian life. If some of them should prove stiff-necked, what of it? After all, we ourselves are not all good Christians either.[13]

Luther stuck to this position for most of his life, arguing that Jews would soon be converting in large numbers to a reformed church. But by his final years, when it had become painfully clear that this was not happening, he turned against the Jews in exasperation. We see the change clearly in his two major commentaries on circumcision, published only about four years apart.

The first appears in his *Lectures on Genesis*, part of an extensive series of discourses on biblical texts. His lecture on Genesis 17, delivered early in 1539, reveals none of the fury and bitterness that would emerge just a few years later. Commenting on Genesis 17:11 ("You shall circumcise the flesh of your foreskin"), he observes that the Jews claim the foreskin to be the only "superfluous" part of the body—proof of their "extreme blindness" (standard Christian polemic and the only negative comment in this text). No, the foreskin is not superfluous, and God knew exactly what he was doing by choosing that part of the male body for removal. The "historical and true reason" for the command was that God had singled out males for punishment, since, by consenting to Eve's offer of the apple of knowledge, Adam alone was responsible for original sin. Even here, though, God expressed his everlasting mercy, for although "he seems to condemn the entire member, yet He preserves its use" (i.e., ability to procreate). Women were spared the pain of circumcision (but not its analogue, the pain of childbirth) in honor of the Virgin Mary: "Because of her God spares the entire sex, and with this seemingly foolish law He burdens only the males." Luther concludes with a mild expression of established doctrine, following Thomas Aquinas and others: "circumcision was not given as an everlasting law but for the preservation of the seed of Abraham until Christ should be born from it." With the coming of Christ, "not only circumcision but the entire law, with its ceremonies and forms of worship, came to an end."[14]

Aside from the conventional reference to Jewish "blindness," nothing in this commentary can be characterized as remarkably hostile to Jews or Judaism. Quite the opposite is true, though, of the pamphlet *On the Jews and Their Lies*, published in 1543, toward the end of Luther's life. This is perhaps the most notorious anti-Jewish polemic in European history, popular to this day among antisemitic fringe groups and a source of discomfort for liberal Christians. It must be acknowledged, though, that despite its inflated rhetoric and gratuitous accusations, the pamphlet includes a telling critique of ritual circumcision.

Luther opens the section on circumcision with a frontal assault on Jewish particularity and ethnic pride—the "chosen people" claim. The Jews "despise all mankind," he declares, simply because they are not circumcised: "My God, what we Gentiles have to put up with in their synagogues, prayers, songs, and doctrines! What a stench we poor people are in their nostrils because we are not circumcised!" Moreover, he continues, they "disdain, despise, and curse the foreskin on us as an ugly abomination which prevents us from becoming God's people, while their circumcision, they claim, effects all."[15] But how about Ishmael and his descendants, all circumcised? And how about the descendants of the six sons of Abraham's second wife, Keturah (Genesis 25)—didn't the command for circumcision apply to them also, and shouldn't they too receive all the blessings?

> For it is one and the same circumcision, decreed by one and the
> same God, and there is one and the same father, flesh and blood or

descent that is common to all. . . . Therefore it is not a clever and ingenious, but a clumsy, foolish, and stupid lie when the Jews boast of their circumcision before God, presuming that God should regard them graciously for that reason.

Perhaps, he continues, the Jews will insist that they are specially privileged because they observe the rite of circumcision more strictly than other peoples—and here he makes clear that he knows about *peri'ah* and realizes that it was a rabbinic addition to the original rite:

> In addition to cutting off the foreskin of a male child, the Jews force the skin back on the little penis and tear it open with sharp fingernails, as one reads in their books. Thus they cause extraordinary pain to the child, without and against the command of God, so that the father, who should really be happy over the circumcision, stands there and weeps as the child's cries pierce his heart. We answer roundly that such an addendum is their own invention, yes, it was inspired by the accursed devil, and is in contradiction to God's command.[16]

Running on at some length with the traditional arguments on "circumcision of the heart," Luther launches another angry polemic: the Jews pay no heed to spiritual circumcision:

> [R]ather they think that God should behold their proud circumcision in the flesh and hear their arrogant boasts. . . . These blind, miserable people do not see that God condemns their uncircumcised heart . . . and thereby condemns their physical circumcision together with their boasting and their prayer. They go their way like fools, making the foreskins of their heart steadily thicker with such haughty boasts before God and their contempt for all other people.[17]

The full section on circumcision, read in its entirety (nine pages in English translation), conveys better than I can here the obsessive quality of Luther's assault on Jewish "boasting," "arrogance," and "pride." One senses also an undertone of indecision: perhaps the author is not entirely certain that there is nothing to all that Jewish arrogance. Was it really God's intention, he seems to be asking himself, that circumcision should forever designate a specially favored people? No, that was impossible; the coming of Christ had revealed the sole path to salvation, and Paul had long since settled the circumcision question. Here again the covenant theme fades into the background as Luther reshapes the Genesis narrative to fit a Christian interpretation of what God truly had in mind when he issued the command to Abraham. Yes, the Jews were "chosen" to receive the original message; but they cannot understand that the physical circumcision of which they boast so relentlessly was only a preliminary representation of the genuine spiritual circumcision to be embodied in the life and death of Christ.

"The Weapons for Our Salvation": Contemplating the Circumcision of Jesus

We've seen that Paul, and all who followed his line of reasoning, viewed circumcision as worse than useless, nothing better than an impediment on the path to spiritual perfection. But when it came to the circumcision of the infant Jesus, Christian exegetes focused attention (as had the rabbis) on the redemptive power of circumcision as blood sacrifice. The Gospel of Luke records, almost in passing, that Jesus was circumcised: "And at the end of eight days, when he was circumcised, he was called Jesus, the name given by the angel before he was conceived in the womb."[18] Although this is the only notice of the event in the New Testament, for Christian theologians it presented both a challenge and a matter rich in prospects for interpretation. The challenge was self-evident: if, as Paul had argued so eloquently, circumcision was not only meaningless but even contrary to life in the spirit, why would God permit it to be inflicted on his divine son? Was this not conveying precisely the wrong message at the very beginning of the Savior's earthly life? Confronted with this unwelcome reference to the particularistic Jewish rite, theologians endowed it with new Christian meaning. Even though one might grieve over the infant's suffering, the Circumcision (capitalized in accord with its theological weight as a unique event) was actually a prefiguration of the even greater suffering to come: This was the Savior's first sacrificial act; the pain and bloodshed of the Circumcision foreshadowed, or anticipated, the pain and bloodshed of the Crucifixion. Jesus's first "gift" to humanity, the first time he willingly shed his blood, prefigured the ultimate redemptive gift, his blood shed on the cross.[19]

Consider, for example, a late medieval text, *Meditations on the Life of Christ*, a popular manual believed (probably incorrectly) to have been composed by the thirteenth-century Italian cardinal, Saint Bonaventura. In a chapter entitled "Of the Circumcision of Our Lord Jesus Christ," we learn that though the infant Jesus understood the meaning of this anticipatory sacrifice, he suffered in a fully human manner. The author meditates on appropriate sentiment for January 1, the date of the "Feast of the Circumcision":

> From the very first, He who had not sinned began to suffer pain for us, and for our sins He bore torment. Feel compassion for Him and weep with Him, for perhaps He wept today. On this feast we must be very joyful at our salvation, but have great pity and sorrow for His pains and sorrows. . . . And hear that today His precious blood flowed.

His flesh was cut with a stone knife by His mother. Must one not pity Him? Surely, and His mother also. The child Jesus cries today because of the pain He felt in His soft and delicate flesh, like that of all other children, for He had real and susceptible flesh like all other humans.... Then out of pity for the mother the Child stopped sobbing. And the mother wiped His eyes and hers, laid her cheek on His, nursed Him, and comforted Him in every way she could.... From that time corporal circumcision was abolished and we have baptism, of more grace and less pain.[20]

Here Jesus, already solicitous of his mother, restrains his crying so as not to cause her more pain. Mary cries along with her suffering infant in a fifteenth-century Provençal hymn, "Cantinella in Natali Domini" ("Song at the Birth of the Lord"). The composer knew that a ritual circumcision meant sacrificial bloodshed:

> When he was circumcised
> He was given a name,
> *Savior of the World,*
> He was called.
> And when he was cut
> He began to bleed,
> His mother seeing this,
> Began to cry.
> When the child felt
> The stone cutting him
> He was in great pain
> And began crying loudly.
> The flesh detached,
> The blood gushed out
> Here is the New Year's gift
> He wishes to give us.[21]

Christian clergy declared that among all for whom the Circumcision bore a message, it spoke especially to those heretics, long dead but not forgotten, who had argued that Jesus's body was wholly spiritual, physical only in appearance, hence that he had not endured a human form of suffering when circumcised or crucified. In a sermon preached at the Vatican in 1484 in celebration of the Feast of the Circumcision, Bernardino Carvajal had this reply to the heretics: "By circumcision he showed himself to be truly incarnate in human flesh.... [And] surely, if blood was flowing, there was pain, aggravated in the infant flesh. Truly therefore the human flesh of Christ has been most fully demonstrated by his circumcision."

A year later, Antonio Lollio joined even more passionately in the defense of orthodoxy:

> O Basilideans, who deny that Jesus suffered...look upon the cir-
> cumcised boy, hardly come into the light....O Apellites, who say that
> Jesus was an illusory man, hear the voice of the crying boy, and
> believe now that he suffered an inflicted wound....O Valentinians,
> O Alexandrians, O Manichaeans...and all you heretics and proclaim-
> ers of false doctrine—spew out now the old dudgeon...and consider
> the clemency of the boy Jesus who, in need of milk and the nurse,
> afflicted his most holy and pure flesh with the pain of circumcision.[22]

Here, in plain contrast to rabbinic texts, the Christian approach emphasized pain and agony as positive evidence of Jesus's humanity.[23] But this most
momentous of circumcisions was interpretable in frankly triumphalist terms:
the infant Jesus had not simply suffered; he had achieved a transcendent
victory over nonbelief, over lust, and over heresy.[24] Moreover, the date of the
Feast of the Circumcision, January 1, came eight days after December 25, in
proper Jewish fashion. Of course, this marked also the beginning of each new
year in the era of Christian grace. Hence Jesus's circumcision prefigured his
resurrection, and the appropriate frame of mind on January 1 was not sadness
but optimism and rejoicing.[25]

Optimism was certainly the dominant theme in other fifteenth-century
Vatican sermons celebrating the Feast of the Circumcision. "Declaiming at
Solemn Mass before the Pope," says the historian Leo Steinberg, "the preachers
revel in the exegetic tradition, and rejoice in directing their eloquence to Christ's
sexual member." Here is Giovanni Antonio Campano, orating sometime
around 1460: "Today he began to open for us the door and to make accessible
the entry to life. At the moment the boy was circumcised, the weapons for our
salvation appeared for the first time in the blood of that infant."[26]

A key image here—"opening"—appears with elaboration in the sermon
(partly quoted earlier) delivered for the same occasion by Antonio Lollio
in 1485:

> Today is opened for mankind the book of the Circumcision, the first
> volume of the most bitter Passion. Here issues the first blood of our
> redemption....Let us enter through the gate which circumcision
> has opened for us, and which today lies open even wider through
> baptism....Let us venerate this most sacred day of the circumcision,
> which we can call the gate that opens the way to Paradise.[27]

Note the similarity to the interpretations of medieval Jewish mystics, who
believed that uncovering the penile glans through circumcision opened a
"gate" through which men passed on the way to envisioning God. "Revealing"

the glans by circumcision "opened" Jewish males to viewing the divine emanation: not so different from Jesus's circumcision, the "gate" that for Christians opened "the way to Paradise."

"Carne Vera Sancta": Sacred Foreskins

Although the rabbis spoke of foreskins with contempt, for Christians the
foreskin of the circumcised infant Jesus came to be treasured among the most
precious of relics—this despite the fact that there were at least a dozen or so
available for veneration. Between the eleventh and sixteenth centuries, churches and abbeys in France, Italy, and other parts of Europe harbored sacred
foreskins (each of course the only true relic)—priceless not only because of
their ineffable holiness but because relic displays were a dependable source of
income. The Lateran Council of 1215, recognizing the need to exercise some
control, ruled that relics could be displayed only on feast-days and only in
reliquaries. But in 1424, in response to complaints from churches that they
were losing revenue, Pope Martin V decreed that relics could be displayed at
any time in appropriately reverent contexts.

The best-known foreskin was on display in the Vatican basilica (the papal
cathedral), housed in a jeweled gold reliquary, floating in oil along with
Jesus's umbilical cord. It was said that an angel had carried both relics from
Jerusalem to the court of Charlemagne, where they remained until his grandson, Charles the Bald, brought them to Rome. Some popes appear to have
been uneasy about claims of this kind; in the early thirteenth century, Pope
Innocent III declared that only the Lord knew for certain which relics were
genuine. But in the late fourteenth century Saint Bridget (Birgitta), a Swedish
nun and mystic, received a vision of the Virgin Mary, who settled such
questions, assuring Bridget that the Vatican foreskin and umbilical cord were
indeed true remnants of the body of the infant Jesus.[28] The foreskin was
believed to have been stolen in 1527, when an army of Charles V attacked and
plundered Rome. Later, after a former soldier confessed on his deathbed that
he had stolen and buried the foreskin, the pope ordered a search. Sure enough, an Italian woman found the reliquary; but as she tried to open the
container, her hands stiffened, and she and other witnesses sensed a de-
lightful odor. Finally a young girl (presumably a virgin) succeeded in opening
it, and the foreskin was returned to the Vatican. I don't know whether it
remains there now.

Another renowned foreskin was on display once every seven years at the
monastery of Charroux, in Poitou. (The name Charroux was said to derive from
chair rouge, "red flesh," signifying their most precious possession.) In the early
twelfth century, the Charroux monks traveled to Rome, bringing the foreskin,
a piece of the true cross, and Jesus's sandals for a special viewing by the pope.
The relic was lost during the sixteenth-century religious wars, when Huguenots

partly destroyed the monastery. But in 1856 reliquaries were discovered in a wall, and the local bishop eventually concluded that one of them did indeed contain the sacred foreskin. The French Ministry of the Interior financed construction of a new church to house the relic, and in 1862 it was transported to its new home amid a crowd of witnesses. The bishop preached an inaugural sermon, declaring that he had perceived on the foreskin some of the Savior's coagulated blood.

Yet another noteworthy foreskin resided in the Benedictine abbey of Coulombs, near Chartres. In 1421 it traveled to England when Catherine of Valois married Henry V, to be placed in the marital bed as a fertility charm! Many others were on display at various times in a number of French churches, as well as in Belgium, Germany, and Italy.[29]

The sacred remnant may have had especially profound significance for nuns. Saint Catherine of Siena, a prominent fourteenth-century mystic, remarked often in her letters that Christian women were wed to Christ, "not with a ring of silver but with a ring of his flesh" ("non con anello d'argento, ma con anello della carne sua")—carne (flesh) here having the same dual meaning as basar in the Hebrew Scriptures.[30] Agnes Blannbekin, a late thirteenth-century Austrian mystic, had an even richer imagination. Although she ate no meat, she described a vision in which she swallowed Jesus's foreskin: "She feels a small membrane on her tongue, like the membrane of an egg, full of exquisite sweetness"; and "so great was the sweetness at the swallowing of this membrane that she sensed a sweet transmutation through the muscles and organs of her whole body."[31]

Christian theologians, although wary of offending the pope, nevertheless felt obliged to raise questions about foreskin authenticity. Catholic dogma held that Jesus ascended into heaven with his entire body, including his foreskin, complete and perfect in every detail (tamim!). But if his foreskin remained on earth (at the Vatican!), had he truly retained unblemished physical integrity? Some commentators argued that the foreskin was an insignificant fragment of skin, no more essential to bodily integrity than saliva or sweat. The same principle applied, they noted, to the blood shed at circumcision and the Crucifixion. Proof of the argument: Jews viewed the foreskin as worthless "excrement"—and Jesus was a Jew. Others maintained, however, that it was madness to suggest that Jesus reigned in heaven with the "disgraceful Jewish mark" still on his body. Jesus's resurrected body, being not that of an ordinary human, was capable of achieving perfection by growing a lost part. But such arguments in the higher circles mattered not at all to the faithful, who hungered for a view of sacred relics.[32]

In 1900 the Vatican, apparently sensing that foreskin veneration was becoming an embarrassment, issued a ruling that anyone referring to "true sacred flesh" (carne vera sancta) would be subject to excommunication. Nevertheless, priests of a church in the Italian village of Calcata, near Viterbo, continued to display their foreskin each January 1 until 1983, when it was stolen—probably to obtain its three-hundred-year-old reliquary, fashioned in the likeness of angels bearing a jeweled silver vase. The local bishop announced that it would be best to let the matter drop.[33]

"Tell Us the Truth": Circumcision in the Popular Imagination

As ordinary Christians moved from the countryside into towns, they became aware of Jews for the first time—and sometimes there were surprises. One thinks especially of house servants, mostly unsophisticated women who would soon learn enough about Jewish practices to raise eyebrows of anyone hearing their reports. Aside from pork avoidance—surely incomprehensible in a world where pigs were a principal source of meat—ordinary Christians were most fascinated by two Jewish practices: kosher slaughtering and circumcision. Both, obviously associated with knives and blood, confirmed the general view that Jews were not only inscrutable but dangerous. Kosher animal slaughter, with its emphasis on extra-sharp knives and abundant blood flow, was a strange enough practice to attract attention; still, the victims were only cattle and sheep.[34] But circumcision—probably witnessed most often by impressionable maidservants—was another matter. Think of how a young woman, recently arrived from the country, might have reacted to the sight of a ritual circumcision, especially when the mohel appeared with his mouth and beard bloody from *metsitsah*. If Jews could inflict such frightful injury on their own infants, what might they not do to hapless Christian boys who fell into their hands?

"Ad Suum Remedium": Circumcision and the Blood Libel

On Christmas Day in 1235, the five sons of a miller in the German town of Fulda were found dead in the ruins of a fire that had destroyed their mill. Townspeople claimed that local Jews had murdered the boys (then presumably set the fire to hide their crime—the narrative is unclear on this point). For nearly a century, ever since 1150, when Jews in Norwich, England, were charged with abducting and ritually murdering a Christian boy, Jews in various parts of Europe had been falsely accused of similar crimes. The charge usually centered on fantasies about ritual crucifixion, the point being that Jews were performing perverse imitations of the deicidal crime of their ancestors. But in Fulda a distinctly new claim arose; now it was said that Jews had killed the boys to obtain their blood: *ad suum remedium*, to heal themselves. As to what required healing, opinions varied. In 1267 Thomas of Cantimpré, a French monk, explained that Jews had suffered from periodic hemorrhages ever since they told Pontius Pilate "His blood be upon us and upon our children." They believed, said Thomas, that "only Christian blood" would cure them—failing to understand that only the sacrificial blood of Jesus could "cure" or redeem them.[35]

The notion that Jews thirsted for Christian blood took hold, and during the next two centuries, ritual murder accusations, usually embellished with tales of bloodletting, recurred throughout Europe, particularly in German territories. There were any number of explanations for what Jews were said to do with the blood: they swallowed it or smeared it on themselves to prolong their lives, to cure chronic hemorrhages peculiar to Jewish men and women, to rid themselves of their foul Jewish odor, to protect against leprosy.

Then, in 1470, in the course of a ritual murder trial at Endingen, in southwestern Germany, a new explanation appeared. Soon after someone found the remains of four members of one family who had disappeared years earlier, several local Jews were charged with their murder. The accused men confessed under torture and were subsequently executed. The record of the interrogations makes clear that confessing to their alleged crime required the Jews to conjure up the kinds of answers their examiners expected. Apparently the first man to be interrogated, perhaps sensing from his tormentors' questions that he faced a new elaboration on the old theme, satisfied them by saying that "Jews require Christian blood at their circumcisions, as an unguent." That left the second accused in the unfortunate predicament of having to discover what his interrogators were now determined to hear:

> Mercklin was asked as to why Jews need Christian blood. To that he answered in many words, saying at first that Jews need Christian blood because it has great healing power. We would not be satisfied with this answer and told him he was lying, that we knew why they need it because his brother Eberlin had told us already....Mercklin then said further that Jews need Christian blood for its taste because they themselves stink. But we would not be satisfied with the answer and told him he was lying, and must tell us the truth, because his brother Eberlin told us a different story; now he must also tell us the truth. To this he answered badly that he wanted to tell us the truth, that he saw it cannot be otherwise ... but that Jews need Christian blood for circumcision.[36]

Before long, it became common to include circumcision as a feature of the alleged assault on the victim (who was always a boy). The Jews shed blood from a victim's penis, so ran the new claim, not just for treatment of their own children's circumcision wounds but for its own sake, as an essential prelude, or accompaniment, to the ritual sacrifice of the Christian boy. This fusion of fantasies is expressed vividly in artistic representations of a notorious trial held in Trent, a town in northern Italy near the Austrian border. On Easter Sunday in 1475, a young boy named Simon, son of a tanner, disappeared and was later found dead. His father accused local Jews of the crime; and despite evidence pointing to a Swiss man as the murderer, a number of local Jews were tortured and, after having provided the required confessions, executed. Simon achieved instant martyr status and was later sainted, his tomb a revered site for pilgrimages. For centuries the Trent cathedral displayed relics and reminders of the boy saint's sacrificial death: a little gown, a knife, a basin in which his blood had been collected, two containers filled with blood, and a glass from which the Jews were said to have drunk the blood.[37]

The record of the interrogations at Trent shows that the victims were driven to testify that Jews needed blood "to celebrate Passover when the Red Sea turned into blood and destroyed the Egyptian army," and "to scorn Christ and to prepare matzo."[38] But an official account of the proceedings devoted "considerable attention" to description of what the authors claimed had been done to the boy's genitals, and this was true also for at least some of the popular art that soon emerged to commemorate the episode. The most widely reproduced illustration, a woodcut from a popular "world chronicle" published in 1493, shows the boy surrounded by nine Jews, including several women, all with name tags. He stands on a low table. Seven of the Jews are either holding him or witnessing the affair without evident emotion. One man applies a wicked-looking curved knife to the child's penis, from which blood pours into a pan held in position by another. The focus on cutting the boy's genitals is unmistakable—suggesting that circumcision may have fascinated the artist more than the ostensible murder.[39]

Two other late fifteenth century illustrations of the same scene, cruder and even more explicit, show the victim being bled from multiple wounds with knives and sharpened prods. Again, assault on his penis features prominently. In one especially unpleasant engraving, the victim, disproportionately enlarged and grotesquely speckled with puncture wounds, lies on a sacrificial table while one of his Jewish tormentors applies a long, prominently displayed knife to his penis.[40]

These features of ritual murder accusations confirm again that fantasies about circumcision have played a far more influential role in the history of Christian attitudes to Jews than is generally understood. The key to understanding Jewish ritual circumcision is recognizing the meaning of its focus on genital bloodletting. Christian folk belief centered on this also; but in Christian folk culture, blood imagery connected with Jews ramified well beyond anything expressed in Jewish literature.

Claudine Fabre-Vassas, a historian of European folk beliefs and customs, points out that a basic element in *kashrut*, Jewish law regarding kosher meat, requires that all blood be removed before meat is consumed. Orthodox Jews prepare meat by salting and soaking it. Why, Christians asked themselves, were Jews so intent on avoiding blood? Was it perhaps because they were trying to repress an actual craving for it—compulsive avoidance weakly defending against unacknowledged lust? That rabbis so often functioned as circumcisers and animal slaughterers only confirmed in the folk mind the conviction that Jews were singularly attracted to blood.[41]

Central to the entire constellation of Christian beliefs about Jews was the practice that exemplified Jewish obsession with bloodshed. To be sure, the infant Jesus himself had endured circumcision, as a foreshadowing of the more profound agony and bloodshed of the Crucifixion. But as Christians saw it, whereas his sacrificial death had brought release from circumcision through baptism, Jews not only persisted in inflicting this bloody torment on their own children but yearned for opportunities to do the same to Christian boys. The image of the rabbi-circumciser-slaughterer, rooted in actual observation but interpreted in a folk-cultural framework, linked circumcision to beliefs about deicide and blood lust. Perhaps the most vivid personification was the bearded mohel, his mouth stained with blood after he had sucked the wounded infant penis. To dismiss such imagery and the deep-seated repulsion it engendered as just further manifestations of groundless antisemitism would be to fail to recognize a singular element in the history of the Jewish-Christian encounter.[42]

"What Will the Rabbi Do to Him?": Fantasies about Emasculation

Although ritual murder accusations emerged sporadically during the early modern centuries, more often it was through humor and satire that Christians now expressed their abhorrence of circumcision. An occasional eyewitness reported what the rite actually entailed, the best-known account being that of Montaigne, whose travel journal includes a detailed description of a circumcision he witnessed in Rome in 1581.[43] But for most people it was popular culture and folklore that provided information on Jews and their peculiar religion. In Italy, as early as the fourteenth century and continuing into the eighteenth, publicly performed farces called *giudiata* ("Jew drama") featured pantomimes in which actors, dressed to represent rabbis and endowed with oversized "priapic" noses, raced about the stage bearing long knives, threatening to slice off the other men's "monstrous appendages." A French traveler to Italy in the eighteenth century described a Punchinello farce called "Punchinello Plays the Jew":

> I saw one in which Punchinello becomes a Jew. The songs, the prayers, the ceremonies of this religion emanating from God are turned to ridicule. A Rabbi, the circumcision knife in hand, frightens Punchinello, causing the girls to ask, What will the Rabbi do to him?[44]

Note that the knife-wielder is a "rabbi." The notion that Jewish religious officials were likely to be expert with knives was based on simple observation of Jewish culture, particularly in small towns where relatively few men were eligible for ritual duties. Quite often the rabbi did indeed perform circumcisions, and in some communities he might function also as ritual slaughterer (*shochet*). This was the case, for example, in towns in Provence, where some men were even formally designated "rabbi slaughterer." That both slaughterers and circumcisers had extra-long thumbnails—the one for testing blades, the other for tearing the foreskin from the glans—may have added to images of Jews as wielders of knives.[45]

In short, we find in popular culture a blend of fact based on simple observation and fantasy rooted in Christian teachings: Jews, seen to be associated with knives and blood, and thought to be guilty of deicide, were imagined to be plotting physical assault on the genitals of innocent children and perhaps even unwary men. At times such beliefs resulted in violence, torture, and executions; at others they seem only to have inspired an uneasy mixture of laughter and anxiety. But whether dreaded, ridiculed, or both, circumcision sat firmly in the Christian imagination as the sinister mark of Jewish difference.

"An Insult to the God of Nature": Early Modern England

"So Base and Uncleane a Thing"

In his illuminating study of attitudes toward Jews in early modern England, James Shapiro remarks on the striking manner in which most historians and literary critics "have steered around the questions of *how* and *why* the English were obsessed with Jews in the sixteenth and seventeenth centuries." Moreover, he notes, "the one feature of the myth of ritual murder most peculiar to English versions (it was nowhere near as central to accusations made elsewhere in Europe) was that Jews circumcised their young male victims." He judges their "obsession with this detail" to be "nothing less than extraordinary."[46]

For example, about one-fourth of Samuel Purchas's comments on Jews in *Purchas His Pilgrimage* (1613) recounts tales of Jews who supposedly circumcised Christian boys before murdering them. One of his most revealing narratives is a distorted version of a notorious thirteenth-century episode in Norwich in which it was said that a Christian child was circumcised. The story tells of a Jew who abducted a boy named Edward "as he was playing in the street, and carrying him to his house, circumcised him," changed his name to Jurnepin, "and there detained him one day and night," until the boy's father forcefully retrieved him. The child's "circumcised member" was "swollen"— a point that was confirmed by "a great company of priests" who examined him. When the Jews insisted that the boy be examined again, he was found to have an intact foreskin; but this convinced no one, "seeing by surgery the skin may be drawn forth to an uncircumcision."[47]

The peculiar name at the center of this narrative is a clue to its historical origin—although the entire story is highly suspect. In 1230, a boy named Odard, son of Benedict (possibly a converted Jew), was said to have been abducted while at play, taken to a Jewish home, circumcised, and renamed Jurnepin.[48] Next day a woman found him wandering by a riverbank, crying and saying that he was now a Jew. She took him to her home, rather than to his own. A day later Jews came to her home and demanded that she give them the boy, whom they called Jurnepin. But the child's father was hiding in another room, and when he emerged young Odard acknowledged his true name and parentage. The Jews, frustrated in their attempts to make off with the boy, warned the woman (still unaccountably in charge) not to feed him pig's flesh. They also protested to the local constable and bailiffs, claiming that Christians were trying to abduct a Jewish child. The boy was examined by a coroner, who testified later that he had been circumcised. The affair lingered without definite outcome for four years, until 1234, when thirteen Jews were brought to trial, first before local justices and clergy, then eventually in what appears to have been a major show trial held before King Henry III, the archbishop of Canterbury, and a host of bishops and barons. The Jews are said to have given the king a gold coin, asking that the boy be examined, but he was again found to have been circumcised (although remember that, according to the Purchas version, he was actually intact). Many of the accused were imprisoned and fined heavily, and eventually some were hanged. On several occasions in 1235 and 1238 there were assaults on Jews in Norwich, presumably in connection with these accusations. As the historian V. D. Lipman has observed, the "true story behind this case is not easy to determine."[49]

Considering their fragile status and vulnerability in medieval England, it seems extremely unlikely that any Jews would have acted as brazenly as was claimed, or that they would have insisted on a second examination if they knew that the boy had in fact been circumcised.[50] If the story is to believed, their actions from the beginning ensured a disastrous outcome. I read the episode not as an actual instance of forcible circumcision but as evidence of how most ordinary English folk viewed Jews, and how likely they were to fantasize about circumcision as emblematic of what might be the fate of innocent Christians who fell into Jewish hands.

The English knew that circumcision diminishes sexuality. In a sermon preached on New Year's Day, 1624, in honor of the Feast of the Circumcision (i.e., the circumcision of Jesus), John Donne chose as his text the verse in Genesis 17 saying that "Abraham was ninety-nine years old when he circumcised the flesh of his foreskin." One thing we learn from this, he observes, is that when God commands, we must "return to the first weaknesse of Children" and obey without question. But he imagines Abraham wondering about the purpose of this puzzling "mandatum in re turpi" (command regarding something obscene):

> [W]hy does God command me so base and uncleane a thing, so
> scornfull and misinterpretable a thing, as Circumcision, and Cir-
> cumcision in that part? . . . Why will God command me so trouble-
> some and incommodious a thing as this? . . . What use is there of this,
> in my Body, which is now dried up and withered by 99 yeares? . . . If
> *Abraham* had any such doubts, of a *frivolousnesse* in so base a seale,
> of an *obscenity* in so foule a seale, of an *incommodiousnesse* in so
> troublesome a seale, of a *needlessnesse* in so impertinent a seale; if
> he had these doubts, no doubt but his forwardnesse in obeying God,
> did quickly oppose these reasons to those, and overcome them: That
> *that* part of the body is the most rebellious part; and that therefore,
> onely that part *Adam* covered, out of shame, for all the other parts he
> could rule. . . . In this rebellious part, is the root of all sinne, and
> therefore did that part need this stigmaticall marke of Circumcision,
> to be imprinted upon it.[51]

The English seem also to have associated circumcision with the threat of
emasculation. In the centerpiece of his book, a keen analysis of *The Merchant
of Venice*, Shapiro points out that until the confrontation between Portia and
Shylock in the trial scene (IV.1), we know nothing about the site of the "pound
of flesh" other than that Shylock had proposed that it "be cut off and taken /
In what part of your body pleaseth me" (I.3.146–47). The term "flesh,"
Shapiro reminds us, is the biblical euphemism for penis, a familiar point to
readers of the time, and it seems quite likely that Elizabethan (and later)
audiences took this to be Shylock's meaning, at least initially. Only at the trial
do we learn that the flesh is "to be by him cut off / Nearest the merchant's
heart" (IV.1.230–31). But, of course, circumcision of the "heart" was precisely
what Paul had advanced as the spiritual improvement on circumcision of the
"flesh." Viewed in this light, says Shapiro,

> Shylock's decision to exact his pound of flesh from near Antonio's
> heart can be seen as the height of the literalism that informs all his
> actions in the play, a literalism that when imitated by Portia leads
> to his demise. . . . Shylock will cut his Christian adversary in that part
> of the body where the Christians believe themselves to be truly cir-
> cumcised: the heart.

When Antonio, freed by the clever Portia from Shylock's vengeance, demands
that the Jew convert to Christianity, he has gained "consummate revenge
upon his circumcised adversary . . . a punishment that precisely reverses what
Shylock had in mind for him." Shylock's baptism "will metaphorically un-
circumcise him," and "the circumcising Jew is metamorphosed through
conversion into a gentle Christian."[52]

Whether Shakespeare's audiences interpreted the play this perceptively is open to question; but by redirecting our attention from ducats to flesh Shapiro places circumcision at front and center stage in the most memorable of all confrontations between Christian and Jew.

"That Unmanly Ceremonial": A Satire by Alexander Pope

In 1716 a bookseller named Edmund Curll published a set of mediocre "Court Poems" that he falsely attributed to Alexander Pope. In revenge, Pope issued three satirical pamphlets, the last of which was entitled "A Strange but True RELATION HOW *EDMUND CURLL*, . . . Out of an extraordinary Desire of Lucre, went into *Change Alley*, and was converted from the Christian Religion by certain Eminent *Jews*: And how he was circumcis'd and initiated into their Mysteries."[53] Especially interesting here is the association between circumcision, greed, and emasculation. The Jews in this tale insist that Curll be circumcised if he is to be permitted to join in their financial speculations, promising that "immediately upon his Conversion to their Persuasion he should become as rich as a *Jew*." Curll agrees, renouncing Christianity "for the *Mammon* of Unrighteousness," bartering "his precious Faith for the filthy Prospect of Lucre in the present Fluctuation of *Stocks*." With each enticement of financial gain, he agrees to relinquish another item in his heritage: the Apostles' Creed, the Four Evangelists, and so on. But eventually they reach the bottom line: Curll must give up *"Black-Puddings"* (a sausage made of pork and pig's blood), and he must be circumcised—"for both of which he would have been glad to have had a Dispensation."

But no such luck; and so on the designated day Curll appears at a tavern to undergo the dreaded operation. On entry he sees "a meagre Man, with a sallow Countenance, a black forky Beard, and long Vestment," holding a large pair of shears and "a red hot Searing-Iron." Curll tries to escape but is held by six Jews, who unbutton his "Breeches" and force him onto a table, "a pale pitiful Spectacle."

> He now entreated them in the most moving Tone of Voice to dispense with that *unmanly* Ceremonial, which if they would consent to, he faithfully promis'd that he would eat a Quarter of *Paschal Lamb* with them the next *Sunday* following. All these Protestations availed him nothing, for they threat[e]ned him that all Contracts and Bargains should be void unless he would submit to bear all the *outward* and *visible* Signs of *Judaism*.

Resigning himself to his fate, the "Apostate" spreads his legs and awaits the operation; "but when he saw the High-Priest take up the *Cleft Stick*, he roared most unmercifully, and swore several Christian Oaths, for which the

Jews rebuked him." The terrified Curll defecates, but the undeterred "Old *Levite*" carries on with his work—"when by an unfortunate Jerk upward of the impatient Victim, he lost five times as much as ever Jew did before." Finding that "he was too much circumcis'd," which disqualified him altogether, the Jews "refused to stand to any of their Contracts" and "cast him forth from their Synagogue." Curll became "a most piteous, woful and miserable Sight," with his wife ("poor Woman") in despair over her own fate, "wringing her Hands and tearing her Hair." But "the barbarous Jews" have held on to their trophy—"the Memorial of her Loss, and her Husband's Indignity"—which they display publicly.[54]

This contribution to English literature is followed by a "Prayer," which begins as follows: "Keep *us, we beseech thee, from the Hands of such barbarous and cruel* Jews, *who, albeit, they abhor the Blood of* Black Puddings, *yet thirst they vehemently after the Blood of* White ones."[55]

"The Best of Your Property": British Reactions to the Jew Bill

By the mid-eighteenth century there were some eight thousand Jews in England, in a population of about eight million—a tenth of one percent. Nevertheless, Jewish merchants of Sephardic background were contributing measurably to the British economy. Most, having been born in England, were legally classified as non-Anglicans, which barred them from holding public office, voting, or taking university degrees. Though excluded from retail trade, they could engage in wholesale transactions. They could not own land or participate in the colonial trade, and they could engage in foreign trade only by paying very high duties. In April 1753, a bill was introduced into the House of Lords providing that "Persons professing the *Jewish* Religion" who had resided in Great Britain or Ireland for at least three years could become naturalized citizens "without receiving the Sacrament of the Lord's Supper." The bill was aimed not at altering the status of the general Jewish population but only that of the relatively small number of Sephardic Jewish merchants who were handicapped by restrictions attached to their alien status. The rather modest purpose of the bill was to grant these merchants the status of naturalized citizens so they could participate more freely in commerce.[56]

The legislation, which became known almost at once as the "Jew Bill," passed in the House of Commons in May. But although this represented only a modest gain in legal status for Jews, the ruling generated so much public protest that by December it was repealed. The opposition came from many directions: urban merchants who feared new competition, conservative rural gentry who disliked all foreigners, Tories who saw an opportunity to discredit the Whigs who had promoted the bill, and conservatively inclined Whigs. In the course of the raucous debate inspired by the bill, says the historian Roy Wolper, "the Jew was scored for being dishonest, obstinate, blasphemous, clannish, ambitious, cunning, arrogant, traitorous, vengeful, and cruel"—the last of these probably attached to beliefs about ritual murder and circumcision as well.[57] In his history of Jewish life in early modern England, David Katz remarks that, despite the furor, "the storm passed over mid-eighteenth-century England like a dark cloud and left little trace behind nor any lasting effect on Anglo-Jewish relations."[58] Nevertheless, it seems indisputable that the episode revealed deep-seated hostility to Jews and fear of what their enhanced status might signify.

Much of the rhetoric arising in opposition to the Jew Bill was satirical and humorous, but the rancor and its attendant anxiety were no less evident for that. Circumcision was an obvious target, apparently a source of more dread than any other feature of the Jewish presence. Derogation of circumcision was nothing new in England, but now "what had been an occasional stone became an avalanche, and the rite came to symbolize the separation between Jew and Christian."[59] Moreover, although it was common knowledge that Jews circumcised infants, it was probably also known that adult Conversos, former converts to Catholicism or their descendants who had emigrated from Spain or Portugal, underwent circumcision when they reentered the Jewish community, and this may have underlain fantasies about Jewish designs on all adult male genitals. English men, says James Shapiro, "were repeatedly warned to guard their threatened foreskins."[60]

The fictitious name Moses Ben Amri entered the popular imagination as that of a zealous circumciser. The *London Evening-Post*, which led the newspaper assault on the bill and its supporters, carried this sham advertisement:

> MOSES BEN AMRI, Surgeon,
> *At his House near* Moor-gate
> *Begs leave to inform the* PUBLICK
> That He
> CIRCUMCISES
> In the Safest, Easiest, and Most Expeditious Manner,
> N.B. *He will wait on* People of Quality *at the other End of the Town, at their own Houses, on proper Notice.*

A letter, also from "Moses Ben Amri," to a man who was apparently thought to be seeking Jewish financial support in his bid for political office, warns that he might be in for more than he bargained for: "you have not *resolution* enough to undergo the *painful Operation of Circumcision*."[61]

Another satirical advertisement in the *Evening-Post* announced that since members of Parliament who had supported the bill were already "Christian Jews," they should proceed with "fulfilling the Law," since there was no longer any need to fear "the Pain and Confinement attending the Mosaick Rite of Circumcision":

This is to inform the Publick,
That there is just arriv'd from Holland, Mr. Ishmael Levy, who had
the Honour of being Circumciser to the Synagogue at Rotterdam
upwards of Twenty Years. This Gentleman gives as little Pain in the
Exercise of his Art as the Italian Tooth-drawer. . . . All such Venerable
PERSONAGES, N[obleme]n, M[ember]s of P[arliamen]t, etc., there-
fore, who are already circumcis'd in their Hearts, may now have an
Opportunity of becoming Apostates from Christianity to all Intents
and Purposes, without Hindrance of Business or the least uneasy
Sensation.[62]

Among the most revealing items was an anonymous satirical pamphlet
entitled *The Christian's New Warning Piece: Or, A Full and True Account of the
Circumcision of Sir E. T. Bart.*, which described the fictitious circumcision of a
minor Whig politician (one Edward Turner, possibly also the target of the
Moses Ben Amri letter), who was said to have submitted to the operation as a
condition of receiving Jewish financial support in his bid for a seat in Parliament. "E. T." is portrayed as bearing "a very great *Restlessness, and Uneasiness of Temper*" leading to a "*Wandering Disposition*," which was "thought
to have foreboded the present Manifestation of his Inclination to *Judaism*."
Having decided to finance his bid for Parliament by "forming an Alliance
with those Enemies of *Christianity*, the *Jews*," he applied to a "*Mr. G-d-n*"
(Gordon?):

That courteous Gentleman reply'd, that if the Rite of *Circumcision*
were comply'd with, and he were once in Possession of Sir E. T.'s
Foreskin, every Thing else would soon be made easy, and they might
command their own Terms. On the Return of the *Messenger*, Sir E. T.
seem'd much perplex'd at the Thoughts of *Circumcision*, but being
encourag'd by those about him . . . he at last consented to undergo the
Operation. All Matters being thus settled, and the Day of *Circumcision*
fix'd, Mr. *G-d-n* came down, the Night before . . . and brought with
him the famous Mr. *Moses Ben-Amri*, so celebrated for his easy and
expeditious Method of performing this *Mosaical Ceremony*.

The group assembles on a Saturday (the Jewish Sabbath, when such an event
would never take place). When the doors have been locked—"*for Fear of the
Christians*"—the mohel delivers a sermon on the slaughter of the men of
Shechem following their agreement to be circumcised: an example, he advises
the prospective convert, to be emulated. "The Charge being ended, which
was receiv'd with great Applause by the whole Assembly, Sir *E. T.* rising from
his Chair, all pale and trembling, and with some Hesitation of Voice, (which
was suppos'd to proceed from Mr. *Moses Ben-Amri*'s inadvertently producing
the *Circumcision Knife*, just at that Juncture)" expresses uncertainty and

anxiety about whether submitting to circumcision will indeed guarantee him the desired support. Whereupon his Jewish patron, "fearing that the Business he came upon might be entirely frustrated," assures the trembling politician that "as soon as the *Jewish Polity* was establish'd in England," E. T. would become "*Member of Parliament* for the NEW JERUSALEM."

> Upon this the little *Baronet*, with great Agility, mounted the Table, and, unbuttoning his Breeches, laid himself on his Back, the *Jewish Operator* attending on the right Side of him, and Mr. *J--nk--n* on the left, who very prudently held a *Bed-pan* under his *Br--ch*, for Fear of Accidents from that Quarter. Then Mr. *Moses Ben-Amri* approach'd with great Solemnity, with the *Forceps* in one Hand, and the *Circumcision Knife* in the other, and having mutter'd some Words in *Hebrew* (which Dr. *H.* the only Person that understood them, interpreted to be nothing more than a Sort of *Grace before Meat*) he lifted up the flaccid *Prepuce*, and at one dexterous Stroke sever'd it——never more to return to the *Stump* on which it grew.

The victim is so terrified that he urinates right into the mouth of the unfortunate Jenkinson.

The Jews had been promised the "*concised Prepuce*" as a trophy, but one of the onlookers stole it, apparently in the belief that, properly prepared, it would serve either as an aid in seduction of women or perhaps to guarantee a firm erection. He carried it away to his "Chambers," where "he wash'd it, and squeez'd it, and twisted it, and turn'd it, and hung it from his Window, on a Stick, to dry. Then again he soak'd it, and stroak'd it, and again he dry'd it, and stretch'd it, and try'd it (in Manner of a *Chinese Ring*) about the Neck of *Young Mr. Boots.*" The expectation is that young women "shall feel unusual Raptures from his fond Embraces, and bless the kind invigorating Contrivance." The narrator laments "that the same Portion of Matter, which was wont to contribute to filling up the Measure of chaste connubial Love, shou'd now (sad Change of Employment!) be destin'd to be the Instrument of rank Debauch, and *Priestly Leachery.*" The Jewish negotiator, having been deprived of his trophy (intended for the same purpose?) declares himself "absolv'd from the *Contract*," leaving the hapless "E. T." with neither finances nor foreskin.[63]

The debate on the Jew Bill also gave rise to doggerel identifying circumcision as the mark of the Jew's ineradicably alien status. Any Christian who supports naturalization for Jews, proposed one versifier, deserves circumcision for himself:

> That I hate ev'ry Jew,
> Believe I speak true,
> Nor shall they be naturalized;
> For them if I vote,

> Or e'er turn my Coat,
> I myself will be first circumcised.[64]

Shapiro records these specimens:

> Lord how surprised when they heard of the news,
> That we were to be servants to circumcised Jews,
> To be Negroes and slaves, instead of True Blues.
>
> In brave Edward's days they were caught in a gin,
> For clipping our coin, now to add sin to sin,
> As they've got all our pelf, they'd be clipping our skin.
> Those foes to the pork of old England,
> Oh! the old English roast pork.

This last verse recalls King Edward's expulsion of the Jews from England in 1290, following charges that they were shaving metal ("clipping") from coins.[65]

Another on the pork theme traded on the notion that circumcisions were celebrated with foreskin consumption:

> When mighty Roast Pork was the Englishman's Food,
> It ennobled our Veins and enriched our Blood.
> And a Jew's Dish of Foreskins was not understood.
> Then Britons be wise at this critical Pinch
> And in such a Cause be not Cowards and flinch,
> But the best of your Property guard ev'ry Inch.[66]

Finally in this regard we have a verse urging women to help defend that in which they had considerable investment:

> That the Children of Aaron
> Should mangle and tear one,
> So shocking a Thought is sufficient to scare one.
> Think well Lady S———n of this Operation
> And join with good Christians in saving—the Nation.[67]

Despite the lighthearted tone of much of this material, it seems clear that the prospect of Jews becoming Englishmen was, to say the least, unwelcome, and that circumcision was perceived as a cardinal sign of a difference that would never disappear.[68] Moreover, not all commentary was so jocular; some critics expressed their discomfort more frankly, wondering whether this despised practice might insinuate its way into English life. For instance, a column entitled "News for One Hundred Years hence in the *Hebrew Journal*," appearing in a number of publications, described an England ruled by Jews. "Last Week," announced one entry, "twenty-five Children were publickly

circumcised at the Lying-in Hospital in Brownlow street." In another periodical, a "Christian Freeholder" imagined the worst:

> [Jews may] become Owners of the greatest Part of the Esays in
> the Kingdom. And . . . if we should ever live to see a Jewish King upon
> the Throne, with a Jewish House of Lords, and a Jewish House of
> Commons, the least they would do against the Christian Part of the
> People, would be to exclude them all Places of Power and Trust,
> unless they would submit to be circumcised.[69]

In an even more hostile fantasy, two of seventeen imagined victims were
hapless Irishmen who refused to be "curtailed" of their Christian heritage:

> On Wednesday last 17 Malefactors were *crucified* at Tyburn, pursuant
> to their Sentence, among whom were Bryan Macmanus and Thady
> O Sullivan, born of honest Parents in the Kingdom of Ireland, where
> they were unhappily educated in the Errors of the Christian Religion,
> to which they were bigotted to the last, and chose to lay down their
> Lives rather than be curtail'd of the Honour of their Ancestors by the
> Act of Circumcision.[70]

Finally, another pamphlet, also anonymous, entitled *Seasonable Remarks
on the Act Lately Pass'd in Favour of the Jews*, declared that Jews "have not
forgot their old practices of circumcising, crucifying, etc.," and that "nothing
less than our flesh as well as our money will satisfy their unchristian appe-
tites."[71] As Roy Wolper remarks, the entire belief system surrounding circumcision "threatened castration; defense was therefore something more
than innocent."[72]

"A Barbarous Violation": Late Eighteenth-Century England

Despite the demise of the Jew Bill, anti-Jewish literature continued to appear
in England, with circumcision always a favorite target. In 1787 a pamphlet
appeared attacking Joseph Priestley, the pioneering chemist remembered for
his discovery of oxygen. Priestley was also a prominent Unitarian minister,
and in that role had publicly advocated friendly dialogue with Jews as the
most promising strategy for converting them to Christianity. *The Reply of the
Jews to the Letters Addressed to them by Doctor Joseph Priestley* was attributed to a
"Solomon de A. R." (representing a Sephardic name) but was probably written
by one of Priestley's most vocal opponents, a clergyman named George
Horne. Priestley had suggested that Jews might be persuaded to accept Christ
if they could preserve their traditional practices. Well then, said the supposedly Jewish author, show us the way by sharing our religion as we shall share
yours: accept circumcision "with the boldness and confidence of a man," and

"without fancy that the operator's hand may slip," for we know how to do the job efficiently:

> A table is prepared, something in the form of a hog's back.... Upon this the subject is laid, and incurvated to the upmost of his bent.... Across his neck, his hands and arms, and legs and thighs, are thrown proper ligatures, which fasten him so completely to the table, that he can neither shrink downwards nor jerk upwards. But this is not all. After he is thus fastened to the table, side boards are applied close to his body, and screwed up as tight as possible, which take from him entirely all power of wriggling or motion of any kind, except in thought; and in this posture, the operator being secured against all hazards of interruption in his operation, it is performed with the utmost safety and expedition.[73]

At about the same time, another pamphlet (possibly by a Jewish convert) launched a frontal assault, unmitigated by any pretense at humor. Circumcision, declared the anonymous author, is

> a barbarous violation of the principles of Humanity, and an insult to the God of Nature. For what can be more unhuman, than to punish an Infant by a cruel operation on a part of its body, done by a bungling Butcher of a Priest! Or what can be more insulting to the all wise Creator, than for a stupid Fool of a Fellow, to presume to correct His workmanship, by finding one superfluous part, and taking that away to reduce the subject to perfection?[74]

"In the popular imagination," concludes the historian Frank Felsenstein, circumcision signified "the perpetual stigma of the Jewish people in their self-inflicted Otherness."[75] As we have seen, it also appears to have threatened those many Englishmen who seriously feared that accepting such Others into the nation might end with imposition of their most frightening practice on native sons.

"Not Worth Calling in a Surgeon": Tristram Shandy's Mishap

In December 1759, six years after the repeal of the Jew Bill, there appeared the first two volumes of a work that would include a singular fantasy about genital mutilation: Laurence Sterne's novel *The Life and Opinions of Tristram Shandy, Gentleman.* Although the definitive misfortune of Tristram's life occurred when he was five years old, we learn about it only in the midst of the fifth volume of Sterne's rambling nine-volume masterpiece. The accident would never have occurred had the window-sashes in Tristram's home been properly hung:

——'Twas nothing,—I did not lose two drops of blood by it——'twas
not worth calling in a surgeon, had he lived next door to us——
thousands suffer by choice, what I did by accident. . . . The chamber-
maid had left no ∗∗∗∗∗∗∗ ∗∗∗ under the bed:——Cannot you
contrive, master, quoth *Susannah*, lifting up the sash with one hand,
as she spoke, and helping me up into the window seat with the
other,—cannot you manage, my dear, for a single time to ∗∗∗∗ ∗∗∗ ∗∗
∗∗∗ ∗∗∗∗∗∗?

    I was five years old.——*Susannah* did not consider that nothing
was well hung in our family,——so slap came the sash down like
lightening upon us;—Nothing is left,——cried *Susannah*,—nothing
is left—for me, but to run my country.——[76]

Ten chapters further along, we find Tristram's father, Walter Shandy, musing
on whether the damage should be taken seriously or simply disregarded:

——If it be but right done,—said my father, turning to the *Section—
de sede vel subjecto circumcisionis*,——for he had brought up *Spencer de
Legibus Hebræorum Ritualibus*—and *Maimonides*. . . . ——Very well,—
said my father, ∗
∗ ∗ ∗—nay, if it has that convenience——and so without stopping a
moment to settle it first in his mind, whether the *Jews* had it from
the *Egyptians*, or the *Egyptians* from the *Jews*,—he rose up, and rub-
bing his forehead two or three times across with the palm of his hand,
in the manner we rub out the footsteps of care, when evil has trod
lighter upon us than we foreboded,—he shut the book, and walked
down stairs.—Nay, said he, mentioning the name of a different
great nation upon every step as he set his foot upon it—if the
EGYPTIANS,—the SYRIANS,—the PHOENICIANS,—the
ARABIANS,—the CAPADOCIANS,——if the COLCHI, and TROG-
LODYTES did it——if SOLON and PYTHAGORAS submitted,—what
is TRISTRAM?——Who am I, that I should fret or fume one moment
about the matter?[77]

5

"Trembling of the Hands"

Radical Challenges in a Pivotal Century

> The Jewish body, and specifically the male body,
> lies at the heart of anti-Semitism.[1]

Think of this book as pivoting on a central chapter, the one you're about to read. Until now, I've been contrasting two distinct belief systems regarding circumcision: Jewish praise and devotion, Christian condemnation and rejection. I've tried to show that from ancient times to the late eighteenth century, nothing demonstrated more clearly the sharp difference in world view between the two religions, and nothing more starkly exemplified the unbridgeable gap between them. This was destined to change—but only gradually, and not in directions that could have been predicted—as one among the many complex social and cultural changes set in motion by the European Enlightenment and the French Revolution. The capsule term for these changes is *modernity*; and the key event (if such can be isolated in the flow of historical time) in the transition to modernity was the French Revolution—a social transformation so profound that its impact reverberated throughout the nineteenth century and indeed well beyond. Along with so much else, the Revolution radically transformed Jewish life in western Europe. For the first time, Jews who were more progressively inclined could raise questions about traditional Judaism; and their most pointed question was whether circumcision was still an appropriate practice for a modernizing people.

The nineteenth century was also a time when Gentile views on circumcision took an astonishing turn, but that story will come later. In this chapter I'll focus on events in the Jewish world, because Jews still "owned" circumcision, as it were, and it was in Jewish communities that the foundations for new perspectives and new attitudes emerged.

Jews were among those most profoundly influenced by the definitive feature of the transition to modernity: elimination of rigidly stratified and segregated social classes and categories. The Revolution created a nation of "citizens," independent persons with *individual* rights and responsibilities. Although Jews comprised only a tiny fraction of the French population, their status received inordinate attention, simply because they represented in starkest form the essential distinction between the old, prerevolutionary society and the new. A delegate to the French National Assembly, speaking on the question of what "emancipation" would mean for Jews, said it all in a few words: Jews must be "denied everything as a nation," he declared, "but granted everything as individuals." In the new France there could no longer be a place for "a nation within a nation," no room for people who intended to remain apart from other French men and women. Jews, he insisted, must become individual citizens, with exactly the same duties and privileges as everyone else—no more, no less.[2]

For centuries Jews had lived in a premodern world in which their status was rigorously defined and circumscribed. They lived in *corporate* communities, self-identified, internally regulated, and treated by political authorities as distinct social groups, with *collective* rights and collectively imposed taxes, social requirements, and legal sanctions.[3] Their social and cultural lives were shaped and controlled by rabbis who held the power to decide on all issues not involving relations with the outside world. When it came to the question of circumcision, a parent (that is, a father) did not freely *decide* to have his infant son circumcised, since were he not to do so, he and the boy would be permanently excluded from membership in the community—all but tantamount to exclusion from human society. A moment's thought suggests how profoundly this situation might change when corporate communal life was replaced by life in a world of independent individuals. How much change actually occurred—and, even more remarkably, how much did *not*—will be a guiding theme in this chapter.

Although the transition to modernity began in France, our attention will center on Germany—more accurately, the various German states and principalities that eventually coalesced to form modern Germany—because the Jews of Germany were the largest and most prominent Jewish population in western Europe. It was among them that the idea of Jewish "Enlightenment" (Hebrew *haskalah*) first took hold, and it was they who exercised the most far-reaching influence on other Jews in central and eventually even eastern Europe.[4] Jews shared in the general understanding of "Enlightenment": individual responsibility, confidence in human reason, skeptical attitudes to dogma. But for Jews in particular it also meant cultural modernization, entry into middle-class occupations and social status, and adoption of "respectable" dress and deportment—becoming proper Germans.

Inevitably such radical change was accompanied by widespread defection from traditional Jewish customs, challenges to previously unquestioned religious regulations, and indifference to the rulings and strictures of rabbis when these seemed in conflict with changing social and behavioral standards. A new distinction arose: The traditional religion was now called Orthodoxy, while those who favored modernization created their own modified version of Judaism, Reform. The foundations of Reform lay in the desire of many German Jews for religious worship appropriate to their new bourgeois style of life. Central to their self-identification was rejection of the idea of Jewish nationhood. Reform Jews presented themselves as Jewish Germans (not German Jews) who differed from other Germans only in their adherence to "Mosaic" religion—that is, the original religion of the Old Testament and its prophets, but not that of medieval rabbis and the Talmud. In line with this, they distanced themselves from rabbinic Judaism by calling their places of worship "temples" rather than synagogues. Insisting that they were simply part of a *religious* denomination within German society, not a distinct *people* (or "nation"), Reform Jews also rejected the fundamental concept embodied in the term "people of Israel," which appears repeatedly in the Orthodox liturgy. What they declared themselves decidedly *not* to be was an exiled nation residing in German territory; they were Germans who adhered to the earliest form of biblical religion. (Note, though, that their definition of Old Testament religion certainly did not include animal sacrifice or other obviously anachronistic practices.)

The implications for attitudes to circumcision seem obvious. If circumcision was an indelible sign of peoplehood and particularity, how could it be construed as an appropriate rite for modern Jewish Germans who rejected the idea of separate peoplehood? In other words, if circumcision was not a mark of *German* national identity, why should *any* Germans practice it? What is truly remarkable is that, despite what would appear to have been inescapable logic, a very large number of German Jews—not just the Orthodox (for whom there was no question) but probably most in the Reform movement as well—continued not only to practice circumcision but to defend it as an inviolable command and an indispensable rite of incorporation into the Jewish community.

This is even more remarkable when we realize that circumcision endured throughout the century (and longer) as "the most salient popular image of the Jew's body"—an unambiguously negative image that in many Gentile minds defined Jews as ineradicably different and unassimilable into Christian society.[5] There were Jewish challenges to the practice, to be sure; but the history of their fate only underscores the essential lesson: Of all the traditional practices that might have been singled out as particularly anachronistic and inappropriate for a modern people—dietary taboos, premodern costume, prohibition of intermarriage, residential self-segregation, restrictive Sabbath regulations—circumcision seems to have been the most durable, the most resistant to even modest critical consideration.

"The Very Core": German Jews in the German Imagination

If many German Jews now supposed that they had become truly German, that was not the way most other Germans thought. They saw Jews—specifically *male* Jews—as a categorically different breed, regardless of any amount of behavioral modification. For in the final analysis the distinction was physical. The "Jew" (in this categorical sense) was a peculiar kind of male—one whose body had been irreversibly disfigured by circumcision. For nineteenth-century Germans, says Sander L. Gilman, circumcision was "the very core of the definition of the Jew," not only for "medical science" but also in the popular mind.[6]

Did this idea—that Jews differed in the most literal physical sense— influence the self-image of German Jews? Gilman suggests that it did: "the internalization of the sense of their body's difference cannot be underesti- mated." Thus, he says, even though late nineteenth-century German Jews were virtually indistinguishable from other western Europeans, in "language, dress, occupation, location of their dwellings, and the cut of their hair," even in such physical characteristics as hair and eye color, it seems likely that in their own minds, as well in those of other Germans, they were indelibly different. And the "major sign" of that difference was the circumcised penis of the Jewish male—an imposed mark, to be sure, but a mark with immense implications. Jewish men were imagined as bizarre, unnatural specimens of masculinity—seemingly male but with mutilated genitals. Obviously, men of this sort could hardly be taken for genuine Germans.[7]

Here, then, was the making of a dilemma for German Jews. Was cir- cumcision so intrinsic to their identity, so essential to Judaism, that pre- serving the rite should outweigh all other considerations? Or might it be wise to conclude that this practice, like so many other customs, had outlived its time and should now be discarded as an anachronism standing in the way of social and cultural advancement?

"The Expression of an Outlived Idea": German Jews Debate Circumcision

The Society of the Friends of Reform

The first group to follow the logic of Reform with complete candor (too com- plete, as it turned out), and to call for a truly revolutionary path for modern Judaism, was a small assembly of German Jewish laymen, constituted in

Frankfurt in 1842 as the Society of the Friends of Reform (Verein der Reformfreunde).[8] They declared their intention to renounce "allegiance to all objectionable commands and to all antiquated customs": to endow their religion with "a worthier form" by preserving only its "pure content" and removing "everything which has degraded and dishonored it in the eyes of thinking men."[9] In its initial formulation the group's platform, prepared only for internal consideration, was indeed a call for reform. It said that the reformers recognized the "Mosaic religion" to be capable of "continuing development." They felt no longer bound by the various dietary and other regulations connected with "corporal practices" deriving from the "ancient polity"; thus they considered circumcision no longer "binding as a religious act or a symbol." Moreover, they rejected the authority of the Talmud, and they no longer awaited a messiah "who would lead the Jews back to Palestine," but regarded the country of their birth and citizenship as their only homeland.[10]

The most threatening items were those referring to "corporal practices." The Verein members were wise enough to remove both from the published version, leaving only the statements about unlimited development, disavowal of talmudic authority, and unqualified loyalty to the German homeland. These items alone would have been enough to bring down the wrath of the many German rabbis, including even advocates of Reform, who soon entered the fray. But what most upset nearly everyone and led to "agitation that shook the Frankfurt community from center to circumference" was the unpublished statement on circumcision. Word of this had leaked out, and in no time furious responses to the very idea of challenging this bedrock custom left every other objection far behind.[11] The rabbis in particular outdid themselves in declaring their outrage; even some of the most progressive drew the line at the very notion that circumcision was open to question.

Hoping to quell the agitation, a Verein member prepared a pamphlet (under a pseudonym) titled *On Circumcision in Historical and Dogmatic Consideration*. He advanced three arguments: First, a father who did not circumcise his son was not liable for any kind of punishment. Second, when an uncircumcised boy reached maturity, he should be accepted as a full member of the Jewish community, provided only that he profess Jewish identity and observe the Sabbath and holidays to the best of his ability. Finally, whereas circumcision was suited to the political condition of the ancient Israelite nation (Spinoza's thesis), it should now be replaced with a ceremony more appropriate to modern conditions. He ended with a proposal for such a ritual, to be called "Sanctification of the Eighth Day" and conducted if possible in a gathering of at least ten "Israelites." Having received the infant, boy or girl, from the godfather, the father would raise it up and recite a prayer praising the Lord for "having sanctified us by your commandments" and having "commanded us to lead our children into your covenant with Abraham and with Moses."[12] But for all the acceptance accorded to this document, the author might as well have proposed that crucifixes be placed along the inner walls of temples.

The controversy was limited at first to arguments over whether circumcision was meaningful for Jews in a modernizing society. Matters came to a head, though, in 1843, when the Frankfurt Health Department, aware that several prominent Jewish physicians publicly opposed circumcision on medical grounds, and having been informed that several infants had died after being circumcised, announced that in the future everyone performing this operation would have to demonstrate appropriate medical knowledge and surgical skill, and that a licensed physician must be in attendance. Although this alone would have been threatening enough, what aroused most reaction was the third paragraph of the ordinance, which said that "Israelitish citizens and residents, in so far as they wish to have their children circumcised," could employ only approved individuals. The phrase "in so far as they wish" (*insofern sie . . . wollen*) probably had no significance for the Health Department officials; but for Solomon Abraham Trier, the community's elderly rabbi, it was yet another red flag. He declared, correctly of course, that this was an open invitation for individual Jews to decide for themselves whether they wanted their sons circumcised.[13] Until then, although the *civil* authorities had never insisted on circumcision or any other ritual practice, Jews had taken for granted that only circumcised males could be accepted in the Jewish community. And since Jews in Frankfurt were classified officially as "Jewish citizens," a man's civic identity was predicated on his being circumcised. In effect, the only choice was between circumcision and baptism; one could not live in a "no-man's land."[14]

The embattled Rabbi Trier appealed to the Frankfurt Senate, explaining that circumcision symbolized a covenant so essential to Jewish identity that if a father failed to circumcise his son, it was incumbent on the community to do so. He asked therefore that the Senate issue a "correct decree, namely, that no child of Jewish parents may be admitted into the local Jewish association as a member of the Jewish community and the son of an Israelite citizen if he has not been circumcised."[15] Not surprisingly, the Senate declined, explaining that the ordinance was intended simply to ensure medical safety, not to challenge a Jewish "religious ordinance."

Rabbi Trier now addressed a message to eighty European rabbis, denouncing the Friends of Reform as a dangerous "sect" and a threat to Judaism, and soliciting their opinions on how to deal with faithless fathers who refused to have their sons circumcised. He received forty-one responses, all but one telling him what he wanted to hear. In 1844 he published twenty-eight of the forty positive responses in a volume entitled *Rabbinic Opinions on Circumcision.*[16]

The respondents differed on details, but they were almost entirely in agreement that recalcitrant fathers should be properly punished. As one declared, men who rejected "the sign of the covenant" had in fact rejected Judaism and their own ties to the "Israelite religious community." Everyone was bound to shun such persons and to guard children from exposure to "such a dangerous principle." If a violator entered the synagogue, he should be accorded only the respect one would offer a stranger. But he could not be counted among the required number of ten male worshipers (*minyan*), nor could he participate publicly in the service (e.g., be called to recite blessings during Torah readings). Sinners who became mortally ill and formally repented should be forgiven and properly buried; but those who refused to repent should be buried in isolation, like executed criminals.[17] Another warned especially against contracting marriages (for daughters) with such heretics; for "just as in former times immoral, heathenish people had to be expelled from the Promised Land, so also now must the House of Jacob not tolerate in its midst those who have abandoned Judaism."[18]

The "Science of Judaism" Scholars

Since the rabbis responding to Rabbi Trier were Orthodox, it's not surprising that they reacted so vehemently. But the fact is that prominent rabbis on the Reform side were almost equally unwilling even to consider the circumcision question.

Leopold Zunz was the leading light of the new critical scholarship—*Wissenschaft des Judentums* (science of Judaism)—based on the principle that Jewish history and religion should be subject to modern standards of scholarly research. Nevertheless, when it came to circumcision he was as cautious as his Orthodox counterparts. Unlike other transgressions, he argued, a single refusal to circumcise had lifelong consequences, and it was unlikely that an uncircumcised boy would grow up to think of himself as Jewish. Circumcision entailed far more than a mere ceremonial cutting; its real significance lay in *being* circumcised for the rest of one's life. In contrast to other ritual acts, which could be performed later if accidentally omitted, failure to perform a circumcision at the designated time constituted a "continual transgression." Rejecting this single commandment, he continued, would mean abandoning the Jewish past and future, destroying the very life of Judaism: "Suicide," he declared, "is not reform."[19]

Abraham Geiger, an equally distinguished *Wissenschaft* scholar, was more radical but hardly more forthcoming. In a private letter to Zunz, he confessed to an opinion that he was never willing to express openly. He did not approve of publicly attacking a practice so widely treasured as the "innervating foundation (*Grundnerv*)" of Judaism. Nevertheless, he continued:

> I am unable to support circumcision with any conviction, just because it has always been so highly regarded. It remains a barbaric,

bloody act [*ein barbarisch blutiger Akt*], which fills the father with
anxiety and subjects the mother to morbid stress. The idea of sacrifice, which once consecrated the procedure, has certainly vanished
among us, as it should. It is a brutal [*rohes*] practice that should not
continue. No matter how much religious sentiment may have
clung to it in the past, today it is perpetuated only by custom and fear,
to which surely we do not want to erect temples.[20]

Finally, there was Samuel Holdheim: equally eminent and respected, but
with a reputation for outspoken advocacy of positions that others deemed
dangerously radical—and prepared to go beyond nearly all his Reform colleagues in frank repudiation of circumcision. He argued that although
the Scriptures were divinely inspired, they were a human creation subject
to interpretation in the light of modern reason and ethical standards.[21] In
a pamphlet entitled *Concerning Circumcision, Primarily in Religious-Dogmatic
Consideration,* published in 1844, in the midst of the circumcision controversy, Holdheim presented responses to three fundamental questions. First,
was an uncircumcised man born to Jewish parents a Jew nonetheless? Definitely yes, he said: Circumcision was a sign of the national component of
Judaism, the part that was no longer operative, since modern Jews were not
an independent nation (Spinoza's argument again). It is birth to a Jewish
mother, not circumcision, that makes a man Jewish (an accepted rabbinic
principle). Second, was a father who refused to have his son circumcised, or a
youth older than thirteen who insisted on remaining uncircumcised, still to be
considered a Jew? Obviously the answer was again yes, for the same reason.
Finally, how should rabbis respond to someone who did not circumcise an
infant? Should they try to force him to do so, perhaps even calling on civil
authorities for assistance? Of course not, declared Holdheim; the duty of
rabbis was to teach, not to attack those acting according to the dictates of
conscience.[22] He did not argue that circumcision should be entirely eliminated; but since it was no longer integral to Judaism, it had become a matter
for personal choice. Arabs and others practiced circumcision, he noted, but of
course that did not make them Jews. It was birth to Jewish parents, for
women and men alike, that constituted entry into a particular covenant with
God.[23]

Holdheim appears to have been especially angry at Isaac Noah
Mannheimer, a Viennese rabbi who had taken a firm conservative stand in his
response to Trier (no registration for uncircumcised boys, no bar mitzvah, no
Jewish marriage, no burial in a Jewish cemetery). Holdheim lashed out in a
particularly harsh paragraph, declaring that such rabbis intended to officiate
as though in a medieval Jewish court, appointing themselves as "guardians of
faith" and "protectors of morality," determined to impose their will on the
"benumbed masses" (*verblüfften Menge*). But they were entitled only to teach

and admonish, not to threaten or coerce. Every individual Jew now had the right to exercise his "freedom of conviction and conscience," free from attempts at "violent intrusion" by self-appointed judges.[24]

A few years later, Holdheim accepted an opportunity to declare himself again. In 1848 a group of Hungarian Jewish reformers asked him whether they could rely primarily on the Ten Commandments when adopting a number of major reforms, including elimination of dietary restrictions and circumcision. Holdheim's response indicated how far he was willing to accept reinterpretation of the entire tradition. Religious regulations and practices pertaining to an exclusively Jewish state were no longer meaningful, he replied; Jews everywhere now obeyed the laws of the countries to which they belonged by birth and citizenship. Circumcision was meaningful for ancient Israelites united by belief in a covenant that had singled them out for divine favor. But in the conditions of modern life that belief now appeared as "the expression of an outlived idea" that "self-conscious" Jews must necessarily reject. Holdheim therefore declared himself "opposed to circumcision on principle." He assured those who trusted his religious understanding and conscience that they could remain "true and complete" Jews without obligation to circumcise their sons.[25]

It is no exaggeration to say that this was the most forward-looking statement on the subject in the nineteenth century. Couching the argument entirely within a theoretical framework contrasting nationalist and ethical elements in Judaism, Holdheim showed exactly what he meant by saying that circumcision was "the expression of an outlived idea." Although agreeing with Geiger's privately expressed view of the practice as anachronistic and repugnant, publicly he argued only that a rite holding significance in the distant past did so no longer. But his position was largely dismissed as altogether too radical, and his ideas came to nothing.

"Good Intentions": Reform Conferences and Synods

Between 1844 and 1871, rabbis of the Reform movement held a series of conferences and synods, at each of which questions arose about circumcision. Increasingly the medical aspects of the practice came under discussion. But not once did the attendees seriously consider the essential question of whether the rite should be continued. At the first conference in 1844 they promptly dismissed a resolution declaring that "those who do not observe the command of circumcision are to be considered members of the Jewish religious community despite this." Instead, everyone accepted the president's proposal that, since circumcision aroused so much emotion, it would be wise to avoid exciting passions that might disrupt the conference.[26] This was to be the characteristic response to statements on circumcision at every conference and synod thereafter.

At the second conference the rabbis were asked to consider a letter from a physician who wrote that circumcision could cause such afflictions as "sexual diseases" and impotence. He requested that the practice be abandoned or at least better controlled. The rabbis replied that, although they recognized the writer's "good intentions," other medical authorities disagreed with his claims; moreover, it was common knowledge that Jewish marriages were "very fruitful." They would "undoubtedly take up the subject at some future time" and would then take the doctor's letter into consideration.[27]

The third conference, in 1846, faced an even more pointed medical challenge but responded according to form. A physician informed the rabbis that his first son had almost bled to death following circumcision, and that the second had in fact died. Must a future infant son, he asked, also be circumcised? "Will it not suffice if I have him named in the synagogue and have the customary benediction pronounced? Can the state, can the congregation, raise any objection to such an initiation of my sons into Judaism, considering the experiences I have had?" Following a lengthy discussion, the conference adopted a set of resolutions on circumcision: First, every mohel was to "take a thorough course of instruction from a competent physician," pass an examination, and be licensed. "Permission to circumcise must be denied to any mohel who, because of bodily defect, such as trembling of the hands, near-sightedness, etc., is unfit to perform the operation." The mohel or the physician could decide whether to perform *peri'ah* with a sharpened thumbnail ("as is the traditional custom") or with a surgical instrument; but *metsitsah* was to be no longer permitted. Medical examination should precede a circumcision to make certain that the child was able to endure the operation; and a physician was to conduct the "after-treatment." Finally, whenever a physician testified that "a child has died or has sustained lasting injury from circumcision, and it is therefore a fair supposition that danger to life and health threaten a second child of the same parents," the circumcision was to be postponed until it was certain that the second child was out of danger. The rabbis, historian David Philipson remarks, "did not discuss for a moment" whether circumcision should be considered an absolute requirement for Jewish boys. The resolutions "had the purpose simply of reforming certain abuses and of preventing as far as possible any ill effects from the operation."[28]

This was the last conference for a number of years, but in 1869 and 1871 rabbis met again, and again questions regarding circumcision came up for consideration. In 1869, a prominent Viennese physician submitted two questions, by then familiar to everyone: Was an uncircumcised son of a Jewish mother to be considered a Jew? If so, how should he "be treated on ritual occasions . . . both subjectively and objectively?" He reported that cases had arisen in Vienna and Prague where Jewish fathers refused to have their children circumcised but intended to raise them as Jews. When the rabbis in Vienna refused to register one boy, his father appealed to the civil authorities,

who ordered the rabbis do so. Eventually the rabbis decided that uncircumcised males could be counted as Jews; but when asked for details—for example, whether they could receive ritual honors in the temple or could be
married in Jewish ceremonies—their responses were vague and confusing.
The questions were again assigned to a committee for consideration.[29]

At the synod held in 1871 the assembled rabbis, after affirming "the great
importance of this sign of the covenant and its maintenance as a symbol
among Jews," and having deplored the fact that at times it was being "neglected," unanimously adopted yet another resolution: Accepting "without
any reservation the supreme importance of circumcision in Judaism," they
nevertheless agreed that an uncircumcised boy born to a Jewish mother was to
be considered Jewish and to "be treated as such in all ritual matters, in
accordance with the existing rules regarded binding for Israelites."[30]

Although it was more charitable toward the uncircumcised, there was
nothing truly innovative in this statement or any that preceded it, since the
rulings were in plain agreement with talmudic dicta. More noteworthy is the
fact that leading representatives of Reform Judaism—men who were willing
to accept far more radical reinterpretation of Judaism than anyone before
them, and who had long since accepted modifications or outright abandonment of any number of ritual regulations—still insisted on "the supreme
importance of circumcision." Most remarkable of all, they delivered this statement, as in the past, without providing anything beyond the most superficial
explanation or justification.

"Sanitary Principles": Challenges from Jewish Physicians

Beginning late in the eighteenth century, and culminating in the nineteenth,
a new kind of European discourse about Jews emerged—not replacing the old
but running parallel with it and at times becoming dominant. The new discourse was biological, medical, and racial, and its focus was not on Jewish
spiritual capacity but on the Jewish *body*. Moreover, while Gentile biologists
and racial theorists played an expectable role, the somewhat surprising fact is
that Jewish physicians, a newly influential element in German-Jewish society,
not only joined the chorus but often led it.

Jews were already respected as physicians in medieval times, and despite
antagonism and discrimination, they maintained the tradition throughout the
early modern centuries. By the early nineteenth century, Germany had become the world center for scientific medicine, and Jews studied medicine in
such numbers that physicians were soon among the foremost participants in
the German-Jewish Enlightenment. These men (and they were all men) played
a unique role in the profound changes taking place among their German-
Jewish contemporaries. A key concept for Enlightenment advocates was

Bildung, "formation" or "cultivation," here meaning development of personal character: dignity, integrity, upright behavior. The goal, of course, was to become respectable citizens whom others would accept without reservation or prejudice.

As the historian John M. Efron has pointed out, the new class of Jewish physicians—men trusted and esteemed well above the ordinary—were not just *products* of this social and cultural modernization, they were among its foremost *creators,* pioneers in advocating and exemplifying steady Jewish progress toward bourgeois respectability. But whereas religious reformers of the time emphasized the need for Jewish spiritual regeneration, physicians argued for physical betterment—urging their fellow Jews to consider for the first time what Efron calls "the physical nature of Jewishness" and, most tellingly, to compare their own bodies with the stereotypical image of the ideal German—always imagined as male. We can anticipate the contrasting images: German men were sturdy, muscular, virile; Jewish men, frail, weakly, effeminate.[31]

For Germans who promoted biological theories about the ineradicability of Jewish difference, circumcision was the obvious target. Some even surmised that centuries of circumcision had resulted in Jewish males occasionally being born circumcised—a made-to-order case study for those interested in the question of whether induced physical characteristics could be transmitted to offspring.[32] For Jewish physicians, focusing unfavorable attention on the most firmly established of all Jewish ritual traditions was clearly unwise. They could take note, though, of diseases to which Jews seemed especially susceptible; and from there it was a short step to raising awareness of infant pathology attributable to circumcision.[33]

Although most physicians who wrote on the subject avoided calling for an end to circumcision (whatever may have been their personal beliefs), they launched a frontal assault on mohels whose practices caused rates of infant morbidity and mortality that no conscientious physician could overlook. For example, one physician reported that in 1837 all infants circumcised in Vienna by a particular mohel died. The historian Jacob Katz remarks that other observers "could tell of similar tragedies, and there is no doubt of the veracity of their testimony." Moreover, he continues, it is likely "that these incidents were nothing new, and that similar tragedies had occurred throughout the generations"—although people were so inclined to accept infant deaths as "natural" events that there had been no public reaction.[34]

The physicians identified several problems calling for immediate attention. Mohels were ignorant about sanitation or indifferent to it; many were surgically incompetent; and they engaged in dangerous practices that could no longer be tolerated. One major concern was hemorrhage; physicians received emergency calls to attend infants who bled uncontrollably when mohels accidentally cut penile arteries, and sometimes these children died.

Even more often encountered were life-threatening infections and infectious diseases. Mohels used their sharpened thumbnails to perform *peri'ah*, tearing delicate bleeding tissue with contaminated nails and fingers. They used dirty surgical instruments, wiping wounds with pieces of lint from other circumcisions, violating principles of sanitation that were now central to physicians' image of proper medical procedure.

The most objectionable practice of all was *metsitsah*. Mohels were sucking wounded infant penises with mouths contaminated by infected gums, ulcers, and, most egregiously, syphilis and tuberculosis. Not only was this extremely dangerous, the physicians declared, it was also repulsive.[35]

A Manual for "Self-Instruction"

Representative of the approach of Jewish physicians of the time was a popular manual designed for a general audience, published in Vienna in 1845. The author was Gideon Brecher, a physician from Prossnitz, a town in Moravia, where he performed circumcisions as part of his medical practice. The booklet was entitled (in characteristically neutral fashion) *Israelite Circumcision, described from historical, practical-operative, and ritual aspects, primarily for self-instruction.* Although Brecher urged improvements in the performance of circumcision, rather than its abolition, his antagonism to incompetent mohels (and perhaps his ambivalence about the rite itself) was evident in his foreword. He singled out *metsitsah* as the most urgent problem, declaring that it was his "sacred duty" to speak out in opposition to the practice. From a theological viewpoint its elimination was permissible, he argued, and only self-deluding persons could accept its continuation.[36]

Right at the beginning Brecher guarded against reaction from the rabbinate. Following his foreword was a twenty-page "Letter of Approval" by a prominent Prossnitz rabbi, Orthodox but inclined toward moderate positions. He said that he himself no longer performed *metsitsah*; it was a nonessential practice, recommended by talmudic authorities only for medical reasons that were no longer operative. In addition to considerations of sanitation, he wrote, on religious grounds *metsitsah* should be "abolished and prohibited."[37]

Most of the booklet dealt with noncontroversial topics: historical commentary and technical information on performance of the operation. Only in an "appendix" entitled "On Abolition of Metsitsah" did the author return to what must have been his real purpose in writing. He defended his position again by noting that a number of rabbinic authorities had agreed that the practice was not essential to a ritual circumcision. But the essential argument against *metsitsah* was medical. Often infected mothers gave birth to infants studded with venereal ulcers. What was the expectable result when a mohel then sucked on an infected penis? (Brecher used a euphemistic term for penis: *Schamglied*, literally "modesty member.") Moreover, mohels could transmit their own infections when their mouths came into contact with bleeding infant genitals.[38]

Two additional appendices, one providing a detailed account of male genital anatomy, the other a complete description of the circumcision liturgy, in Hebrew and German, indicate again that despite his determined opposition to *metsitsah*, Brecher hoped to be seen as a conscientious physician with strictly medical motives. Clearly he did not want to challenge circumcision as such. (We recall that he performed circumcisions himself.) Since his goal was saving infant lives, not reforming Judaism, he chose to focus on a single argument: although circumcision would endure, *metsitsah* must not.

"It Must Be Demanded": A Call for Immediate Reform

A pamphlet published by another Jewish physician in 1886—more than forty years after Brecher's manual—shows how little had changed. The author, Julius Jaffé, chose a carefully balanced title: *Ritual Circumcision in Light of Antiseptic Surgery, with Consideration of the Religious Regulations*. But the key term was "antiseptic": the work of men like Pasteur and Lister now had to be taken into account. The opening pages reflect awareness of the developing literature in comparative ethnology; in addition to ancient beliefs and practices, Jaffé noted that various peoples in Africa, South America, Australia, and the Pacific islands also practiced circumcision. (He did not comment on the fact that in no other society were *infants* circumcised.) But despite the variety of explanations found in such cultures, he continued, for Jews only two matter: hygienic value and religious significance. Note that here he subtly departed from the Orthodox Jewish position, which declared (and still declares) affirmation of the biblical covenant to be the sole meaning and purpose of the rite, and accepts medical or hygienic justification only incidentally. But, like Brecher, Jaffé obviously intended to be as conciliatory as possible by accepting ritual circumcision, even as he prepared to demand that medically (and ethically) unacceptable features of the practice be eliminated.

The pamphlet dealt almost exclusively with medical issues. Jaffé cited claims for the medical value of circumcision that were becoming current by his time: treatment of "phimosis" (here meaning foreskin constriction) and prevention of a variety of relatively uncommon ailments. He cited French medical reports on penile cancer (a topic that would achieve widespread attention in the next century) and discussed research suggesting that circumcision helped protect against syphilis. He also noted claims that circumcised boys were less inclined to masturbate. (I discuss these topics later.) Thus, he concludes, circumcision "can be credited with many positive qualities."[39]

But having dutifully acknowledged the possible benefits, Jaffé launched into a lengthy, horrifying description (seventeen of his forty-three pages) of complications and severe adverse consequences of circumcisions performed by incompetent mohels. He described deaths and near-deaths from hemorrhage, infections (syphilis, tuberculosis), gangrene, erysipelas, mutilation, and other calamities. Some children were rescued, he reported, only when a physician intervened before all was lost. But despite the grim litany, the author insisted that he did not condemn circumcision; he only wanted assurance that a qualified physician would always be in attendance, to ensure that the procedure would be carried out in accord with proper medical standards: "It is impossible to demand abandonment of a ritual that has existed for millennia and constitutes an indispensable requirement for admission into the Jewish religious community. It must be demanded, however, that this be performed in a manner that endangers neither the life nor the health of children."[40]

The pamphlet closed with detailed recommendations for improving the operation. Circumcision should take place in an uncrowded room at home, Jaffé urged, not in a synagogue. The operator should be either a physician or a properly qualified mohel with knowledge of sanitation. Such traditional practices as sucking and use of sharpened thumb- and fingernails must be discontinued; only clean instruments should touch the penis.

Whatever his personal religious views, then, Julius Jaffé, like most other Jewish physicians who dealt with ritual circumcision, chose not to confront the rabbinate by challenging the practice itself. He went further than Gideon Brecher, however, by explicitly blaming incompetent mohels for endangering infant lives, and by calling for physician supervision of all circumcisions performed by mohels. I cannot overemphasize the importance of this pamphlet, and of others like it, as indicators of the growing influence of physician opinion. Despite its moderate tone, it was an uncompromising demand for rigorous medicalization of a ritual procedure that for centuries had been immune to intervention by anyone outside the religious establishment.

"The Custom of Israel Is Law": The Rabbis Respond

Criticism of circumcision, particularly by physicians—men with immense prestige in Jewish communities—posed formidable problems for the rabbinate, especially the Orthodox. Viewed in somewhat broader perspective, challenges to the traditional practices of mohels, and to the outright incompetence of some, were to be expected among people who were embracing reform in every aspect of their religious lives. For the rabbis, Reform and Orthodox, the bottom line was a straightforward question: How do we respond when statements by respected physicians appear to contradict talmudic mandates? One possible path to resolution, adopted by the more liberal, was to conclude that there were no contradictions after all; one could accommodate to medical requirements with moderate changes that seemed compatible with talmudic directives. But among the Orthodox were those who would have none of this. The ancient sages never erred, they declared; their rulings and instructions were not subject to challenge, revision, or reversal by physicians or anyone else. These men maintained (not unreasonably) that once the door to change opened even a crack, more change was certain to follow. They were prepared to give way on improvements that impinged on nothing essential—basic sanitation, adequate training for mohels—but that was the outer limit.

Not surprisingly, the conflict centered on *metsitsah*. Washing hands and using fresh lint for each infant were one thing; eliminating an established (and dramatic) feature of every circumcision was quite another. As many Orthodox rabbis saw it, conceding on *metsitsah* would be tantamount to accepting the triumph of Reform, which would signal the death of authentic Judaism and its replacement by an illegitimate pseudoreligion. Discourses on transmission of venereal diseases and such were of little or no interest to them; they had only to decide how the sages would have responded to the new challenges, and to follow faithfully along the mandated path.

The key to the question, as they understood it, was precisely what the sages had meant by their statements about circumcision on the Sabbath. The Mishnah mentions *metsitsah* only in passing, saying that a circumcision performed on the Sabbath (when nonessential "work" is prohibited) includes three acts: "cut," "tear," and "suck" (as it would at any other time). Since sucking had been included as part of a Sabbath circumcision, this alone indicated that it was an essential component of the rite. A talmudic rabbi had added commentary that was taken to be confirmatory: "If a surgeon does not suck, it is dangerous and he is dismissed. . . . Just as when one does not apply a bandage and cumin there is danger, so here too if one does not do it there is danger." The point was that sucking seemed to be not only permitted but expected as a necessary part of a circumcision whenever it was performed, including on the Sabbath.[41] Thus, the German rabbis concluded, a legitimate circumcision requires sucking.

A pivotal ruling emerged in 1837, after Rabbi Eleazar Horowitz of Vienna received a letter from the chief physician at the Jewish hospital notifying him of infant infections and deaths following circumcision—possibly but not necessarily attributable to *metsitsah*. Whatever the immediate cause of the deaths, however, the physician wanted *metsitsah* eliminated—not only because it was medically dangerous but also because it was a "disgusting" (*ekelhaft*) practice. Horowitz, inclined to leniency, decided that rather than sucking the circumcised penis, mohels might wipe it with a sponge dipped in wine or water. He wrote to the leading talmudic authority of the time, Rabbi Moses Sofer (1762–1839), asking whether such an innovation would be permissible. Sofer replied that, in his opinion, *metsitsah* was only a recommended therapeutic practice, not an essential requirement, hence that it might be omitted if something better took its place. If physicians said that sponging was an adequate substitute for sucking, so be it.[42] This ruling stood as authoritative and was widely followed, even by many of the most conservative Orthodox rabbis and mohels. But others took a firm stand against any change whatever. One rabbi in Hungary spoke for this contingent when he declared that "Moses certainly received the law at Sinai in this form" (i.e., with *metsitsah*), hence nothing justified new rulings on medical grounds.[43]

Leading the counterattack against sponging or any other change was Jacob Ettlinger (1798–1871), an influential rabbi who founded two journals (one in German, the other in Hebrew) specifically to defend Orthodoxy against every challenge. Since Moses Sofer had died in 1839, Ettlinger had to proceed judiciously in contradicting the senior rabbi's ruling, but contradict he did: "although one does not answer the lion after his death, if he was still alive I would have argued with him while sitting at his feet." He called on his colleagues to "examine how far things will go if you decide in favor of the scientists' view over what we have received from the Sages of the Talmud. . . . God forbid that everything will be overturned, and most of the Torah, as it is practiced in all the diaspora of Israel, will be abolished."[44]

Ettlinger held the line even on use of fingernails for tearing adhering foreskin tissue (*peri'ah*), although he conceded that mohels need not be prohibited from using surgical instruments. Innovative technology, he ruled, was in the same category as elimination of *metsitsah*, just another form of assault on "the holy covenant." It was enough that Maimonides had mentioned fingernails—"and in any case the custom of Israel is law."[45]

From midcentury onward, most Orthodox rabbis, fearful that any concessions would encourage calls for further change, closed ranks and followed Ettlinger's lead, refusing to accept the authority of outsiders, medical or governmental, and insisting that the rite of circumcision be maintained strictly in its traditional form. Their position was epitomized in a statement issued around 1855 by Moses Schieck, rabbi of a small Jewish community in Slovakia. When the opinions of physicians conflict with those of the sages, he declared, the words of the sages are binding. "We cannot apply the concept of changing times," he declared, "to anything which is a law to Moses from Sinai, for the word of our God is eternal."[46]

The ostensible justification for *metsitsah*—that it helped to stop bleeding—was now irrelevant; the Orthodox rite *required* that the mohel suck blood. Pressure for reform continued, however, not only from physicians but from governmental authorities intent on modernizing medical practices. In 1887, Michael Cahn, rabbi of the town of Fulda in central Germany, designed with the aid of bacteriologists a small glass tube that would enable a mohel to suck blood without direct oral contact with the penis. Within a year the tube had been manufactured and tested, and had gained the approval of authoritative Orthodox rabbis. By the turn of the century this solution had been widely adopted in western and central Europe, and the practice of direct mouth-to-penis sucking was largely abandoned.[47]

Most eastern European rabbis refused to budge at all, however, so that the presence or absence of traditional *metsitsah* became a cultural dividing line between eastern European Jewry and communities to their west. Typical of the eastern faction was the rabbi of Lvov, in the Ukraine, who said that the physical act of sucking expressed love for the commandment of circumcision. But on one point nearly every rabbi, east and west, Orthodox and Reform, traditional and acculturated, agreed: they would defend "the basic symbols of identification with the community, first and foremost, circumcision."[48]

"This Last Remnant of Asiatic Custom": A Call for Abolition

Most German-Jewish physicians adopted a cautious strategy, criticizing only the medical practices of mohels but not questioning ritual circumcision as a Jewish tradition. One man departed from that approach, however, with a publication that stands out in this history as the most fiercely phrased of all critiques. Eugen Levit, a physician from a town in Bohemia, wrote with anger and passion rooted in painful personal experience. In 1874 he published a pamphlet modestly (and somewhat deceptively) entitled *Israelite Circumcision, elucidated [beleuchtet] from a medical and humane standpoint, by an elderly physician*. It aroused immediate attention in the medical world.[49]

Right at the start Levit declared that he was writing "to oppose a barbaric custom of our nation and to protect thousands of innocent creatures from torture and mutilation [*Entstellungen*]." His first son, probably born in the 1840s, had died after his circumcision became infected. When a second son was born in 1849, Levit decided not to have the boy circumcised—even though he was not intentionally rebellious. "I led the child along the Jewish path," he wrote. "I was called by name to the Torah on Sabbath, had the infant named, and vowed publicly and solemnly to have my child raised in accordance with Jewish principles." The town rabbi, standing on tradition, challenged the father's right to have the boy's name recorded in the Jewish registry, but the local authorities and the regional governor decided the case in Levit's favor. The boy was duly registered with the notation "uncircumcised." Eventually Levit, still optimistic, enrolled his son in a Jewish school for religious instruction. But in 1857 a new rabbi reopened the challenge, this time with more success: Levit was ordered to have the boy either circumcised or baptized. "I obeyed this draconian order," he reported; "I led my only son to the altar myself, to baptize him, just as Abraham led Isaac to the altar to slaughter him." Fortunately, he continued, now that the government was more enlightened, a parent no longer had to choose between two objectionable alternatives.[50]

Levit said that in his thirty-five-year medical practice he had witnessed six deaths and more than twenty mutilations [*Verstümmlungen*], even though most of the circumcisions had been performed by physicians. Similar tragedies occurred often when "clumsy, old, often trembling" mohels used contaminated instruments and sucked on wounded penises with unclean mouths, causing bleeding and infection.[51]

After further pages of medical argument, Levit turned to cultural and religious considerations, and here he expressed his outrage even more forcefully: "Fanatical zealots, supposedly honoring God or from a sense of guilt, may punish their own bodies with fasting, waking vigils, lashing, all sorts of self-denial and mortification; but to impose asceticism on the body of someone else, especially an innocent, defenseless child—that no one has the right to do." It is not circumcision, he reminded readers, but belief in one God that makes someone a Jew. At a time when organizations protected animals against mistreatment and teachers were forbidden to impose physical punishment on children, "torture of an innocent baby" could not be justified by contending that a "bloody sacrifice" was a sacred act.[52]

This was followed by some of the most vehement condemnation of circumcision ever written:

> What cultivated people would ever consider regarding bloody, mutilated genitals as a divine cultural symbol? Indeed, whenever I have attended this ceremony, I have never perceived a devout, solemn attitude in any participant. Every time, to be certain, I have seen the pale, trembling father offering his sacrifice to the mohel, while the shocked, delicate mother awaits in anxious agony the return of her passionately loved infant. I have seen many of those in attendance fall in a faint—yes, even a simple, coarse peasant servant girl, the wet nurse, shedding tears at the scene she witnessed....A ceremony dripping with blood, eliciting cries of pain and agony, arousing pity and dread in some, revulsion in others, a sacrificial oath offered with a body part, overcoming considerations of purity, good breeding, modesty, and sensitive feelings, something that only anatomists and physicians should discuss openly, and that even lascivious jesting in frivolous conversation hardly dares allude to—only fanatic Oriental zealots could call such an event a consecration.

The term "Oriental" is a clue to Levit's mindset. He was appealing to the sensitivities of Reform Jews whose fundamental goal, as I've shown, was to redesign Judaism to accord with contemporary German cultural standards. By contending that circumcision was an anachronism in nineteenth-century Europe, Levit argued that the rite was a worthless survival from the "barbarous" past, a rejection of the principles underlying the Reform movement. He underscored this point:

> The contemporary generation, whose feelings and ways of thought have been conditioned by education, upbringing, scientific knowledge, art, lectures, and the radiating influence of enlightened,

purified European culture, and who have been permeated by the Christian-Germanic moral environment, cannot be edified by, reconciled to, or divinely inspired by a horrible blood symbol.[53]

Why be so hypocritical, he asked, as to claim biblical justification for circumcision when so many of us no longer feel constrained by other biblical mandates? The time had come for circumcision to be criminalized, and it was the duty of Jewish physicians to initiate action. Levit urged formation of "organizations for the abolition of this abusive practice" (*Vereines zur Abschaffung dieses Missbrauches*), led by influential persons and dedicated to providing information to the public. After all, he remarked, would any modern society and government now accept a religious sect insisting on a bloody act of this sort as its rite of initiation?[54] He closed with a return to his central argument:

Only by doing away with this last remnant of Asiatic custom will every boundary wall finally fall, and Israelites will step openly into the European community. Finally, I hope still to witness [a time when] governments will prohibit circumcision on sanitary principles, and the perpetrators of this grave physical assault will be brought to account.[55]

A Pivotal Publication: Religion and Medicine Fused

Although some physicians in Vienna and elsewhere took note of Levit's pamphlet and sympathized with his arguments, the work had no lasting influence on attitudes to circumcision among the German-Jewish laity, let alone the rabbinate. "Abusive" or not, medically dangerous or not, culturally appropriate or not, the rite of circumcision survived every critique, every challenge. Moreover, by the final decades of the century, a counterdiscourse had emerged among German-Jewish physicians, reflecting parallel developments in England and the United States (the subject of my next chapter). Some began to maintain that, far from being harmful, circumcision was in fact a beneficial medical procedure that protected against a number of afflictions and even cured some. So while physicians on one side continued to stress the danger of infection, hemorrhage, and the like, others became advocates, arguing that circumcision was not only a religious imperative but also was advisable on "hygienic" grounds.

In 1896 a large jointly written volume exemplified this new approach. The editor and principal author was Abraham Glassberg—not a physician himself, but supported by contributions and assistance from a number of physicians and academic specialists. Offering a comprehensive overview of circumcision "in its historical, ethnographic, religious, and medical significance," the book was clearly designed to convey authority and legitimacy. It was dedicated to Glassberg's "highly esteemed patron," Adolf Rosenzweig, a distinguished Reform rabbi in Berlin. The dedication confirms what is evident throughout the volume: that Glassberg and his associates were well-educated Reform Jews committed to a strictly conservative position on circumcision.

The perspective was uniformly positive. An introductory statement by M. Rawitzki, a Berlin physician, entitled "On the Usefulness of Foreskin-Cutting [*Vorhautschnittes*] in Newborns," set the dominant tone. Rawitzki's approach was solely medical, without even a mention of religion; he presented a lengthy account of a variety of problems attributable in his view to an excessively tight foreskin, most notably including cancer of the penis. The unsaid implication was clear: circumcision was highly advisable for all male infants, Jewish or not.[56]

Next followed a discourse on "Ritual Circumcision from a Medical Perspective" by two physicians (one a mohel), dealing frankly with medical dangers and recommending that mohels be examined and certified as medically knowledgeable. It included a brief description of *metsitsah*, noteworthy as evidence that even some Reform mohels were still performing circumcisions in the traditional manner, without use of a glass tube: "Now the mohel, after taking a sip of wine in his mouth, sucks repeatedly with his lips on the bloody wound, each time spitting the blood mixed with wine onto the floor. Finally, he sprays some of the wine on the sucked wound."[57]

The core of the book, taking up nearly 200 of its 355 pages, was almost certainly written mainly or entirely by Glassberg himself. This was a learned theological discourse, citing sources in Latin, Greek, and Hebrew, ranging from discussion of ancient history, through an account of how the Church Fathers viewed circumcision, to thorough analysis of the talmudic and midrashic literature. The ultimate purpose of the book is evident in the concluding section, again almost certainly by Glassberg, entitled "Circumcision in Modern Times." The author provided an overview of the circumcision debates since the 1840s, noting that "many parents," caught up in a "modern, all-denying trend, refused to permit their newborns to be circumcised," either because they viewed the rite as a "pagan-barbaric mutilation" or because they feared that the operation might be damaging. He recounted the history of the turmoil in Frankfurt, and discussed Holdheim's position in order to reject it. All attacks on circumcision, he concluded, had been unsuccessful; neither physicians nor "destructive theologians" had demonstrated that it was harmful or dangerous. Perhaps the state should abolish the practice if harm could be convincingly demonstrated; but in fact the opposite was the case: circumcision, properly performed, provided "very significant prophylaxis against many evil, fatal afflictions [*Leben zerstörende Uebel*] and should be legally instituted for non-Jews." Moreover, circumcision was so "deeply rooted in the religious consciousness of the Jewish people" that the very existence of

Judaism depended on its retention. He closed by quoting Leopold Zunz's statement on the vital importance of circumcision, including that author's ringing declaration: "Suicide is not reform!"[58]

Here again, it is hard to overstate the historical significance of this document, appearing as it did in Germany at the end of the century. Its noteworthy feature is that, possibly for the first time in that country, the volume fused medical and religious arguments so thoroughly that readers might well conclude that circumcision was not only divinely mandated but medically rational. As I mentioned, the Orthodox rabbinate were indifferent to medical arguments, whether favorable or unfavorable. But here from the Reform side was an end-of-century defense of circumcision employing *medical* authorities to bolster a *theological* discourse, all culminating in a declaration that not only must circumcision be retained as a Jewish practice but its benefits should be extended to Gentiles as well. We should also note, though, Glassberg's acknowledgment that "many" parents were refusing circumcision for their infant sons—indication that while physicians, rabbis, and other public figures debated the merits of circumcision, some German Jews were quietly deciding the question for themselves. But I know of no evidence on actual numbers.

This volume represented a trend that was already plainly visible elsewhere; in fact, it was the German version of a new approach to circumcision that had emerged in England and the United States, and that would achieve its ultimate expression in twentieth-century America.

"So Painful an Operation": France

The German-Jewish Enlightenment spread slowly but steadily to other parts of Europe, and although information on attitudes to circumcision in other countries is thin, what little there is points to the same general reactions: modest opposition or occasional outright rejection from some acculturated Jews, conservative attachment to tradition by the majority. The large Jewish population of Russia and Poland in particular remained generally more conservative into the twentieth century. Modern ideas and aspirations reached there also, however, influencing many young men and women to turn away from traditional religious beliefs and practices. There too I've found no evidence suggesting that embracing modernity necessarily meant rejecting circumcision. But absence of evidence is not evidence. Secularized European Jews, east and west, having rejected religious orthodoxy, would have been unlikely to seek the services of a mohel. The simplest course would have been to dismiss circumcision as a pointless survival from the premodern past and leave one's sons intact, but not to challenge the practice openly.

As I've shown, Jewish "emancipation" began in France soon after the Revolution, and most French Jews, as eager for social acceptance as their

German counterparts, abandoned religious practices deemed incompatible with the modern way of life. But, again like the Jews of Germany, most French Jews appear to have remained loyal to circumcision, come what may. For the first few years after the Revolution they encountered no significant governmental opposition to the practice, but during the Reign of Terror (1793–94) there were demands for its abolition. Despite the dangers inherent in defying a punitive regime, circumcision endured. Zosa Szajkowski, a historian of French Jewry, cites a filial memorial to a rabbi who "risked his life for the sake of the commandment of circumcision ... [w]hen Robespierre and his associates prohibited circumcision and the practice of the other precepts and sought to obliterate their memory."[59]

But that was a voice from the Orthodox side. The most outspoken on the opposite side was Olry Terquem, a thoroughly assimilated but respected religious reformer who called for liberation of Judaism from "Asiatic forms and formulas" preventing Jews from integrating into "the great French family."[60] In a series of publications under the pseudonym "Tsarphati" (Hebrew for "Frenchman"), he argued that many biblical and talmudic precepts and regulations had to be radically revised, or in some cases abandoned entirely, if French Jews were to achieve a level of cultural development appropriate to modern citizens.[61] He aimed some of his most caustic commentary at circumcision. In a letter published in 1838 he remarked:

> If I were to tell you that, in a certain country, there exists a population which attaches a religious importance to mutilating, to slashing, to lacerating the weak creatures as soon as they enter life, to submitting them to so painful an operation that sometimes death follows it ... with no protest ever being raised in favor of the victims, if I let you guess the country, would not your ideas naturally point to an African country, inhabited by some savage race? Such is not the case. It concerns our *patrie*, France, and a notable segment of its inhabitants.[62]

As in Germany, most members of the "notable segment" were unwilling even to consider abandoning the sign of the covenant. But Terquem fought on, protesting especially against peri'ah and metsitsah, demanding that they be eliminated and that mohels be required to receive formal medical certification. Anticipating what has now become a familiar argument, he declared that "the authority of the Talmud ceases where the rights of humanity begin."[63]

Like Holdheim in Germany, Terquem faced so much opposition that most of his effort went nowhere. He probably expected no better. In France, control over Jewish religious affairs was vested in supervisory councils called consistories. In 1844 a royal ordinance for "organization of the Israelite religion" (*culte Israélite*) declared that each local consistory was to exercise complete control over ritual circumcisions. This was almost certainly a response to growing awareness of medical problems, perhaps to physician protests. Only men authorized by the consistory were to be permitted to practice as mohels, and they were to obey regulations issued by the consistory with the approval of the central consistory. In August of that year, the local Paris consistory, uneasy about news accounts of syphilitic infection and mortality associated with circumcision, asked seven mohels to declare under oath that they would obey regulations for sanitation and would no longer perform *metsitsah*. Four agreed and were duly authorized. One asked for time to think it over; two others declined, but one of these soon changed his mind and took the oath. Several weeks later it turned out that one of the men who had taken the oath was still performing *metsitsah*. Called before the consistory to explain himself, he said that lawyers and rabbis had informed him that he was free to practice as he chose—that the consistory could no more prohibit *metsitsah* than they could prohibit fasting on Yom Kippur or observing the Sabbath. The consistory turned to the police for help but apparently got nowhere. Orthodox groups in Paris, supported by rabbis in Alsace-Lorraine (home to large numbers of Orthodox Ashkenazic Jews), urged that the consistory choose mohels with care but not try to alter traditional practices. In fact, the central consistory supported the local reform efforts, and by midcentury sanitary regulations were promulgated everywhere. Nevertheless, it appears that many mohels continued to practice *metsitsah*.[64]

The sequence of events in France resembled that in Germany: fairly widespread (if grudging) recognition of medical dangers associated with circumcision; arguments by a few reformers for complete elimination of the practice; particular discomfort with *metsitsah*; determined resistance by the Orthodox; eventual introduction of moderate reforms and controls designed to avoid the most adverse (and publicly noted) consequences; but almost no willingness even to consider the question of whether circumcision served a valid religious purpose.

"A Sanguinary Protest Against Universal Brotherhood": Italy

Among the most outspoken opponents of circumcision in the late nineteenth century were two Italians, Cesare Lombroso (1835–1909) and Paolo Mantegazza (1831–1910), both trained physicians with interests and careers spanning a variety of disciplines. Lombroso, who was Jewish, made his reputation as a criminologist and prison reformer; a self-described "experimental anthropologist," he is remembered now mainly for his theories on the physical characteristics of criminals. Mantegazza was a versatile and rather flamboyant scholar best known for his writings on sexuality, considered bold for his time but recognizable now as early ethnology.

In 1894, Lombroso ventured beyond his usual scope with a book entitled *Anti-Semitism and Modern Science*, ostensibly a refutation of the racist theories of the time but in fact a call for Jewish assimilation. In the key chapter, entitled "Defects of the Jews," he cited the usual stereotypes of Jewish characteristics, then focused on several customs that he saw as epitomizing the Jewish propensity for self-segregation: eating matzah on Passover, wearing phylacteries (*tefillin*) at morning prayers, and circumcision:

> It is time for the Jews to persuade themselves that many of their customs belong to other epochs.... If, in accord with the times, all other religions have modified not just their surface appearance but their essence, why can't they [the Jews] modify at least the surface? Why do they not renounce that truly savage wounding [*vero ferimento selvaggio*] that is circumcision?[65]

Though Jewish himself, Lombroso seems to have known about circumcision only from what he heard at second hand. In another passage he remarks that the ritual circumciser "even reaches the point of using his teeth as well as stone knives for the cruel practice of circumcision, as did our cave ancestors."[66]

Mantegazza's most widely read book was *The Sexual Relations of Mankind* (1885), a comparative ethnology that was translated into several languages and appeared in at least eleven editions. A chapter entitled "Mutilation of the Genitals" opens with a brief paragraph on "artificial phimosis," then turns to circumcision: "Circumcision is a mark of racial distinction; it is a cruel mutilation of a protective organ of the glans and of an organ of pleasure; it is a sanguinary protest against universal brotherhood." Civilized people, he continued, look upon circumcision as "a shame and an infamy"; and although he was "not in the least anti-Semitic," in fact had "much esteem for the Israelites," he would "shout at the Hebrews" until his final breath:

> Cease mutilating yourselves; cease imprinting upon your flesh an odious brand to distinguish you from other men; until you do this, you cannot pretend to be our equal. As it is, you, of your own accord, with the branding iron, from the first days of your lives, proceed to proclaim yourselves a race apart, one that cannot, and does not care to, mix with ours.[67]

As we'll see shortly, by the time these two men wrote, circumcision had already become a popular medical procedure in Britain, the United States, and to some extent even in Germany. The two Italian authors seem to have known (or cared) nothing about this; their focus was strictly on ritual circumcision as an anachronistic sign of ethnic separatism—perhaps a reflection of the fact that the Jewish population of Italy was small and relatively well integrated.

Remembering the Covenant in the New World

In her history of mid-nineteenth-century Jewish Americans, Hasia R. Diner says that, despite obstacles, Jewish immigrants did their best to maintain traditional religious practices in the New World. Before 1840 there was no rabbi anywhere in the country, and it was not until decades later that most communities could hope to employ an ordained rabbi. Until then they had to be content with a general religious practitioner, someone who could lead services, provide basic religious education, slaughter animals in the kosher manner, and circumcise newborn males. But whatever the challenges, the immigrants tried to live Jewish lives and to raise their children as Jews. "No element," she continues,

> demonstrated Jewish commitment to tradition more boldly than their retention of *milah*, the circumcision of infant sons. . . . In upstate New York, in the Rocky Mountain West, or in the Deep South, [mohels] linked dispersed Jewish communities and attested to this tradition's persistence. Circumcisers traveled hundreds of miles to attend to the ritual. Parents considered the ceremony a crucial, unalterable part of their lives.[68]

Nevertheless, there is considerable evidence that over the course of the nineteenth century loyalty to traditional practices steadily eroded, and that the overall trend was toward lax observance or none.[69] The reasons are self-evident. Aside from a few cities like New York, Philadelphia, Baltimore, and Cincinnati, most Jewish communities were insignificant enclaves within overwhelmingly Gentile environments. In small towns in the South, Midwest, and West, pioneer Jewish settlers found even the most basic forms of observance—Sabbath services, kosher food, religious education for children—difficult to arrange or simply beyond reach. Moreover, mid-nineteenth-century immigrants, like their later counterparts, hoped to win acceptance as full-fledged Americans. They abandoned customs and practices marking them as alien or unattractively distinctive, and gravitated toward "Americanization" of traditional practices: substitution of English for Hebrew in religious services, lax observance of kosher food regulations, willingness to conduct business on Saturday. More than a few men, particularly those living far from centers of Jewish life, married Gentile women, and some of their children were raised as Christians.[70] Contrary to Diner's account, many Jewish boys remained intact, either because their fathers chose to disregard the requirement or simply because there was no one to perform a circumcision. Gentile wives would probably have objected to circumcision. Jeremiah J. Berman (a rabbi-historian) cites a circumcision performed in New Orleans on three boys, aged seven, four, and three, after the death of their Gentile mother.[71]

But the evidence is mixed. In a study of midcentury Jewish American religious observance, Berman, taking a position more like Diner's, says that early immigrants were "men of strong Jewish loyalties" who "generally adhered to traditional Jewish practices." He cites as an example a letter published in a Jewish periodical in 1870 from a man in Pueblo, Colorado, who, having begun serving the local Jewish community as a kosher slaughterer, was now also performing circumcisions:

> Of course as yet we have no Synagogue, and the Sabbath is not
> observed, but there is a prevailing feeling that we should be Jews in
> fact, as we are in name. Another advantage we are beginning to
> have is as it regards circumcision [sic]. We were formerly compelled to
> send young ones 120 miles to have that rite performed, and now I
> have already officiated several times with success.[72]

Berman says that most communities expected their all-purpose functionaries to perform circumcisions. The few men who specialized as mohels in outlying regions often traveled widely and advertised their readiness to do so.[73]

In his account of Jewish participation in the midcentury gold rush in California, Robert E. Levinson reports that, although many boys were circumcised, these were not necessarily ritual circumcisions. In Nevada City, California, there were enough Orthodox Jews to engage a Reverend Samuel Laski of San Francisco, who traveled to the town on occasion to slaughter animals and perform circumcisions. The editor of the local newspaper reported on a circumcision he had attended in 1857:

> We were induced to witness the rite of circumcision at the house of
> a Jewish friend, on Wednesday. The officiating priest was the Rev.
> Mr. Laski of San Francisco. The ceremony consisted of first lighting
> a couple of candles, putting on of hats by the whole company present,
> procuring a glass or two of wine, and reading a portion of Hebrew.
> Second, introduction of the child, nipping in the bud, and a short
> ceremony of reading. Third, partaking of hospitalities, more reading
> which was all Hebrew to us, and adjournments. Those curious in
> such matters are advised to obtain further information by seeing for
> themselves, or consulting a rare old book a part of which is said
> to have been written by Moses.[74]

Despite the friendly tone of this brief account, one senses also an "ethnographic" perspective, as though the editor were reporting on the exotic doings of a distant tribal people. Note that he was not *invited* to witness the rite but "induced."

Since mohels were in short supply in the Western territories, circumcisions were often performed on boys of an age well beyond eight days, and occasionally even on young men. In 1872, when there were only about eighty or ninety Jews in New Mexico, a Reverend Fleischer of Denver visited the territory on invitation "and circumcised a large number of children at an advanced age." Another mohel came to Santa Fe in 1875 to circumcise two boys, one eight days old, the other four weeks.[75] This kind of accommodation to scarcity seems to have been the pattern wherever Jews had settled in small numbers.

In his history of the nineteenth-century Jewish community in New Orleans, Bertram W. Korn describes the career of a man who became a circumciser with no qualifications other than readiness to try anything. Albert J. Marks was an itinerant actor of limited talent who served the New Orleans Jewish community from about 1839 to 1842 as their religious factotum. A theatrical manager for whom he worked described him as "a short, fat, round-faced, good-natured little Jew" who "occasionally officiated as a rabbi, being of the tribe of Levi, and a lineal descendant from Aaron, the ancient high-priest." Another manager noted that Marks had been "for many years high-priest of the Jews in New Orleans and parts adjacent, receiving a handsome income from the chosen people for the performance of marriage ceremonies, funeral rites, and other *little* operations indispensible [sic] to the proper starting of young Jews of the male sex into their second week's journey of life."[76]

Another man of the same ilk was Abraham Galland, a quack medical practitioner and nostrum salesman who is said to have taken whiskey for courage to perform circumcisions, "at which profession he excelled." Galland served congregations in several California communities in the 1850s and 1860s. In 1867, he circumcised the first triplets born in San Francisco. The synagogue was filled with Jewish and Christian onlookers, including a senator, a general, and the governor-elect. The boys were named Abraham, Isaac, and Jacob.[77]

Parental resistance to circumcision, even in major cities, caused consternation in conservative circles. The first ordained rabbi to arrive in the United States was Abraham Rice, a firmly Orthodox immigrant from Bavaria, who served a congregation in Baltimore from 1840 to 1849. Rice struggled to preserve rigorous religious observance at a time of increasing preference for the more liberal tenets of Reform Judaism. A year after his arrival, he was already responding to queries regarding burial of uncircumcised boys or men. He ruled that a boy dying before age thirteen was entitled to Jewish burial; however, just as an infant who died before the eighth day of life had to be circumcised before burial, the same principle applied here. Intact males over age thirteen, however, were guilty of an unpardonable violation, thus ineligible for Jewish burial. Moreover, the circumcised son of a Gentile mother remained a Gentile until he underwent a ritual circumcision and immersion in a ritual pool (*mikveh*). A medical circumcision was unacceptable even when followed by immersion, he added, since the surgery had no religious legitimacy.

Aside from the burial questions, could uncircumcised men participate in religious services? Anyone over age thirteen who had willfully violated the command by remaining uncircumcised, Rice ordered, must be excluded from participation in the community. Such a boy or man was to be regarded as an alien (*ben nakhor*, literally "son of a foreign land"). He could not be counted in the quorum of ten men (*minyan*) required for public prayer, and he and his neglectful parents were to be regarded as apostates with no share in "the world to come." Only a hemophiliac whose two brothers had died after circumcision could be excused.[78]

Since many mohels were self-appointed and medically ignorant, circumcisions sometimes went badly. In January 1871, a New York City Jewish periodical published a tactfully worded notice from the registrar of medical records:

> Within about a month some half dozen deaths have occurred in this City from haemorrhage after circumcision of Hebrew infants. I am informed that numerous unskilled and unscrupulous persons have taken to performing this operation for a small fee among the poorer Jews. I write to you to beg that you call attention to those having authority in your denomination to so unwarrantable a sacrifice of human life.
>
> Permit me at the same time to assure you that no one has a greater respect than myself for all religious observances.[79]

In 1881, a New York mohel, plainly on guard against lawsuits, required that a widow sign a legal release before he circumcised her three sons, ages eight, six, and four. It read in part as follows:

> I do agree to keep the said Rev. Susskind Moses Finesilver, his servant, servants, assistant or assistants free from all harm, damage, suit, or other actions, by reason of any unforeseen accident or happening by reason of said operations so to be performed upon my said Sons . . . for any loss, disability, sickness, medical attendance, death, loss of service or loss of any kind or nature.

But despite the peril—surely far more menacing then than now—many parents continued to seek circumcision for their sons, perhaps because both Jews and Gentiles were beginning to believe in its "prophylactic value." Two mohels in Atlanta said that in 1885 they had performed two-thirds of their circumcisions on Gentile infants.[80]

It seems, then, that, while a large number of Jewish immigrants and their descendants abandoned most religious regulations, relatively few rejected circumcision for their sons. Why? The answer, I suggest, is that a circumcision is a one-day event and a circumcised penis is publicly invisible. Many Jews perceived ritual regulations as impediments to integration into mainstream American society and culture. Eating in restaurants or in Gentile homes, even living in towns where kosher food was unavailable, meant putting dietary regulations aside. Conducting a successful business in a society where shops did well on Saturday but closed on Sunday required that the Sabbath become a day of busy activity. On the other hand, some customs—for example, fasting on Yom Kippur or gathering for a family Passover seder (with or without ritual readings and practices)—were more likely to endure, simply because they made little or no difference in the larger picture. The same applied to circumcision. True, some Gentiles knew about the rite and even attended on occasion, but in the reasonably tolerant environment of a pioneering society this appears to have mattered little if at all. (The substantial number of intermarriages, almost all between Jewish men and Gentile women, may also say something about Gentile indifference to circumcised genitals.) Moreover, by the late nineteenth century circumcision was gaining remarkable popularity in the general American population—not because it was a Jewish practice but because many Americans, notably physicians, had come to believe that it bestowed significant medical and "hygienic" benefits.

Defending Against "Sinful Seceders"

Abraham Rice's biographer reports that on the very day Rice arrived in America, Isaac Leeser, the equally conservative leader of the Philadelphia Jewish community, lamented that Jewish parents were refusing to have their sons circumcised. Leeser, not a rabbi but a passionate campaigner for preserving orthodoxy, had already publicly reprimanded the members of his Philadelphia congregation. They would be "shocked," he declared in a sermon, if anyone were to try to convert them to another religion, "to forswear directly your allegiance to Jacob's God." Yet they showed no regard for their "children's future happiness" when they denied them membership in "the congregation of the faithful." What could justify such negligence?

> The covenant can do them no bodily or mental injury; it is only an
> acknowledgment that in the flesh they belong to the house of Israel;
> and surely it is their right, as well as it was yours at your birth,
> that nothing should be done by their parents which of necessity must
> make their entrance into the great body of Jews more painful and
> more difficult, and consequently more uncertain, than it ought to be.
> You were children of the covenant, and yet you rebelled; let your
> own children have the same choice; ... but let them never have cause
> to say, as many no doubt have said: "It is my father's and mother's
> fault that I am not an Israelite."[81]

In 1843, Leeser founded a monthly periodical, the *Occident and American Jewish Advocate*, dedicated to defending strict orthodoxy. The issue of

September 1844 included an editorial, unsigned but almost certainly written by Leeser, attacking the Frankfurt Society of the Friends of Reform as "a body of sinful seceders ... whose abrogation of circumcision proves that they mean to destroy the law of Moses." The editorial included a long extract from a letter published in a German-Jewish Reform periodical (*Orient*) fulsomely applauding wives of Society members as defenders of the faith. Particularly regarding circumcision, the writer noted, "their religious sentiment is displayed in the strongest manner, and they manifest in this point a powerful opposition to their husbands." As proof of feminine resolve he told this story: When a member of the Reform Society refused to have his son circumcised, his wife "employed all means of persuasion to obtain from her husband the permission to have her child entered in the covenant." But when her "weeping eye" and "mild petition" failed to influence him, she threatened "entire dissolution of the tender bonds of love." At that point the husband "left the field" and permitted the circumcision to take place—"without, however, sanctioning this holy consecration by his presence." Such was the "discord" ensuing in a society "whose only divinities" were "reason and progress."

Leeser added his own expression of gratitude: "Thanks, noble daughter of Jacob! thanks in the name of all Israel; how gladly would we make public the name of her who so nobly withstood the mandate of her domestic tyrant! ... Our cause is not lost whilst there are such defenders."[82]

In the October 1847 issue of his journal Leeser upheld the "cause" with another inspirational letter. This one came from Augusta, Georgia, where a correspondent reported that five boys had recently "entered into the Jewish covenant, and three of these under circumstances of peculiar interest, and the most gratifying character." These boys, declared the writer, were "worthy examples ever to be emulated ... appropriate models for universal imitation ... guides for the youth of this and future generations," whose story should be an inspiration "wherever the followers of Moses lift up their voices in prayer."

The models for universal imitation were three boys, aged nine, ten, and thirteen, born to Jewish mothers and Gentile fathers, "in spots far removed from any Jewish congregation." Living among peers "of a different sect," and "encompassed by the prejudices of a Christian community," the boys had received a bare minimum of Jewish education to prepare them for their courageous decision. Having lost their fathers while still young (a matter left unexplained), the boys "naturally began to cling still closer to the maternal bosom," until, "unmoved by persuasion, unbiassed by the hope of reward, and unshaken by parental entreaties," they "boldly stepped forward, and from a self-conviction of its propriety, conformed to the ancient rite. Voluntary sacrifices!! The offerings of pious hearts!"

Apparently the boys' mothers (less noble daughters of Jacob) had opposed their decision. Nevertheless, following the operation, reported the writer, one boy displayed his "religious zeal" and "manly resolution" by exclaiming, "If God requires it I will go through it again." Only one, though: a discreetly worded further comment suggests that, in fact, not only the mothers but two of the boys had resisted: "It was a novel and beautiful sight, to witness a boy of *ten*, the pioneer in this movement, arguing with his companions, as to the propriety of observing the Jewish ordinance, and they convinced by his reasoning, and their own reflections, yielding at last a willing assent." Declaring his certainty that no account of a circumcision could surpass this one "in the purity of purpose and moral sublimity of the acts," the writer called for the event to be "conspicuously enrolled in the annals of Judaism."

Isaac Leeser added his own note of approval of "the above cheering incident." He hoped that

> should this article reach the eyes of those who have in violation of
> the law left their children uncircumcised, (of which we regret to
> say there are several in this country,) we would earnestly beg of them
> to reflect on the momentous omission of which they have been
> guilty. It is the privilege of every Jewish child [*sic*] to be initiated in the
> covenant of Abraham; so that it may have the option of being an
> Israelite or not when it arrives at maturity. And what right have
> parents to stand in the way of their son's future prospects, by ne-
> glecting to initiate him in the Jewish church? If they themselves are
> wicked Jews, though circumcised, their children can follow their
> example in this respect, despite of their circumcision [*sic*]; and if, on
> the contrary, the latter wish to be strict observers of the Mosaic law,
> why deny them the opportunity of being so? . . . Let all our readers
> who are pious Israelites, urge upon those whom they know to have
> neglected the law, to remedy the omission without delay.[83]

Leeser's awkward prose and tortured logic seem to express his uncertainty about how to persuade parents bent on assimilation to "initiate" their sons into the "Jewish church." It also suggests the magnitude of resistance to circumcision. The reference to "several in this country" was surely a gross understatement. Had Leeser known of only "several" resisting parents in the entire country, he would not have afforded this much attention to a letter from Georgia.

The April 8, 1870, issue of another widely circulated periodical, the *Israelite*, included a letter from a "Gentile friend," a condescending harangue explaining why Jews so often met with antagonism. "Perhaps my remarks may appear too harsh," mused the friend, "but I do not mean them to be so. I speak as to brethren whom I wish to serve."

> Here then allow me to speak regarding one or more tenets of
> your faith, which, if removed, I think would open the way to a large

accession to your ranks. First, "circumcision." This certainly belongs only to an age of ignorance and barbarism. No argument in its favor, that I have ever seen or heard of, has any weight compared with the following statement which all created things sustain me in asserting, viz: "If God had considered the results, claimed by this practice, to be beneficial, He would have so made man as to render it unnecessary." Now, *you* presume to improve His work—the very masterpiece of His omnipotence and wisdom.

To this the editor of the *Israelite*, Isaac Mayer Wise of Cincinnati, the nation's leading Reform rabbi, replied in equally ponderous, and equally aggressive, prose. "We can do away with circumcision," he declared, "which is only a sign of the covenant, whenever the object thereof being realized, the covenant shall be necessary no longer."

We do not maintain to improve human nature by the light of this sign of the covenant. Whenever this light shall have fully triumphed over the darkness of idolatry and its remains in the doctrines of trinity, incarnation, immaculate conception, vicarious atonement, salvation by faith, universal depravity, heartless condemnation of all who believe otherwise, and the barbarous perversion of the understanding and the morals growing out of those doctrines; whenever the world will believe in one First Cause who is wisdom, power, goodness and justice absolute and infinite, and renounce their corruptive phantoms of devil and evil spirits; whenever the dignity of human nature, the majesty of justice, the divinity of virtue, the sovereignty of righteousness and the dominion of love, truth and light will be acknowledged, and the Satanic doctrines of priestly arrogance and human wretchedness be disavowed; whenever hell, brimstone and eternal torment shall be abolished here and hereafter, on this globe first and beyond them [sic]; in brief, whenever the human understanding, conscience and consciousness shall be restored and their fiends be banished, Israel's covenant is fulfilled, the world is God's chosen people, and we will cheerfully discard with the rite of circumcision [sic], as we now maintain, he who walks in the light of the Lord is circumcised and has entered the covenant of God with Israel.[84]

6

Good Sanitarians

Circumcision Medicalized

> No one who has seen the superior cleanliness of a Hebrew
> penis can have avoided a very strong impression in favour of
> the removal of the fore-skin.[1]

> Again, look at the custom of circumcision, one of the most salutary
> regulations that was ever imposed on a people.... What wisdom was
> shown by Moses, and by Mahomet in later times, in retaining this
> wholesome custom as a religious rite, and thereby securing its
> perpetuation.[2]

> It is a well-known fact that the most forlorn and mouse-headed, long-
> nosed glans penis will, within a week or two after its liberation from
> its fetters of preputial bands, assume its true shape.[3]

In nineteenth-century Germany, the principals in the circumcision
controversy were nearly all Jewish, and the debate centered on
whether modernizing Jews should continue the practice as a religious
obligation. But during the same century in the Anglophone world
(Britain, the Commonwealth nations, the United States), an entirely
new kind of discourse developed—mainly (but not entirely) among
Gentiles, and with attention directed at the foreskin itself, which was
now vilified as a source of countless serious afflictions. Particularly
during the second half of the nineteenth century, attitudes toward
circumcision in these countries changed utterly, from ridicule and
rejection to praise beyond anything imaginable in earlier centuries.
The transformation began neither in Christian theology nor popular
culture but in the medical profession. Reputable physicians became

convinced that the foreskin—the precious possession that eighteenth-century Britons had been so intent on guarding—was responsible for everything from childhood masturbation to syphilis, orthopedic and neurological disorders, cancer, insanity, and more. As the century unfolded, the number of afflictions attributed to this part of male genital anatomy seems to have been limited only by the imaginations of physicians and surgeons who became ever more determined to remove it. The result was that male infant circumcision became a widely recommended procedure, wholly divorced from doctrinal religious considerations, usually performed by physicians with little knowledge of the anatomy and physiology of the prepuce—and accepted by Christian parents, who seem to have forgotten Paul's warning to the Galatians.

The sequence of events seems even more remarkable when we realize that nowhere else in Europe, or, for that matter, in any non-English-speaking country, did circumcision ever gain anything beyond the most limited acceptance. Medical historians have attributed the difference to Victorian notions about sexual morality and bodily "hygiene" as public health concerns, combined with poor understanding of the role of the foreskin in sexual gratification and normal adult sexual functioning. But whatever the main reason or reasons for this peculiar outcome, the United States and England, along with Canada and the other Commonwealth nations, became the only countries to institute infant circumcision as standard medical procedure.[4]

Health, Morality, and Elongated Foreskins: Nineteenth-Century Britain

Although the conventional image of Victorians as puritanical and sexually repressed oversimplifies a complex behavioral code, many mid-nineteenth-century British men and women were concerned, some to the point of obsession, with sexual morality and control of sinful inclinations. Men were believed to be imperiled by excessive sexual indulgence, women by the prospect of illegitimate pregnancy and decline into promiscuity and prostitution. Both genders faced the ultimate horror, venereal disease, particularly syphilis.[5] Class prejudice obviously underlay such observations; the personal hygiene, sexual restraint, and robust health of the privileged class stood opposed to what were perceived as the deficiencies of those low on the social ladder: their unsanitary habits, their sexual immorality, and their susceptibility to fearful diseases.

Raising children, particularly boys, to become disciplined, productive participants in the economy required that their sexual proclivities be rigorously tamed and channeled into risk-free diversions: sports and other "manly" activities. Youths had to learn that semen was a precious substance embodying finite amounts of energy, and that its reckless expenditure would result in listlessness and nervous illnesses. The most formidable obstacle on the path to respectable manhood, the most demanding challenge to parents, teachers, and physicians, was masturbation. Curbing masturbation was not just a matter of defeating sinful impulses, though that was certainly necessary. Beyond that, many were convinced that masturbation could cause severe physical debilitation and even mental deterioration to the point of insanity. This notion had already appeared in the early eighteenth century, when an anonymous English publication entitled *Onania, or the Heinous Sin of Self-Pollution, And All Its Frightful Consequences, in Both Sexes*, informed readers that masturbation led to any number of afflictions: impaired growth, physical weakness, impotence, ulcers, epilepsy, and finally, early death.[6] By 1750, the book had appeared in nineteen editions and about thirty-eight thousand copies had been sold. In 1760 the alarm sounded again, when another book appeared in France, this one by a Swiss physician named Samuel Tissot, entitled *L'Onanisme, ou Dissertation physique sur les maladies produites par la masturbation*. Soon translated into English, German, and Italian, it was still being reprinted as late as 1905.[7]

But it was not until the mid–nineteenth century that British physicians began focusing attention on masturbation as a threat not only to moral discipline but also to actual physical health and even sanity. Beliefs about insanity as possession by evil spirits were no longer credible; now physical afflictions were thought to be the real causes of mental disability. Many physicians subscribed to a theory called "reflex neurosis," which held that disease or malfunction in any body part could act reflexively to damage any other part of the body or even the mind. "Nervous signals" from an affected organ were said to travel through the spinal cord to a "target organ" in another part of the body. Dysfunctional reproductive organs and genitals, particularly but not only in women, were believed to be frequent sources of all sorts of neurological and other systemic illnesses.[8] In accord with this theory, "erotic sensation was redefined as *irritation*, orgasm was redefined as *convulsion*, and erection of the penis was redefined as *priapism*." Hence, "stimulation of the genitals could cause disease in distant parts of the body." Moreover, physicians sometimes saw men in mental institutions masturbating; and rather than recognizing this as expectable behavior for anxious, disturbed individuals confined without privacy, they concluded that masturbation had caused their patients' problems in the first place. The fixation on genitals developed to the point that any and all seminal emission was labeled pathological—an imaginary condition called "spermatorrhea."[9] As I noted, semen was believed to be a precious substance in limited supply, the source and reservoir of male strength and vitality; its depletion—even for the most acceptable of purposes, procreation within marriage—endangered a man's health and virility. It was physicians' responsibility to prevent seminal loss via sexual promiscuity, masturbation, or nocturnal emissions. Some who issued these warnings were quacks, but capable physicians also joined the chorus.[10]

How could physicians stave off such calamities? The logical place to look for answers was the penis itself. Was there anything about penises that might be amenable to medical correction—some anatomical feature that could cause "irritation" and unseemly genital "excitability"? A glance often answered the question. Many male babies and young boys have long, tapering foreskins, attached firmly to the underlying glans; now their entirely normal genitals were perceived as inordinately, almost obscenely, prominent. Was all that unsightly (and excitable) tissue really necessary? Suppose it were to become infected or inflamed, causing pain and perhaps even urinary obstruction? To identify this newly discovered danger, physicians attached the label "phymosis" to any foreskin that appeared too long, too likely to cause harmful stimulation or irritation—an ideal candidate for surgical removal. Phimosis (the current spelling) was not a new diagnosis. In his *De Medicina* the first-century Roman encyclopedist Celsus had described it as abnormal thickening of the foreskin. But the term went generally unnoticed until the eighteenth century, when several medical authors defined the condition as inflammation or excessive tightness of a prepuce such that it could not be retracted. These authors realized, though, that a long adherent prepuce is normal for the penis of an infant or young child. Their nineteenth-century successors now proposed that normal infant foreskins be removed to preclude hypothetical trouble at an undefined future time.[11]

If foreskins were indeed a prime source of mischief, how about Jewish men—were they resistant to venereal disease and perhaps even sexual immorality, as one would anticipate for men whose foreskins were long gone? And was masturbation as much a problem among Jewish boys as for others? Comparative studies might yield answers to these vital questions, and might contribute to the campaign for public health and morality.

By the mid–nineteenth century, some 35,000 Jews, mostly immigrants from Germany and Holland and their descendants, were already a presence in Britain—in London, of course, but also in Manchester, Leeds, and a number of other towns. From about 1870 onward, immigrant Jews of distinctly alien cultural type—Yiddish-speakers from eastern Europe—added a major new element to the Jewish population, especially in London; after 1880, some three or four thousand arrived in that city yearly. Clustered in well-defined Jewish neighborhoods from which they seldom ventured, and with distinctive cultural and religious practices, they remained largely isolated from mainstream society. Even though some Jews were more acculturated and socially integrated, in the British mind they all embodied difference—an alien people ideally suited for defining British identity through contrast with its opposite. They were equally well suited as subjects for study in the comparatively new field of public health.[12]

Since the 1840s, public health had been the domain of sanitary engineers and municipal planners; but during the final decades of the nineteenth century, physicians appropriated this field as their own professional concern and responsibility. Large Jewish populations concentrated in urban neighborhoods offered ideal possibilities for comparative study of disease incidence and distribution. In a sense British physicians viewed Jews as "specimens," an exotic population that might provide comparative information. And of course the most intriguing Jewish practice was circumcision. Physicians knew that circumcision led to thickening and hardening of the surface of the glans. Might that not protect against venereal infection? If it turned out that such was indeed the case, wasn't it conceivable that the Jewish religious practice, viewed for centuries as bizarre, was actually farsighted? Did the rabbis know more about these matters than anyone had suspected? Considering the feverish reaction of eighteenth-century Englishmen to the prospect of even limited association with circumcised Jews, it may come as a surprise to learn that by the middle of the nineteenth century British physicians were asking such questions. But, determined as they were to win the battle against venereal disease, ask they did, and their conclusions were to have long-term consequences for British and American medical history.

"Our Hebrew Brethren": The British Circumcision Campaign

In November 1855 a British medical journal published a brief article entitled "Congenital Phymosis," by J. Cooper Forster, a surgeon at London's Royal Infirmary for Children. Cooper Forster defined phymosis as a pathological condition arising from "nature having been too prolific in the supply of skin at the extremity of the penis." Young boys afflicted with this condition, he reported, had "lengthy, puckered, and contracted" foreskins, along with symptoms of "urinary irritation." Attempts to draw the foreskin back over the glans caused much pain (as indeed it would if still attached to the glans). Even though the urine of such patients was "quite natural" and they were in "perfect health," Cooper Forster anticipated future problems. Nurses should be directed, he urged, "carefully to wash away the secretion that may form, which may easily be done by withdrawing the prepuce from the glans." If it was too late for that remedy, he was convinced that circumcision was "the surest means of relief." Indeed, he continued,

> I think if this operation was more frequently performed upon young
> children, even when suffering from much less severe symptoms
> than I have described (if the above-named precautions have not been
> adopted by the nurse), it would do much to prevent the occurrence
> of many of the diseases and troubles that occur in after-life.

Every surgeon had seen adult patients with "the annoyances of retained secretion, syphilitic sores under the prepuce," and "the swelling accompanying gonorrhœa." Moreover, Cooper Forster had "no hesitation" in saying that this "malformation" (i.e., a long prepuce) was nearly always found in patients with cancer of the penis. "No doubt the most natural state of the penis is with a covered glans," he acknowledged, "but, at the same time, the prepuce becomes a source of evil where the glans cannot be uncovered for the purposes of ablution [*sic*]." He went on to describe his own method of circumcising, which he said caused very little trauma: "in the course of a few days the whole unites, and leaves a very elegant organ for after use." Still, he added a mildly worded caveat: "I need hardly give the caution not to slit up the urethra, which I have known accidentally done."[13]

A month later an article appeared in the same journal, by the man who would become the most influential British advocate for circumcision, Jonathan Hutchinson (1828–1913). Among the most distinguished physicians and surgeons of the century, admired by colleagues for his diagnostic acumen and eclectic knowledge, Hutchinson received numerous honors culminating in knighthood. A specialist in diseases of the skin and eyes, he was recognized as an authority on venereal diseases, and it was on that subject that he published his thoughts on circumcision. Several years earlier, he had published a brief statement on phymosis and circumcision, but Cooper Forster's article seems to have persuaded him that it was time to present more detailed conclusions based on his recent research. Working at the Metropolitan Free Hospital, situated in a part of London with a large Jewish population, Hutchinson had been struck by differences between his "Jew patients" and others. Of the 330 patients in his sample, 58 were Jewish. But whereas the Gentile patients presented with 165 cases of syphilis and 107 of gonorrhea, among the Jewish patients there were only 11 cases of syphilis compared with 47 of gonorrhea. In other words, although Jews were at least as susceptible to gonorrheal infections as anyone else (which proved that "superior chastity" or reluctance to seek medical treatment could not be explanations), they exhibited noteworthy resistance to syphilis. The two populations differed physically in only one obvious respect: "The circumcised Jew is then very much less liable to contract syphilis than an uncircumcised person." No one who was familiar with "the effects of circumcision in rendering the delicate mucous membrane of the glans hard and skin-like," Hutchinson remarked, would "be at a loss for the explanation of the circumstance." The conclusion was inescapable:

> Taking then this fact as established, it suggests itself as probable that circumcision was by Divine command made obligatory upon the Jews, not solely as religious ordinance, but also with a view to the protection of health. . . . One is led to ask, witnessing the frightful ravages of syphilis in the present day, whether it might not be worth while for Christians also to adopt the practice.

"Such a proposition," Hutchinson continued, "if intended only to protect the sensualist from the merited consequences of loathsome vice, would, it is to be hoped, be dismissed at once by every right-thinking man." But the fact was that innocent wives and children suffered because of the sins of husbands and fathers. Here again, though, the evidence was impressive: While only one in twenty-four Jewish children with "surgical diseases" also had syphilis, one in six Gentile children was afflicted. The findings for women were similar.[14]

Cooper Forster and Hutchinson were pioneers on a theoretical path that soon became dominant: circumcision as *prophylactic* surgery—to protect against infectious diseases (and, according to Cooper Forster, cancer) in adult life. At this early date, however, neither would or could have based the claim on germ theory. By the mid-1850s, syphilis was believed to be caused by a poison that entered the body through cuts in the skin. The soft surface of the glans and foreskin was said to be vulnerable to abrasion and especially susceptible to penetration.[15]

But it was not until the 1870s and 1880s that Pasteur's germ theory, Koch's research into the bacterial causes of disease and wound infections, and Lister's publications on the need for antiseptic measures in surgery began to penetrate medical consciousness enough to influence theorizing about circumcision. As advocates became aware of Lister's work, their attention shifted from claims about circumcision as *treatment* for all kinds of illness to focus on its putative value as *protection* specifically against sexually transmitted diseases. The old beliefs lingered, of course, and were still being defended into the twentieth century by unsophisticated practitioners and quacks; but by the final decades of the century the emphasis had clearly shifted toward claims that prophylactic infant circumcision protected men for life.

The advent of germ theory had other consequences, however: harsh critique of Jewish circumcision on the same medical grounds as in Germany. By the 1880s, physicians were publishing accounts of infant patients infected with syphilis or tuberculosis by ritual circumcisers, probably caused mainly by sucking. Although most infants recovered when treated in time, the large number of cases was an obvious cause for concern. One physician remarked that it was "surely time that steps should be taken among Jewish communities to obviate the recurrence of similar catastrophes."[16]

Hutchinson also took a dim view of mohels. In his authoritative text on syphilis, published in 1887, he commented on a New York physician's report of four children circumcised by a single mohel, with severe consequences: all developed inflammation and ulceration of the wound, followed eventually by the death of three. Hutchinson reported having seen similar cases, all attributable in his judgment to syphilitic infection. The most likely "source of contamination," he thought, "was the lining of the box in which he kept his stores of lint." He urged that mohels "abandon the filthy custom of taking home the prepuce in the same box with their dressings."[17]

But Hutchinson remained steadfast in advocacy of physician-managed circumcision. By 1893 he was expressing approval of the procedure as a general prophylactic measure. In a "Questions and Answers" contribution to the *Archives of Surgery* he posed the question, "Under what circumstances is the operation of circumcision in infancy desirable?" His answer:

> It is imperatively required whenever the prepuce is unusually long and contracted at its orifice. The surgeon should, however, avail himself of every possible opportunity of inducing parents to have their male children circumcised. The operation confers great advantages in several different directions. If properly done, it has no drawbacks whatever.

But since in fact the operation was not always "properly done," there were "drawbacks," and Hutchinson was careful to specify them. To his third question, "What special risks attend it?" he replied: "By far the most important risk is that of hæmorrhage.... Many children have died after the operation in consequence of carelessness in this matter. The only other risks are poisoning of the wound by unclean instruments, and the introduction of syphilis by the dressings, &c."[18] Nevertheless, in 1900 he was still firmly advocating the procedure, for "moral" as well as medical reasons. For adult men the main consideration was reduced susceptibility to syphilis. For children the main problem was "cleanliness," and the danger was that uncircumcised boys might be inclined to roll back the foreskin in order to wash beneath it: a practice that would be "injurious to the morals of the child." Yet accumulated secretions could become "a source of annoyance and irritation" that might lead to "reflex excitement of an undesirable character." Hutchinson granted that the foreskin might contribute to adult sexual pleasure. But that advantage might "well be spared," and if foreskin removal resulted in "some degree of increased sexual control...one should be thankful."[19]

Increasingly among the general run of physicians the inclination was to recommend the practice for every male infant. By the final decades of the century in Britain, disease prevention and sexual discipline were so thoroughly conflated that many physicians viewed circumcision as a double-barreled weapon in the battle for public health and public morality. Prophylaxis for rampant sexuality and its frightful medical consequences was an urgent responsibility. The solution was to cut penises down to size.

"An Imperial Phenomenon": Protecting Future Servants of Empire

The Jews of London were not the only exotic population attracting the attention of British physicians; there were also the diverse and far more numerous peoples of the Empire, particularly in India and Africa. Imperial officials in Africa knew about male (and, vaguely, about female) genital cutting there, of course, but civilized Britons could hardly be expected to imitate the practices of "primitive" tribesmen. India was another matter, though;

there British administrators and medical officers generally considered Muslims cleaner and more sophisticated than Hindus. Muslim circumcision
probably contributed to that image. Moreover, as the social historian Ronald
Hyam notes, British men stationed in India contracted venereal diseases in
disturbing numbers, and some physicians, convinced that the tropical climate
encouraged infectious growths beneath the foreskin, urged that upper-class
English boys—future members of the overseas ruling elite—be circumcised to
avoid trouble later. Physicians at home followed this advice. British circumcision, says Hyam, was "an imperial phenomenon," performed mainly on
infants of the "upper and professional classes." By the 1930s a high percentage of upper-class boys—but only about 10 percent of working-class boys—were
being circumcised.[20]

"A Source of Annoyance, Danger, Suffering, and Death": The American Scene

"Preternatural Elongation": A Crusade Against Phimosis

In 1845—earlier than Cooper Forster or Hutchinson—an American surgeon,
Edward H. Dixon, published a popular medical volume entitled *A Treatise on
Diseases of the Sexual Organs: Adapted to Popular and Professional Reading, and
the Exposition of Quackery, Professional and Otherwise.* Dixon remarked that he
had omitted illustrations so as not to "excite prurient ideas" in young readers;
he wanted no mistaken association with "filthy and obscene publications." A
chapter on "Phimosis and Circumcision" described "natural phimosis" as a
"deformity" of "those who have naturally too long a foreskin" and defined
pathological phimosis in familiar terms as inflammation and thickening of a
nonretractable prepuce.[21] Dixon explained his surgical methods for both
conditions:

> We are in the habit of using a forceps with its two chaps curved, and an
> inch in length, at right angles with its shafts; these greatly facilitate the
> operations upon this part; they enable us to grasp the corners, and
> remove them with mathematical certainty at a single clip of the scis-
> sors, instead of the repeated and irregular incisions with the knife. [22]

In addition to inflammation, which he thought was caused most often by
venereal infection, Dixon also mentioned cancer of the penis as an affliction
associated with phimosis. His recommendation: "Nothing is more common
to the practical surgeon than these affections [sic], and there is no doubt that
the humane and enlightened rite of circumcision, if practised on all male
children, would render them very infrequent, as they are generally caused by a
preternatural elongation of the prepuce."[23]

Not only did these recommendations come early in the century; they differed from anything we encountered in the British record. In Britain, physicians were reporting on experiences with Jewish *patients* and speculating about the implications of their possible differences with Gentiles. But here was a physician characterizing the Jewish *rite of circumcision* as an "enlightened" prophylactic procedure—not because it initiated infants into Abraham's covenant but because it removed troublesome foreskins. Later in the same chapter Dixon used similar wording in advising that Christians should adopt "the ceremony of the Jewish people" as "a most effective means in preventing the spread of syphilis."[24] Obviously, he meant not the ceremony but the surgical procedure. Language of this kind, reinterpreting a "covenant" rite as a medical procedure—and in effect conflating the two—was the earliest expression of what would become one of the most distinctive features of the American discourse on circumcision. Now it was to be not only Jewish patients but Jewish ritual practice that provided valuable lessons for the medical profession.

From this point on, we need to distinguish between two kinds of claims. Dixon, like Hutchinson soon afterward in Britain, promoted circumcision as a *preventive* measure. Judging from the absence of American publications on the subject over the next quarter-century, it appears that, although some physicians were undoubtedly aware of Hutchinson's claims, and perhaps of Dixon's as well, few were drawn to the idea of practicing circumcision as prophylaxis.

Curing Reflex Paralysis and Spinal Anemia:
Lewis Sayre's Pivotal Publications

But 1870 was the annus mirabilis for circumcision in America—the year in which an entirely new kind of claim gained widespread attention. At the annual meeting of the American Medical Association, a distinguished New York orthopedic surgeon named Lewis A. Sayre (1820–1900) delivered an astonishing announcement: he had *cured* a five-year-old boy of paralysis in both legs by removing part of his foreskin. Having concluded that the problem was paralysis, not contraction, Sayre had decided on application of galvanic battery current. But in the course of treatment, the child's nurse urged Sayre not to touch the boy's "pee-pee," which was "very sore." She reported that the boy complained frequently of painful penis, and that the friction of his clothes caused erections. Now Sayre suspected the fundamental problem: "As excessive venery is a fruitful source of physical prostration and nervous exhaustion, sometimes producing paralysis, I was disposed to look upon this case in the same light, and recommended circumcision as a means of relieving the irritated and imprisoned penis." Next day he operated (with anesthesia), assisted by two other physicians and with students in attendance as observers. The wound healed in less than two weeks, Sayre reported, and "the penis was immensely increased in size." In light of what we now know about Sayre's twentieth-century successors, his next comment was noteworthy: "The [remaining] prepuce was sufficiently long to cover the glans, and could be readily glided over it without any irritation whatever." In other words, much of the boy's foreskin remained. Sayre declared that the child had improved immediately and dramatically—ate better, slept better, looked better, and could fully extend his legs; within less than two weeks he was walking alone, and was soon entirely well. Sayre made clear that he had used no treatment other than "quieting his nervous system by relieving his imprisoned glans penis."[25]

In light of his special prominence in this history, it is essential to realize that although Sayre used the term "circumcision," this did not mean to him what it means to us now. He did not practice or recommend complete removal of foreskins unless he judged such a radical procedure to be necessary. Referring to two later cases, boys aged about seven and nine, whom he claimed to have cured of "hip-disease," he emphasized that "the prepuce was easily *torn* back with the thumb and finger nails," after which he removed impacted foreskin secretions. "This slight operation," he remarked, "together with cleanliness and frequent moving of the parts to prevent adhesions, answered all the purposes of circumcision, and at once quieted their nervous irritability." He continued with an unmistakable warning:

> In many cases this latter operation of *tearing* the prepuce from
> the glans, aided by a slight nick in the frenum, and, if necessary,
> another in the prepuce on the dorsum of the penis, will answer all the
> purposes of circumcision, without its mutilation, leaving the prepuce
> to cover the glans, which as a matter of taste and ornament is
> sometimes desirable; circumcision only being necessary when there
> is a great redundancy of prepuce.[26]

The term "mutilation," which *opponents* of circumcision now generally avoid in public statements, may appear here for the first time in the literature on circumcision—introduced by the physician whose name customarily heads the roster of American advocates![27]

Sayre continued with dramatic new discoveries thereafter: "spinal anæmia" and paralysis caused by "irritation of the genital organs," cured by circumcision; "paralytic club-foot," markedly improved by circumcision; equally marvelous cures for hernia, bladder inflammation, tuberculosis of the pelvic joint, spinal curvature, epilepsy, and insanity. He also claimed to have achieved significant improvement in two girls, aged three and five, both with limb deformity and spastic paralysis, by excising the clitoris.[28] Note that none of these children had genital problems; instead, this highly respected surgeon was claiming cures for everything from major orthopedic disabilities to neurological and mental illnesses.

In a paper published in 1887, originally read that year at the Ninth International Medical Congress, Sayre not only called attention to his conservative methods but again declared his unease about what he now realized was an increasing problem: other physicians were going much too far. He had relieved "paralysis, and various other nervous symptoms...by simply removing the *constriction* from the glans penis, and the retained and concrete smegma from behind the corona, and so arranging the prepuce that it could glide *easily* to and fro over the glans without any constriction." A properly performed operation, he continued, leaves

> the organ in a normal condition, with the glans partially covered with
> its prepuce, but which can be easily uncovered, as it should be,
> and not mutilated and disfigured, as I have frequently seen it, by a too
> free removal of the prepuce, thus leaving the glans entirely unpro-
> tected. While, therefore, I may be responsible for bringing this sub-
> ject so prominently before the profession, I wish to raise my voice in
> protest against this unjustifiable mutilation, as well as against the
> indiscriminate performance of the operation in cases where it may be
> of no avail. [29]

In short, having pioneered in recommending conservative foreskin surgery for various forms of "reflex paralysis," Sayre now realized that he had unintentionally encouraged widespread adoption of more radical procedures essentially identical to what we now call "circumcision." While I cannot be precise, it seems clear that between about 1870 and 1885, a significant number of physicians began not just loosening foreskins but removing them entirely.

Sayre's 1887 paper included a number of letters from physicians attesting to the value of his discovery; many used the words "circumcision" or "circumcised," but the operation was seldom described sufficiently to determine what these words meant.[30] Although Sayre spoke positively about the authors of the letters, he must have understood that, while some had followed his recommendations, others had not. In a discussion following his presentation at the medical congress, a Dr. Willard of Philadelphia commented that Sayre's "former enthusiastic advocacy of circumcision" had led "many rash and unthinking physicians to advise this operation in cases where it is entirely unnecessary," and had also led them "to overlook serious central lesions [i.e., in the brain or spinal cord] in cases where an adherent prepuce has been but an accidental coexisting condition." Willard reported that he had dealt conservatively with hundreds of cases, and that "I now very rarely circumcise a young child....I am an advocate of discriminate circumcision, but not of indiscriminate." He continued with sharply worded comments on a claim that Sayre himself appears never to have mentioned:

It is idle to class this operation among Mosaic sanitary laws. It
was ordered long before the time of Moses, not upon hygienic, but
upon religious grounds, as a distinctive mark. Its adoption by other
nations was undoubtedly due to the fact that their superstitious
minds easily accepted the theory that by thus mutilating themselves,
the acknowledged blessings showered in past time by the Almighty
upon this "peculiar people" might be secured to themselves, since
this was the only outward and visible sign of difference. Such barbaric sacrifices are not infrequent, and those who practice this rite are
certainly not noted either for their morality or cleanliness.[31]

Willard's comments were followed by the quite different recommendations of
a Dr. Love of St. Louis:

It has been my judgment and my practice for many years in these
reflex irritations to pursue the radical course of circumcision. I
believe thoroughly in the Mosaic law, not only from a moral but also
from a sanitary standpoint. All genital irritation should be thoroughly
removed.... Dr. Sayre takes a more pronounced position on this
subject than the majority of those who have discussed his paper. An
improper performance of a surgical procedure is no argument
against the operation, but rather against the operator. For the reasons
I have given, I am in favor of the radical application of the Mosaic rite
of circumcision.[32]

As we'll see shortly, the comments of these two physicians were not
the first to introduce Moses into the developing controversy about circumcision.
Love may or may not have been Jewish; in any event, his call for general
adoption of "the Mosaic rite of circumcision," peculiar though it may sound
now, was an early example of what would soon become a standard feature
of circumcision advocacy: conflation of medical recommendations with references to the Hebrew Scriptures. Sayre responded positively to Willard's
statement, but not to Love's: "As to complete ablation of the parts under all
circumstances, as recommended by Dr. Love, I must enter my strongest
protest."[33]

Sayre's revelations were confirmed time and again, as physicians outdid
one another with reports on their own ventures in reductive genital surgery.
They too now discovered that "congenital phimosis" could cause any number
of neurological and infectious afflictions, all markedly relieved or even cured
by circumcision. As they knew from the theory of reflex neurosis, pathologic
impulses originating in a long, "irritable" prepuce could travel everywhere
from feet to brain.[34]

I cannot say whether most physicians followed Sayre's lead by removing
only part of the foreskin or whether some were already practicing more radical

versions of circumcision similar to what is now routine in American hospitals; probably both. In any event, many physicians believed that removing the prepuce, whether fully or in part, removed the problem. Theories and claims of this kind represented a momentous departure from the relatively modest recommendations of their British colleagues. Now it was not only the claim that pathology of the sexual organs, particularly venereal disease, might be reduced in prevalence by preventive surgery; rather, the *very presence* of a foreskin became a pathological condition causing any number of severe afflictions in every part of the body.

Moses the Good Sanitarian

Among the many who followed Sayre's lead was Norman H. Chapman, a Philadelphia neurologist. In 1882, he recommended circumcision as a cure for "nervous affections" caused by "neglected congenital phimosis." Secretions could accumulate in an "elongated and tight foreskin," he reported, causing "local irritation, which is usually sufficient to keep the organ almost constantly in a state of undue excitement." Children who had been "brisk and cheerful" became "peevish, fretful, and discontented," with loss of "mental energies," decline in school performance, loss of appetite, and disturbed sleep. In the most severe cases the nervous system became so "undermined" that the child developed chorea (uncontrollable spasmodic movements) or forms of "reflex or peripheral palsy." Chapman had effected cures with a combination of circumcision, massage, "galvanism," tonics, and improved diet. He claimed also that circumcision cured strabismus (misaligned eyes, as in "cross-eyed")—the rationale again being that these were "reflex palsies" originating in genital irritation. He concluded with a sweeping recommendation:

> I conceive that it is always good surgery to correct this deformity [i.e., a long, "tight" foreskin], wherever it is at all aggravated, as a precautionary measure, even though no symptoms have as yet presented themselves. . . . Moses was a good sanitarian, and if circumcision was more generally practised at the present day, I believe that we would hear far less of the pollutions and indiscretions of youth; and that our daily papers would not be so profusely flooded with all kinds of sure cures for loss of manhood.[35]

This may have been the first reference to Moses as a "sanitarian"—a new role for the biblical lawgiver. Note that Chapman referred to Moses rather than Abraham. Since Moses was thought to have authored the Torah (the "Five Books of Moses"), advocates could now maintain that he had introduced the account of Abraham's circumcision, and had ordered the post-exodus circumcisions said to have been divinely commanded to Joshua—all to promote his own medical goals. So in contrast to the traditional Jewish emphasis on Abraham as the originator of circumcision in response to a divine command, Moses now emerged as a brilliant proto-physician who had lighted on the procedure as a public health measure!

Biblical sanctions for modern medical recommendations now meshed comfortably with growing concerns about physical and moral "hygiene," and with the incorporation of public health into the professional domain of physicians. Moreover, beliefs about "reflex neurosis" and the like were on the way to replacement by a more credible theory and a more convincing justification for foreskin removal. Growing awareness of germ theory meant that tissue beneath the foreskin could be portrayed as a lurking vector of infection. "Smegma," the normal physiological secretion protecting the glans and facilitating the foreskin's gliding function in intercourse, was transformed into "infectious material." Whether a physician accepted the new revelations about germs or clung to notions about reflex irritation, the conclusion would be much the same: foreskin removal was exemplary medical practice. And the man credited with this momentous discovery: none other than Moses.[36]

Members of the Tribe: Jewish Physicians Add Their Voices

A MESSAGE FROM A MODERN MOSES. With Gentile physicians now praising circumcision as a medical panacea, their Jewish colleagues beheld new vistas. If it was turning out that the ancient practice was not just the sign of Abraham's covenant but also a nearly miraculous treatment for everything from paralysis to insanity, wasn't it reasonable to welcome its acceptance by the general community? At a time when Jews were intent on becoming full-fledged Americans, what could have been so gratifying as the prospect of everyone's adopting the most problematic sign of Jewish difference?

This is indeed what happened. But asking *why* raises another question. Most Jewish American physicians in the decades from about 1870 to 1940 were the sons of immigrants. Although they were of course aware of their personal status as ethnic Jews in multiethnic America, it appears that when it came to circumcision, their primary reference group was their fellow physicians. But they might well have been gratified to see circumcision lose its reputation as a peculiar badge of Jewishness and become instead an emblem of modern standards of hygiene and sound moral values. These years, we recall, were the age of "melting pot" ideology, when the ultimate immigrant achievement was to become wholly and undeniably American. Insistence on difference—not only in penile anatomy but with the claim to "chosen" status that circumcision was commonly taken to signify—was no more the path to acceptance in the New World than it had been in the Old.

But another possibility comes to mind. If blending in and becoming indistinguishable was the primary goal, why not advocate *elimination* of Jewish circumcision, by focusing on its dangers and complications, rather than its ostensible benefits? In contrast to Germany, where that position found only very limited Jewish support, in America there was less communal pressure, more freedom to decide for oneself, more room for maneuvering around ritual regulations. But even here resistance to change in this one ritual domain appears to have been about as firm as in Germany.

When challenges to circumcision came from within Jewish ranks, conservative Jewish physicians responded as physicians—with medical arguments. In October 1871 (just one year after Lewis Sayre's initial report), a well-regarded physician named Montefiore J. Moses published an article in the *New York Medical Journal* defending *ritual* circumcision strictly for its therapeutic and prophylactic virtues. Its bland title, "The Value of Circumcision as a Hygienic and Therapeutic Measure," doesn't do justice to the article's pivotal role in this history.[37] Here, probably for the first time, the aptly named author exhorted his fellow Jews to remain loyal to circumcision, *regardless of their religious views*, as a step on the path to lifelong good health.

Moses began with reference to an article that had appeared in a Jewish periodical "condemning the practice of confiding the operation of circumcision to persons who, entirely ignorant of the first principles of anatomy or surgery, yet perform the act under dispensation from a religious sect."[38] But he did not defend mohels; rather, he advocated circumcision as a procedure residing properly in *medical* hands—even though he knew that mohels were not the only operators liable to inflict damage on infants:

> While the intention of the writer [of the first article] was, to impress upon the Israelitish community the necessity of having their children attended to by surgeons, many have accepted the article, and the exposition of the danger incurred by the children, as an argument against the "barbarity" of an "old prejudice," and adduce it as a strong reason for urging the abrogation of a ceremonial rite, the origin of which is coeval with the earliest civilization, and the value of which has borne the criticism of ages, and the tacit sanction of science, in almost every age and country.

Word of a recent "accident" (his quotation marks) during a circumcision by a local "medical gentleman" had encouraged "dissenters" to renew their attacks. Speaking as an "Israelite" and a physician, Moses chose to write in a medical journal, so as not to be "trammelled in [his] expressions"—as he "necessarily would be" if he wrote for an "ordinary" (Jewish) publication.[39]

Skipping briskly past ancient theological debates, Moses asked his readers to view the Jewish "ordinance (the divine origin of which I do not propose to discuss)" as "a human law"—that is, as a medical directive—and listed several questions for consideration, including the "value of the operation," whether it was painful, and the number of "accidents" and their causes. The plain value of the operation was prophylactic: children with foreskins often fell victim to the "ravages" of "the solitary vice." The "little sufferer[s]" were readily recognizable by their "haggard faces and extreme nervous irritability." Examination disclosed "a long, contracted, and irritated prepuce" hiding "fetid sebaceous matter." With circumcision "the devil [was] at once exorcised": the child stopped masturbating and soon recovered.

Moses had never seen a case of masturbation in a young Jewish child, except those who associated with boys whose "covered glans" had "naturally impelled them to the habit." Without doubt, cleanliness was "the key to health."[40] Pain was not a problem. Moses reported having operated on "sleeping children, who only awakened at the first incision, relapsing into a tranquil slumber during the completion of the operation."[41]

As for "accidents," he pointed to the "late Dr. Abrahams, who probably did the operation oftener than any one [sic] of his time, and who on his visit to the Holy Land . . . offered the best testimony of success, in depositing several thousand foreskins in the shrines at Jerusalem." Moses knew of no deaths among Abrahams's cases, and supposed that if there were any, they were "so trifling a percentage" of the total as to have been lost.[42] True, hemorrhage and the rare cases of tetanus were dangers, but only when the operator was careless or inept: "Circumcision is an operation of the simplest nature, and the mutilations we often see are no more necessary than is amputation of the forearm, for the cure of a diseased finger-nail."

The "object of the ceremony, as ordered in the Mosaic code," was "to liberate the glans from its close mucous covering." When done properly, Moses assured possible skeptics, "the sacrifice of some *little* tissue is necessary, but so little, in fact, as to be scarcely appreciable." When performed by "rabbinical appointees," however, the operation "frequently involves the loss of *too much* tissue" and resultant hemorrhage.[43] So the message to this point was clear: adherence to "the Mosaic code" required the skilled hands of a physician, who could be trusted to "liberate the glans" in a proper manner.

Here Moses was apparently following Sayre's recommendation for conservative treatment and implying, quite incorrectly, that this corresponded to requirements for ritual circumcisions. Many physicians, however, were guided neither by Sayre's warnings about "mutilation" nor by what the biblical Moses supposedly ordered, but by what they learned about circumcision from Jewish practice. And the implication that a ritually proper *Jewish* circumcision need result in very little tissue loss was simply untrue. It was not "the Mosaic code" that directed the actions of mohels but the long-established rabbinic regulation demanding *complete* foreskin removal.

Moses continued with his answer to a rhetorical question conflating biblical mandate with medical prescription: "What special diseased conditions are frequently due to a neglect of the ordinance?" The answer was the familiar litany of genitourinary and venereal diseases, "nocturnal pollutions," "spermatorrhea," and nervous illnesses "amounting to absolute mania"—all curable or preventable by circumcision.[44] In conclusion, he warned that "Jews of the enlightened (?) school [sic]" were "inaugurating a dangerous reform" when they proposed eliminating circumcision. He urged his "professional brethren, of other creeds" to instruct their "Jewish patrons" on "the value and *safety* of maintaining circumcision, if not as a religious duty, as a hygienic measure, the importance of which probably influenced its institution as a ceremonial law."[45]

Thus, circumcision, the emblem of difference between Jew and Christian, was now to be defended as nothing more nor less than "a hygienic measure" for Jewish traditionalists and skeptics alike. Although at first Moses appears to have been addressing only colleagues with Jewish patients, by the end of the article readers would surely have concluded that circumcision was highly advisable for all infants.

Moses died of nephritis in 1878, at age thirty-six. An obituary in a medical journal characterized him as "a gentleman of exceedingly pleasing address and fine professional and scholarly attainments, as well as of the most exemplary character."[46] His article was still being cited years after his death—in support of *general* circumcision—and we can only speculate about how much additional influence he might have exercised had he lived longer.[47]

DELIVERING RITUAL CIRCUMCISION FROM "MEN OF NOT OVER-CLEANLY HABITS." Moses' argument was extended in an article published three years later, again in the *New York Medical Journal*, by a Dr. L. H. Cohen, of Quincy, Illinois. Cohen, who identified Moses as "my friend," was responding to a recently published article by R. W. Taylor, a specialist in dermatology and venereal diseases. Taylor had been asked by the New York City Board of Health to investigate the cases of four infants, all circumcised by the same mohel, who had developed ulcerative lesions of the penis. Three of the children died, two before Taylor could examine them; the fourth survived. The immediate questions were whether the lesions were syphilitic, and, if so, whether they had been transmitted by the circumciser. Taylor's report, the work of a capable and conscientious physician, was thorough and convincing. He concluded that although syphilis might be transmitted by circumcision, particularly if a mohel were incompetent and was carrying the infection, he had found no evidence that the mohel in question had ever been infected. He did determine that one of the boys (the one who survived) had indeed developed an unmistakable syphilitic lesion; but this had appeared two months after the circumcision, when the wound had apparently healed. The three boys who died had not contracted syphilis (although it is obvious that they had contracted ulcerative lesions severe enough to cause disability and death—a point that Taylor apparently considered beyond the scope of his inquiry).

Taylor urged that "performance of the rite should be absolutely confined to responsible and educated persons"—either a physician or "a physician assisting an officiating rabbi, or a circumciser of recognized merit." Following this recommendation, he concluded, "will render a rite, which has useful sanitary bearings, less liable to fall into disrepute among those upon whom it is obligatory."[48]

In addition to the skillfully diplomatic conclusion, Taylor demonstrated throughout the report that he was an open-minded, scientifically objective researcher whose sole aim was to get at the truth. He did, however, exculpate a mohel whose operative methods may very well have led to the deaths in question. Perhaps he phrased his recommendations so cautiously because he had been asked to determine only whether the lesions were syphilitic. In any event, he seems to have gone out of his way not to offend Jewish readers.

Cohen was not offended but he was uneasy; he feared that Taylor's article, "while written in the interests of science, would be apt to prove a mischievous, perhaps a dangerous tool in the hands of some pretended Jewish reformers who would fain abolish the practice." Citing M. J. Moses as recommended reading, he carried the argument further. Although Taylor had not demonstrated transmission of syphilis in his reported cases, Cohen acknowledged that infections could be transmitted by circumcision "as practised by some men of not over-cleanly habits." Taylor had mentioned "the practice of sucking the wound," but Cohen was "happy to say that in the West this disgusting part of the ceremony is almost always omitted." He recalled only one instance in which the mohel "took the glans in his mouth, or spurted the styptic therefrom upon the wound."[49]

Note this new twist: a Jewish physician was defending *ritual* circumcision, initially against mildly phrased critical recommendations by a Gentile physician, but, following the lead of M. J. Moses, also against unidentified Jewish critics (probably not physicians) who had declared outright opposition to perpetuating the Jewish rite. The medical debate on circumcision as a therapeutic or prophylactic procedure was now too entangled with the Jewish debate on ritual circumcision for anyone to confidently distinguish them. All these men agreed on one point: either physicians, or mohels carefully supervised by physicians, should perform circumcisions. Like M. J. Moses, Cohen wanted to rescue ritual circumcision by medicalizing it—taking the procedure out of the kind of hands he had "many a time seen, with shockingly dirty fingers tipped with ebony-edged nails." Such unpleasant business was enough to disgust first-time witnesses whose "feelings of delicacy and refinement [were] severely tried, to say the least, by the rough, boorish, frequently brutal conduct and bearing of the operator."[50] Cohen seconded the recommendation of his predecessor that the operation should be performed by a surgeon. He did feel obliged to add, though, that Moses "was a little unjust in the remarks that closed his otherwise excellent and truly valuable article." It was true that "some

few 'enlightened' Jews in the city of New York protest[ed] against the ceremony of circumcision as 'barbarous—a relic of the past, that it is time to
abolish,' etc., etc." But theirs was a minority opinion. Cohen (a Midwesterner)
belonged to a "very ultra-reform Jewish congregation," whose members
"hail[ed] with joy the birth of a male child" and celebrated with a circumcision
on the eighth day. He knew, though, that most agreed "that the ceremony
should be performed by an educated medical man." Once this opinion became
accepted by "the mass of Israelites throughout the land," there would be no
more objections from would-be reformers and no need for investigations into
disease transmission.[51]

Apparently Cohen did not know, or did not care, that a nonritual circumcision performed by a physician had no validity in Jewish religious law.
Unless the procedure was conducted on the eighth day by a physician capable
of reciting ritual blessings, and with a mohel or rabbi in attendance to ensure
that everything proceeded properly, the surgery had no religious significance.
We see here the beginning of the belief that foreskin removal in itself is
sufficient to "mark" a male infant as Jewish. Since by this time many Gentile
infants were also being circumcised, Cohen was in effect recommending that
the Jewish rite be "Americanized" out of existence.

By the late nineteenth century, then, while a few Jewish Americans were
arguing that ritual circumcision should be abolished, many physicians, Jewish
and Gentile, with little or no interest in Jewish religious controversies, were
advocating adoption of circumcision as a public health measure. At the same
time, others called not for abolition of the Jewish rite but for its medicalization,
urging that physicians replace mohels as operators, or insisting that at very
least there be adequate physician supervision. But although many physicians
were disturbed by reports of rotting teeth in mohel mouths, filthy nails on
mohel thumbs, and caked blood on mohel instruments, few suggested that
circumcision itself might be medically worthless.

THIS "CAN NOT BE CONTEMPLATED WITH INDIFFERENCE": A DISSENTING
VOICE. There were a few in the Jewish medical community, however, who
rejected all circumcision outright. In 1869, a leading Baltimore Jewish physician, Abram B. Arnold (1820–1904), published a comprehensive article
expressing serious reservations about circumcision as ritual or routine practice. Although Arnold had performed many circumcisions—at least eight
hundred since 1850 by his reckoning—he indicated that he felt uneasy about
what he himself was doing.[52] Calling circumcision "this species of mutilation," he remarked that although some authors conjectured that Moses "instituted the rite of circumcision" as prophylaxis against genital diseases, he
could not "believe that a painful, and sometimes a dangerous operation,
should have been adopted by a whole nation, for the mere purpose of avoiding
a few rare and not serious local complaints."[53] Although circumcision could

be "a very simple affair," occasionally it was "formidable enough," owing to "the remnants of the vicious surgery of a past age"—"squirting of wine on the fresh wound, followed by the sucking of blood with the mouth."[54] He reported on badly mismanaged cases that had ended in severe and permanent mutilation or death.[55]

Seventeen years later, in 1886, Arnold expressed even more unease about the increasing popularity of circumcision. Nevertheless, he was still performing the operation himself, apparently in the main on Jewish infants. In one of the most carefully argued papers in the medical literature of the time, he opened with a tellingly phrased statement: "An esteemed medical friend, who is a member of the [New York Medical] Academy, informed me some time ago that the subject of circumcision, as indiscriminately practiced by the Hebrews, was exciting considerable interest in certain quarters, under the impression that this operation possessed some value as a prophylactic measure." It isn't difficult, he continued, "to divine the purposes of the prepuce.... A better provision than the anatomy of the prepuce can not be conceived for shielding the very vascular and sensitive structure of the glans from external sources of irritation and friction, that might rouse the sensibility of this organ."[56] As the final phrase suggests, Arnold argued counter to the widely accepted (and correct) position that the prepuce facilitated masturbation; he thought that an exposed glans was more likely to be "affected by chance titillations." Noting that some physicians had taken the opposite position, he argued that accumulation of "sebaceous secretion" was harmless, and that the frequency of "irritation" from such accumulation had been overstated. And he was skeptical about claims for the "hygienic" value of "indiscriminate circumcision":

> I doubt whether a bloody operation will ever become the fashion for the prevention of a possible trivial affection [sic]. It is to me extremely questionable if circumcision originated from considerations of bodily cleanliness, for people who are indifferent to filth will hardly resort to a mutilation to keep it off from one part of the body.[57]

Neither was he convinced that the operation was effective in "moderating the amorous instinct" (although it appears that he would have found that desirable). He knew that Hutchinson had found that the procedure conferred "comparative immunity" from syphilis among Jews and granted, with characteristic reserve, that "the reputation of circumcision as a prophylactic against syphilis has a chance of being established." But he recommended a more dependable preventive: "Fortunately, there is one sure way of keeping the disease at a distance [i.e., prudent sexual behavior], whatever may be the outcome of the numerical comparisons."[58]

Although he accepted circumcision as the appropriate treatment for "congenital phimosis," Arnold took careful note of "the accidents attending the Jewish rite of circumcision"—fortunately uncommon, he added, but a matter for concern:

> It must be admitted that an operation consisting of an extensive incision and laceration, the opening of arteries, the possibility of inflammation and suppuration, and the infliction of intense pain in a child but eight days old, can not be contemplated with indifference. Hebrew mothers not seldom date the bad health of their little sons from this operation.

Citing cases of fatal hemorrhage, severe mutilation of the penis, fatal erysipelas, and other horrors, Arnold made it clear that he would have liked to see circumcision in both its ritual and "indiscriminate" forms disappear entirely.[59]

INVESTIGATING THE "SURGEON-IN-CHIEF." Other Jewish physicians, uneasy about ritual circumcision in particular, confined their comments to the deficiencies of mohels and called for their replacement by qualified physicians and surgeons. Representative of this group was Henry Levien of New York, who published an article in 1894 entitled "Circumcision—Dangers of Unclean Surgery," the dangers being those attending surgery performed by mohels ignorant of modern antisepsis. Like Arnold, Levien was no friend of ritual circumcision. Jewish circumcisions, he began, are "practised as a purely religious rite," maintained since Abraham's time "as a peculiar sacrifice which is acceptable to God."[60] He followed with an exceptionally detailed description of the rite. Despite its scrupulously ethnographic quality, no one could have missed the ironic tone. Levien described "certain peculiarities of a rather fanatic nature"—for example,

> the custom of hanging up slips of paper, written or printed, containing a psalm and some cabalistic names of some angels, designed to protect child and mother from the grasp of the devil. These slips are to be seen attached to the bed, walls, and doors of the bedroom, and remain there for about twelve weeks, the time limit for the satan [sic] to exert his demoralizing influence upon the new-born and his mother.[61]

When the big day arrived, one knew that "something remarkable" was ahead:

> To comfort the weary and hungry visitors the father, greatly agitated, goes from one guest to another, telling them that "he" will come soon. By "him" is meant the chief personality of the day, the surgeon-in-chief, the Mohel. He is a busy man. . . . But who is he? Where did he study? Why is he entrusted with the life of a human

being? Nobody can tell. All we know is, that he witnessed this operation several times, and announced himself competent enough to perform the same.... Lister, being born in this century, could not have imparted his ideas to the surgeons of the Talmudical era; consequently the Mohel, who receives his information on this subject from that source only, bravely goes to operate without any knowledge of asepsis and antisepsis.

Levien invited readers to join him in inspecting the operating equipment of the self-certified surgeons:

All you find is a wooden case-box, with one double-edged knife in it. It is not hard to discover on the knife suspicious spots of dried-up blood, left from some previous operation or operations. I recently called the attention of the Mohel to the condition of his instrument, upon which I discovered a few bloody spots; to satisfy me he tried to rub the blood off with his finger-nails, and believed asepsis was fully attained.

Describing a typical operation performed by a mohel, complete with *metsitsah* by a mouth that might be "full of decayed teeth and purulent gingivitis," Levien asked readers to contemplate the "dangers of infection the new-born has been exposed to." In larger cities, he continued, mohels, operating without supervision, suck the infant's blood through a glass tube. Some also employ "a metal plate with a long and narrow hole," used as a clamp: the foreskin is pulled through the hole while the plate is forced downward toward the glans. But this instrument adds to the possibilities for infection. Levien "found on this metal piece dried up blood, and had to insist on its disinfection."[62]

Levien issued a warning to "colleagues who are engaged in obstetrical practice among the Hebrews, to make it their business and a matter of conscience to be present at every operation, and supervise the whole procedure." He described two cases, one fatal, of infants who suffered severe hemorrhage and infection—"mutilations from the hands of ignorant people"—following ritual circumcisions. But despite such calamities, he felt reluctant to prohibit "a process, though a depletory one, in a nation in whom the depletion for hereditary reasons may be a necessity for the well-being of the race, and may prove disastrous if this operation is denied"—presumably acknowledgment of the commonly held belief that circumcision is necessary for Jewish "survival." He proposed that there be "a law that, at each and every operation, a duly registered and practising physician shall be present" to oversee the operation and to be the "responsible party." Circumcision, he concluded, "is an operation requiring as much care and dexterity on the part of the surgeon as in any other surgical work, and should be performed by a competent surgeon, or at least under his direct supervision."[63] The term "surgeon," used twice with "operation" and "surgical," in this single sentence, along with the earlier reference to Lister, underscored the argument that circumcision could not be accepted as just another religious ceremony.

A Dr. R. Hochlerner, almost certainly Jewish, responded in the same journal with a rebuttal:

> That delicate little procedure or operation, as Dr. Henry Levien would have it, circumcision, is again attracting the attention of our profession, and I believe there is no operation that has been so much discussed or spoken of for centuries as this rite of the Hebrews; and it is not surprising that it is the bête noire of our progressive Hebrew physicians imbued with the spirit of Listerism.

Severe complications of the kind reported by Levien were very rare, insisted Hochlerner; and when it came to prevention of infection, mohels did better than physicians. This might be explained, he thought, by the mohel's "dexterity, the swiftness with which he performs the only operation he is able to, and which he has performed thousands of times." Contrary to Levien's claim, he knew that "country" mohels used antiseptics and iodoform gauze. Moreover, "even the poorest Hebrew" always sought out the most competent and experienced mohel, and those who could not afford the fee would be assisted by others, "thus paying for the opportunity to be present at a God pleasing rite."[64]

Following in the Footsteps of Moses

By the 1890s, calls for adoption of circumcision as a medical panacea, for children and adults, had become a commonplace in American medical literature, still with references to the biblical Moses.[65] A short article published in a Chicago medical periodical in 1889 by A. U. Williams, a physician in Hot Springs, Arkansas, informed colleagues that he had cured genital infections in more than four hundred adult men by circumcising them. Williams advocated universal prophylactic circumcision: "I would follow in the footsteps of Moses and circumcise all male children."[66]

Another of Moses' admirers was J. Henry C. Simes, a prominent Philadelphia urologist. It was generally recognized, he declared, that "one of the most prevalent causes" of masturbatory misbehavior was "an abnormally long and contracted prepuce," since the "very great amount of nervous element in its anatomical structure makes it a part which is very susceptible to the slightest irritation." In adolescents "the morals of the individual" might be "decidedly affected by the condition of his prepuce." Simes had encountered young men who were "very much demoralized" by frequent nocturnal emissions. Examination often revealed "an elongated prepuce, the removal of which terminates all the trouble."[67] From moral benefits it was a short step to hygiene, then to a recommendation that everyone adopt the ancient "Jewish rite":

> The hygienic advantages, which are the result of the operation of circumcision, none can doubt. Leaving aside the religious signifi-cance of the operation when performed by the Jews, there is no doubt that it was commanded to be done for its hygienic effect, and that the first and great teacher of hygienic medicine, Moses, certainly had this view in his mind when he gave forth the order, that all male children of Israel must be circumcised.

Considering how many "pathological conditions" were curable by cir-cumcision, Simes found it "strange" that "the custom of the Jewish rite" had not been more widely "adopted by the Christians."[68] He seems to have taken for granted that Jewish religious laws had been instituted in the service of hygiene and morality. Christians would be wise, therefore, to ignore Paul's warning that circumcision was worthless and adopt *universally* the most *particularist* of Jewish rituals.

Here we see why Jewish circumcision, with its two distinctive features—performance soon after birth and removal of all possible foreskin tissue—became standard in American medical practice. Following in the footsteps of Moses meant taking the lead from his Jewish descendants, who surely knew best about the proper time and way to perform a circumcision. No one ques-tioned the appropriateness of such surgery for a neonate, nor did anyone propose removing only the loose tissue at the tip of the foreskin. Despite the well-documented unsanitary practices of mohels, and the realization that *peri'ah* could cause dangerous complications, American physicians, Jewish and Gentile, modeled their own practices on the centuries-old Jewish method. America, an overwhelmingly Christian nation, was on the way to becoming the site of more circumcisions in the Jewish manner than any place on earth.

By the end of the century, circumcision advocacy had become routine. In 1893, a New Orleans physician named Mark J. Lehman published an article titled "A Plea for Circumcision," crediting Abraham, rather than Moses, with medical clairvoyance. "If sacred and profane literature is critically analyzed it appears that Abraham and his contemporaries, wise men in their day, dem-onstrated a knowledge of Hygiene in adopting by 'special mandate' the ceremonial of Circumcision." Any physician "of average intelligence," he continued, has observed "the various neurotic diseases of childhood in males, incontinence of urine, phymosis, paraphymosis and other ills, wails and woes traceable to a peculiar prepuce, either in texture, formation or other anatomical abnormalities." Should circumcision therefore be widely adopted? Well, said Lehman, anyone familiar with the healthy state of "the Jewish type" knew the answer. And it was only now, as physicians recognized "the intimate relations between the genitals and brain centers" (the old reflex neurosis theory), that everything was falling into place. Frequently he had treated distressingly "puny, ill-nourished baby boys," whose therapeutic circumcision was "followed by the fretting infant becoming a model of the plump, good baby—a mother's joy and a father's pride." Moreover, it was "an open question" whether tuberculosis, cancer, syphilis, and "scrofula" were not "one and the same disease," and whether "such a simple measure as general circumcision" would not be the answer to the entire plague of "insidious and filthy diseases." Lehman urged his colleagues to tarry no longer: "Experience proves its utility, its necessity, and its universal adoption should be urged at once."[69]

By the final decade of the century, then, the medical debate on circumcision was following two partly intersecting paths: On one side, Jewish physicians argued—mostly among themselves, though in the pages of medical journals—the merits of ritual circumcisions and of mohels, enlisting tradition, "hygiene," and harm in diverse combinations as justification either for or against the traditional rite. On the other, a steadily growing number of both Gentile and Jewish physicians urged that this ancient form of genital surgery be widely adopted as a prophylactic procedure for afflictions beyond count.

"Mouse-Headed" and "Corona-Deficient": Doctor Remondino's Magnum Opus

In December 1889, a San Diego physician named Peter Charles Remondino (1846–1926) delivered a paper at a meeting of the Southern California Medical Society entitled "A Plea for Circumcision; or, the Dangers that Arise from the Prepuce." The paper included only a fraction of the material he had been accumulating. Two years later he published a book, more than three hundred pages in length, entitled *History of Circumcision from the Earliest Times to the Present. Moral and Physical Reasons for Its Performance.*[70] I can say without exaggeration that this was and is the most exuberant, and the most renowned, of all panegyrics to circumcision. Probably no single publication ever reached a wider audience or exercised more influence on physicians and laity alike. Garrulous and rambling in style, laden with polemics, replete with hyperbole and undocumented claims, the book still has to be taken seriously, if only because it became so influential. In any event, it's entertaining!

A Protestant Italian American who had immigrated at age eight, Remondino was a widely published author, a journal editor, the first president of the San Diego Board of Health, and a vice-president of the California State Medical Society: a respected mainstream physician. The prepuce, he declared, was nothing better than an "outlaw" appendage, a useless relic surviving from the time when man lived "in a wild state," when "in pursuit of either the juicy grasshopper or other small game, or of the female of his own species to gratify his lust, or in the frantic rush to escape the clutches, fangs, or claws of a pursuing enemy, he was obliged to fly and leap over thorny briars and bramble-bushes or hornets' nests, or plunge through swamps alive with blood-sucking insects and leeches." Back then, had it not been for "the protecting double fold of the preputial envelope that protected it from the thorns and cutting grasses, the coarse bark of trees, or the stings and bites of insects," the average penis would have resembled "a battle-scarred Roman legionary." But with advances in civilization and the advent of clothing, the prepuce became not only a "superfluity" but a "nuisance, as its former free contact with the air had retained it in a state of vigorous and disease-resisting health which was now fast departing."[71]

The prepuce, therefore, was not a functioning part of the male genitals; it was simply an inert piece of skin covering the actual organ (a view congruent with that of the authors of the Talmud). But for civilized men prepuces were worse than useless; they were a pernicious hindrance to normal intercourse and conception. It was well known that many women suffered from "uterine displacement" due to wearing of corsets, "habitual constipation," miscarriages, "irregular menstruation," and so on. Was it not self-evident that uncircumcised penises were ill-adapted for impregnating such women? "Just imagine one of these conditioned females and one of the mouse-headed, corona-deficient, long-pointed glans males in the act of copulation!"[72]

The ancient Hebrews, declared Remondino, were far wiser than Christians have realized; they understood the benefits of circumcision so well that they instituted it as a divine command. Indeed Paul, intent on creating a religion attractive to potential converts in the Gentile world, did them and everyone a lasting disservice when he dismissed circumcision as a worthless rite.[73] The fact was that by every reasonable standard the Jews—the one people in America and Britain who remained loyal to circumcision—were remarkable for their longevity, their overall good health, and their freedom from venereal diseases, none of which could be convincingly explained unless their ancient practice was taken into account. Moreover, Jews exhibited little inclination to "criminality, debauchery, and intemperance," nor did they commit such "silly crimes" as "indecent exposures" or "assaults on young girls." Why these differences? Even after allowing for the influences of family life, social customs, and the like, there remained "a wide margin to be accounted for."[74]

Jews enjoy health, longevity, and disinclination to self-destructive behavior, Remondino argued, not because of their way of life but despite it. They are temperate with alcohol but certainly not "abstemious." And when it came to eating, they were second to none.[75] Moreover, historians had demonstrated conclusively that Jews were remarkably resistant to just about every major affliction of suffering humanity. Time and again they had escaped epidemics of plague, typhus, and dysentery—so strikingly, in fact, that gullible men imagined them to have made a pact with the devil.[76] But might it have been the case that Jewish vigor was attributable ultimately to their most distinctive practice? Physicians and statisticians had repeatedly documented Jewish longevity, low infant mortality, and resistance to tuberculosis and syphilis. It was clear, moreover, that these "exemptions" and "benefits" were not solely attributable to "social customs."[77] The conclusion was inescapable: Jewish health, longevity, and resistance to infection must be the reward for loyalty to circumcision.

Remondino's book almost certainly contributed more than any other publication to convincing a large number of physicians and general readers that the custom so often reviled by Christians was in fact the supreme Jewish gift to civilized, medically enlightened humanity. When everyone recognized the immense worth of foreskin removal and accepted it for themselves and their children, it would be the Jews above all whom they should thank.

Resistance from skeptics led Remondino to renew his crusade in 1902 with a wide-ranging, characteristically flamboyant article on "circumcision and its opponents." Responding to an unnamed article "which professed to see no benefit whatever in circumcision," he reported the case of a middle-aged man who had recently died of metastatic penile cancer—because he had not been "fortunate enough either to have been born a Jew or a Turk." Remondino included an unsettling photograph of the patient, who had obviously been very unfortunate indeed. From there he recounted a conversation with "an intelligent but irascible Scotch gentleman" whose circumcision had cured his "neurasthenia and resulting ill health," all resulting from "reflex conditions due to a tight prepuce." Although brought up on the Bible and "a wholesome fear of the Lord," the gentleman advised Remondino of his anger at Saint Paul:

> I have been brought up and educated to look upon Saint Paul, the founder of Christianity, with awe and admiration, but, by God, sir, if I had Saint Paul here now, sir, I would shoot him, yes, sir, I would shoot him. He had no biblical warrant nor no business to summarily abolish circumcision as he did. . . . Saint Paul was more of an evangelist and not as scientific a man as Moses, and I may be wrong in wanting to shoot him. He probably did not know the harm he was entailing on Gentile humanity by abolishing circumcision. Still, when I think of the agonies I have been made to suffer through his carelessness, I feel that he ought to be shot, sir.[78]

Granted, continued Remondino, he had seen his share of "unfavorable results" and "complications" resulting from the actions of incompetent operators; but if the problems he had witnessed could "all be rolled into one spasm of physical pain or concentrated into one pang of mental anguish, they could not be compared to the pain, anguish and sufferings" of patients with cancers that could have been prevented by circumcision. Moreover, with modern methods of local anesthesia, sterile dressings, and improved sutures, circumcision was a safe operation, no more "barbarous" than vaccination.[79]

Following a grim catalog of infections and cancers that circumcision would have prevented, Remondino proceeded to a discussion of "reflex diseases" caused by the very "presence or existence" of a prepuce: "Hydrocele, hernia, hip joint disease, epilepsy, asthma, disturbances of speech or of sight, and a whole category of diseases can often be traced to their origins in some preputial irritation or cause." He underscored the point with another disturbing photograph, this one of a man with massive hypertrophy of the prepuce. Remondino had cured a wide array of such afflictions simply by removing an offending foreskin.[80] He closed with a few words of partial appeasement. Unconvinced physicians were "by no means all blindly dogmatic and unreasonable," since some opposed circumcision only when performed on "seemingly perfectly normal subjects." But there was "danger" from "those narrow, inelastic and unbending understandings" for whom opposition to circumcision was "such a creed, that they have steeled themselves against its performance." These physicians were akin to the "anti-vaccinationists," who saw only risks and "accidental evil results," while failing to recognize "immunities and advantages." But eventually there would be no place for such "one-sided views."[81]

Note that Remondino's claims hardly take account of the germ theory of disease, which by 1891 was certainly familiar to physicians. But although it might be easy to dismiss him as a true believer whose claims for cures of "reflex diseases" and the like now seem fanciful, the fact is that many physicians of his time took him quite seriously. The medical periodical that published his 1902 article—the American Journal of Dermatology and Genito-Urinary Diseases—was no "quack" publication. Moreover, physicians continued for years to cite Remondino's book, and even today one encounters an occasional citation, although more likely now in nonprofessional publications. More than a century after its appearance, this most zealous of all assaults on the foreskin still has a place in circumcision advocacy.

The Finishing Touches

By the first decade of the new century, circumcision of infants and young children had become so routine that the discussion had advanced into procedural details. Thus we find a physician informing colleagues that children "only a few years old may be held by two assistants and the operation done without any anesthesia." Alternatively, he recommended "bandaging the child to a board after the Indian method of strapping the papoose." One required only a "narrow cushioned board and a few bandages . . . to hold the child firmly in place until the operation is ended."[82]

In New York City ritual circumcision came under complete medical supervision. In 1914 the New York Kehillah, the Jewish community council, created a Milah Board, composed of physicians, rabbis, and mohels, empowered to license mohels and to oversee all ritual circumcisions. They sponsored courses, prepared a handbook (endorsed by the city's health commissioner), and examined candidates for licensing. The standards for certification were rigorous: candidates received thorough personal and medical investigation; they were required to undergo medical instruction; their operations were regularly observed by physicians; and they were reexamined at two-year intervals. The names of certified operators and rejected candidates were published in newspapers and periodicals, and sermons and editorials warned against patronizing men on the blacklist. In 1917 a New York pediatrician commented that in that city the practice of ritual circumcision was "on a higher plane than anywhere else in the world."[83]

Still, not every physician was ready to go along. A brief protest in the form of a letter to the editor of the *Medical World*, a monthly periodical, appeared in 1915 from an Omaha physician, M. D. Pass. "Tho a Jew by birth," he began, "I am decidedly opposed to circumcision as practised by the Jews on their eight-day-old male infants. This operation, as performed by the orthodox Jewish rabbis, without asepsis or anesthesia, is filthy and cruel." Pass announced that he had begun "a movement toward the abolition of the ordeal upon helpless babes," and asked for "the moral support of the medical profession." He asked his "brethren" for their opinions: "What benefit has universal circumcision conferred upon the Jew? Shouldn't this practise, of savage origin, be abolished in this day and generation?"[84]

The letter generated a lively response—all from physicians with non-Jewish names—extending over the next five issues. Of the twelve who wrote, three supported Pass, nine opposed him. Although Pass had clearly focused on Jewish circumcision, most respondents mentioned this only in passing if at all, and the only one who did refer to ritual circumcision came down firmly on Pass's side. The advocates, mostly from small towns in the Midwest and South, had nothing to say about Jews or their ritual practices; instead, they extolled the medical virtues of physician-managed circumcision and its potential contribution to sexual continence and marital bliss.[85]

It appears, therefore, that by 1915 a substantial number of American physicians, probably a majority of those who had considered the question, had concluded that, whatever the possible objections to some ritual practitioners, circumcision should no longer belong to Jews alone. Rather, that people's ancient medical discovery would now benefit boys throughout America.

7

"This Little Operation"

Jewish American Physicians and Twentieth-Century Circumcision Advocacy

> One nice thing about circumcision is that when it is done it is finished. The foreskin never grows back.[1]

> The advocacy of neonatal circumcision cannot be considered as a cut and dried issue.[2]

New Claims, New Champions

By 1910, more than a third of all male infants in this country were being circumcised, and the rate was steadily rising. Claims for miraculous cures were no longer popular; now it was prevention, first of one illness, then another, that held center stage. When one claim proved insupportable, there was always another to take its place. The ancient Jewish-Christian controversy now held relatively little importance in American life. And since circumcision was no longer a noteworthy distinction between Christian and Jew, questions about its spiritual meaning or value had also faded away. When an occasional physician mentioned Abraham or Moses, it was to portray them not as men to whom God spoke but as proto-physicians who, realizing that circumcision prevented venereal diseases and other genital afflictions, informed their innocent followers that God had ordered this surgery for all male children. In the imagination of these physicians, biblical heroes were reborn as medical visionaries and distinguished colleagues.

The only lingering question of concern—when there was any—was whether foreskin removal was truly beneficial to health.

That was a question for physicians to answer, of course, but to say that they were undecided would be an understatement. Although occasionally someone mentioned possible damage to sexual physiology and sexual sensation, it is remarkable how little this seems to have mattered. But after all, these physicians (almost entirely male) were concerned with medical diagnosis and treatment, not sexuality. Those participating in the discussion were urologists, pediatricians, and obstetricians, with a sprinkling of general surgeons, general practitioners, and the occasional female nurse or midwife. Urologists generally favored the procedure. Some were inclined to chide pediatrician opponents: you see only children; we see adult men with infections, ulcers, and cancers. Pediatricians were divided; some opposed the practice, others favored it, while many seem not to have thought much about it one way or another. As for obstetricians, they were inclined to accept circumcision as a simple (and moderately profitable) accompaniment to deliveries, often performed almost immediately after birth—at times without even requesting parental consent. Of course, since obstetricians saw neither boys nor men as patients, they had no investment in assessing the long-term effects of foreskin removal on health or sexual functioning. But all kinds of physicians, from experienced surgeons to egregiously unprepared hospital interns, performed circumcisions, seldom with any provision for pain relief other than gauze soaked in sweetened water.[3]

Perhaps the most noteworthy feature of all is the immensity of the medical literature on this supposedly minor procedure—a seemingly limitless outpouring, throughout the century, of professional committee statements, articles, review essays, editorials, and letters to the editor, pro and con; most carefully measured and capably documented, but a few frankly polemical, sometimes expressed with undisguised anger and disdain for opponents.[4] Assessment of the sheer volume of this literature suggests that, despite the putative simplicity of the operation, circumcision was understood to be no ordinary medical procedure—that social and cultural considerations weighed heavily on even the most well-intentioned medical judgment. Among much other evidence for this are the statements issued by such organizations as the American Academy of Pediatrics and the American College of Obstetricians and Gynecologists, trying to walk a fine line between qualified advocacy and qualified rejection. Usually they conclude with a nod to the right of parents to make the final decision—a situation unique in modern medicine, as though physicians were throwing up their hands and saying, you decide, we can't and would rather not try.[5]

A change in medical practice during the first half of the century had profound consequences for attitudes and practices connected with circumcision. Childbirth in hospitals, supervised and controlled by male physicians assisted by nurses, became increasingly the norm, accepted first by middle-class women, then eventually by nearly everyone. While fewer than 5 percent of births took place in hospitals in 1900, by 1920 hospital births in many cities already ranged between 30 and 50 percent or even higher. The rate rose steadily thereafter, so that by 1960 all but a few rural childbirths took place in hospitals.[6] Mothers and their newborn infants were now subjected to depersonalizing procedures and routines extending well beyond the delivery room. Women complained of being treated disrespectfully, even cruelly, by physicians and nurses who saw their expressions of pain and anxiety as nothing more than nuisance behavior, unseemly interference with procedures that had to be completed as efficiently and expeditiously as possible.[7]

With hospitalization came medicalization of newborn infant "management." Rather than resting at its mother's breast after birth, the infant now lay alone in a bassinet, located in a separate nursery, where it might cry or not as it pleased. And before long infant circumcision took its place as another hospital procedure, a routine operation performed very soon, sometimes even immediately, after birth, often by the very obstetrician who had just completed the delivery. Parents, including women in labor, were asked to sign circumcision consent forms at the hospital (if they were consulted at all), and most did so, on the not unreasonable assumption that anything that was medically recommended must be medically advisable. One parental signature sufficed.

Circumcision rates thus rose along with those for hospital births. Whereas in 1910 about 35 percent of male infants were circumcised, by 1940 the rate had risen to about 60 percent.[8] By then circumcision had become such an integral part of the American hospital scene that probably few Americans still thought of it as a particularly Jewish procedure. Increasingly, even Jewish infants were circumcised by physicians in hospitals—a procedure with absolutely no ritual significance.[9] Moreover, during World War II, military and naval physicians often ordered circumcision for men judged to have prominent foreskins that might make them susceptible to venereal disease or other infections. Thus, many men who had remained intact as children now had the oversight corrected—subsequently increasing the number of fathers who would accept circumcision for their own sons. Mohels continued to practice, of course, but at times even they performed in hospitals, in rooms set aside specifically for this purpose (though not always maintained with adequate antisepsis).[10]

The decades between 1880 and 1910 had seen circumcision often touted as *cure* for illnesses that seemed especially tenacious and resistant to treatment: epilepsy, paralysis, and so on. But by 1920 few physicians still subscribed to the reflex neurosis theory or to extravagant claims for cure of orthopedic and neurological ailments. Faith in circumcision as protection against sexually transmitted diseases persisted to a degree, although eventually, with the advent of antibiotics in the 1940s, syphilis and gonorrhea became less frightening and moved off center stage. But the title-holding disease of the twentieth century, unchallenged as the most fearsome, was cancer. So it is hardly surprising that the century's most resolute circumcision advocates discovered evidence that the procedure conferred benefits more wonderful than ever. It was, they believed, the weapon against cancer that everyone longed for: a readily available *preventive* procedure.

Two physicians were largely responsible for introducing and initially publicizing these claims: Abraham L. Wolbarst and Abraham Ravich. They were not prophets in the wilderness, though; many others—urologists and obstetricians especially, but also a few pediatricians and general practitioners—concurred, until by the 1950s most American parents were convinced that acquiescing to circumcision for their infant sons meant protecting them, and even their potential spouses, from the most dreaded of illnesses. In time, as claims for cancer prevention were in their turn called into question, new claims arose, and the terms of the century-old debate shifted yet again. But over the long span between the 1920s and 1980s, the message was unmistakable: of all its ostensible benefits, the most impressive was that circumcision might reduce cancer rates. The most publicized claims applied to cancer of three organs: penis, prostate, and uterine cervix. The medical literature on this topic alone is extensive almost beyond belief—which in itself says something about how controversial the notion has been, and about the determination of physicians on both sides to make their voices heard. But before turning to the literature I must address a fundamental question.

The Role of Jewish American Physicians

Considering what we now know about the role of circumcision in the history of the Jewish-Christian encounter—particularly its centuries-old status as the most reviled and ridiculed of Jewish practices—the question arises: Did Jewish and Gentile physicians react differently to the adoption of circumcision as a routine procedure in American hospitals? Although I must qualify my answer, I think we can recognize significant patterns of difference. I realize, of course, that we enter sensitive territory here (one that others have understandably avoided), but without frank consideration of the historical evidence we miss an important part of our story.

To begin, let me establish a crucial point regarding physician attitudes. On the one hand, most physicians, Gentile and Jewish alike, simply *accepted* circumcision without much consideration one way or another, since by the 1940s it had become as routine as the tonsillectomies that had also become ubiquitous in American medical practice.[11] On the other hand, a few physicians engaged in active debate over the medical value of the procedure. Some were dedicated *advocates* and *promoters* who campaigned passionately for "universal circumcision" and advanced numerous justifications for its continuation. Others, equally determined *critics* and *opponents* of the practice, conducted research and published articles arguing that there were no demonstrable medical reasons for removing normal tissue from hundreds of thousands of infants. So our question is, were twentieth-century Gentile and Jewish physicians significantly more prominent in one cohort or the other?

As for Gentile physicians, many believed routine circumcision to be wise medical practice, and some recommended it earnestly. But only a very few became consistent advocates, while a significant number published articles critical of the practice. In contrast, it seems beyond question that Jewish physicians have been disproportionately prominent as advocates. In particular, they were largely responsible for promoting claims for circumcision as a cancer preventive. Admittedly, we're looking at a mixed picture—noteworthy patterns, not absolute differences. But although all these men surely acted with what they considered to be sound medical judgment, some Jewish physicians may have been influenced also by nonmedical considerations.

Since this topic, perhaps more than any other, lends itself to misunderstanding or misinterpretation, I want to explain the essential argument as clearly as possible. Jewish names—Wolbarst, Ravich, Weiss, Fink, Schoen, and others—will appear disproportionately in the discussion, not because I've chosen arbitrarily to focus on them but because Jewish physicians have been disproportionately prominent in circumcision advocacy. Nevertheless, I do not maintain that these few men were personally responsible for the widespread adoption of circumcision in this country; nor can I or anyone be certain about their motives. The fact that many Gentile physicians initiated and participated actively in the campaign for routine circumcision is enough to refute simplistic explanations or conclusions. Moreover, Jewish physicians have also been among the most outspoken opponents of circumcision.[12] I do propose, however, that the cultural background of many Jewish circumcision advocates predisposed them to view the practice in a positive light, to welcome evidence that the most problematic custom of their people was proving (in their view) to be medically beneficial, and to dismiss arguments to the contrary. The presence of a large and influential population of Jewish physicians in this country, their concentration in leading centers of research and publication, and their remarkably active participation in the century-long debate on circumcision seems too obvious and too significant to be rejected out of hand, or, worse, to be avoided because it might be wrongly interpreted as gratuitous defamation.

To begin, I'll discuss the publications of two physicians—both distinguished New York City urologists, both named Abraham, and both representatives of a late nineteenth to early twentieth-century rhetorical style that is now out of fashion. The two were Abraham L. Wolbarst (1872–1952), the most forthright advocate in the early decades of the century, and Abraham Ravich (1889–1984), whose lavish prose style in his book *Preventing V.D. and Cancer by Circumcision* stands second only to that of the matchless Peter Charles Remondino. Wolbarst and Ravich belonged to the first numerically substantial generation of Jewish American physicians. I find in their publications two definitive characteristics: defensive posture regarding circumcision as a Jewish practice; and, linked with that, far-fetched speculation about health practices of the ancient Hebrews and extravagant praise for the biblical Moses as a brilliant proto-physician. Their articles, it must be emphasized, were professional statements addressed to fellow physicians; they appeared not in popular magazines but in first-rate medical journals. Rhetorical style aside, these men were the first to advance highly influential, and in Wolbarst's case seemingly imperishable, claims for cancer prevention. Much of the later medical literature was generated by their supporters and opponents.

"A Serious Menace": Abraham L. Wolbarst and Penile Cancer

By 1914 the infant circumcision rate in this country had already reached about 40 percent, and of course the overwhelming number of those children were Gentile.[13] That year the nation's most widely read medical periodical, the *Journal of the American Medical Association*, published an article by Abraham Wolbarst entitled "Universal Circumcision as a Sanitary Measure." Wolbarst was a widely published and inventive surgeon, hailed in a British surgical journal as a "great authority on venereal diseases."[14] Here he announced his support for all circumcisions, whether performed by mohels or physicians, and not just for Jewish infants but for every boy in America.

"Of late," he began, "there has been noticeable a decided tendency on the part of some medical men, mostly pediatricians, to condemn the ancient practice of ritual circumcision." The particular opponent he had in mind was L. Emmett Holt, an influential Columbia University pediatrician, who had just published an article on transmission of tuberculosis by infected mohels practicing *metsitsah*.[15] The real problem, Wolbarst insisted, was not circumcision but "careless or ignorant operators," of whom there were undoubtedly a few who had to be controlled or eliminated. But considering "the millions of Jewish and non-Jewish children" who had been "subjected to this ritual operation" without complications, it was evident that the problem lay elsewhere. He would "demonstrate that circumcision, far from being the menace that some of these observers would have us believe, is, on the contrary, a most beneficent practice from the sanitary aspect, and that it should be encouraged in every possible case, whether it be done as a ritual act or as a purely sanitary measure."[16]

Note how the phrasing conflated *religious rite* with *medical practice*. Not only Jewish but Gentile children had undergone the "ritual operation," and "ritual act" was now hardly distinguishable from "sanitary measure."

Wolbarst didn't defend mohels who spread infection; to the contrary, he agreed that some should not be permitted to practice. However, mohels themselves, "anxious to avoid any untoward accidents in the performance of this little operation," were ready to cooperate in "weeding out" diseased or ignorant members of their profession. Moreover, their "skill and dexterity" surpassed that of surgeons. So let's eliminate incompetent operators, he urged, but not attack circumcision.[17]

Regarding *metsitsah* ("merely a relic of ancient times"), Wolbarst had been assured by an experienced rabbi-mohel that this practice was obsolete, and that mohels now used cotton and gauze saturated in antiseptic solutions to control bleeding. His foremost purpose, though, was not to discuss outdated practices but to alert every physician to the medical value of the Jewish custom: "Not only am I heartily opposed to any curtailment of the practice of ritual circumcision, but I also advocate its universal employment in all male children, whether Jewish or Gentile, from a purely sanitary and health-giving point of view." Having seen for himself the benefits of circumcision as a preventive of venereal disease, he had concluded that "universal circumcision" was "an absolute necessity, when we consider the general welfare of the race."[18]

Wolbarst continued with a point-by-point exegesis of seven reasons for adoption of universal circumcision: "a great aid to cleanliness," prophylaxis against a variety of venereal diseases, "diminished tendency to masturbation," and so on. Regarding venereal diseases, he cited sixteen physicians (most with non-Jewish names) who had responded to a questionnaire on the subject, all but one essentially in agreement that circumcision was an effective preventive measure. A Cincinnati physician wrote that, although he had noted nearly equal numbers of venereal infections among circumcised and intact patients, this was because it seemed that "the circumcised temperamentally are more given to lascivious vice and expose themselves to a greater degree than the uncircumcised." (He offered no opinion as to why this might be so.)[19] A New York physician thought that chancroid (genital ulcer) was less frequent among "Judaeus Apella" (literally, "Skinless Jew"). Another reported that in "the great number of amputations of the penis" that he had performed for "epithelioma of the glans," all but one of the patients had "long foreskins."[20] Only one physician, M. W. Ware (identified by Wolbarst as "my one-time preceptor"), dissented, declaring that "circumcision is absolutely no safeguard against any of the venereal diseases that human flesh is heir to," and that it was nothing better than "a fetish surviving from ancient times." To this Wolbarst replied that, notwithstanding the "deference" due his former teacher, closing one's eyes "to the utility of this little operation because it is a relic of ancient times brings to mind the similarly ancient custom of biting one's tongue to spite the nose." Since "the vast preponderance of modern scientific opinion" now strongly favored circumcision, objection need be raised only against those who failed to perform it properly.[21] He concluded with a final paean and a pointed but ambiguously phrased reproof of fellow Jews who rejected the procedure:

> Circumcision must be considered one of the most beneficent mea-
> sures ever devised for sanitary purposes in human beings, and it is to
> be wondered at that there should exist, at this late day, physicians

who stand ready to condemn the practice. It is indeed a curious fact
that many, if not most, of those who oppose ritual circumcision are
themselves Jews, and I can recall a conversation with an eminent
physician, the son of a famous American rabbi, who boasted that he
would not permit his sons to be circumcised. It seems passing
strange that men should go so far in their worship of the unattainable
as to forget that "all that glitters is not gold," even though it be such a
worthy appendage as a prepuce. They also seem to forget that the
Tenth Commandment specifically forbids us to covet that which our
neighbor possesses, and in this general prohibition, we may surely
include the prepuce.

Therefore, it was "the moral duty of every physician to encourage circumcision in the young," performed either "as a religious rite or as a purely sanitary
measure."[22] Whether or not Wolbarst was being facetious in designating the
prepuce "a worthy appendage," his reference to coveting what others possess
suggests that, all his arguments notwithstanding, he realized that the prepuce
might not be entirely useless after all.

Once again he virtually fused "religious rite" and "sanitary measure." By
characterizing infant circumcision as the physician's "moral duty," Wolbarst
added his influential voice to the chorus of physicians advocating the procedure as a cornerstone of public health policy. Jewish and Christian theological
dogma had receded into the background; the key themes now were sanitation
and prophylaxis.

The 1914 paper was only the beginning of Wolbarst's contribution to the
circumcision discourse. After a twelve-year silence he returned to the subject
in 1926 with two articles, one a repeat of his earlier arguments, the other
breaking new ground. The first, entitled simply "Circumcision in Infancy:
A Prophylactic and Sanitary Measure," appeared in *American Medicine*, a
periodical on topics of general interest to the profession. Here Wolbarst expressed his gratification that, despite lingering resistance by uninformed
physicians—those who portrayed circumcision as "merely a relic of the barbaric past and an unnecessary mutilation of the preputial tissue"—there was
"an increasing tendency among intelligent non-Jews to have their male children circumcised—not on the eighth day, to be sure," but during early
childhood. He cited with approval an English physician's statement that
"Moses was right in making circumcision compulsory" and establishing a law
that "only later developed a religious significance." He hoped that if any
antipathy toward ritual circumcision remained "because of its historical, racial
or religious aspects," it would soon be "relegated to that limbo to which all
racial and religious prejudices belong at this day in human history."[23]

That same year Wolbarst published in the journal *Cancer* a paper that was
to be as influential as his call for "universal" circumcision—but this time with

an entirely new argument. Picking up on an observation that had been noted repeatedly over the years, he announced that infant circumcision not only protected against infectious disease but also prevented one variant of the most dreaded of all diseases. The article was entitled "Is Circumcision a Prophylactic Against Penis Cancer?" and the answer was yes.[24] Penile cancer, an uncommon disease afflicting mainly elderly men, was known to occur only rarely among Jews and Muslims. The reason, said Wolbarst, was obvious: these two groups practiced male infant and child circumcision. Penile cancer could be eliminated "by the simple expedient of circumcising all male infants ... 'a consummation devoutly to be wished for.' "[25] The prepuce, he argued, "is an ideal cancer grower; not only does it provide the soil upon which the cancer may grow, but it also furnishes and retains the essential irritating secretions which accumulate in the preputial cavity and there fructify into the full blossomed cancer."[26] And if it was wise practice to remove troublesome adult foreskins, wasn't it "the greater part of wisdom to remove it in the infant and thereby secure to every male all the sanitary and prophylactic advantages which are conceded to the circumcised?"[27] The time had come to recognize that, although the foreskin might have "served some useful purpose in the early days of man's existence on earth," it was "difficult to offer a single plausible reason for its [continued] existence. . . . Not only is it useless, it is absolutely dangerous and a serious menace to present day man."[28]

By this time cancer had replaced venereal disease and tuberculosis as the most feared of all diseases; so even though penile cancer was uncommon, a claim of this kind was bound to attract notice. On January 1, 1927, an unsigned editorial in the leading British medical journal, the Lancet, acknowledged Wolbarst's "rather impressive line of argument" but commented with appropriate reserve:

> If it could be shown that universal circumcision would remove this cause of death and disability there would be an excellent case for adopting it as a prophylactic measure. . . . If Dr. Wolbarst is right in his conclusion as to the comparative freedom of the circumcised, his argument for universal circumcision is a strong one. . . . It is to be hoped, therefore, that practitioners will place on record any cases in which they have seen the condition in Jews or Gentiles circumcised in infancy.[29]

Wolbarst waited five years before responding. This time his article, published also in the Lancet, bore a more assertive title: "Circumcision and Penile Cancer." To "clear up the doubt" expressed in the editorial, he offered a six-point argument, the gist being that cancer of the penis never occurred in circumcised Jews and rarely in "Muhammedans" circumcised between ages four and nine. Since there was no evidence for "racial immunity" in these groups, the only shared practice explaining the immunity had to be "circumcision in early life."[30] He had done his homework. Assisted by two statisticians, he had sent a questionnaire to all skin and cancer hospitals, all Jewish hospitals, and 1,250 of the nation's largest general hospitals, requesting data on penile cancer in Jews and others over a five-year period. Hospitals replying with usable information reported a total of 837 cases of penile cancer, all but one in Gentiles. The single case of penile cancer in a Jew was recorded for a man who had not been circumcised. Adding information from other physician reports, Wolbarst arrived at a total of 1,103 cases, not one in a circumcised Jewish man. He followed these revelations with equally convincing data on Muslims culled from studies conducted in India and Java, all pointing again to the conclusion that early circumcision prevented penile carcinoma.[31] Prospects for eliminating the disease in America were steadily improving. "It is a gratifying sign," Wolbarst concluded, "that the practice of non-Jewish parents of having their male children circumcised early in life is rapidly growing in the United States, despite the myopic opposition of medical men who persist in regarding the foreskin as something holy and sacred."[32]

Whether consciously or not, this twentieth-century urologist mirrored ancient rabbinic predecessors who had condemned the foreskin and declared its removal a religious mandate. Did that matter to him? Would he have been so intent on circumcision advocacy if foreskin rejection had not been integral to his ethnic heritage? Although I find nothing in his personal record or publications to suggest that he was motivated by religious piety, it can be said that he certainly found intact penises offensive. In an article on circumcision contributed in 1936 to a sexual encyclopedia, he remarked that "no amount of washing and cleansing seems to be able to eradicate the secretions of the foreskin and their penetrating odor." Following a litany of old and new medical claims for circumcision, he closed by recommending the procedure as "a most valuable hygienic measure and a great aid to personal cleanliness."[33]

Prevention of penile cancer was only the first ostensible contribution to the war against cancer on which circumcision advocates would soon focus; but despite the fact that Wolbarst's conclusions have been repeatedly challenged, his claim remains alive and well to this day. Indeed, the medical literature on this single feature of the circumcision controversy is probably more extensive, and more contentious, than any other. The first major challenge to the reigning orthodoxy on this subject came only decades later, in 1964, when Charles Weiss, a specialist in microbiology, tropical medicine, and public health, reviewed the literature and concluded that there was no convincing evidence that foreskin secretions were carcinogenic or that infant circumcision protected men against penile cancer.[34]

But neither Weiss's article nor any other was enough to stem the tide of enthusiasm, and today the debate goes on. Wolbarst's name is still occasionally in the medical news, and many physicians remain convinced that among the justifications for routine circumcision is its value as a preventive against penile carcinoma. Attributing the disease to lack of circumcision is probably an instance of spurious correlation—that is, pointing to a variable of secondary significance as the primary cause. More recent studies have cited other variables closely connected with risk for penile cancer: poverty, poor personal hygiene, sexual promiscuity, genital infections, smoking, and excessive alcohol drinking.[35] Circumcision correlates with social class: infants from higher-income families are more likely than others to be circumcised; and since most circumcisions in the earlier decades of the century took place in private hospitals, American men fitting the high-risk profile were probably disproportionately intact. (That is, they were born at home or in public hospitals, where they were less likely to be circumcised.) Moreover, penile cancer rates in European countries, where routine circumcision is unknown, are very similar to our own. Finally, a telling argument often advanced by opponents: How, they ask, can the procedure be justified in cost–benefit terms? Should physicians circumcise hundreds of thousands of infants in order to prevent occurrence of a few cases of penile cancer (often curable) in adult men?[36]

Despite all the opposing arguments, however, the most determined advocates continue to this day to cite prevention of penile cancer among the justifications for routine circumcision. Most resolute in recent years has been Edgar J. Schoen (b. 1925), a California pediatrician about whom I'll have more to say shortly. In 1990 he published one of his numerous articles, in the prestigious *New England Journal of Medicine*, reviewing the history of the "status" of circumcision and reminding physicians of its many benefits. Schoen duly cited Wolbarst's 1932 paper, by then nearly sixty years old. Since 1947, he claimed, there had been "six major studies" in the United States involving more than 1,600 patients with penile carcinoma, none of whom had been circumcised in infancy.[37]

A few years later, Paul M. Fleiss, a pediatrician, and the medical historian Frederick M. Hodges sent a letter to the *British Medical Journal* responding to a recently published article (not by Schoen) that had "mistakenly repeat[ed] the myth that neonatal circumcision renders the subject immune to penile cancer." Again, the principal reference was Wolbarst's 1932 paper. That author, said Fleiss and Hodges, had "invented this myth and was directly responsible for its proliferation." He had based his claims "on unverifiable anecdotes, ethnocentric stereotypes, a faulty understanding of human anatomy and physiology, a misunderstanding of the distinction between association and cause, and an unbridled missionary zeal." They pointed out that sophisticated epidemiological studies had shown the rate of penile cancer in North America to be very low, and that in fact penile cancers had been diagnosed repeatedly in neonatally circumcised men in this country.[38] Schoen responded promptly, with unconcealed annoyance, saying that he was "amazed" that anyone could still maintain that "no link exists between circumcision and penile cancer." His reading of the "overwhelming evidence" yielded "a ratio of 5000:1 for the incidence of penile cancer in uncircumcised to circumcised men." Fleiss and Hodges replied in turn with their own reading of the same evidence, commenting that "it would be equally valid to claim that abstinence from pork prevents penile cancer." A more promising preventive, they thought, would be a campaign against smoking.[39]

No argument seems sufficient, though, to place this controversy at rest. In 1999 a "Task Force on Circumcision" of the American Academy of Pediatrics issued a statement concluding that the procedure was not essential to a child's "current well-being." The next year Schoen and two other prominent advocates published a rebuttal arguing, among much else, for the "overwhelming protection of circumcision against penile cancer" (though, since penile cancer occurs predominantly in elderly men, this is hardly a matter involving any child's current well-being).[40] And as recently as July 2001, the Centers for Disease Control and Prevention issued a report on circumcision declaring, among other claims, that the procedure reduces the incidence of penile cancer.[41] Nearly eighty years after his original publication, Abraham Wolbarst's singular contribution to the circumcision debate lives on.

"A Second Epochal Opportunity": Abraham Ravich's Viral Theory of Carcinoma

Wolbarst's successor in the campaign against the foreskin was another New York urologist, Abraham Ravich. In 1941 Ravich discovered that cancer of the prostate was far more common among his uncircumcised Gentile patients than among Jewish men. Research into the medical literature soon revealed that his findings could be correlated with those of two predecessors to yield a striking conclusion. First, of course, there were Abraham Wolbarst's publications on penile cancer. Second, a gynecologist named Hiram M. Vineberg had reported in 1906 that his Jewish patients exhibited a remarkably low incidence of cancer of the cervix. Vineberg had been uncertain what to make of this information; he thought it might have something to do with religious regulations requiring abstinence from intercourse during and after menstruation and after childbirth.[42] But for Ravich everything came together in a single stunning insight: Cancers of the genital organs might be caused by a virus lurking in the smegma (normal foreskin secretions) of intact men.[43]

His first publication, appearing in the *Journal of Urology* in 1942, announced at the start that this was no run-of-the-mill medical report. "Mystery still shrouds the cause of most human cancers," he began, but an "accumulation of apparently unrelated observations" might "hasten the day when this greatest of all scourges will be mastered. Our greatest hope in overcoming cancer is to eradicate the etiological factors that tend to produce it." Then the revelation: Although it was well known that cancer of the penis was rare among Jews and Muslims, among his predominantly Jewish patients he had encountered remarkably few cases of cancer of the prostate. Aware that the generally reported incidence of cancer in patients with obstructive prostatic disease was 20 percent, Ravich had long been "perplexed" by the gap between this figure and his own experience. Between 1930 and the time of writing he had treated 768 Jewish and 75 Gentile men for prostatic obstruction. Among the Jewish patients only 13 suffered from cancer, while 755 had the more common benign prostatic hypertrophy. But of his 75 Gentile patients, 15 proved to have a malignant cancer. The difference—20 percent of the Gentile men versus 1.7 percent of the Jewish—was obviously far beyond chance. Since Jews and Gentiles were alike "morphologically," it seemed logical to conclude that circumcision protected Jewish men against cancer of the prostate.

As for why this might be so, Ravich proposed a tentative explanation: "It is entirely conceivable that the process may be that of some parasitic, virus or other carcinogenetic agent that infests or involves the urethra and migrates along its lumen into the prostate in more or less the same manner in which gonorrhoeal prostatitis so often complicates gonorrhoeal urethritis." Further research should be the next step. Moreover, since Jewish women rarely suffered from cancer of the cervix, it seemed "logical to suppose" that both cancers "might be transmitted by some parasitic or other carcinogenetic factor by direct contact and that the best prophylactic measure would be a more universal practice of circumcising male infants."[44] Ravich's theory was approvingly reported in the science section of a June 1943 issue of Newsweek, where it was noted that his work was "receiving widespread attention" because it might "shed light, indirectly, on the cause of all cancer."[45]

Expectably enough, this revolutionary idea, completely at odds with mainstream medical thought, was "bitterly opposed," Ravich reported later, by a number of cancer researchers, "steeped in the old idea that cancer was caused by some mysterious inborn internal factors." Opposition came also from "uninformed prejudiced physicians, laymen and editors" who had been "misled on religious and emotional grounds."[46] But he pressed on, certain that he had achieved a major breakthrough on the medical challenge of the century. He coauthored another paper with his son (a psychiatrist), who presented it at an international cancer congress in Paris in 1950; this was published the following year in a New York medical journal. Ravich had now gone all out with a claim that circumcision prevented cancer of the prostate, penis, and cervix. It was clear that there was a much lower incidence of cervical cancer among women in "ethnic groups" practicing male circumcision "as a religious ritual."[47] A research team had discovered that smegma (from horses) injected subcutaneously could produce cancer in mice.[48] And his own research, as well as that of others, had demonstrated conclusively that cancer of the prostate was relatively uncommon (although not absent) in Jewish men. It therefore appeared "incumbent upon public health agencies, obstetricians, pediatricians, and all other physicians concerned with the problem to insist upon the simple and harmless surgical procedure of circumcision as a routine measure in all male infants."[49] Considering that Ravich, like Wolbarst, enjoyed a well-justified reputation as a capable urologist, it is easy to understand why physicians who read this article would have found it persuasive.[50]

In 1973, aged eighty-four and retired in Miami, Ravich published a volume combining autobiography and medical information with doses of polemic. Entitled *Preventing V. D. and Cancer by Circumcision*, the book not only repeated the old arguments but also passionately attacked his opponents. Recently (during the 1960s and early 1970s), Ravich reported, the most zealous critics, alarmed by the growing realization that early circumcision protects against cancer, were doing their best to discredit foreskin removal with alarmist claims that it was worthless and even harmful. Brooding over the growing number of skeptics, he reflected on his own setbacks, particularly at the hands of "a small group of misguided pediatricians with a flair for writing on controversial subjects." It was they, he suspected, who were behind "the refusal during 1966, by the two leading Pediatric journals" to publish papers submitted "for the purpose of clarifying the situation for these specialists." As for what might be motivating this "tenacious desire to retain the foreskin," Ravich thought it might be attributable to "false pride, distorted phallic veneration, anti-semitism, ignorance of the real reason for the original ban against circumcision or surrender to misleading propaganda."[51]

With the hyperbole of an elderly man intent on securing his place in medical history, Ravich added a new twist to century-old rhetoric, comparing his own achievements with those of the biblical Moses. The "paramount purpose" of Jewish circumcision, he insisted, had always been "hygienic"; the ritual aspect was simply a way of ensuring that it would be accepted and maintained.[52] Although many non-Jews still believed that circumcision was a "relic of some ancient barbaric rite, grafted into the Jewish religion by some accident and not as a carefully thought out hygienic measure of prevention by the Jewish patriarchs long ago," the fact was that Moses was a "brilliant sanitarian" who, having recognized the connection between foreskins and infections, stressed "cleanliness, hygiene and prophylaxis." As a young man he had "pored over the medical papyrii" in the royal palace, and from this had "fashioned the Mosaic Code," while the Pharaoh had "caroused and had fallen prey to religious superstitions, witchcraft and magic." Moses' "keen insight into medicine, almost modern in scope," his challenges to the learned men of his time, and his "attention to the sick" had "earned him the titles of Great Master and Divine Healer." Indeed, the entire medical profession was "indebted for its advancement to the Hebrew religion, to a greater extent than is generally believed"; for while "the Church" retained its "spiritual dominion and let science slumber in darkness," Jewish physicians, "led by the teachings of [their] religion alone," conducted "the study of medicine in a scientific manner."[53]

In fact, both Abraham and Moses had paved the way. Realizing that his "Hebrew followers" were being decimated by "widespread venereal infections," Abraham decreed that infant circumcision was "God's Will." Moses, an equally perceptive proto-physician, observed during the "forty-year flight from Egypt" that "his uncircumcised Israelite followers frequently suffered severe illnesses and death after sexual orgies with the native women they encountered on their trek through the Sinai Desert.... For this reason, toward the end of their trek he re-instituted compulsory circumcision among his followers and progeny, again as an Act of God, to assure compliance."

Centuries later, in his eagerness to win converts, Paul "discontinued the rite," and his "unauthorized willful act has been blindly followed by most Christians ever since at a frightful and needless loss of life in the millions." But the time had come for decisive rethinking, based on Ravich's own observations in Brooklyn. In fact, his "opportunity for comparative study" had been "somewhat similar to that confronting Moses about 3600 years ago"— and their conclusions were essentially identical.[54]

At this distance it is impossible to know whether Ravich may have been motivated from the beginning by desire to demonstrate the medical value of Jewish circumcision. There are no explicit claims of this sort in his medical publications, and I see no evidence that he was anything other than sincere in his belief that the cause of many forms of cancer was a virus lurking beneath the foreskins of intact males. The theory of a viral origin for some carcinomas has received tentative support, in fact, but not Ravich's prediction that a carcinogenic virus would be discovered in foreskin secretions.[55]

Cancer of the penis is relatively uncommon and usually curable; yet circumcision advocates still cite Abraham Wolbarst's claims. In contrast, although prostatic cancer is far more prevalent and often fatal, nearly all physicians have dismissed the theories of Abraham Ravich.[56] A prominent pediatric urologist, George W. Kaplan, and a colleague conducted a thorough study of records in a Chicago hospital between 1958 and 1964, comparing Jewish and Gentile patients (many of the latter also circumcised) with either benign prostatic enlargement or prostatic cancer. Their conclusion: "There did not seem to be a difference in the incidence of carcinoma of the prostate between circumcised and noncircumcised Gentiles. This tends to refute the contention that circumcision is responsible for the differing incidence in Jews and Gentiles." In a comprehensive "overview" of the circumcision controversy published eleven years later (in 1977), Kaplan stood by the conclusions of his earlier study.[57] His view represents the consensus to this day.

A "Comforting Conclusion": Circumcision and Cervical Carcinoma

No claims for the virtues of circumcision have generated as much public interest as those regarding cancer of the uterine cervix. The story begins once again with comparison of Jewish and Gentile patients. The first physician to call attention to the rarity of cervical carcinoma among Jewish women was the man whose article had attracted Ravich's notice: Hiram N. Vineberg, a gynecologist with a large dispensary practice among Jewish immigrants at Mount Sinai Hospital in New York. In 1906, Vineberg reported that among some 18,500 Jewish patients seen over a period of fourteen years, he had found only nine cases of cancer of the cervix. What especially interested this perceptive physician was that nearly all his patients exhibited the social and economic characteristics then thought to be associated with the disease: poor, prolific, overworked, and malnourished.[58] Why the very low incidence of cervical carcinoma in a population expected to display the opposite? Vineberg thought it might be attributable to "their marital relations," which were "restricted by the Mosaic and Talmudic codes" prohibiting intercourse during and after menstruation, and for a time after childbirth—regulations preventing "the irritation caused by the sexual act at unfavorable times."[59] Perhaps because his attention focused on women patients, he did not think of circumcision.[60]

In 1954, a medical research team from leading institutions in the United States and India published a paper alerting physicians to a possible association between cervical cancer and uncircumcised male partners. The research was directed by Ernst L. Wynder, a physician who came to the United States as a refugee from Nazi Germany in the 1930s and became prominent as a cancer researcher. His paper, cautiously worded and conservatively titled, appeared in the *American Journal of Obstetrics and Gynecology*, but it had already attracted notice when initially presented at a meeting of the New York Obstetrical Society in November of the preceding year. Prompted by reports that comparative studies of cervical cancer in the United States, India, and Fiji had revealed much lower incidence of the disease among Jewish and Muslim women, Wynder and his associates evaluated the information and conducted interviews of additional patients.[61] They uncovered a number of characteristics of cervical cancer patients that seemed to be either causative of the disease or at least contributory. As a group these patients were more likely to have begun intercourse earlier than average, to have married earlier, to have been married more than once, and to come from low-income families. Their male partners were significantly more likely to have poor penile hygiene and to be uncircumcised. The researchers noted, however, that cervical cancer had also been diagnosed "in women exposed only to circumcised males and in virgins." They concluded, therefore, that there had to be causative elements other than "those involving coitus and lack of circumcision."[62] In short, their findings, though suggestive, were far from conclusive.

Wynder's style of presentation was so prudent that he cannot really be called an *advocate* for circumcision. A disciplined researcher who reported his findings with all possible qualifications, he can't be held accountable for what others made of his research. But although his article did not appear until October 1954, his research had already been reported—actually misreported—in an April 1954 issue of *Time* magazine. As the title, "Circumcision and Cancer," foretold, the column focused so heavily on circumcision that only the most careful and critical reader would have grasped the actual conclusions of the research. The opening sentence set the stage: "The fact that 85 percent of the boy babies born in U.S. private hospitals nowadays are circumcised, regardless of the parents' religious beliefs, may be an important factor in reducing cancer of the uterine cervix (neck of the womb) in years to come." Wynder had reached this "comforting conclusion," the article continued, after discovering "striking differences" between married Jewish and non-Jewish women. Although the article mentioned early intercourse and number of marriages, two key findings—that cervical cancer occurred most often in low-income patients whose husbands or sexual partners had poor personal hygiene—were ignored in the simplistic conclusion: "circumcision may be a big help in preventing both [penile and cervical cancer], presumably because it facilitates personal cleanliness."[63]

Wynder published another article in 1960, reevaluating his earlier conclusions. Recent studies from Israel and elsewhere, he noted, claimed that male circumcision alone explained the low incidence of cervical cancer in Jewish and Muslim women. However, statistical studies had yielded equivocal results. Investigators were beginning to realize that statements by wives—and even by men themselves—about circumcision status were often incorrect. Wynder had conducted a study revealing that taking account of inaccurate reporting reduced a supposed tenfold relative risk for wives of uncircumcised men to about twofold. He and his colleagues acknowledged that they could not prove conclusively that circumcision had any effect on incidence of cervical cancer. Nonetheless, they advocated newborn circumcision, particularly for "low income groups," as the best way to promote "good personal hygiene."[64]

By that time, however, other researchers had conducted a reliable study that reached different conclusions. Edward G. Jones and colleagues examined the possible causative role of a number of physical and behavioral variables, most of which—including "circumcision of marital and other partners"—proved to be statistically insignificant. They concluded instead that adverse socioeconomic conditions, "domestic and marital instability," chronic "psychophysical stress," early sexual maturation, and early intercourse and pregnancy all occurred significantly more often in women "destined to develop uterine cervical carcinoma" than in other comparable women.[65]

Although most physicians seem to have let both the Jones report and Wynder's second article fall into limbo, the *Time* article had far more enduring influence with the public. Many parents still believe that circumcising an infant son may protect his future wife from cervical cancer. Moreover, although the most committed circumcision advocates no longer afford a prominent place to the claim, they often include at least some mention of it, and an occasional physician still declares this to be a prime justification for continuing the procedure.[66]

The search for cancer causes and cures dominated American medical research for nearly the entire twentieth century. How does the circumcision controversy appear when viewed in wider historical context? Was circumcision a major element in the story, or does my attention here exaggerate its prominence? Judging from historical studies of cancer research, the answer must be that the debate was a minor affair. Two histories, by Robert N. Proctor and James T. Patterson, barely mention the subject.[67] There is no index entry for circumcision in Patterson's book, and the two entries in Proctor's refer only to incidental mentions. Perhaps most tellingly, although both authors cite *other* research by Wynder on tobacco and lung cancer, they say nothing about his publications on cervical cancer; and neither Wolbarst nor Ravich receives so much as a sentence.

"An Enduring and Unexpected Success": Gomco and Mogen Clamps

Some mohels pride themselves on their ability to perform rapid circumcisions, using a shield to protect the glans, cutting tissue with a scalpel, and tearing away the remainder with index fingers and sharpened thumbnails. But nearly all physicians, as well as many mohels, use clamps, devices designed to reduce or eliminate hemorrhage by crushing tissue before removal. The two most frequently employed, called the Gomco and Mogen clamps, both apply immense pressure to the extended foreskin, producing necrotic tissue that can then be excised without significant bleeding. Although the procedure takes longer than the traditional method—anywhere from about eight to twenty minutes or more for the Gomco, less for the Mogen—clamps are favored because they minimize the possibility of hemorrhage, the most immediate danger.

Circumcision clamps were already in use by the late nineteenth century; but none achieved widespread popularity until 1934, when a Buffalo inventor of medical instruments, Aaron Goldstein (1899–1945), developed a clamp in collaboration with Hiram S. Yellen, an obstetrician and gynecologist. Goldstein was a successful inventor specializing in medical instruments; it was probably Yellen who suggested that he design a more efficient circumcision clamp.[68] In 1935, Yellen reported that he had performed more than five hundred circumcisions with Goldstein's new clamp. He praised it as an "efficient instrument" that could be employed by a single operator: "The technic [sic] is quite simple, and the time required is less than that by any other method."[69] Goldstein marketed the device under the name Gomco (Goldstein Manufacturing Company). It continues to be among the most widely employed circumcision instruments.[70]

In a laudatory article published in a urology journal in May 2002, Julian Wan, a pediatric urologist, explained the clamp's mechanical virtues "considered from an engineering standpoint":

> The clamp is an amalgamation of two classic simple machines: the lever and the inclined plane. The arm is a lever with the fulcrum placed to yield a two-to-one mechanical advantage. The screw nut is a modified inclined plane. Its mechanical advantage is calculated as $2 \times \pi \times$ the radius of the nut divided by the distance between the threads. There are 32 threads per inch on the screw nut, and it has a radius of 0.5 in. This yields a further mechanical advantage of 32π or roughly 100-fold. When these mechanical advantages are combined, they yield a 200-fold (2×100) increase in force. The average adult can exert 40 to 100 lb. of force turning the dominant wrist in a pronation-supination action to drive the screw nut. The GOMCO clamp converts this force into 8000 to 20,000 lb. of hemostatic force against the prepuce.[71]

Despite the claims of Yellen and his successors that the clamp is safe and efficient, not everyone has agreed. A physician named Isaac B. Lefkovits, who had apparently used the clamp in performing ritual circumcisions, published a pamphlet in 1953, in Hebrew with English translation, condemning it for causing "dreadful pain and extreme suffering similar to that caused by the crushing of a finger caught in a door," and possible brain damage caused by sharp rise in blood pressure and congestion of vessels in the brain.[72] Much more recently, in August 2000, David W. Feigal, Jr., director of the Center for Devices and Radiological Health of the Food and Drug Administration, issued an internet warning about potential for injury with use of Gomco and Mogen circumcision clamps. Feigal reported that in the period July 1996–January 2000, the Center had received 105 reports (an average of two or three each month) of injuries during use of the clamps; he did not specify how many injuries were reported for each. Another recent report, by four pediatric surgeons in Boston, described two cases of "degloving injuries to both the prepuce and penile shaft from a Gomco clamp."[73]

Wan, who practices at Children's Hospital of Buffalo, views the clamp more positively. It has proved to be "an enduring and unexpected success," he says, still selling well after nearly seventy years:

> The simplicity in appearance and use of the Gomco clamp belies its clever design and its history. Things that are encountered routinely and function unobtrusively tend to be unappreciated because of quiet familiarity. The products of human imagination do not generate spontaneously but grow from, and reflect the character, thoughts, experiences, and dreams of, their creators.[74]

The *Mogen* (Hebrew for "shield") clamp was devised in 1954 by a Brooklyn rabbi-mohel, Harry Bronstein. The clamp is a hinged shield with a bar-and-cam lever at the open end; it opens only to a width of three centimeters, which minimizes the danger of trapping a small section of glans. The operator first separates the prepuce from the mucosal tissue joining it to the glans (using hemostats, one for traction, another for separation). Then the prepuce is pulled forward and outward, and the clamp is applied to the foreskin just above the tip of the glans at a forty-five-degree slant (to protect the exquisitely sensitive frenulum on the underside of the penis). The jaws are shut and left in place for one or two minutes in infants, longer in older males. After removing the clamp, the operator excises the foreskin tissue along the crush line and presses the remaining tissue back over the base of the glans. The complete procedure is said to require about three to twelve minutes; mohels, many of whom favor the Mogen, usually claim to need the shorter times.[75] Typical of general opinion was a 1994 article by five Jewish physicians, reporting on 319 circumcisions performed with this clamp at a hospital in Mexico City. They concluded that circumcision with the Mogen "is an easy, quick, and safe procedure to learn."[76]

Here again, though, there are critics. The FDA report on injury, cited above, said that this clamp "may allow too much tissue to be drawn through the opening of the device, thus facilitating the removal of an excessive amount of foreskin and in some cases, a portion of the glans penis." The report by the Boston pediatric surgeons described three cases of injuries to the glans with use of the Mogen.[77] But although using circumcision clamps obviously involves risk of serious damage to the glans, the Gomco and Mogen clamps are favored because they have proved to be the best in their class—and they do help prevent hemorrhage.

"Chronic Remunerative Balanitis": Opposing Voices

By the 1960s and 1970s, with the circumcision rate at about 80 percent and still climbing, most physicians, as well as parents—especially white middle-class parents—took the procedure for granted. Nevertheless, there were physicians who maintained that circumcision was medically worthless. It seems certain that these authors saw Jews (including Jewish physicians) as the most dedicated supporters of circumcision. Typically they tried to neutralize anticipated Jewish reaction in advance, by focusing on hospital circumcision and referring only obliquely to ritual circumcision as a separate matter not their concern. Their choice of words is instructive.

Among the most provocative publications was a 1965 piece entitled "The Rape of the Phallus," which appeared in the *Journal of the American Medical Association*. The author, William K. C. Morgan, a British-born Baltimore pulmonary physician, obviously intended to stir the waters. Why circumcision? he asked. "One might as well attempt to explain the rites of voodoo!"[78] The only real indication, he continued, "seldom mentioned in the surgical textbooks," was "chronic remunerative balanitis" (i.e., diagnosis of penile inflammation as justification for financially profitable circumcision).[79] Why then did parents accept circumcision with such "equanimity and enthusiasm?" Partly because of pressure from physicians, but also because "the procedure has become customary—one has to lop it off along with the Joneses." He concluded with a remark suggesting who he felt were his most likely critics:

> This commentary must not be construed as a crusade against cir-
> cumcision. The teaching of the Koran and Bible, the mistaken beliefs
> of many of the medical profession, the intuition of woman, and,
> above all, folklore, tradition, and health-insurance agencies support
> this ritual. Nevertheless, let us remember that 98 times out of 100
> there is no valid indication for this mutilation other than religion.

Ninety-eight times out of one hundred. It hardly needs remarking that, even though he first named the Koran (which does not mention circumcision), the religion Morgan had in mind was Judaism, and that the two "validly" circumcised infants were those born to Jewish parents.[80]

The article drew expectable criticism, and Morgan reported that he had received "abusive, scurrilous, and anonymous letters": "It has even been suggested that I should be hauled before the House Un-American Activities Committee." He defended his article as having been "intended and, in the main, received as satire—a form of writing which is meant to appeal to reason rather than emotions."[81]

In a widely noted paper entitled "Whither the Foreskin?" published in 1970 in the *Journal of the American Medical Association*, E. Noel Preston, a pediatrician, remarked that it was "the duty of the medical profession to lead, rather than follow a community's standard of health care." But when it came to circumcision, physicians had become followers. Routine circumcision was nothing better than a worthless fad, destined to join such "antiquated curiosities" as tonsillectomy and radiation of the thymus gland in "medicine's attic." Like Morgan, however, Preston shied away from condemnation of ritual circumcision. "Obviously," he added, "circumcision performed on the basis of religious beliefs is beyond the scope of this discussion."[82]

In response to the article, a Dr. C. J. Falliers, apparently originally from Britain or Europe, wrote that in the years since his arrival in the United States he "continued to be shocked at the arbitrariness of the thoughtless mutilation of so many boys." He advanced an argument that had (and has) received remarkably little attention from physicians:

> The *sensory* pleasure induced by tactile stimulation of the foreskin is
> almost totally lost after its surgical removal. . . . Consequently, the

fundamental biological sexual act becomes, for the circumcised male, simply a satisfaction of an urge and not the refined sensory experience that it was meant to be.

Writing for the other side, a California physician, Lawrence D. Freedman, cited the usual arguments on smegma and cancer, and commented (without ironic intent) that "wise physicians" who performed routine circumcisions had "saved innumerable young men countless hours of having to perform the constant task of retracting their foreskins and extracting their smegma. Perhaps some of these young men have used this time in more profitable and pleasurable pursuits."[83]

Later, Preston repeated his disclaimer on ritual circumcision, obviously addressing Jewish readers: "I continue to respect religious convictions, and would not presume to interfere with a religious ceremony." In a letter published the next year he remarked that some correspondents had misinterpreted his article "as being anti-Semitic, anti-Communist, or even pro-Communist, and still others have made other various miscellaneous derogatory responses."[84] It appears that in the minds of at least some physicians, opposition to infant circumcision implied religious intolerance and unacceptable political sentiments.

Preston's rhetorical strategy was characteristic for opponents of circumcision: refer to the ritual version only to exempt it from consideration. But Gentile physicians were not the sole opponents. In 1978, Sydney S. Gellis, a prominent Boston pediatrician, delivered a brief but passionately argued call for an end to circumcision. Commenting on two recent reports on complications following circumcision, Gellis dismissed the penile cancer argument and all medical justifications as spurious. He acknowledged (reluctantly, it seems) that listing the hazards would not deter parents who insisted on circumcision "for religious reasons," but for all others, physicians needed to be "much more vociferous" in discouraging the practice.[85]

Targeting the "Cesspool": Defending Circumcision at Century's End

"Unhindered by the Scientific Necessity of Proof"

Calls for an end to circumcision met with resistance, of course; and here again Jewish physicians were the most prominent defenders. Although these men (and, as before, they were all men) limited themselves for the most part to orthodox medical arguments, one embellished his claims with brazen chauvinism, employing a prose style worthy of Abraham Ravich. Gerald N. Weiss (not to be confused with Charles Weiss), a Louisiana surgeon, championed circumcision as a Jewish gift to the medical profession, publishing not only articles addressed to other physicians but also a booklet for parents.[86] In an early publication, a 1968 article entitled "The Jews Contribution to Medicine" (sic), which appeared in a popular magazine for physicians called *Medical Times*, Weiss, like his predecessors, transformed Moses into a public health physician, adding some fresh imaginative touches:

> The noble idea of God the Healer was the touchstone of Jewish medicine. The holier the man, the healthier was he. Health was linked closely to religious practice, and nowhere is this fact better demonstrated than in the regulations laid down by Moses. This reverent, tough, awesome field commander led 600,000 Jewish men, their wives and children through a wilderness for four decades.... In the Torah, we meet the first great proponent of prophylaxis or the prevention of disease. Moses has been titled the "first public health officer" by men of medicine.... Administering the sanitary regulations of the community were an impressive array of officials or "health wardens."... There was a health chief for each thousand Israelites and under him were ten lieutenants—"able men, reliable men who could not be bribed," "who would practice their profession with the greatest skill and precision." The Jews were also among the first to recognize the value of preventive medicine in individual illness.[87]

Much of what follows is an account of the accomplishments of Jewish physicians, their "medical acumen" based on "the teachings of the Scriptures as the bedrock, and the acceptance of the ultimate destiny resting in an all-wise and all-knowing God who both guides the physician and determines the span of the sufferer."[88] Perhaps the most remarkable feature of this first article is that it includes no mention whatever of circumcision.

Eventually, though, Weiss compensated abundantly for the oversight. In 1985, by which time he was in his sixties, he entered the circumcision controversy for the first time, with an article revealing limited familiarity with the subject: Too many physicians, he declared, overlooked the "wisdom" of the "prophylactic surgery" practiced by the ancient Egyptians and Hebrews; instead, they would "rather risk disease and later attempt to correct it, at great expense and often unsuccessfully." As Weiss saw the matter, misguided "economic bias" regarding the initial cost of the procedure outweighed recognition of its prophylactic value and the long-term savings that resulted. He repeated the usual claims and urged adoption of routine circumcision "even when it is not a medical imperative."[89]

That was the entry of an amateur contestant into a field of experienced gladiators. But in 1994 he reappeared with a better-documented article in the journal *Clinical Pediatrics*, coauthored with Elaine Weiss, a retired nurse (presumably his wife). Here he began to display his prowess in biblical interpretation, although with some difficulty in keeping to the subject. "The eternal debate" on circumcision, the authors began, "has not waned in contemporary America. Loud, emotionally charged voices have come with the communications explosion to confuse physicians, parents, and the thinking male as to the merits and demerits of the procedure.... With computer technology allowing access to centuries of available information, it can be shown that the world's most common operation represents the essence of prophylactic surgery."[90] Citing such predecessors as Remondino and Ravich, as well as a popular book by a contemporary ally, Aaron Fink (whom I'll discuss soon), they repeated the usual claims about prevention of cancer and sexually transmitted diseases. Weiss also cited a paper of his own, published in 1993 in the *Israel Journal of Medical Science*, in which he reported on research claiming (erroneously) that the prepuce was deficient in Langerhans cells, which provide immunity against infections—additional evidence, Weiss declared, that "the rite of circumcision concept needs replacement with the right of posthectomy [foreskin removal]."[91]

Turning next to the "religious connection," the Weisses instructed their pediatrician audience on how to interpret biblical history:

> By the biblical Covenant of God with Abraham, the "father of the
> Hebrew nation," the operation was to be performed on the seventh
> neonatal day. This predated the discovery of the blood-clotting
> mechanisms in infancy. We know now that the clotting factors be-
> come functional by the seventh neonatal day in the healthy infant.
> Thus, benefits of the early operation conform not only to clotting
> and pain considerations but also reduce the chances of certain
> childhood diseases, later-life complications, and the pain of adult
> male surgery.

But despite "these remarkable discoveries by a primitive Hebraic culture," the apostle Paul, eager to gain pagan converts to Christianity, misrepresented circumcision as "mutilation or castration." A question, then, for Gentile readers to ponder: "Is it any wonder that the Christian concept of circumcision remains a dilemma to this day?"[92] From there the authors proceed to a "sociopolitical viewpoint":

> If circumcision, as the respected physicians Maimonides and Freud
> contend, reduces the sexual drive—by whatever means—then more
> self-control of the male organ might promise societal relief from
> related violent crimes with the associated sexually transmitted dis-
> eases.... Aside from ritual circumcision, which may benefit specific
> societies, shouldn't neonatal circumcision be the choice for just the
> health benefits alone?[93]

Why did *Clinical Pediatrics* accept an article interpreting biblical history and advocating infant circumcision to promote "self-control of the male organ"? That question occurred to some readers, including Paul Fleiss, a Jewish pediatrician, whose response, along with others, led to a protracted exchange. Fleiss's first letter made a point that should have been apparent to the journal's editors: "If circumcision can free society from violent crime and disease by decreasing sexual desire, why have the levels of violent crime and sexually transmitted diseases increased in direct proportion to the increase in the number of sexually active circumcised males in American society?" Other readers weighed in with additional objections. Robert Van Howe, a pediatrician specializing in statistics on infectious diseases, systematically challenged each of the Weisses' medical claims, including their statement that there was no need for concern about pain in newborn infants. The authors of another letter, one a British physician practicing in South Carolina, the other a Canadian, declared that "science rather than history and religion should provide the basis for modern medical treatment."[94]

The Weisses replied with a lengthy defense of their arguments and added a warning to their critics:

Pediatricians who fail to advise of the need for neonatal circumcision could possibly be held liable on a public health basis for STD [sexually transmitted disease] transmission through the covert foreskin that harbors herpes viruses, chlamydia, pathogenic bacteria (e.g., Group B streptococci), and now possibly the HIV-1 virus. Pediatricians should be proactive in prevention of diseases, be it the need for vaccinations or circumcisions![95]

An obviously exasperated Fleiss returned to the attack:

Attempts to legitimize Bronze Age blood rituals under the guise of modern medicine are unethical. One of the social functions of medicine is to free humankind from harmful and useless customs and to encourage science-based medical and social practices. If the Weisses care to attempt to justify ritual penile reductions in terms of theology, let them try—but not in the pages of a medical journal. Attempts to justify the forced circumcision of non-consenting individuals in the name of medicine must fail or risk further discredit and disgrace to modern American medical practice.

To which the Weisses replied that in "this wonderful country of ours, there is room for disagreement."[96] This article and the subsequent exchange took place, it will be recalled, in 1994 and 1995, and not in a popular magazine but in *Clinical Pediatrics*. To the best of my knowledge, no modern medical journal has published this kind of discourse on any other subject.

Weiss must have paid some attention to Fleiss's critique, because his next major publication seems more conversant with the professional literature, though it still featured fanciful language, extravagant claims, and minilectures on "Hebraic history." This was an article published in 1997 (when Weiss was in his late seventies) in another leading pediatric journal, this one specializing in infectious diseases. "The global resurgence of old familiar infectious diseases" (e.g., malaria, infant diarrhea, schistosomiasis) and the advent of the HIV crisis had led him to remind pediatricians that prevention was still "the most effective weapon against infections." Following lengthy discourses on the virtues of "primitive health care" (i.e., circumcision) and on "circumcision facts of ancient history," particularly "the Hebraic code of disease prevention" (based largely on early twentieth-century articles and the writings of Will Durant), Weiss informed his readers that "modern research using the World Wide Web and Net opens the way for an accurate scientific medical/surgical answer" to old questions. "Lost through the ages in a body of religious literature," he continued, "is the real reason for posthe[c]tomy" (circumcision): "unhindered by the scientific necessity of proof of an etiologic disease agent or its pathophysiology," the "ancients" realized that foreskin removal was the logical treatment for bloody urine or inability to urinate.[97]

"Unhindered by the scientific necessity of proof": seemingly Weiss's own preference as he elaborated on history as recorded in the "Holy Scriptures." After Abraham circumcised himself and his son Ishmael, his elderly wife, barren all her life, became pregnant and bore Isaac. He must have understood that circumcision would ensure reproduction and group survival. Weiss proposed a urological explanation:

> As a surgeon in practice for greater than half a century, I find it logical to speculate that it was Abraham's foreskin that prevented conception with Sarah in his later life.... Might it have been the foreskin adhesion problem causing a constriction over the glans that impaired erection and thus caused unsatisfactory intercourse after a desert life of repeated irritations and infections?[98]

Once again, why, so recently, did a journal on children's infectious diseases publish fantasies about "impaired erection" in a mythical old man and his inability to have frequent, productive intercourse with his very elderly wife? One wonders why an editor did not politely inform the author that speculation about the sexual lives of biblical characters was inappropriate for a modern medical journal.

There was more: Weiss discoursed next on schistosomiasis (also called bilharzia), a systemic tropical disease acquired through contact with a water-borne parasitic flatworm. "Children bathed in the contaminated waters of the Mideast oases," he hypothesized, "the foreskin allowing for a pooled pocket of infected water to harbor the cercaria [worm larvae] and allow invasion of the body through the immunodeficient area of the mucosal prepuce."[99] From that speculation he proceeded to a triumphant conclusion:

> It seems that a primitive but intelligent and discerning culture could well have used circumcision to remove an obstructing or grossly diseased part, the foreskin. By observing children's urinary signs and symptoms with schistosomiasis, it was a bold, calculated step by the discerning Hebraic sages and prophets who initiated the measure in 8-day-old Hebrew infants. This innovation, so medically significant to the Hebrew culture, became a mandatory health measure through its inclusion in the Bible.[100]

Weiss favored the image of the prepuce as a "cesspool," a contaminated "sac" or "pocket" harboring dangerous pathogens: "The very anatomy, gross and microscopic, of the preputial sac speaks of the nature of a cesspool. In this pocket, completely exposed only when the glans penis is revealed, by erection or by mechanical manipulation and cleaning, reside all the secretions, excretions, sloughing debris and whatever else accumulates at the terminal end of the male penis."[101] Lest anyone misunderstand the distinction between ritual regulations and medical science, he concluded with a few words of reassurance: "Neonatal circumcision has been perpetuated in many societies and cultures, not because of the Jews and their Covenant of Circumcision, but because of its merit as a secular surgical prophylactic health measure."[102]

Weiss's final contribution to the advocacy cause, a booklet entitled *Circumcision: Frankly Speaking*, appeared in 1998, apparently published by himself.[103] Written in a breezy popular style, it offered historical tidbits on biblical topics and the ostensible origins of circumcision, along with the usual claims for the benefits of circumcision as preventive surgery. A summary list of benefits includes everything from "sanitary convenience" and relief of "excessively narrowed foreskin opening" through prevention of cancer and AIDS to avoidance of "zipper injury," and "Finally, just a good reason: 'To be just like DAD!' is common reasoning!!!"[104]

The language in a chapter entitled "Pain" suggests that Weiss may have found this topic especially problematic:

> Just thinking of the word can make some folks wince. Of course there are other situations that evoke "pain": a sore neck, or even an insult or co-worker that gets on your nerves can cause anguish and pain. An important thing to remember is that pain is often confused with sensation. Have you ever seen a comedy routine where

a male gets hit in the groin and the audience sympathetically coils in
mock pain? . . . This is the sympathetic pain, which is a scenario
many parents may face when they learn that newborn circumcisions
are routinely performed in a hospital setting without anesthesia.
It seems unpleasant in nature, but actually newborn nerve receptors
are not fully developed and they do not feel what we adults have
come to know as "pain."[105]

As in this passage, the overall tone of the booklet is confident and reassuring. Parents reading it without further inquiry might well decide that
they owed it to their infant sons to endow them with the benefits of foreskin
removal. All things considered, it seems reasonable to conclude that this kind
of popularization may have contributed more to the perpetuation of routine
infant circumcision than any number of factual counterarguments in medical
journals. I don't know how widely the booklet was distributed, but I obtained a
copy readily on the internet.[106]

"A Life-Sparing Path": Aaron J. Fink's AIDS "Hypothesis"

Another late entrant into the fray was Aaron J. Fink (1926–1994), a California
urologist. Sometime around 1985 Fink realized that some physicians were
condemning circumcision as "barbaric and unnecessary" surgery "advocated
only by the uninformed"; but as he saw it, *they* were the uninformed.[107] Further
aroused by a 1986 decision by Blue Shield providers in several states to discontinue coverage for routine circumcision, he sent a manifesto entitled "In
Defense of Circumcision" to the *New York Times* and the *San Francisco Chronicle*, repeating the customary claims for benefits; neither published the letter.[108]
    By then Fink had come up with a novel idea: What if circumcision pro-
tected against infection with HIV, the virus that causes AIDS? In 1986 he sent
a modestly titled letter—"A Possible Explanation for Heterosexual Male Infection with AIDS"—to the prestigious *New England Journal of Medicine*, asserting (erroneously) that since genital herpes and syphilis occurred more
commonly in uncircumcised men, and since these infections entered through
abrasions or breaks in genital skin, it seemed likely that "the cervical secretions of a woman infected with AIDS" could be readily transferred to a
male "when the skin surface is a delicate, easily abraded penile lining, such as
the mucosal inner layer of the foreskin." In short, the toughened glans of the
circumcised male resisted infection, while the foreskin tissue and tender,
moist glans of his intact counterpart were ideal ports of entry. The letter
continued with a striking proposition: "I suspect that men in the United
States, who, as compared with those in Africa and elsewhere, have had less
acquisition of AIDS, have benefited from the high rate of newborn circumcision in the United States." Fink thought it likely "that the presence of

a foreskin predisposes both heterosexual and homosexual men to the acquisition of AIDS."[109] Note, though, that he focused on the possibility that *heterosexual* men might be infected through contact with "cervical secretions" (this at a time when very few American women were HIV-positive). Since it was generally known that AIDS afflicted mostly homosexual men in America and heterosexual men in Africa, Fink had in effect delivered a radical new claim for circumcision as prophylactic surgery—and partly shifted the focus of attention from this country to the African continent.

The proposal—newsworthy, to say the least—soon appeared in media throughout the United States and Canada. Asked about his "theory" by a United Press reporter, Fink replied, "This is nothing I can prove." That didn't discourage other physicians from conducting research leading to a steady stream of widely publicized articles arguing that circumcised men were indeed less likely to contract HIV—with the result that prevention of HIV infection has now surpassed even cancer prevention as the most popular claim of circumcision advocates.[110]

Fink repeated his argument in a small book on circumcision, addressed to parents and published (by himself, it appears) in 1988.[111] The double sense of the title—*Circumcision: A Parent's Decision for Life*—was probably unintended. The focus was on sexually transmitted diseases, which Fink declared to be "no longer a matter of morals" but "an issue of life or death." Defeating the threat, he informed prospective parents, called for immediate action: "The facts now point to circumcision, cutting off the foreskin, as a life-sparing path to public and personal health." And lest anyone doubt the urgency of the situation, he added questions likely to generate unease in the most skeptical reader:

> Will your infant son have a problem practicing daily cleaning of
> his penis? Will he be promiscuous? Will he visit prostitutes? Will
> he be at greater risk of acquiring sexually transmitted diseases,
> including AIDS? Will he use a condom? Will he live in a tropical,
> humid land? Will he be a diabetic?[112]

"Having a foreskin," he continued, "may be linked to acquiring the deadly virus that causes AIDS"; scientific evidence in support of this "connection" was accumulating. If his book were to "provide the knowledge and insight that might save even one life from the tragedy of AIDS," the effort was worthwhile.[113] Since one of the book's seven chapters was entitled "Preventing AIDS: Another Benefit of Newborn Circumcision," the average reader might well have concluded that this was fact, not supposition.

In 1987, Fink filed a resolution entitled "Newborn Circumcision as a Public Health Measure" with the California Medical Association, saying, among other claims, that "it has been recently hypothesized that a circumcision [*sic*], preferably in the newborn period, may lessen the acquisition and in turn the spread of AIDS, a sexually transmitted disease." The association's advisory panels on pediatrics and urology concluded that the arguments for adoption were "not sufficiently convincing"; and although the urologists stood by circumcision as "an acceptable preventive health measure," both panels recommended against adoption of the resolution. The association's Scientific Board declined endorsement, and the resolution was not adopted.[114] Fink returned in 1988 with a repeat resolution with the same title, but much lengthier and heavily documented. The Scientific Board again recommended against adoption, but this time the resolution passed by a voice vote.[115] The following year, John W. Hardebeck presented a counterresolution entitled "Newborn Circumcision: Medical Necessity or Useless Mutilation?" saying that newborn circumcision "is a procedure without factual, demonstrable, supportable medical indications in the overwhelming majority of cases," and that "most medical authorities worldwide feel that newborn males have a right to remain 'intact' except in rare instances."[116] This was rejected.

Fink's success before the medical association brought an unanticipated reaction. In response to the controversy surrounding the Fink resolution and Hardebeck's attempt to counteract it, a group of circumcision opponents held a conference in a hotel across the street from the one housing the medical meeting. The conference organizer was the nation's leading opponent of infant circumcision: Marilyn F. Milos, the founder and director of the National Organization of Circumcision Information Resource Centers (NOCIRC).[117] The three-day conference, labeled the First International Symposium on Circumcision, was so successful that six more symposia, resulting to date in publication of four volumes based on the proceedings, have been held since then, in locations as diverse as Lausanne, Oxford, and Sydney.[118] So it might be said that Aaron Fink unintentionally created a vigorous new expression of opposition to circumcision.

Fink wrote once more on AIDS prevention in a letter to a British medical journal, prompting two hostile replies, both from Leeds physicians.[119] After publishing another letter to the same journal in 1991—this one claiming that infants appear to have no memory of painful events until age six months or older (hence that circumcision has no lasting psychological effects)—he seems to have abandoned the controversy.[120] He died in 1994. But the campaign to link HIV infection to foreskins is still very much in the news. Although it is common knowledge that circumcised American men are susceptible to HIV infection, physicians and the media have accorded wide currency to claims that circumcised men in Africa are somehow resistant.[121]

The Urinary Tract Infection Hypothesis

One non-Jewish physician has pursued circumcision advocacy with something of the determination displayed by the men discussed to this point. In

1982, two physicians reported in the journal *Pediatrics* that of one hundred male infants they had treated for urinary tract infections, ninety-five had not been circumcised.[122] This attracted the attention of Thomas E. Wiswell, a neonatologist (a pediatrician specializing in management of the newborn) at an army medical center in Texas, who until that time had been *opposed* to routine circumcision and had even coauthored an article evaluating methods of counseling parents against the practice.[123] Wiswell and two colleagues studied the medical records of 2,502 infants born at the medical center during an eighteen-month period in 1982–83. They found that those who had been circumcised had a urinary tract infection (UTI) incidence of 0.21 percent (four cases in 1919 infants), while those who remained intact had an incidence of 4.12 percent (twenty-four cases in 583 infants). All twenty-eight infants with UTI responded promptly to antibiotic treatment and had sterile (normal) urine within two to four days. Wiswell proposed that if the infections were shown to have long-term adverse effects (serious kidney disease later in life), this would have obvious implications for the debate on routine infant circumcision.[124]

That report appeared in 1985. The next year Wiswell followed with another paper, based on a much larger sample, presenting "corroborative evidence" for the accuracy of his initial conclusions, and from then on he produced a series of publications on what soon became his unique contribution to the circumcision controversy.[125] Consistent with his earlier negative assessment of the procedure, he avoided hyperbole and recommended informed decision-making. For example, in a paper on risks from circumcision published in 1988, he reported that while "short-term complications" following surgery were "rare and mostly minor," bacterial infections occurred later "with significantly greater frequency" in intact boys. But he continued with a warning: "Foreskin ablation is controversial, to say the least. The literature abounds with emotional defenses for and against circumcision. There are far fewer data-based reports." He concluded by quoting with approval an earlier statement by a Canadian physician: "There must be more light and less heat in discussions regarding circumcision."[126]

By 2000 he was citing studies claiming that infant males treated for UTI were significantly more likely to develop severe or even fatal renal disease in later life. When several physicians challenged these findings, Wiswell stood his ground, but he conceded that additional carefully conducted research was needed.[127]

Wiswell's articles have been characterized by a degree of moderation and "circumspection" (his term in a 1997 article) that has been notably lacking in much of this literature. Asking why leads only to speculation, but it is worth considering whether this physician has less personal investment in circumcision advocacy than is evident in the publications of Abraham Wolbarst, Abraham Ravich, Gerald Weiss, and Aaron Fink.

"The Final Decision Is Theirs": Voices from the Academy

By 1970 the American Academy of Pediatrics (AAP), the professional organization representing nearly all certified pediatricians, recognized the need for
an authoritative statement on routine neonatal circumcision. The following
year the Academy's Committee on Fetus and Newborn said that there were
"no valid medical indications" for the practice.[128] In 1975, responding to
objections from some physicians, the organization created an Ad Hoc Task
Force on Circumcision to reconsider the earlier conclusion. Their report,
published in the journal *Pediatrics* in October 1975, said that they had found
"no basis for changing this statement": there was "no absolute medical indication for routine circumcision of the newborn." But they added a crucial
qualification:

> Nevertheless, traditional, cultural, and religious factors play a role in
> the decision made by parents, pediatrician, obstetrician, or family
> practitioner on behalf of a son. It is the responsibility of the physician
> to provide parents with factual and informative medical options re-
> garding circumcision. The final decision is theirs, and should be
> based on true informed consent. It is advantageous for discussion to
> take place well in advance of delivery, when the capacity for clear
> response is more likely.[129]

"The final decision is theirs." In the history of American medicine this
statement is surely unique. The pediatricians declared that their colleagues
should be willing to perform a surgical procedure lacking adequate *medical*
rationale, provided only that *parents* (actually, *a* parent) request or agree to it—
and "well in advance of delivery," a situation that often does not obtain. Even
tonsillectomy, the closest competitor to circumcision for the label of unnecessary surgery, had been justified by the belief that it prevented serious throat
infections. But of course circumcision bore entirely different meaning and
associations: The pediatricians sanctioned performance of that operation for
"traditional, cultural, and religious" reasons, "on behalf of" uncomprehending newborns. In short, *a group of well-qualified pediatricians accorded to parents
exclusive right to authorize physicians to perform surgery on infants for explicitly
nonmedical reasons.* To say that this was extraordinary is an understatement.

In 1983 the Academy's Committee on Fetus and Newborn, in collaboration with the American College of Obstetricians and Gynecologists, issued
Guidelines for Perinatal Care, which included repetition of the 1975 recommendations. This attracted the attention of Edgar J. Schoen, a California
pediatrician who, like Weiss and Fink, seems to have discovered circumcision
promotion fairly late in his career (in 1983 he was age fifty-eight) but soon

earned his present reputation as the nation's foremost advocate.[130] In 1989 Schoen chaired another Task Force on Circumcision, which produced yet another report. As one would expect, although this one paid due attention to "contraindications" and "complications," the overall tenor leaned decidedly toward positive assessment. The report discussed phimosis, paraphimosis, cancer of the penis and cervix, and infections as matters on which there were still no final conclusions. It characterized circumcision as "a rapid and generally safe procedure when performed by an experienced operator." Infants were said to respond with "transient behavioral and physiologic changes." The conclusion was studiously equivocal: "Newborn circumcision has potential medical benefits and advantages as well as disadvantages and risks. When circumcision is being considered, the benefits and risks should be explained to the parents and informed consent obtained."[131]

One can almost hear members of this six-person task force arguing over wording—some sympathetic to the earlier reports, others siding with Schoen. Notably absent was the 1975 statement about "no valid medical indications." Moreover, the final three words—"informed consent obtained"—were obviously oriented toward acceptance. Although it would be inaccurate to characterize the report as solely a brief for circumcision, unquestionably it was much more positive than its predecessors.

There were predictable objections from circumcision opponents, and in 1999 yet another task force—seven members, including one from the American College of Obstetricians and Gynecologists, and chaired for the first time by a woman—issued a new "Circumcision Policy Statement." This one evaluated all claims, pro and con, in greater detail and addressed several new topics, including "ethical issues." The concluding statement aimed for the impossible goal of satisfying everyone:

> Existing scientific evidence demonstrates potential medical benefits of newborn male circumcision; however, these data are not sufficient to recommend routine neonatal circumcision. In the case of circumcision, in which there are potential benefits and risks, yet the procedure is not essential to the child's current well-being, parents should determine what is in the best interest of the child.... It is legitimate for parents to take into account cultural, religious, and ethnic traditions, in addition to the medical factors, when making this decision.[132]

The statement did not satisfy Edgar Schoen. He soon issued a critique, coauthored with Thomas Wiswell and Stephen Moses, a Winnipeg physician who advocated circumcision as prophylaxis against HIV infection. Characterizing the new statement as "cause for concern," they presented the arguments on everything from penile cancer to HIV, and called on the Academy leadership to "quickly address the narrow, biased, and inadequate data analysis as well as the inappropriate conclusions" of the report and the corresponding "Information for Parents" available on the internet.[133] The task force replied with a cautiously conciliatory statement: While they recognized "potential medical benefits" to circumcision, these were not "sufficiently compelling" when weighed against the "evidence of low incidence, high-morbidity problems" associated with the procedure. They said again that they favored "leaving it to the family to decide whether circumcision is in the best interests of their child."[134] In reply to this, Schoen and his colleagues insisted that their remarks were "not meant to represent an overzealous procircumcision stance"; they wanted only to make certain that parents received "an accurate presentation of scientific evidence," so they could make a well-informed decision.[135]

Meanwhile, other respondents, including not only pediatricians but mohels and activists on both sides, weighed in with the inevitable objections to statements they found unacceptable. A San Francisco pediatrician, Thomas Bartman, reminded his colleagues that they had earlier issued a statement "condemning the mutilation of female genitalia" and asked why the task force "failed to afford the same protection to our male patients."

> Just as no surgeon would perform a medically unnecessary appendectomy just because the parents desire one for their child, so should we, as the protectors of children, refuse to perform unnecessary mutilating procedures on our patients simply because of their parents' desires. Remember, we are not "religious" or "cultural" or "ethnic" practitioners. We are physicians who should practice medicine, not rituals.

Bartman called on colleagues to join him in "declining to perform medically unnecessary procedures to alter *either* male or female genitalia," and he asked the Academy's Committee on Bioethics to review the policy statement. A letter from Frederick M. Hodges and Paul Fleiss cited the substantial evidence that the foreskin, not the glans, is the most sensitive part of male genitals, arguing that attention should focus on the "sensory deficit" caused by foreskin removal.

In their reply to Bartman, the task force said that "the critical distinction between female genital mutilation and male circumcision" was that the latter had "potential medical benefits"; moreover, the bioethics committee had approved their statement. They ignored the central argument of the Hodges and Fleiss letter. Speaking for the other side were a mohel and a urologist from Los Angeles, who reminded pediatricians that, in contrast to hospital circumcisions employing clamps and analgesia, the "traditional Jewish neonatal bris" was the "fastest and most humane," since it took only about ten seconds and avoided the pain caused by crushing tissue.[136]

Schoen returned to the fray once again with a June 2003 letter to the journal *Pediatrics*. Arguing that "new data" had accumulated in support of most of the customary claims—protection against penile cancer, HIV infection, urinary tract infections, phimosis, and penile skin lesions, as well as improved "genital hygiene throughout life"—he urged that the 1999 AAP report be reconsidered, and that a new report be issued to provide "a comprehensive picture of disease prevention from birth through old age."[137]

Aside from the relative merits or demerits of the arguments, there are lessons in the history of these reports. First, I think it certain that no other contested procedure in American medical history has generated so much seemingly endless attention, so much argument and counterargument, or so much passion. If until now anyone has doubted that male infant circumcision is a procedure like no other in the minds of the very physicians who perform it, surely the American Academy of Pediatrics has provided an answer. Second, as I've said, perhaps the most remarkable feature of this story is that, in obvious contrast to all other medical decisions, when it comes to circumcision it is *parents*, not physicians, who are expected to determine that a surgical procedure is in a child's "best interests." It seems indisputable that despite the years of debate about cancers and infections, we're looking here at something more complex than ordinary disagreement on medical questions. The vaguely phrased references to "cultural" and "religious" considerations (whose culture? whose religion?) speak also to the discomfort and uncertainty attached to surgery that began as a Jewish ritual practice and became an American hospital routine.

Finally, a matter on which I've said little until now: comparisons between female and male genital alteration. Some feminists, fearing that attention to male circumcision may dilute awareness of the problem of female genital alteration in Africa and elsewhere, insist on calling one, but not the other, "mutilation"—the double standard in reverse. But the real issue is not terminology. Viewing conflict on this question as needlessly divisive, opponents of circumcision argue that the question is not what should be called "mutilation" but whether anyone has the right to authorize or perform surgery on the genitals of *any* child without compelling, unequivocal medical justification.[138]

A Seemingly Endless Controversy

Although articles pro and con on circumcision continued to appear in medical journals during the 1980s and beyond, one gets the impression that many, perhaps most, physicians consider the matter settled; either they accept circumcision or they do not. But if circumcision rates are any evidence, the arguments of opponents must have attracted public notice. As I noted earlier, the rate peaked around 1980 at about 85 percent or possibly higher; by 1990 it had declined to about 60 percent; since then it has decreased slightly, though the sharp decline seems to have ended, at least temporarily.[139]

In 1996, a team of Winnipeg pathologists, John R. Taylor and colleagues, published a paper breaking new ground. Remarking that even opponents of circumcision defended the prepuce as protection for the glans rather than "as a tissue worthy of preservation in its own right," these researchers demonstrated that circumcision removes tissue richly supplied with nerves and blood vessels, including a band of ridged mucosa (the "ridged band")—highly specialized sensory tissue located at the junction of the penile skin and smooth mucosa.[140] In plain language, they concluded that circumcision destroys not just a bit of "superfluous skin," as is so often claimed, but a vital sensory component of the male genitalia, essential for normal sexual sensation and functioning.

Nevertheless, the practice lives on in American hospitals, maintained largely by custom and inertia—and perhaps some monetary interest. The religious debate on "spirit" versus "flesh" initiated by Paul nearly two thousand years ago, the image of circumcision as the indelible mark of the Jewish male, recourse to the language of "covenant" and "chosen people" status, subconscious fears of circumcision as akin to castration,[141] rejection of the practice as an anachronistic blood rite: all are largely forgotten, submerged in an interminable and inconclusive medical discourse claiming or denying the benefits of genital surgery for infants who express their own opinions in the only way they can.

8

Unanswerable Questions, Questionable Answers

Justifying Ritual Circumcision

The operation itself is so trifling that in a society where any physical symptom provokes exaggerated anxiety, it arouses no concern.... In the old tradition, the greatest honor of all is that of the *metsutsa*, performed by a venerable and pious man who sucks the first drop of blood. Then the wound is tied around with cotton, to be changed daily by the mohel until within a few days it has healed. Nobody worries about that part and even the baby makes little of it.[1]

Some amount of bleeding is a necessary part of the ritual circumcision. To suggest that I do them without any bleeding is damaging to my reputation in the Jewish community.[2]

"Nobody Worries About That Part"

The first epigraph is from *Life Is with People*, a 1952 study of immigrant memories of early twentieth-century Jewish life in the small towns of eastern Europe. Most of those immigrants were more attached to traditional European Jewish culture than were their children, but when it came to circumcision there was little if any difference in attitude. Infant sons had to be circumcised, and no one thought afterward about "that part." What did change for many, though, was the setting of the operation and the professional qualifications of the operator. Jewish parents with minimal knowledge of their religious heritage, and with very little commitment to religious observance, knew only that circumcising an infant son was somehow necessary to "make him Jewish." But by the latter decades of the century, a circumcision performed at home by a mohel was no longer the norm. Circumcision had become a widespread *American* practice. Since so many Gentile infants were being circumcised in hospitals, the operation had lost its specific connection with Judaism and Jewish particularism. Nevertheless, many Jewish parents, knowing next to nothing about Gentile infants, still believed that circumcision was definitively Jewish. Often, however, they decided on an "American-style" circumcision by a hospital physician, rather than ritual surgery of uncertain significance performed by a mohel with possibly old-fashioned methods and standards. Moreover, aside from signing a consent form, a hospital circumcision required nothing on the parents' part: no scheduling with an unknown religious functionary; no mysterious rite; no need to witness the surgery; no house party to plan. Performed out of sight, the matter was soon happily out of mind (at least for the parent who avoided diaper changing).

This was not the case, of course, for the minority who continued on the Orthodox path. Medical rationalizations had no place in their world; they circumcised their infant sons, with full ritual accompaniment, because God had mandated that they do so. But in the course of the century Jewish Americans steadily fell away from Orthodoxy; and we know that the great majority are now relatively indifferent to formal religious observance.[3]

Depending partly on who is and is not counted, the "core" (clearly identifiable) Jewish American population numbers about five and a half million—only about 2.2 percent of the American population. But when it comes to definitive attitudes and behavior—religious observance and ethnic self-identification—this is a very diverse group, more than other Americans may suppose. The differences are usually understood and described in terms familiar to Christians: just as there are Baptists, Methodists, Catholics, and the rest, so among Jews there are Orthodox, Conservative, and Reform. Those who know more may add the ultra-Orthodox Hasidim and, at the other end of the spectrum, the small progressive segment called Reconstructionists.[4] But the truth is that denominational categories, although useful to a degree, not only fail to describe the Jewish population completely enough but actually blur distinctions that probably matter most.

Over the past couple of decades, sociologists have provided a portrait of Jewish Americans taking account of divisions that often matter more than the conventional denominations. Their most significant single finding is that the overall trend is away from religious orthodoxy and ethnic particularism, toward assertion of "American" as primary identity. To put this somewhat differently, most members of this population are best understood as Jewish Americans, not as American Jews.[5] The distinction matters. It's common knowledge that "Jewish" is both a religious and an ethnic label. But ever since the onset of modernity, with its emphasis on individualism and personal choice, it has been possible to separate those two forms of identity—to maintain ethnic Jewish identification without necessarily accepting any of the beliefs or practices of Judaism. Aside from the relatively few who still adhere to strict Orthodoxy, beliefs and customs connected with religious particularism— "chosen people" ideology (long since discarded by most), dietary restrictions, the ban on intermarriage, residential separatism, and so on—are now little more than history. Moreover, even moderately affiliated Jews—typically, middle-aged and older people who identify as Conservative or Reform—feel that they have the right to individual choice with regard to adherence to religious regulations.[6] In short, the truly operative divide is between, on the one hand, those whose lives center on strict ritual observance and ethnic particularism and, on the other, those who express Jewish identity mostly in a more "secular" manner, through aspects of social and cultural style— supplemented, perhaps, by occasional attendance at a synagogue service, a bar mitzvah, or a Passover seder. Of the two groups, the latter is by far the larger; most have only a smattering of Jewish knowledge—and beliefs about an ancient covenant between God and the Jewish people are simply absent from their cognitive world. Nevertheless—and this is an all-important point—it appears (albeit in the absence of reliable data) that most weakly affiliated Jewish Americans, despite their indifference to virtually all religious regulations, continue to believe that their sons should be circumcised. As I've said, this is certainly explainable in part by the prevalence of circumcision as an American custom, and by the ease with which one can agree to a hospital circumcision (worthless though that may be in Orthodox eyes). But there seems also to be a remarkably tenacious residue of belief that circumcision is still the "Jewish thing to do"—even when this may stand alone as the last acknowledgment of a tradition that has been otherwise abandoned.

What stands out in Jewish American discourse is the emphasis on circumcision as a guarantee of Jewish "survival" in the most literal sense. No one really explains why, at a time when nearly 60 percent of all American male infants are circumcised, ritual removal of infant foreskins will ensure the survival of the Jewish people. No one, moreover, has explored the question of whether Jewish men who were circumcised at birth by hospital physicians are any more or less self-identified and affiliated than those who underwent a ritual circumcision. Finally, of course, the inescapable question: Are Jewish women, all of whom escaped "birthright" surgery, any less committed as Jews than their circumcised male counterparts? Claims for the indispensability of ritual foreskin removal ignore critical social variables that may well be far more influential. But having made this single concession to tradition, parents may then feel that they have done their part for Jewish continuity and need do no more. Does this suggest why circumcision alone seems to be such a uniquely defended Jewish practice? Is it simply a matter of making a decision for infant sons and leaving it at that?

To provide a clearer idea of contemporary attitudes and circumcision practices among those who have at least some denominational affiliation, I'll discuss three widely divergent groups within the spectrum: first, strictly Orthodox Jews, now less than 10 percent of the Jewish population; next, Reform Jews, the largest denominational group and still growing, with membership spanning every age category; and finally, Humanistic Jews, a very small group, liberal and essentially secular but committed to preservation of Jewish ethnic identity. This does not cover the full range of differences, particularly since it says nothing about the large nonaffiliated category, but it will tell us something about attitudes toward circumcision among Jewish Americans who maintain varying degrees of religious affiliation.[7]

Harnessing "Man's Worst Animal-Like Urge":
The Orthodox Perspective

Although Orthodox Jews occasionally cite medical claims as incidental benefits of circumcision, in the final analysis no medical consideration influences their conviction that newborn boys must be ritually circumcised. Circumcision of other people's infants may require medical justification, but circumcision of *theirs* requires none. All that need be known is in the seventeenth chapter of Genesis; the rest is commentary. Nevertheless, circumcision manuals addressed to the Orthodox faithful add a great deal of commentary, products of the creative rabbinic imagination.

Typical of this literature is *Bris Milah*, by a rabbi-mohel named Paysach J. Krohn, issued in 1985 by a leading Orthodox publishing firm in its popular "ArtScroll Series." Krohn offers a host of explanations, interpretations, and homilies derived from rabbinic and kabbalistic sources as well as folk traditions. Adopting a confident, inspirational tone throughout, he declares that circumcision is the precious birthright of every Jewish boy. In the world of this rabbi and his readers, non-Jewish practices and concerns are of no interest whatever. Those who work their way through his book's nearly two hundred pages find nothing about medical controversies, let alone legal or ethical arguments.

The book begins with an "Overview" authored by another rabbi, Nosson Scherman. He reminds readers of the great Rabbi Akiba (here Akiva, ca. 45–135 CE), who taught that it is our duty not only to perfect the universe but also to become fully human by transforming our animal nature. But if God prefers circumcised men, why did he not create us that way? The term *orlah* (foreskin), says Rabbi Scherman, which we apply to the "small bit of surplus flesh," signifies an obstruction. The human soul yearns for reunion with the divine holiness it enjoyed before it experienced the base animality and greed of human life; but to make this possible we must first remove the obstruction.

Adam was born circumcised because he was so close to God, with nothing intervening between the divine spirit and his own physical body; the organ representing "man's worst animal-like urge" was completely "harnessed" to the Lord's will. But when Adam fell into the trap of physical desire and temptation, he forfeited his right to physical purity. The symbol of that purity, his naturally circumcised penis, came to be covered by impure flesh: a fore-skin that, unfortunately for all men, became part of the male body as a reminder of the fall of the first man. For twenty generations thereafter, mankind failed to achieve redemption, until Abraham earned the privilege of circumcision for himself and his progeny.[8]

But why, Scherman continues, did Abraham not circumcise himself much earlier in life? Because he had to wait until his accumulated merit entitled him to overcome the disgraceful impediment imposed by Adam's sin. When the proper time came, he circumcised himself at the divine command and promised that all his male offspring would be circumcised for eternity. Thus Abraham became "father of God's nation" and earned for his people the pledge that "the Land" would be theirs.[9] Moreover, circumcision empowers every Jewish man to overcome his "urges" and to transcend his "animal instincts," thereby achieving circumcision of the heart. For just as *peri'ah* requires removing every remnant of tissue to ensure that foreskin will never again cover the glans, so must men rid themselves of every trace of their "base passions." Each circumcision thus affirms once again Abraham's covenant with God and repeats the hope that someday mankind will return to Adam's original state of grace. This is why, in defiance of all obstacles, the Jewish "soul and psyche" welcome circumcision as a joyful celebration of the Lord's supreme gift to his chosen people.[10]

Rabbi Krohn enlarges on this message. First there is the child's name, which is bestowed immediately after he is circumcised. Just as Abram became a new man named Abraham after his circumcision, so the infant now becomes a newly named person.[11] A section entitled "A Tapestry of Eights" offers a kabbalistic-style numerological discourse similar to those of ancient com-mentators. When the infant enters for his circumcision, the witnesses greet him with *Baruch haba* (Blessed be he who comes). As I've shown, Hebrew letters have numerical equivalents: a (*aleph*, א) corresponds to 1, b (*bet*, ב) corresponds to 2, and so on, with letters after the value of 10 representing 20, 30, and the rest. The letters of *haba* (הבא) come fifth, second, and first in the alphabet, respectively—hence $5 + 2 + 1$. The mohel's knife, called *izmail*, is a combination of two words: *az*, "then," and *mal*, "to circumcise." The letters of *az* equal 1 plus 7—signaling that the child is to be circumcised on the eighth day. Moreover, the child must wait seven days so that he can live through a Sabbath, a spiritual experience fortifying him for entry into the covenant.[12]

From there the rabbi carries his readers into realms far distant from genital surgery: Chanukah is an eight-day holiday; the high priest wore eight special garments when presiding over temple rituals; Joshua, who circum-cised Hebrew men entering the Promised Land, belonged to the eighth generation after Abraham; and so on. In addition, each tassel attached to a man's prayer shawl (*tallit*) consists of eight strands, reminding him against sinning with any of the eight sources of danger in the body: eyes, ears, nose, mouth, hands, feet, genitals ("place of gender"), and heart. Thus the number 8, symbolizing purity and perfection, represents the bond between the Lord and his people.[13]

A special virtue of circumcision, says Rabbi Krohn, is impairment of sexual sensation. Sensual desire is a legacy of Adam's fall from grace. The "holy mark" on the Jewish penis signifies that God created this organ not for gratification of lust, but to enable Jewish men to achieve spiritual perfection and to bring souls of the chosen people to earth.[14]

Readers who recall the discussions of rabbinic and mystical texts in earlier chapters will have recognized Krohn's style of interpretation. Note that he speaks here not only to Hasidic readers but to all Orthodox Jews, none of whom care much about secular rationales for circumcision, since they view the practice as divinely ordained. Mystical and numerological interpretations fully satisfy their desire for explanation.[15]

Removing the Evil Husk

In response to the interest in mysticism and kabbalah among some younger Jewish Americans, a few authors now use kabbalistic texts to attract readers to traditional Jewish practice. One of the best-known writers in this genre is the late Aryeh Kaplan, who left a promising career in physics to devote himself to religious scholarship. I was introduced to his commentary by a young Jewish mother; after we had discussed her son's circumcision, she sent me excerpts from a 1990 volume entitled *Innerspace*.[16] In a section on "The Mitzvah [commandment] of Circumcision" Kaplan reflects on three "basic functions" of the (male) "organ of procreation": procreation, sexual pleasure, and uri-nation ("disposal of waste matter"). Why, he asks, are procreation and uri-nation combined when there is no biological explanation (so he believes) for the association? His answer is that the Yesod, the divine emanation re-presenting the phallus (as described in the Zohar), contains the "Divine influx"—the "creative power with which God sustains and directs the world." In fact, this was his *"primary purpose* in creating the world." But God also had a secondary purpose: permitting evil (i.e., male sexual desire) to be nourished through the Yesod, so that men would have maximal "free choice and hence reward" for resisting its expression. The biological energy sustaining evil is "waste matter."[17]

Another interpretation of the commandment, says Kaplan, was offered by the sixteenth-century kabbalist Isaac Luria, who explained that the two "legs" of the letter *chet* (ח) represent the Yesod, the right leg by expressing positive procreative ability, the left, negative waste matter and evil. But if the left leg is broken at the top, the result is another letter, *heh* (ה), representing a purified Yesod, free of evil inclinations. If Adam had not succumbed to sexual desire, he would have successfully dislodged the "left channel" and overcome the evil aspect of his human nature. Instead, the two channels "converged," and Adam's Yesod (his phallus in its original pure form) was covered by a *klipah* (husk) "from which evil could draw its nourishment."[18] Now we understand, concludes Kaplan, why only a circumcised Jewish male has a "share in the World to Come": In that world "the concept of Yesod will be completely without a foreskin," and sexual pleasure purely spiritual. An uncircumcised man, cursed with a spiritually bereft soul, cannot enjoy the divine radiance and would experience the joy of the Garden of Eden only as hell.[19]

It will be evident that this kind of interpretation depends not only on acceptance of Genesis as though it were factual history but also on indifference to what is known about human evolution and physiology. Mystical explanations centering on the Yesod encourage religiously inclined readers to conceive of circumcision as a redemptive spiritual experience for the infant and themselves. Books of this kind, addressed primarily to young people with little or no historical knowledge of the Jewish mystical tradition, blend promises of spiritual rewards with threats of miserable consequences for those who defy divine commandments. A related point: Interlaced throughout Kaplan's discourse (and implicit in the entire text) are repeated warnings against illicit (nonmarital) sexual behavior, and indeed any form of sexuality expressing keen physical passion; for such actions contaminate the sanctified circumcised penis, rendering its owner ineligible for rewards in the World to Come. As we've seen, such arguments were common fare in medieval kabbalistic writings; but Kaplan's work is remarkable in that perhaps nowhere else in contemporary Jewish literature is fear of unconstrained sexuality expressed with such deep conviction.[20]

Welcoming the "Tender New Arrival"

For parents accustomed to turning to the internet for information, there is "Mazel Tov," the website of Raphael Malka, a rabbi-mohel practicing in the Washington, D.C., area. For Rabbi Malka, blessed with a cheerful frame of mind, circumcision is a "joyous occasion in a baby's life and that of his family," a way for parents to thank God for sending them the "tender new arrival," their *"bundle from heaven."* No one these days "questions the desirability of circumcision," he assures us, since it is now "standard hygeinic [*sic*] practice." But of course only a properly trained mohel can convert a "surgical act" into a religious experience.[21] Since circumcision, he continues, "has a great spiritual effect on the child," the operator must be not only medically qualified but also "religiously authorized." Enemies of Judaism have tried many times to eliminate circumcision, and now there are those who want to replace the religious rite with a spiritually meaningless surgical operation. For these potential defectors Malka has a challenge: "*Shall we, through indifference, neglect a sacred rite which our forefathers have preserved at all cost?*" If your answer is a determined no, call or fax the rabbi at the numbers provided.[22]

"A Progressive Religion": Reform Judaism and the Move Rightward

As might be expected, many Reform and nonaffiliated Jewish Americans now opt for secular circumcisions performed in hospitals. But, somewhat surprisingly, there has been a counteracting development.

A brief historical reminder: Between about 1820 and 1880, some 150,000 European Jewish immigrants, coming largely from Germany and central Europe, established Reform congregations imitating Protestant standards of religious propriety. Inspired by Rabbi Isaac Mayer Wise (1819–1900), the founder of organized Reform Judaism in America—who had declared, "Whatever makes us ridiculous before the world...may safely be and should be abolished"—they instituted use of English for prayers and sermons, common seating for women and men, organs and choirs, and confirmation ceremonies for girls as well as boys (replacing bar mitzvah).[23] Regulations regarding diet and Sabbath observance, considered a matter for personal choice, were widely disregarded, as was the requirement that men cover their heads at worship services. The conviction that Jews should now live in accord with principles of modernity and rationalism, characteristic of European Reform Judaism from its beginning, prevailed perhaps even more firmly in the United States. In 1885, a conference of Reform rabbis meeting in Pittsburgh issued an eight-point "platform" that still stands as the preeminent expression of the Jewish American Reform movement. The third declaration read as follows:

> We recognize in the Mosaic legislation a system of training the Jewish people for its mission during its national life in Palestine, and to-day we accept as binding only the moral laws, and maintain only such ceremonies as elevate and sanctify our lives, but reject all such as are not adapted to the views and habits of modern civilization.

The fourth declaration rejected all laws regulating "diet, priestly purity, and dress" as "altogether foreign to our present mental and spiritual state," while the sixth defined Judaism as "a progressive religion, ever striving to be in accord with the postulates of reason."[24] Nevertheless, despite the open quality of American life, and despite assurances from the distinguished Rabbi Wise that they were free to eliminate customs that might make them seem "ridiculous" to others, at no time did Reform Jews living in the new world of America formally declare that they need no longer circumcise their infant sons. To the contrary, they held on to circumcision when nearly all else was abandoned.

Over the next seventy years or so, the Pittsburgh principles underlay what is called "Classical Reform"—a religion characterized by liberal interpretation of tradition and de-emphasis of ritual regulations. But since the end of World War II, and particularly during the past quarter-century, American Reform Judaism has been moving slowly in the opposite direction. I can only suggest reasons for this. Fundamental processes of social change—acculturation, integration, partial assimilation, as measured by rising intermarriage rates and evidence of declining religious and ethnic commitment—have led rabbis and Jewish leaders to fear demographic decline and, in the most pessimistic of scenarios, ultimate "disappearance." In response some have turned to renewed emphasis on traditional practices. In addition, the emergence of the State of Israel and, connected with that, the accelerating prominence of Holocaust commemoration, have generated a conservative trend that has permeated the Reform movement along with other parts of the Jewish community. "Classical Reform" has given way to a more cautious "Mainstream Reform" that is actually less open to reform.[25] It must be pointed out, though, that the large number of nominally Reform Jews who are integrating, intermarrying, and showing little if any interest in formal Jewish concerns, can hardly be much concerned about social developments for which they themselves are responsible. The anxiety and apprehension are mainly in the minds of rabbis and self-appointed community leaders.

"O Prosper the Work of Our Hands": The Berit Mila Board

One of the most remarkable expressions of the rightward shift began in 1984, when the three major organizations of the Reform movement—the Central Conference of American Rabbis, Hebrew Union College, and the Union of American Hebrew Congregations—collaborated in establishing a Berit Mila Board (their spelling), empowered to train and certify physicians (women and men) to serve as ritual circumcisers. Led by Rabbi Lewis M. Barth, a professor of rabbinic literature at the Los Angeles branch of Hebrew Union College, the Board was composed of physicians and rabbis—perhaps symbolic of how completely genital surgery and religious rite had merged. In 1988, with increasing numbers of physician-mohels being certified, the group created a National Association of American Mohalim/ot (mohalim and mohalot are plural Hebrew terms for male and female operators). The next year they changed "Association" to "Organization" to create the acronymn NOAM.

The Hebrew term *no'am*, literally "pleasantness," is translated in the Jewish Publication Society version of Psalm 90:17 as "favor": "May the favor of the Lord, our God, be upon us; let the work of our hands prosper; O prosper the work of our hands." This was adopted (with the word "Lord" changed to "ETERNAL" in capitals) as a motto.

The organization conducts courses for physicians throughout the country, from San Diego to Boston and many points between. By 1997, they had certified nearly two hundred physician-mohels who had performed more than 6,500 ritual circumcisions.[26] These men and women are not required or even expected to follow Orthodox practices; they are free to devise their own versions of the rite, introducing whatever might appeal to contemporary audiences. They never mention *metsitsah*, of course, nor do they include traditional readings containing offensive statements or implications—the references to blood and sacrifice, or the story of how Phinehas murdered the fornicators.[27] Instead, their ceremonial readings speak about parental love and support, "entry" into Abraham's covenant, loving memory of departed family members, and so on.

In 1990, the Board published a volume entitled *Berit Mila in the Reform Context*, designed as a textbook for physician trainees.[28] The contributors (mostly rabbis with doctoral degrees in history, sociology, education, etc.) were among the best-educated members of the Jewish American clergy. In his introduction Barth acknowledges that the practice "has come under increasing attack," that physicians seem less accepting than in the past, and that "there has been a resurfacing of terminology such as 'mutilation' and 'castration' to describe it," but he dismisses such "highly charged rhetorical description" as a legacy of "ancient Greek and Roman attitudes." He also recognizes the objections of "feminist thinkers" who have "targeted circumcision as a visible sign of the establishment of patriarchy, of male dominance and denigration of women—excluded by the very nature of the act from the Covenant." But his only response to "these contrary voices" is vague recourse to "the framework of Reform Jewish thought and practice." He has noticed a possible "shift back to encouraging routine circumcision"; but since for Jews circumcision is solely "a religious act," medical considerations are of only incidental interest (even though the book is addressing physicians!).[29]

A few contributors to the volume also sense problems. For example, Sanford Ragins, a rabbi and historian, opens his essay with a reminder that "Classical Reform Judaism was marked by a coolness, if not by outright hostility, toward many traditional Jewish rituals, especially those which, like *berit mila*, are so earthy" (the last adjective a startling reminder of the Christian argument). Then he quotes the third principle of the Pittsburgh platform and comments: "To say the least, such a declaration is not exactly encouraging to those [presumably including himself] who wish to celebrate observances like *berit mila*." The bulk of his essay describes the impact of

Jewish emancipation and modernity on the development of Reform Judaism in Europe. But his conclusion retreats into an illogical argument. Although the founders of the Reform movement may have "ignored or disvalued" some aspects of "our tradition," he assures readers, we perform circumcisions "in fulfillment, not betrayal, of their legacy." By training physicians to "serve Jewry" as ritual circumcisers, he and his colleagues "preserve and extend the achievements of our predecessors."[30]

Unconvincing though their arguments may be, Barth and Ragins are at least writing within a familiar framework of discourse. But what are we to make of an essay entitled "Reflections on Circumcision as Sacrifice," by two Reform rabbis with doctoral degrees in history and sociology? These scholars inform their physician students that the "subject of circumcision draws us into the territory of myth," and that the "particular province of myth most hospitable to the rites of circumcision is sacrifice." Circumcision, they continue, "is manifestly a salvationary rite, performed by the father on his son to save his—the father's—life, to win him—the father—the divine favor." Elaborating on this announcement, they continue on the theme of "circumcision as sacrifice." In its "rabbinic formulation," they explain, circumcision is "an attempt to exact from the male child recompense for the loss of semen by the father" and perhaps also "loss of amniotic fluid and milk by the mother." Having "drained the father of his life-force (semen)," the infant must now repay the debt "by relinquishing his own bodily fluid (blood) in the *berit mila* ritual." Circumcision turns out, therefore, to be not so much an affirmation of Abraham's covenant as "an attempt to rectify the imbalance of life fluids caused by the loss of the ultimate life-force fluid (semen) by the father through the sacrifice of another fluid (blood), which was given directly to the father or his surrogate, the *mohel,* who in turn provided the child with another fluid, wine."[31] So this *is* a medical procedure after all: American physicians, with access to the world's most advanced medical knowledge, must circumcise (Jewish) infants in order to "rectify" an "imbalance of life fluids." Presumably, female infants cause no fluid drainage problems.

Physician-mohels seeking further enlightenment can turn to articles in the *Berit Mila Newsletter,* issued by NOAM in seven volumes between 1989 and 1995. There, for example, they can read reflections on the question of how to deal with infant pain. Dr. Barry Meisel, discounting the "old beliefs that infants do not feel pain or won't remember it anyway," urges use of dorsal penile nerve block to spare infants as much pain and stress as possible. Opponents of circumcision, he remarks, cite several arguments: that it's "an unnecessary procedure"; that infants have the "right to be whole and no part should be taken away any more than one would cut off a baby's ear lobes"; and that it "inflicts pain." The first two objections he ignores. Use of anesthesia, he concludes, "may provide some solace to that group who call circumcision the unkindest cut of all."[32]

In another contribution on pain, Dr. Dorothy Greenbaum says that mohels must address not only the infant's pain but also the "emotional pain of the parents." We circumcise infants, she explains, for several reasons: because "God commanded it," because the rite enables us "to identify with our heritage," and because we realize that "man needs perfecting—even at the stage when we feel that this beautiful newborn baby is nearly perfect."[33] But since there is abundant evidence that infants feel pain, we must try to make the operation as painless as possible. After all, circumcision is a "trauma," and the "fragile and trusting" infant isn't a "willing participant." Although very well informed—her article discusses all the possibilities for pain relief and is followed by an excellent bibliography—Greenbaum admits that she herself relies for pain relief only on "swaddling" and a sucrose pacifier. As for parental and family apprehension, there may be some "benefit": When adults are "frightened for the child," they "suddenly realize how precious he is." So although we should do our best to "guard and protect" infants, the idea of carrying pain relief "to the extreme and whisking the child away into another room where he is circumcised quietly while everyone eats and drinks may in fact totally defeat the purpose of the ritual and sterilize its sanctity." Dr. Greenbaum's conclusion: We should minimize the infant's suffering "but not go so far as to anesthetize the emotional experience of the adults." Since circumcision symbolizes our "responsibility to repair the world," we should aim to "reform the pain but preserve the feeling of Berit Mila."[34]

Greenbaum does not explain why only males are born "nearly" but not wholly perfect. Nor does she elaborate on "repair of the world," or how and why unanesthetized infant foreskin removal contributes to global renovation. Finally, if Jewish adults do indeed require an emotionally draining experience to enable them to "identify" with their "heritage," it might be asked why this should be provided by operating on infants. Is it not usually understood that adults accept stress and discomfort in order to assist children on the path to maturation—rather than the other way around?

Another Berit Mila physician, Dr. Janet Marder, says that although she doesn't "know much" about physician fees, she does know that circumcision fees charged by some of her "rabbinic colleagues" are "scandalous—a blot on the honor of our community." Remember, she urges readers, that our message to the Jewish community should be one of "simplicity, modesty, and restraint." In the final analysis, she continues, life is a "mystery," hard to fathom, and circumcision does indeed pose problems for "medical people, scientifically oriented," when they undertake to perform "a primitive act bound up with dark messages about blood and tribe and the life-force." It's an "awesome task," taking place in a time of "erosion of the sacred":

> It is, most of the time, a black and white, workaday world. Every
> now and then a miracle happens. A child is born and the world

explodes into technicolor. Through the work of your hands, through the words of your mouth, a family of Israel encounters the Holy One. Some of the erosion is repaired. . . . That is the blessing you bring to our community.[35]

Rabbi Sheldon Marder, the physician's husband, follows her article with a personal "confession" regarding that blessing:

> Both times my wife Janet gave birth . . . I greeted with great joy, but also a powerful sense of relief, the doctor's announcement, "It's a girl!" I admit it. I was grateful that I would not have to be a father at a berit. As a rabbi I was ashamed of myself. Not enough, mind you, to cancel out my feeling of relief. [But having thought more deeply about a rabbi's role] I am now very humble in the presence of parents who bravely fulfill this sacred and awesome mitzvah. I am deeply honored to have a role in their lives at a time when they are experiencing one of the ultimate joys of life.[36]

The rabbi seems to have sensed no inconsistency in admitting that he was profoundly relieved to have escaped one of life's "ultimate joys."

"I Smiled to My Congregants": Young Rabbis Face the Personal Challenge

Not only Rabbi Marder but other Reform rabbis seem to share the ambivalence and unease of Berit Mila physicians. Lawrence Hoffman tells what happened in a study group of young rabbis, most with children, when he discussed research that would eventually become part of his book, *Covenant of Blood*. Several participants spoke about the circumcision of their own sons, "about which, it turned out, they frequently harbored intense rage—rage at themselves for allowing it to happen, and in some cases rage at the *mohel* who had done it and botched the job." When Hoffman asked whether anyone had declined to circumcise a son, he met with "silence," then "anger." He had no right even to participate in the debate, the others charged, because at his age he no longer had to face the unwelcome question. "It's easy for you to talk," they told him, while "we still have to worry about it." These young rabbis, comments Hoffman, face "the dilemma of circumcision" each time a son is born to a congregation member, "not to mention to themselves."[37]

Hoffman cites a widely noted article by Michael B. Herzbrun that appeared in a 1991 issue of a prominent Reform journal. The author, a young rabbi in Rochester, described his personal agony when he realized that his infant son was experiencing severe pain: The child's "startled shriek lapsed into a prolonged, gasping, silent wail." Staring at the suffering infant, Herzbrun asked himself:

> What covenant did *his* expression represent? The only promise that he had known during his first week of life was the nurture of his mother's presence. Yet her embrace and warmth were beyond his reach when the ceremony began. And although we both were standing beside him, I had also participated in this "betrayal." I smiled to my congregants in attendance, satisfying their need to know that everything was alright. But what about my son's needs? As he struggled in pain, had I somehow abandoned him for the sake of the ceremony?[38]

Herzbrun raises other questions. Is circumcision "a form of mutilation?" Does the rite serve to reassure fathers, faced with "frightening awareness of their own mortality," as well as doubts about their own "potency and virility" and "psychological dominance in the family structure"? And how about the child's mother? Might her "own potential ambivalence regarding circumcision ultimately affect her relationship with both her husband and her newborn child?" But these questions were not enough to lead him to reject the rite itself. In the final analysis, his sole purpose was to call for relief of pain: not just the pain of the infant but also the pain felt by parents who see the child suffer. Despite "the cutting of the flesh and the pain inherent in the circumcision procedure," he concludes, "the *berit mila* appears destined to remain an inviolate rite within our tradition."[39] That a young rabbi, writing for a periodical managed and read by his colleagues, ventured only this far is no surprise. It seems more remarkable that the editors accepted an article raising such challenging questions.[40]

A Mohel to the Stars

Probably the most widely known graduate of the Berit Mila Board's training program is Fred R. Kogen, a theatrically accomplished physician known as the "Mohel to the Stars" and the "Mohel of Beverly Hills." Kogen performs circumcisions as a full-time occupation, and he is obviously very successful in this role. He has been featured in newspaper and magazine articles, and is one of three mohels celebrated in the 1999 documentary film *L.A. Mohel*. One magazine named him "Bachelor of the Month" when he was in his midthirties, and in July 1999 he was featured in *Los Angeles* magazine, with the label "Expert Cutter," as one of "The Best of L.A."[41]

In the "Goals and Philosophy" section of his website, Kogen distinguishes his surgical method from that usually employed by hospital physicians. Hospital circumcisions may take fifteen minutes or longer; his "takes about 60 seconds, and no one is required to watch, except, of course . . . the mohel!"

There is very little blood and crying, the baby is comforted in the arms of a loved one, then handed immediately back to his parents for the conclusion of the ceremony. A restraining board is usually not necessary to hold the baby. To make the baby as comfortable as possible, I also favor the use of a prescription topical anesthetic, sweet kosher wine or concord grape juice, infant Tylenol, a little pain reliever mixed with antibiotic dressing, and a lot of TLC (tender loving care).

"A properly conducted bris," he continues, "can be one of the most unforgettable moments of one's life and should always be a powerful and wonderful experience. It should reconnect us to our heritage as Jews and you as a family to those beloved departed, all of whom had a bris upon their eighth day of life."[42] Perhaps I need not comment on the rather obvious meta-message. Kogen appears to be saying that *adults* will have a wonderful and unforgettable experience, and that *they* will be reconnected to their predecessors and their ethnic heritage. What has happened to initiation of the *infant* into Abraham's covenant? Moreover, the "beloved departed" are exclusively male, and indeed the entire statement seems to address only men.

In a December 1996 *New York Times* article, Kogen described himself as "the alternative to the guy who shows up dressed like a Hasid and should not be holding a scalpel." Kogen, the article continued, "respects, understands, and, as it were, caters to his clientele. He wears a 'not quite Armani' Italian suit, has call waiting on his cell phone and drives a Lexus. ('If the car's too junky, they think, how serious can he be?')"[43] His website is elegantly designed to provide information and reassurance to clients. Although acknowledging that there is no "compelling reason to circumcise all newborns as a matter of routine," he is well prepared to accommodate parents who request the procedure. He promises to provide "the safest, least traumatic way to accomplish this goal." The website "set-up instructions" for the ceremony, organized from A to F, are the most elaborate I've encountered. I'll quote them in some detail, to provide a sense of how at least one Reform circumciser has redesigned the traditional rite, and how expertly he has enclosed and submerged infant foreskin removal in adult ceremonial proceedings.

A. Contact Kogen's "bris certificate calligrapher," who hand-designs naming certificates.
B. Leave a parking space for Kogen, since he keeps "emergency supplies" in the Lexus.
C. Feed the baby, give him acetaminophen drops, and dress him as desired—but "no snapped one-piece suits."
D. Purchase in advance petroleum jelly, antibiotic ointment, surgical gauzes, and acetaminophen—all available from Kogen's office "if interested in this option."

E. Prepare a "large open room," with raised chandelier, sturdy table, fabric tablecloth ("Please no plastic!"), pillow, adequate lighting, "two tall tapered candles" (red roses instead on Saturday), diapers, blanket, pacifier, bib, prepoured wine, four ceremonial wine cups—one-third full with kosher red wine—and one or two sandek chairs.

F. Choose candle lighters, readers, and sandek in advance, and "if no godparents, then use grandmothers." Fill out a "bris script card" ("Please print clearly!"). Invite guests to prepare to "share special thoughts about the baby." Parents may want to compose "a moral or ethical guide" in the form of a letter or poem, describing the infant's namesake and "what special hopes" they have "for his future." Candle lighters and poem readers are to arrive a few minutes early "to review their roles." ("Remind everyone to bring their reading glasses!") Disconnect the telephone, and place a sign on the door: "Ceremony in Progress. Please enter quietly." Have extra cameras and film available; consider hiring a professional photographer. If the father or grandfather has a prayer shawl, this may be used to wrap the baby. "Scatter flower petals (rose or other types) about the periphery of the table," and possibly also a small flower arrangement "to add a special beauty to the table." Place family photographs— weddings, portraits, and so on—on the front edge of the table, along with other "mementos and heirlooms," such as the namesake's personal effects: "tefilin [sic; phylacteries, worn by Orthodox men at prayer], lighter, glasses, watch, pen, wedding band or wallet."

Finally, Kogen's office will provide suggestions for food caterer, baby nurse, "or even some Klezmer music."[44]

In an article in *Rocky Mountain News*, Kogen described a ceremony (more accurately, an event) that was apparently frequent in his experience: "There are hundreds of people showing up, limousines pulling up, valet parking, full catered event, live band, orchestra, everything else. And we're all . . . standing around this poor little baby, cutting off the end of his penis. It's unbelievable."[45]

Note that the emphasis here is not on Abraham's covenant (which seems nowhere in sight) but on the infant's family, on memory of his deceased namesake, and of course on the entire event as a performance, with Kogen as M.C. and involving many members of the audience. Although Kogen serves a predominantly Jewish clientele, he performs circumcisions also for Gentile parents, particularly film and television actors and personnel. He is not just a ritual circumciser, he is a physician-performer for parents who want a top-quality home event.

Leaning Gently Rightward

Reform rabbis in the United States have been uncertain about whether to require circumcision for adult converts. As far back as 1892, they debated the question at their annual conference; and in a lengthy report issued the following year by a committee headed by Isaac Mayer Wise, they declared that, since circumcision of converts had no "basis in the Torah or even in Rabbinical law," the procedure could be avoided "without endangering the union of Israel and the unity of Judaism." Converts could be accepted, they continued, "without any initiatory rite, ceremony, or observance whatever," provided only that they demonstrated understanding of Judaism and its moral obligations, and that they were entering the Jewish fold of their own "free will and choice."[46] This was still the essential position in 1978; in a formal reply to a question about a "prospective convert who fears circumcision," Rabbi Walter Jacob (chairman of the Responsa Committee) said that although prospective converts "should be encouraged to undergo circumcision," the requirement could be "waived according to the earlier Reform decision."[47]

The rightward trend of the Reform movement was on display at the 2001 annual Reform rabbinic convention. Many rabbis had begun wearing skullcaps, and there was renewed interest in other ritual observances, including dietary regulations, that Classical Reform rabbis had long declared obsolete. As the conference president explained, the group was "leaning toward tradition when it comes to ritual and personal practices." Converts were urged (though apparently not yet required) to accept ritual circumcision and immersion in a ritual bath. Moreover, as the incoming president remarked, whereas thirty years ago, families in his congregation had their infants circumcised by physicians in hospitals, now they were having circumcisions performed by Reform "mohelim" (presumably physician-mohels) on the eighth day.[48]

"No Way of Making a Happy Celebration": Humanistic Judaism

The Society for Humanistic Judaism is a small organization whose members reject supernaturalism and traditional religious services but affirm Jewish ethnic identity and connection with Jewish culture. A 1988 issue of their journal, *Humanistic Judaism*, featured several contributions on circumcision. The lead article was by the group's rabbi, Sherwin T. Wine. Questions about circumcision, he noted, are a relatively recent phenomenon in Jewish American life. But deciding against the practice "is not like eating shrimp," because the "emotional commitment" to the practice is "far more intense than to almost any other Jewish ritual." (He doesn't explain what he means by "almost.") Better, he says, to announce that you're a "ham-eating atheist" than to declare that you will not have your son circumcised, which would be considered "almost next to betrayal."[49]

But having issued the warning, Wine mounts an argument for taking precisely that stance. Why, he asks, was removal of the foreskin, rather than some other body part, chosen as a "sign of the covenant"? Perhaps it was because "in Yahveh's mind, modesty precluded an explanation." Or perhaps he associated "phallic surgery" with his promise to grant "numberless descendants" to Abraham. Speculation about the divine mind doesn't help, though, since the "real reasons" are "lost with the reasoning processes of primitive people in dim antiquity." Perhaps they wanted to appease their gods to ensure fertility, and performed the surgery on infants as a way of protecting them from "hostile deities."[50] Nowadays, he continues, one hears three main objections to the practice: Some claim that circumcision confers no "positive health value"; others—the "civil libertarian" group—argue that, since infants have to "suffer the consequences" of the surgery, no one, not even parents, should have the right to impose it on them; finally, feminists find it "deeply offensive" that "phallic circumcision" is the "only required initiation rite." Regarding the medical question he defers to the judgment of physicians and parents. That applies to the infant's civil rights as well, in that if circumcision is truly beneficial, it can hardly be called a violation of the child's rights. But if parents conclude that it is medically worthless, "they should avoid the procedure for their son." As for feminist objections, Wine declares himself fully in accord and calls for "a new kind of celebration": a naming ceremony for infant girls and boys.

Although Wine aimed for a measured assessment, it seems that by the end of his brief article he had convinced himself that, aside from putative medical benefits, it is impossible to justify continuing ritual circumcision. "There is no way," he concludes, "of making a happy celebration out of the performance of bloody surgery."[51]

Two well-informed mothers who rejected circumcision for their sons contributed articles to the same issue. One, Nelly Karsenty, an immigrant who once studied in a yeshiva in Israel, outlines all the major arguments with clarity and conviction. Soon after coming to this country, she says, she was "stunned to realize that questioning this ritual is the ultimate taboo among American Jews." They don't even want to know anything about it:

> The extent of the repression surrounding this issue is astounding. Anyone who dares to question the *brit milla* [sic] ritual is angrily silenced, laughed at, lightly dismissed, or labelled "a traitor undermining Judaism" . . . .
>
> Astonishingly few people know what the *milla* or surgery really entails. Most Jews would describe it as "the cutting off of a little piece of skin." The words most often used when referring to the ritual are: "joyful," "quick," and "painless." Pointing out that we are talking about surgery performed with no anesthetic, raising issues of pain and possible trauma, makes most Jews angry and very defensive. Mentioning that complications do occur and that not all babies

respond well to the surgery is taboo—as if pretending that this is not reality somehow makes it unreal.[52]

Karsenty continues with a sharply worded critique citing every major objection to the practice: pain, "unnecessary surgery," lack of consent, "genital mutilation," and "feminist issues," all carefully argued. Why then, she asks, do "the vast majority of Jews who show no particular attachment to the details of the Jewish covenant with God so tenaciously defend this particular commandment"? Her reply is that since people "seem to have a powerful need for rituals," many Jews cling to circumcision as their only remaining form of ethnic identification—"a symbolic loyalty oath saying that one belongs to the Jewish tribe." Then, too, there is confusion about supposed medical benefits, and perhaps also the notion that the only way to defy anti-semites, as well as to distance oneself from Christianity, is to remain loyal to this one custom. Although acknowledging that "these concerns are very real," Karsenty declares that Jews and Judaism can surely survive with redesign of circumcision into a "bloodless" naming ceremony.[53]

"Make the Most of It": Popular Literature for Parents

"Danger, Dread, and Death": Reassurance from Anita Diamant

Although contemporary books addressed to Jewish parents favor the cheerful, noncritical perspective characteristic of American advice literature, authors seem well aware of the anxiety and dread surrounding circumcision. Perhaps the most widely read writer in this genre is Anita Diamant, who acknowledges in the preface to her *Jewish Baby Book* that parents may feel "dazed, out of control, and something less than joyful" when faced with a rite requiring genital surgery on their infant sons. Since Diamant describes her book as a guide to "liberal Jewish practice in America," meaning "all non-Orthodox movements," she must assume that her readers will not accept categorical statements about divine commands. Her task is to justify the ways of Judaism to apprehensive parents seeking rational explanation and reassurance.[54]

Diamant begins with admission of her own discomfort. She explains that while *brit habat*, "covenant of the daughter," the recently introduced naming ceremony for infant girls, is a lighthearted event, an infant son's *brit milah* is "elemental, mysterious, incomprehensible and awe-ful [sic]." The warning implicit in the preface is repeated: Although a circumcision *should* mean "joy" and "celebration," parents may feel "more confusion and fear than happiness." But comfort is on the way; she will inform them about the "whys" and "hows" of the rite—to reduce their "fears" and add to their "rejoicing."[55]

A brief discussion of biblical and rabbinic interpretations follows, but Diamant obviously doesn't expect these to offer much enlightenment or solace. The "most striking line" in the liturgy, she notes, is the passage from Ezekiel: "I passed by you and saw you wallowing in your blood." This she interprets as a reminder of the "physical reality" of life, including "danger, dread, and death as well as spiritual aspirations." She notes that the "earthy, disquieting words" often go untranslated at a circumcision, or may even be replaced with less disturbing biblical or talmudic quotations (and indeed she omits the passage in her own account of a representative rite).[56] As for the insistence on bloodshed in a "welcoming" ceremony for an infant, this author has no intention of trying to explain *that*.

By the time prospective parents reach the section on "Modern Questions" they might well be on edge. But little relief is in sight. "Is it safe?" asks Diamant. "Will my baby suffer?" Well, she assures readers, Jewish infants have survived the procedure for 3,500 years (about a thousand years too many, with no information on mortality rates at various times). And after all, she continues, a religion centered on "the sanctity of life and health" would hardly require anything injurious to an infant. Complications (unspecified) are "extremely rare," and infection is unlikely because "the site of the cut is well supplied with blood." As for questions about pain and suffering, Diamant has "no definitive answer." Perhaps, she says, exposure to "cold air" and being placed on his back may cause the infant as much distress as genital surgery (although it isn't clear why a room can't be comfortably warm). Be that as it may, she concludes, one must acknowledge the "discomfort" experienced by *parents*—which seems to return her to more manageable territory.[57]

Should one entrust this unsettling business to a mohel or a physician? While the mohel is often envisioned as "a doddering old man," physicians enjoy "enormous respect." But be forewarned: medical circumcisions are often performed by "inexperienced residents" who may be "doing a few babies one after another." Moreover, if one chooses the medical route, religious protocol still calls for a ritual procedure: *hatafat dam brit*, "shedding blood of the covenant" (translated by Diamant as "ritual drawing of blood from the site of the circumcision"), pricking the foreskin remnant with a needle to draw a drop of blood, accompanied by recitation of appropriate liturgy.[58]

In case parents are not yet sufficiently reassured, Diamant adds commentary on "symbolic castration" and "substitute for infant sacrifice"—lines of thought, she muses, that lead one to ask: "Why haven't we abandoned so barbaric a practice altogether?" Her answer: If we discontinue circumcision, "we stop being Jews."[59] Since in the Orthodox tradition it is birth to a Jewish mother—not circumcision—that identifies any infant, male or female, as Jewish, the statement is baseless. However, this author, well intentioned but out of her depth here, may be excused for inability to provide an adequate guide for the perplexed.

"My Son, My Son, My Son": Rabbi Neusner on "Enchantment"

The same can hardly be said for Jacob Neusner, the former director of a major Judaic studies program at Brown University, an ordained rabbi, and a distinguished authority on early rabbinic Judaism and rabbinic literature. An extraordinarily prolific author, Neusner has written, in addition to countless scholarly volumes, a number of books addressed to general audiences. In *The Enchantments of Judaism*, a book on Jewish "rites of transformation," he defines his main audience as Jews of every kind, observant or not, who seek better understanding of "the reality of living Judaism." (He describes himself as a centrist, "closer to the Reform than the Hasidic.")[60]

Struggling to find "enchantment" in circumcision, this learned scholar sounds as uneasy and ambivalent as Anita Diamant. Although the operation is "a minor surgical rite, of dubious medical value," he begins, it is nevertheless "the mark of the renewal of the agreement between God and Israel, the covenant carved into the flesh of the penis of every Jewish male—and nothing less."[61] As for why a covenant must be carved into an infant penis, Neusner offers only the vague assurance that the ritual liturgy (not the actual surgery) is "the medium of enchantment" that somehow transforms the business of foreskin removal into a spiritual experience for the child's parents: "an event heavy with meaning: a metaphor for something more, for something that transcends." (Unlike some Orthodox commentators, he makes no such claim for the infant's experience.) Then he retreats into an anecdote about his own son's circumcision, performed at home. When his wife's father, holding the child in the role of sandek, sat on the dining room table, it collapsed, sending baby and surgical instruments to the floor. Neusner assures readers that the child survived "nicely" and grew up to play rugby for Columbia—a point repeated, as we'll see, in his closing remarks.[62]

"Enchantment," Neusner continues, "works in a mysterious way to make us do things we should not ordinarily do, to see things we commonly do not perceive." Taking for granted that we know what "things" we'd rather not do, he explains what (Jewish) witnesses are intended to "perceive" during the surgery:

> We see ourselves as—in the setting of Judaism—God sees us: a
> family beyond time, joined by blood of not pedigree but circumcision;
> a genealogy framed by fifty generations of loyalty to the covenant in
> blood; and a birth from the union of the womb of a Jewish woman
> with the circumcised penis of her husband. This is the fruit of the
> womb—my son, my son, my son.[63]

Aside from the confusing syntax, what are we to make of such an attempt at explanation? Why the startling reference to union of womb with circumcised penis? As the author knows very well, Orthodox Jewish doctrine holds that the child of a Jewish woman is Jewish by birth, even if the father is a genitally intact Buddhist or Hindu. Moreover, there is the central question, surely on the mind of any parent seeking instruction: Why foreskin removal? Why does a spiritual covenant, understandable only by adults, require infant bloodshed—and of all places from the penis? As for the bizarre capstone, the triple invocation to "my son," might this signify admission of his own anxiety attendant on the entire procedure? Perhaps I should repeat: Jacob Neusner is one of the most accomplished Jewish scholars of our time, an expert on early rabbinic society and culture; ordinarily he does not write in this vaguely mystical mode.

Neusner focuses on several features of the rite. First is the passage from Numbers 25 about Phinehas (here Phineas) and the "covenant of peace." Although I discussed part of this text earlier, it bears repeated mention here. The story is that when Israelite men were discovered to be "whoring" with Moabite women and worshiping Moabite gods, God imposed a plague on the Israelites and commanded Moses to have the leading transgressors "publicly impaled." But before Moses could carry out the executions, Aaron's grandson Phinehas entered a tent where a man was copulating with a Midianite woman and drove a spear through them both. This deed so gratified the Lord that he relented and ended the plague. The passage continues with the lines quoted in the circumcision rite, Numbers 25:10–12:

> The Lord spoke to Moses, saying, "Phinehas, son of Eleazar son of Aaron the priest, has turned back My wrath from the Israelites by displaying among them his passion for Me, so that I did not wipe out the Israelite people in My passion. Say, therefore, 'I grant him my pact of peace.'"

This is the tale that opens the circumcision ceremony. Rather than dealing with the matter straightforwardly, Neusner quotes another author (Lifsa Schachter), who noted that Phinehas won the Lord's favor by punishing "sexual licentiousness and idolatry." Neusner doesn't explain how or why this message might enchant parents, let alone infants.

Turning to the blessing recited by the father (declaring his readiness to perform the commandment), Neusner explains: "What I do is like what Abraham did. Things are more than what they seem.... my fatherhood is like Abraham's."[64] Finally, "yet a further occasion of enchantment": the obscurely worded passage about sanctifying "the beloved from the womb," setting "a statute into his very flesh," and saving "the beloved of our flesh from destruction." This covenant, says Neusner (by now sounding distinctly uneasy) "is not a generality; it is specific, concrete, fleshly." It has "a specific goal": securing "a place for the child, a blessing for the child," by which "he joins that unseen 'Israel' that through blood enters an agreement with God. Then the blessing of the covenant is owing to the child [sic]. For covenants or contracts cut both ways."[65] In short, the child purchases redemption and divine blessing with his genital blood.

Neusner concludes with additional musing, returning to the scene of his son's circumcision. The blessings accompanying the rite literally enchant:

> I am no longer in the here and the now; time is other than what I thought.... The action is not the cutting of the flesh but the covenant of circumcision. And present are my wife and my father-in-law and my baby son on the floor, surrounded by knives and gauze. Present here, too, is the statement that we are Israel—yet, in the here and now, the dazed father; the bemused, enchanted grandfather; the sturdy son. Varsity rugby for Columbia indeed![66]

Here, then, seems to be the ultimate message: that Jewish parents need not be overwhelmed by feelings of discomfort—or, even worse, fears that this perplexing rite may diminish the masculinity of their sons. Nor should they be concerned if the experience leaves them feeling "dazed." They can feel confident that their sons will recover, that they will grow up to be just as "sturdy" as they had been in their intact state. In short, this highly accomplished scholar seems to offer readers little more than acknowledgment of the profound anxiety he himself experienced when his own son was circumcised.

"Let's Admit It": Explanation from Rabbi Gordis

Lest it appear that Neusner may have stumbled where others stride with assurance, I turn finally to a recently published book, *Becoming a Jewish Parent*, by another prominent rabbi-scholar, Daniel Gordis. While admitting that circumcision can be a "confusing" and disturbing experience, he informs (or misinforms) readers that it is "not a terribly complicated ceremony" after all.

But "the question that we have to ask ourselves," and may eventually have to answer for our children, is "What is this all about?" Well, in order to understand the "power" of circumcision, we must acknowledge that "the whole idea makes people very uncomfortable"—which explains why they "often make silly comments" and "why the *mohel* opens with a joke." His own discomfort is already evident: "There's a palpable tension in the room. The baby is so small, so vulnerable, so innocent. How can we explain the tradition's stipulation that we circumcise him? Now? In this way?" "Let's admit it," he continues, although most Jewish parents choose to have their sons circumcised, "it would be an exaggeration to say that they want to."[67]

Next (like Neusner) he shifts to personal reminiscence—actually a confession. Though he had attended "hundreds" of circumcisions, when it

came to circumcising his own son, he "didn't know what was coming"—
that is, he wasn't prepared for the disconcerting sight of the aftermath: the
infant's "red and swollen" penis. During the week before the circumcision
he had been changing diapers, but at his first attempt afterward he was "too
upset to finish." He left the job to his wife and waited about a week before
even looking again. When a second son arrived, he was again "on diaper
duty" for the first week, but after the circumcision was granted another
"reprieve."

In brief, this candid, well-intentioned rabbi, who had attended innumerable circumcisions, finally realized (apparently for the first time) why
parents are so "conflicted" about submitting their newborn sons to genital
surgery. His "discomfort" made him wonder why male Jewish infants need to
begin life with such a traumatic experience. Of course, God commanded it,
and perhaps that's explanation enough for some, but it won't satisfy everyone.
Feeling that there must be something more, Gordis turns to the circumcision
liturgy for answers—and gets no further than the passage about Phinehas.
"What a strange way to begin the *berit milah!*" he exclaims, now beginning to
sound as though he regrets ever having begun on this topic. Why such a
"strange introduction?" Having chosen to retell the story of what readers
surely perceive as a vicious double murder, Gordis, squirming almost visibly,
repeats his question: "Now, why in the world would the *berit milah* start with a
story like that?" Well, we have to try to "think about this creatively," he urges,
try to understand it "on its own terms." But his interpretive effort is so
painfully convoluted that no sensible reader could feel reassured. Maybe, he
proposes, the rite of circumcision recognizes our "tension and anxiety" and
encourages us to ask ("with Phinehas in mind"): "What in life is so sacred
that we would risk all for it?" Do we believe so deeply in some "causes" that
nothing and no one can discourage us?

Although hoping that "we'll never have to kill for something we believe
in" (i.e., emulate Phinehas!), he continues, perhaps it's "not a bad idea" to ask
what would lead us to do so. In particular, does anything in "the *Jewish world*"
matter that much to us—and could Judaism have survived all this time if
some of us hadn't been willing to sacrifice everything "to keep the enterprise
going?" We're asking "tough questions" here, with no easy answers; but
might it be that the rite of circumcision is Judaism's way of making us think
about tough questions? Or perhaps "the whole point" is to make us "feel
uncomfortable" (us, not the infant!). After all, we don't go through this because we want to; "in fact, we really *don't*." We do it because we must acknowledge that the child isn't actually ours: "In some strange [that adjective
again] but palpable way, he belongs to the Jewish people." Incidentally, since
entering the covenant is "serious business," tell the mohel: no jokes, please.
The "tension" has to be "healthy, productive." The rabbi closes on a note of
resignation: "Make the most of it."[68]

Phinehas was apparently more than enough for this embattled author, who wisely omitted consideration of the other "tough questions" posed by the standard rite, with its references to wallowing in blood and rescue from destruction. That matter aside, though, what are we to make of these attempts at explanation, particularly those by the two rabbis? Both are experienced writers, well grounded in Jewish history and accustomed to explaining Jewish ritual matters to general audiences. Is this really the best they could offer? Perhaps it is significant that each turned so quickly to personal reminiscence and confessed so candidly to personal distress. What is most remarkable is that, having undertaken to explain Jewish ritual practices to a largely Jewish audience, both were stymied when they came up against Judaism's most "mysterious rite."[69]

9

"Deep Feelings of Nervousness"

Circumnavigating the Taboo Topic

> You don't keep the sabbath, you don't go to temple any more, you've stopped keeping kosher and you're going with a shiksa. Ronnie, your Granma is very disturbed. She wants me to ask you, just tell your Granma so she wouldn't worry, are you still circumcised?[1]
>
> Don't do it![2]

Circumcision appears everywhere nowadays in American, particularly Jewish American, discourse—in periodicals, academic literature, fiction, on the internet. It also appears frequently in television sitcoms, where screenwriters, whether Jewish or not, express their own feelings about the practice. Some of this literature centers on ritual circumcision; but since hospital circumcisions are such a common experience for both Jewish and Gentile infants, often the distinction blurs. I'll cover a variety of sources in this chapter, but it is reasonably safe to say that whenever circumcision is discussed in literature addressed to a general audience, the defining motif is uneasiness.

Challenge and Defense in Jewish Periodicals

In periodicals reaching predominantly (but not exclusively) Jewish audiences, the usual practice is publication of paired articles, one opposing circumcision, the other supporting—always in that order. Very little public discussion, pro or con, appeared before the 1990s.

Asking and Answering the "Nagging Question"

One of the first to stir the waters was a young San Francisco mother named Lisa Braver Moss, who published an article in the progressive periodical *Tikkun* in 1990, accompanied by a staunchly conservative response by one of the editors. Braver Moss focuses on infant pain: "The issue at hand is pain—pain, and what it means to be Jewish." It seems safe to say, she continues, that "deep into their eighth-day ritual festivities" most Jewish parents are beset by the "nagging question: 'Why are we doing this?'" But in fact she seems reluctant to tackle that fundamental question, since her article proposes only that if the procedure must continue, let it be made less painful for the infant. Even that modest suggestion meets with resistance, she reports, for she has found it "nearly as hard to generate a dialogue about anesthesia in the Jewish community as to question the practice of *brit milah* itself":

> Bringing up the topic usually elicits responses ranging from the lighthearted and dismissive ("The anesthesia might go to better use on me than on the infant") to the defensive ("I was circumcised without anesthesia and it certainly didn't do *me* any harm"). I sense an underlying anxiety that, if we acknowledge infants' pain and discuss anesthesia, we may call the entire ritual into question. And that's taboo.[3]

Although she seems to shy away from defying the taboo, Braver Moss ventures a bit further in her closing statement. Using anesthesia, she argues, may enable us to "see *brit milah* for what it is—elective surgery on sentient beings." And from there we may be able to begin a discussion "not only of how, but of whether we should continue with this ancient ritual."[4]

A modest proposal—but not modest enough for Rabbi Daniel Landes, professor of "Jewish ethics and values" at Yeshiva University of Los Angeles (and a member of the *Tikkun* editorial board) and his coauthor, Sheryl Robin, identified as a writer with graduate degrees in social work and "human development." Their response, entitled "Gainful Pain," appeared immediately following the Braver Moss article. True to their title, these authors announce that "a wince of (empathetic) momentary pain," along with loss of "a few drops of blood," is precisely what the infant *should* experience if he is to participate fully in his own initiation into Abraham's covenant. The very point, they insist, "is to have the infant *there* as a participant in the event, without being numbed by anesthesia, either general or local."[5] Braver Moss's article, representative of "the contemporary attack," combines the "classical" objection to circumcision (it disfigures "the perfect body") with the Christian (it epitomizes the triumph of "flesh" over "spirit") "in a particularly nasty mixture." Make no mistake, they warn: the real purpose of those who argue for anesthesia and "dialogue" is "junking the whole process."[6] Opponents of circumcision fail to understand that what they see only as painful surgery is actually "the physical manifestation of Abraham's universal message of ethical monotheism." Its purpose, moreover, is "to overcome and harness the natural" by diminishing "the evil inclination" (*yetzer hara*) so intrinsic to male sexuality. By discouraging the "natural propensity" of men to misbehave, circumcision "attempts a *tikkun*, a repair of nature, and affirms the value of sexuality through restraint." For while the foreskin "represents the coarseness of unredeemed existence," circumcision confers refinement and the promise of redemption.[7] The authors conclude with a peroration: "The gaining of freedom, the establishment of community, the initiation of true selfhood, and the evoking of the covenant are not achieved without a cost." That cost is unanesthetized excision of infant foreskins.[8]

The appropriately named Braver Moss returned to the fray in 1992 with an article in *Midstream*, a moderately conservative periodical published under Zionist sponsorship. Once again, what is most noteworthy about her article (even more necessary here, perhaps, if she was to gain editorial acceptance) is its cautious tone, since never does she propose that circumcision be discontinued. Rather, she argues for reconsideration—at least, anesthesia to mitigate the infant's suffering—and modest reform to make the rite more appropriate for contemporary Jewish Americans. Many parents, she points out, accept the procedure without reflecting on its ostensible spiritual meaning, then return to their customary nonobservant lifestyle. They do not ponder the ethical implications of imposing genital alteration on a nonconsenting infant; nor are they likely to wonder about possible complications or diminished sexual capacity.[9]

Characteristic of this author's tactics is her attempt to enlist the writings of Orthodox rabbinic authorities as support for her arguments. Thus she cites statements that the child should be awake and not anesthetized as evidence for her contention that personal intent is important—but that an infant cannot express intent. (Though it might be argued that a screaming infant *is* doing just that.) Having granted recognition to the usual arguments favoring circumcision—that it is the infant's "birthright," his permanent mark of Jewish identity, and that it must be preserved to offset the threats posed by intermarriage and assimilation—Braver Moss counters that "questioning" circumcision has enabled her to experience heightened "meaning" in her own Jewish identity. She urges readers to approach the "task" of reconsideration "with an open mind and a Jewish heart."[10]

The article seems designed for a preemptive defense, anticipating charges of disloyalty, ignorance of tradition, and the like. It might be said, on the one hand, that within the mildly worded questions and proposals is a call for profound reform; on the other, that by concentrating so heavily on pain (admittedly a major issue) Braver Moss left her argument open to challenge by anyone drawing on a wider span of considerations.

This was in effect the tactic adopted in a "rebuttal" by Esther Raul-Friedman, an editorial assistant at *Midstream*, which appeared a few months later. Writing from a resolutely Orthodox perspective, she insists that "Miss Moss" failed to understand the "religious or spiritual significance" of ritual circumcision and omitted or distorted "relevant facts." Raul-Friedman's argument is rooted in claims advanced by mohels (presumably Orthodox) whom she interviewed. Circumcision with a clamp is indeed painful, she acknowledges, but not with the specially sharpened knife of the experienced mohel. More to the point, a ritual circumcision is a man's "holy treasure," an external mark that "activates an inner commitment to God and His commandments."

> Thus, in opting not to circumcise their newborn infant, parents not only deprive their son of his legacy, his tradition, his birthright, but they are condemning him to a life without *shayachut* (belonging). For the Jewish people is one people. No matter where one goes or how far one travels, if you identify yourself as one Jew to another— you will always be welcomed.

Circumcision, she continues, is what one mohel described as "a spiritual life insurance policy," and loyal Jews have always realized that "the physical survival of the Jewish people rests on the perpetuation of this mitzvah" (commandment). Respect for Jewish martyrs and for forefathers, commitment to belief in God, love for children and for the Jewish people: all declare "not only our responsibility but our obligation to continue to circumcise our sons and raise them to be proud of their Jewish heritage." Lest all that not suffice, Raul-Friedman adds a warning: Failure to circumcise a son is punishable by divinely ordained premature parental death.[11]

Like other women who uphold circumcision, Raul-Friedman writes as though Orthodoxy's patriarchal nature and exclusive focus on male infants has never generated questions in her mind. She is content with the principle that the very survival of the Jewish people rests largely on a rite affirming male identity, male centrality, and male privilege.

A Symposium on the "Extremely Difficult Demand"

Moment, more popular in style than either *Tikkun* or *Midstream* and with wider circulation, also entered the controversy in 1992 with a set of five articles on "Circumcision: What It Meant, What It Means."[12] The first, titled "Why Not the Earlobe?" is a trenchant critical essay by the anthropologist-rabbi Howard

Eilberg-Schwartz, whose book *The Savage in Judaism* I discussed earlier. The *Moment* essay, based on his chapter on circumcision, adopts a more polemical tone. The contention that Israelite religion transformed a fertility rite of "so-called primitive religions" by endowing it with transcendent spiritual meaning "is at best misleading," he argues, since the practice "performs the same anthropological functions and has the same meanings" as in African societies that ritually circumcise young boys. In African rites, he notes, the dominant themes are "fertility, virility, maturity and genealogy." Circumcision, in those societies as in that of the biblical-era Israelites, is a powerful symbol of patrilineality—descent through males and preservation of the male-defined lineage, with all that these imply for social organization: "The penis, then, is what makes a boy a male, an adult, a father and a continuator of his lineage. We can perhaps sum this up by saying that one must have a member to be a member."[13]

This is the author's answer, of course, to his not-so-whimsical question about the earlobe. But what about the covenant? Well, says Eilberg-Schwartz, if that was what God had foremost in mind, why, as we learn in Genesis 17:20–25, did he order Abraham to circumcise his first-born son, Ishmael, who was to be endowed with enviable fecundity but excluded from the covenant? No, the primary purpose of circumcision was not creation of a covenant; it was guarantee of abundantly fertile male lineages.[14] Incidentally, this helps explain why Abram's name changed to Abraham when he circumcised himself. The change of name distinguished him from his father and from everyone in the patrilineage, by introducing a "radical disjuncture," in effect "creating a new breed of men."[15]

Finally, of course, male circumcision differentiates the genders, initiating boys into the male world and symbolically releasing the male child from "the impurity of his mother's blood": "His blood is clean, unifying and symbolic of God's covenant. His mother's is filthy, socially disruptive and contaminating." Ritual circumcision thus signifies "the passage from the impurity of being born of women to the purity of life in a community of men."[16]

The overall tone of this article—its unequivocal rejection of claims for the religious uniqueness and ineffable significance of ritual circumcision, its insistence on demonstrating how closely the Jewish rite corresponds in meaning to those of contemporary African peoples—suggests that in the two years between publication of his book and this article, Eilberg-Schwartz may have become increasingly committed to a critical perspective on the practice. In any event, the seemingly benign title gains a sharp edge when one recognizes the import of his argument.[17]

Two essays that follow turn out to be implicit responses to Eilberg-Schwartz's arguments. In an essay titled "The Pain and the Pleasure," Suzanne F. Singer cites the familiar medical justifications for circumcision, focusing on the claims of Aaron Fink (discussed in my previous chapter) but saying very little about medical literature opposing the practice. Characteristic of her approach is her bland comment on the results of pioneering research on infant pain: "They concluded that newborns experience pain during circumcision and that the experience changes their behavior for one or two days." On the question of impaired sexual sensitivity she cites outdated statements by Alfred Kinsey (published in 1953) and Masters and Johnson (1966) but says nothing about recent research on foreskin innervation and function. The argument that circumcision constitutes "disfigurement" may appeal to those who are "attracted to naturalness." In contrast to these relatively trivial concerns, "Jewish parents stand before the immense power of millennia of tradition that began with Abraham." Should Jewish children (i.e., sons) now be denied entry into the covenant of their fathers and grandfathers?[18] Her title seems to mean that infants endure pain and a day or two of changed behavior so that their parents may experience the pleasure of conforming to the "immense power" of tradition.

An essay by Rabbi Joel Roth, titled "The Meaning for Today," addresses Eilberg-Schwartz's anthropological conclusions with the counterargument that, whatever the meaning of circumcision for other people, including the ancient Israelites, its contemporary meaning is the product of centuries of rabbinic interpretation investing it with significance wholly beyond that of any other cultural tradition. Rabbinic religion, Roth maintains, emphasizes the "covenantal element," while the "fertility element" has no role. He acknowledges that for those Jews who "do not think of themselves as bound by the covenant," ritual circumcision may indeed be subject to questions that are not "so easily answered," since justifying the rite "from outside the convenantal frame of reference" is "an extremely difficult demand." But somehow, he continues, adopting a more optimistic tone, most Jews—even those who have abandoned Sabbath observance and the dietary laws—continue to observe this single commandment. Why? Well, perhaps Eilberg-Schwartz has a point after all: "Deep in our collective subconscious, circumcision remains the symbol of our fertility, virility, maturity and genealogy—our physical survival. And physical survival is the barest minimum, for all Jews."[19] As in nearly all essays of this kind, the role of motherhood in Jewish "physical survival" receives no mention.

Another rabbi, David J. Meyer, contributed a one-page essay entitled "Doing It Myself," describing his emotions when he used a knife on his own son (after a mohel had applied a clamp). Meyer admits to "deep feelings of nervousness at that awesome time"—aggravated when he gazed into the child's "wide open eyes" and contemplated his "remarkably trusting and serene" expression (presumably before the clamp was tightened). The rabbi comforted himself with the knowledge that the prophet Elijah, in attendance at every circumcision, might soon announce "the beginning of an age in which the hearts of all men, women and children are turned to each other in love and compassion." He does not explain how removal of his son's foreskin might contribute to that world historical denouement.[20]

Dr. Schoen Explains

In 1997, the editors of *Moment*, perhaps having decided to affirm their support of circumcision, published an essay by the pediatrician I mentioned earlier, Edgar J. Schoen. Noting that some Jewish boys are now intact ("a form of genital chic" associated with "organic, back-to-nature movements"), Schoen warns that parents who fail to have their sons circumcised leave them vulnerable to urinary tract infections and to HIV infection in adult life. Moreover, he assures readers, there is almost no "downside." Yes, the procedure is painful, he acknowledges; but a capable physician or mohel can do the job very quickly, adequate anesthesia is now readily available, and there are "no demonstrated long-term emotional effects." As for why male infants are born with foreskins, we "can only guess." Perhaps, Schoen suggests, recalling Peter Remondino's nineteenth-century argument, the foreskin may have been useful in prehistoric times, when men were "running naked through thornbushes and brambles," but now it is no more useful than the appendix or wisdom teeth. Does the foreskin contribute to sexual pleasure? Schoen thinks not; to the contrary, circumcised men probably do better in that regard, and (according to a single study of Gentiles in Iowa) women prefer the cleaner quality and "more natural" appearance of the circumcised penis. Schoen looks forward to a time in the near future when "the current phenomenon of Jewish boys with foreskins" will come to an end.[21]

Personal Recollections by a Sociologist and a Mystic

Tikkun returned to the subject in 2001 with two more entries in the debate, both drawing on personal experience. Michael S. Kimmel, a sociologist at the State University of New York, Stony Brook, and a specialist on gender politics, contributed an article explaining why, after nine months of soul-searching, he and his wife decided to welcome their son into Jewish life with a nonsurgical ceremony. Kimmel reviews some of the arguments favoring circumcision, most having no relevance to Judaism: "aesthetic" preferences, medical claims, research findings suggesting that circumcised men are more active sexually, and, finally, the weight of Jewish tradition. He finds them all open to refutation. He is more impressed by the evidence on the other side: the peculiar history of circumcision as a putative "cure" for masturbation and venery; its destruction of sensitive genital tissue; and, perhaps decisive for him and his wife, its symbolism:

> Circumcision, it became clear, is the single moment of the reproduction of patriarchy . . . the moment when male privilege and entitlement is passed from one generation to the next, when the power of the fathers is enacted upon the sons. . . . To circumcise our son, then,

would be, unwittingly or not, to accept as legitimate 4000 years not of Jewish tradition, but of patriarchal domination of women.

He and his wife wanted their son "to live in a world in which male entitlement is a waning memory, and in which women and men are seen—in both ritual and reality—as full equals and partners."[22]

In reply, a rabbi named David Zaslow explained his decision to circumcise his previously intact six-year-old son. He and his wife had been "resolute" in their decision not to have the boy circumcised in infancy. Everything changed, though, when, at age forty, Zaslow experienced a "spiritual awakening" and became a rabbi (ordained by the experiential Rabbi Zalman Schachter-Shalomi).[23] Now Zaslow understood the difference between circumcision and *brit*:

> A *brit* is a covenant or partnership with the Divine. I was experiencing this covenant myself. Firsthand. Connecting to the Holy One. Personally. Me. I no longer saw Jewish rituals as symbolic. They were, when administered properly, not symbols but part of a spiritual technology for covenanting with G—d.

Zaslow celebrates his own existential transformation: "Oh, how I had changed!" Wondering how he could persuade his wife to acquiesce in a decision to circumcise their son at such a late age, he "opted for the truth—at least for 'my' truth." But she came around readily. While his own decision was "strictly spiritual" (or mystical—"I believed that G-d's covenant was a real energy pact"), his wife's was "strictly practical": she wanted the boy's penis to look acceptable at Jewish summer camp or on a visit to Israel.[24]

As for the child, Zaslow gave him gifts and "tried to make it special for him," but he admits to some personal unease: "I cannot say how much of a choice this was for Ari, but in his six-year-old wisdom he completely consented." (He doesn't speculate on whether a child of that age could have mustered the self-confidence and composure to resist parental pressure.) The morning after the circumcision (performed by a physician and a rabbi, with general anesthesia), Zaslow and his son lay together on the living room floor, the boy obviously in pain. Zaslow informed the child that had he been circumcised when he was eight days old, "there would have hardly been any pain." He didn't want to cause pain, he assured the child, and he asked for forgiveness:

> His answer still gives me shivers, "Of course I forgive you Daddy. But why didn't you do it then? I wanted you to do it then!" My mind went numb. I thought, "What did he mean...Dare I ask?" I asked. He answered, "I wanted you to do it when I was eight days old." I asked, "You remember?" I was getting zapped by an angel. He repeated his cryptic words again. "I wanted you to do it then!" With tears streaming down both our cheeks we sat together in silence.[25]

Michael Kimmel meant well, concedes Zaslow, but he had it all wrong. A ritual circumcision is not a surgical procedure; it's one of a category of commandments, called *hukkim*, "statutes," which must be accepted on faith because they have no rational explanation. They require that one "put the rational mind aside so that the heart and soul might open." When done properly, he continues, a ritual circumcision "is the most incredible father/son bonding experience." Far from asserting male dominance and entitlement, "it seems to be a means of reproducing male love and compassion." For while women "experience the awesome spiritual bonding power of blood every month," men "have this opportunity only during circumcision." Now, in his role as rabbi and counselor, Zaslow encourages fathers to bond with their sons by holding their hands during the circumcision, "to whisper blessings of love to them," to "carry" the pain for their sons, and "to cry for their sons and for all the pain their sons will experience in their lives." A *brit*, he concludes, "is a bonding ritual which I believe leads to higher levels of consciousness for both fathers and sons."[26]

Tikkun is a progressive journal, addressed to a sophisticated audience, often publishing articles by some of the nation's leading scholars and writers. Here, following an article by a sociologist versed in rational discourse, it gave voice to the musing of a psychologically naive mystic. Surely no well-informed reader could have read the two contributions as a debate between equally matched opponents.

We see in these periodicals a common pattern: opponents (always first) advance secular arguments centering on pain, damage to sexuality, sexist ideology, and the like; supporters (some drawn from editorial boards) respond mainly with theological and mystical arguments. Since the two sides speak from wholly different perspectives, there is no true dialogue.

"Committing a Perfidious Impropriety"

By 1998 the debate had made its way onto the internet. That year the online magazine *Salon* published a two-part article by Debra Ollivier, a Jewish woman who was married first to a French Catholic man, then to a Jewish American. Having become accustomed to the intact European penis, Ollivier resisted the prospect of circumcision for her newborn American son. She didn't realize, she says, "that a tiny but vital part of his penis would touch off deeply held convictions about cultural mores, aesthetics, psychology, hygiene, father-son relations, American identity and thousands of years of biblical traditions." She hadn't thought much about penises since her teenage years, she continues, "when every penis was a circumcised penis and the only issue of overriding concern as the tentative probings of adolescence bloomed into full-blown sexuality was: 'How does this thing work?'" Now she was to learn that by objecting to circumcision she was "committing a perfidious impropriety: refuting both my Jewish and American identity and, in so doing, robbing my son of both." Nevertheless she persisted, asking for explanations from "the astonished Jewish relative, the slightly repelled girlfriend, the perturbed American husband," but hearing nothing to change her mind.[27]

Judging from her article, Ollivier read widely in the historical and medical literature, reaching clear understanding of how and why circumcision gained acceptance in this country. She concluded that the procedure has endured because of three "persistent myths or biases." "The mother of all myths, now locker-room gospel, is that a circumcised penis is more hygienic than an intact one." The second, "popular and profoundly baffling," is that the surgery is painless. Third is the "cultural bias" affirming that a circumcised penis is cosmetically or aesthetically desirable. "In moments of free-associative candor," she reports, "girlfriends have compared the looks of an intact penis to everything from an elephant trunk to a dachshund." Contemplating the American mentality from the perspective of her years in Europe, Ollivier wonders whether circumcision is "in some odd way a metaphor for America itself: sleek and streamlined the way we like our cars and buildings." Perhaps, she continues, "the intact penis is a little too unruly, too Paleolithic, a little too, well, animal." [28] Here we find a contributor to *Salon* reaching an interpretation not so distant from those of Maimonides and his Orthodox successors—but with a far different conclusion.

Challenging the "New Enemies"

The most thoroughly argued *defense* of circumcision I've read appeared in the March 2000 issue of *Commentary*, which has evolved over the years from a progressive journal on Jewish and general issues into the leading medium for neoconservative authors. "The New Enemies of Circumcision" was contributed by Jon D. Levenson, a professor of Jewish studies at Harvard, and author of the book on child sacrifice cited in my first chapter. Levenson is a respected scholar, and *Commentary*, however one regards its present political stance, has long been a prominent periodical; so the article must be taken seriously. Simply to label it tendentious would be understatement; the degree of misrepresentation suggests that some Jewish Americans feel remarkably threatened by any and all opposition to circumcision of infants, Jewish or not. Finally, since *Commentary* is a secular periodical, addressing social and political issues along with fiction and criticism, articles on Jewish topics are ordinarily grounded in a secular perspective; but this one is a striking departure from that practice.

Although Levenson cites the conventional claims for medical benefits (advanced without critical assessment), his essential argument is explicitly theological—and rooted in the "chosen people" myth. Circumcision, he declares, was "commanded by God as part of His gracious offer to bring the

Jewish people close to Him in holiness." Citing the ancient rabbinic interpretation of *tamim* as a reference to physical (rather than moral) wholeness or completion, Levenson notes that only Abraham, not Adam, was enjoined by God to be "complete." Hence, he explains, a genitally intact man can be a "whole person" but not a "whole Jew." This, he proposes, is why Jews who have abandoned most ritual observance still want their sons circumcised.[29]

Levenson focuses on two categories of "enemies": an "alphabet soup" of organizations, and recent publications critical of circumcision. But the members of the organizations he cites are circumcised adult men attempting to restore their own foreskins; although they are understandably opposed to infant circumcision, this is incidental to their objective. He is either unaware of, or chose to ignore, the three major organizations specifically opposed to genital cutting of all male and female children: the National Organization of Circumcision Information Resource Centers (NOCIRC), Doctors Opposing Circumcision (D.O.C.), and Attorneys for the Rights of the Child (ARC). Moreover, he conflates Jewish ritual circumcision, a practice these organizations do oppose but tend to avoid confronting, with the far more widespread practice of hospital circumcision, their most immediate concern. In short, his characterization of "enemy" organizations is misleading.[30]

Levenson is on firmer ground when he turns to critical assessment of literature, although here too he seems to have read only selectively. He may have been galvanized into writing his article by the publication of David Gollaher's book *Circumcision*, which, though indeed unfavorable to circumcision, pays only cursory attention to the Jewish ritual practice. Gollaher is a capable historian specializing in nineteenth- and twentieth-century American medical history. His initial chapter, on "The Jewish Tradition," is not his strongest, and Levenson takes advantage of this to discredit the entire book. But here he reaches beyond what Gollaher actually says to imply that he said something entirely different. Citing Gollaher's prediction that routine hospital circumcision will soon become as antiquated as bloodletting, Levenson observes that ritual circumcision would then again become a unique mark of Jewish difference. And although some might approve of this, he argues, we know that whenever groups are clearly demarcated, the weaker is vulnerable to oppression. So Levenson detects an occasional "whiff of anti-Semitism (and/or Jewish self-hate)" in *any* literature opposing circumcision—perhaps, he suggests, "a harbinger of much stronger odors to come."[31]

Here Levenson quotes Gollaher's statement on the likely disappearance of routine hospital circumcisions, adding *his own* speculative conclusion—that this might make Jews more vulnerable to unspecified forms of oppression; then he proceeds to the unwarranted remark about antisemitism and self-hatred, and the prospect of "much stronger odors" if opponents of hospital circumcisions have their way. (The faulty logic is perhaps obvious: Wasn't circumcision supposed to "demarcate" Jews in the first place? And if that makes Jews "vulnerable," why not propose elimination of circumcision for everyone?) In a letter to the editor of *Commentary*, Gollaher, understandably offended, called Levenson's charge "outrageous" and "libelous if it were not so absurd." Levenson responded with no retraction but by citing another of Gollaher's statements, a naively phrased remark regarding accusations of ritual murder. He assured readers, however, that he had not charged his colleague, Lawrence A. Hoffman, with antisemitism or self-hatred.[32]

Levenson's critique of Hoffman's book is milder but equally misleading. To cite a single example: Without mentioning the illuminating commentary of Howard Eilberg-Schwartz on imagery associated with pruning and fertility, on which Hoffman draws in the course of establishing his own complex analysis, Levenson asserts that there is no evidence that laws regarding fruit trees have anything to do with fertility, or that circumcision was mandated for this purpose. But in the very next paragraph of his article he describes the Genesis 17 covenant approvingly as promising Abraham that he would father a "great nation."[33]

Levenson pays considerable attention to two books by Ronald Goldman, a social psychologist who has written about research on adverse psychological consequences of circumcision—along with much else. Levenson focuses on this single aspect of Goldman's work but says nothing about the books as a whole, which are based on substantial research into the medical literature. Instead, he implies that Bris Shalom ("Covenant of Peace") ceremonies, popular among parents who want to welcome their sons ritually without circumcision, are Goldman's singular creation (he refers to "Goldman's ceremony"), when in fact many others have designed similar ceremonies.[34]

But Levenson's ultimate purpose is not only to discredit "enemies" of circumcision, or to defend Jewish *ritual circumcision* alone, but to argue for the *surgical procedure* itself as a spiritual anchor for *all* Americans anxious to preserve traditional moral standards in these turbulent times. Rabbinic theology, he explains, views human beings (presumably only males) as inhabited by a "powerful appetite for evil" that must be forcefully subordinated and channeled. It rejects celebrations of "natural man and his raw instincts" and stands firmly opposed to "liberal culture," with its glorification of "human rights [!] and the supremacy of personal choice." Instead, the rabbinic tradition upholds "sacrifice, discipline, and obedience." Thus, the real significance of the controversy surrounding circumcision is the struggle between, on one side, advocates of personal autonomy (the "enemies") and, on the other, those who believe in the supremacy of duty (particularly for Jews). And while many Americans now value "pleasure, especially sexual pleasure" and pain avoidance above all else, Judaism teaches readiness "to suffer for a worthy cause" and elevation of "self-control over self-expression." Hence what appears on the surface as a Jewish issue proves to include all of American society, as it undergoes "a painful sorting-through of its own moral and cultural dispositions." Levenson hopes that the nation will turn again to the time-honored Jewish values that all Americans once cherished.[35]

Although the tone of this article is consistent with the political nature of contemporary *Commentary* journalism, it would be a mistake to dismiss it as nothing more than a reactionary polemic, or as a lone expression of marginal opinion. Levenson surely consulted with others about this piece; in any event, he speaks here for those who believe that opposition to any form of circumcision is little more than poorly disguised antisemitism. Remarkably, Levenson never mentions his own book, *The Death and Resurrection of the Beloved Son*, which, as I noted earlier, includes the suggestion that Jewish circumcision "may have once functioned as a substitution ritual for child sacrifice."[36] One wonders about the omission.

Bagels

In May 2001 the "Gotham" column of *New York* magazine featured an article entitled "Live and Uncut," noting that some "squeamish Jews" were conducting nonsurgical ("bloodless") "Covenant of Peace" ceremonies. Illustrating the text was a cartoon caricature of a bearded, potbellied mohel walking off with his knife and tool kit, looking upset and confused, while a cheerful, modern-looking young couple, laughing baby in arms, wave him away. "But is it kosher?" asked the author. "The only knife" in this ceremony, he reported, "is the one used to cut the bagels." Although there is no "hard data that Jews are turning away from it in droves," he continued, it's clear that circumcision is coming increasingly into question, and Jewish activists report widespread interest in alternative rituals. Moreover, some rabbis are "sympathetic." One commented, "Even I get chills. No parents want to intentionally cause pain." A mother who hosted a "Covenant of Peace" ceremony described herself as a "liberal, hippie, cultural Jew." "There's no reason to hurt my child," she declared, "to prove he's Jewish. . . . My son's faith will exist in his heart, just not in his genitals." A man who made the same decision said, "I thought about how I don't go to temple or keep kosher and I began to see that my original attachment to circumcision was arbitrary."

The magazine published four letters in response, two on each side of the controversy. A Jewish Canadian reader declared that he was "thrilled" to see that many of his "co-religionists are seeing the light regarding this abomination." He wrote: "Boys shouldn't be sacrificed like animals just because our genitalia stick out. It is illegal to do this to an animal. Why do it to our children?" (Hardly to the point, since in fact animals are regularly gelded and spayed.)

Speaking for the other side was a "secular and cultural" Jew who felt honored to hold his newborn nephews at their ritual circumcisions. For the mother who did not have her son circumcised he had a message: "She is naive if she believes any normal Jewish woman will ever be comfortable with an uncircumcised man. People like [her] have broken an unbroken chain; they *are* the weakest link! Good-bye."[37] (Aside from the circular reasoning, he appears unaware that many "normal" Jewish women are already marrying intact men.)

The "secular" uncle would have enjoyed the celebrations described in the March 3, 2003, issue of the *New York Times*. In a front-page article in the "Dining Out" section, Alex Witchel presented an enthusiastic account of lavish catered entertainments accompanying some ritual circumcisions in New York, Washington, and Baltimore. Although she uses the term *bris* and describes the events as religious ceremonies, there are no traces of covenants or unbroken chains in these proceedings. "Try 400 people in the Grand Ballroom of the Waldorf-Astoria," she gushes. "Or a luncheon for 30 at the Le Périgord. Or 250 for a buffet dinner at a country club." She does acknowledge that some witnesses, including herself, respond poorly to the surgical reality of circumcisions. Recalling that she "fainted dead away" after attending her younger brother's *bris* many years earlier, she reports that one caterer helps sustain sensitive guests by providing "everything from the bagels to the smelling salts."

The social catering director at the Waldorf-Astoria described a circumcision celebration in the hotel's Grand Ballroom:

> It was called for 8:15 in the morning. At about 9:15, the family went up onstage with the mohel, who took the baby behind a screen. We had a microphone so everyone could hear the baby crying. Then we had a klezmer band—people danced. It was great. The food was dairy—smoked fish, bagels, herring, kugel [noodle pudding]. We have relationships with several kosher caterers. Whatever you want, I make it happen.

Witchel admits that she still doesn't do well at circumcisions. At her nephew's *bris*, her "concentration was centered on not fainting and wrecking the event." The boy "screamed" when the surgery began; but since the reporter's specialty is food, not infant pain, she "left the room." Later, when she unwrapped her personal smoked whitefish platter, she found a small package: "It was a baby-size Barney Greengrass T-shirt. The note, addressed to my nephew, read, 'Dear Ilan, Welcome to the world of lox and bagels!'"[38]

"Jews of a Peculiar Kind": The Feminist Dilemma

In an article entitled "Why Aren't Jewish Women Circumcised?" Shaye J. D. Cohen answers the question forthrightly:

> although Jewish women are Jews, they are Jews of a peculiar kind. The 'normal' Jew for the rabbis, as the 'normal' Israelite for the Torah, was the free adult male. . . . The term 'Jews' means men; Jewish women are the wives, sisters, mothers and daughters of men,

the real Jews. . . . Therefore it should occasion no surprise if only men
are marked by circumcision—only men are real Jews in all respects.[39]

Anyone who has followed this narrative will agree that Cohen's characterization of Rabbinic Judaism as unequivocally male-centered and patriarchal
is accurate. Jewish feminists, recognizing this as the central issue for Jewish
American women seeking personally meaningful religious experience, have
responded with incisive critical commentary and creative innovations ad-
vancing contemporary Judaism toward gender equivalence. But it must be
said that when it comes to circumcision, they seem unprepared to move
beyond bland proposals that sidestep the difficult questions. The two most
widely read feminist books both adopt essentially the same perspective: they
mention circumcision briefly without serious critical assessment, and only to
endorse the increasingly popular practice of "welcoming" ceremonies for
infant girls.

In *Standing Again at Sinai*, a study of "Judaism from a feminist perspective," Judith Plaskow's rhetoric and argument are conditioned by her
adoption of biblical narratives as historical reality. She writes, for example,
that "Abraham and Sarah are my ancestors. . . . I went forth from Egypt and
danced with Miriam at the shores of the sea."[40] She presents no substantial
critique of the patriarchal foundations of rabbinic Judaism, simply urging that
the gendered religious system become more receptive to women. Her brief
comment on Abraham's covenant is, to say the least, modest. How can women
participate in "the covenant community," she asks, "when the primary
symbol of the covenant pertains only to men?" Well, she concludes, "women
are part of the covenant community, but precisely in a submerged and non-
normative way."[41] Her critique ends there. To remedy the problem, she
proposes creation of "birth ceremonies for girls . . . rooted in neither a historical nor a continuing ritual but in a desire to assert and celebrate the value
of daughters, welcoming them into the community with a ceremony parallel
to *Brit Milah* (circumcision)." She suggests placing newborn girls "in the
context of Jewish women's history by telling the stories of some biblical wom-
en who form part of the covenant the baby girl now enters." Some authors,
she notes, "have suggested physical symbols or acts that might conceivably
carry the weight of circumcision." These have ranged from bathing the infant's feet to immersing her in a ritual bath (*mikveh*) and "breaking her
hymen."[42] Plaskow mentions this last proposal without comment.

Sylvia Barack Fishman treats the subject somewhat more fully in her
book, *A Breath of Life*, but here again the discussion is brief and only suggests
critical perspective. Characterizing the rite of circumcision as among the most
meaningful of all Jewish "communal celebrations," she declares that it
"evokes not only the joyous acceptance of a Jewish destiny but also a courageous leap of faith, with both religious and nationalistic overtones." By this

she means that circumcision symbolizes "each parent's willingness to expose his [*sic*] child to the dangers being Jewish might entail," since he is "marked forever as a Jew, in both good and evil times."[43] Presumably she has the Holocaust in mind; but considering that well over half of all male newborns in the United States are circumcised, for Jewish Americans the argument seems unduly pessimistic and gratuitous.

With regard to ceremonies for infant girls, Fishman acknowledges that creating "sacred rituals" is "a complex task" that "often touches on sensitive issues." Precisely what those issues are goes unexplained, however, as she describes proposed life-cycle ceremonies for girls. For infants there is *shalom bat*, "welcoming the daughter," in which "friends gather to listen to talks, eat, sing, and celebrate together" and to announce and explain the child's name. Fishman notes that a woman rabbi, Julie Cohen, insists on the term *brit banot* (covenant of daughters)—not, says the rabbi, "in the sense of copying what boys do [*sic*], but because bringing a child into the covenant is so important, and you would want to do it in front of family, friends, and community." However, Fishman adds, "perhaps because they remind some people of female circumcision, terms making use of the word *brit* are far less popular than variations on *shalom bat*."[44] The remainder of her brief discussion of this topic is similarly neutral in tone.

What is most striking in both these books is unwillingness to address the fundamental question: How should a genuinely feminist critique of Judaism interpret circumcision? Since this practice, perhaps more than any other, highlights the intensely gendered quality of traditional rabbinic Judaism by focusing attention on the penis, and since most women (not wanting to be reminded of female circumcision) agree that girls should be welcomed into the Jewish community with a pleasant, nontraumatic ceremony, why should male infants not be similarly welcomed? Might widespread adoption of a bloodless, gender-neutral, naming ceremony for all newborns contribute positively to the essential feminist goal, integrating women into Judaism with complete equivalence? Might this be a salutary step toward resolution of an otherwise inescapable contradiction?

Why don't Plaskow and Fishman advocate such a gender-neutral ceremony? It might be argued that feminists should focus on the experiences of women and girls, not men and boys; but these authors understand quite well that circumcision, by celebrating the male-centered quality of traditional Judaism, surely contributes to shaping the self-image of Jewish girls and women. Proposing *bat shalom* ceremonies for girls without even mentioning the possibility of parallel *bar shalom* ceremonies for boys (or, perhaps preferably, *brit shalom* for both) leaves the crucial questions unaddressed. But we look in vain in these books for the forthright critical voice characteristic of Jewish feminist writing on other topics.[45]

"Extra Skin": Explaining Circumcision to Young Girls

Two children's books on ritual circumcision, both Orthodox in orientation, and both intended specifically for older sisters, try to explain why baby brothers are celebrated with a special ceremony for boys alone. The girls, aged about five to seven, are portrayed as jealous and resentful, in need of reassurance that they are equally loved and valued. Each story features an adult woman relative who explains matters to the child. In *Baby's Bris*, by Susan Wilkowski, little Sophie, looking wistful and perplexed, wonders what her aunt meant by saying that the day of the infant's birth "was so special for *her* [i.e., Sophie]." Each day brings new revelations. On the fifth day her father and grandparents take her to the synagogue, where they chat with the rabbi (unaccountably arrayed in a prayer shawl): " 'Mazel tov!' said Rabbi Wohlberg. 'I look forward to the bris.'. . . 'Bris, bris, bris,' Sophie cried. 'Was everyone as excited when I had *my* bris?' " Her grandmother explains that her birth was celebrated "in a very special way"—not a *bris*, "because those are just for boys," but with dancing, singing, thankfulness to God, and "a nice whitefish salad." When the eighth day arrives and the mohel appears, Sophie realizes that the big event is about to happen: "It was time." When the mohel announces that the ceremony "is a symbol of our promise," Sophie asks, "Is it my promise, too?" Oh, yes, her aunt assures her, the promise belongs to everyone in the family, even the departed generations pictured on the wall. The operation receives only minimal notice. The mohel recites a prayer, places the infant on the grandfather's lap, opens the diaper, and removes "a small bit of skin." The accompanying illustration shows the infant sleeping peacefully, still apparently clothed, while a calm, smiling grandfather beams down on the procedure. Afterward, when Sophie asks whether the child is all right, her aunt assures her once again: "He's fine, Sophie. He's just fine." The infant appears in two more illustrations, both times sleeping quietly.[46]

The five-year-old heroine of *Rosie and the Mole*, by Judy Silverman, is frankly perturbed and resentful. No one attended her recent birthday party, she complains; so why does this week-old baby get such a big party? And if girls have only a naming ceremony, why should boys have a *bris* as well? "Oh, Rosie," says her adult cousin, "For a five-year-old, you ask the hardest questions. Boys need a bris in order to fulfill the Jewish people's agreement with God. . . . Girls don't need any special sign to be part of the Jewish people. We're born completely Jewish!" Soon the apartment fills with "people talking and laughing and joking." When Rosie hears her father refer to the *moel* (*sic*), she mistakes this for "mole" and imagines that an animal with claws will attack the infant. The mohel, Rabbi Schaeffer—"a short, plump figure in a heavy coat with a fur collar, and a small fur hat," eyes hidden behind dark glasses, hands encased in black gloves—arrives, confirming the girl's fears: "To Rosie, he looked like a gigantic mole," and she "suddenly felt lucky she had never had a bris." The baby finally appears in an illustration, looking blissfully content, but Rosie is apprehensive. Don't worry, her mother reassures her, no one will harm the baby. Rabbi Schaeffer "will remove some extra skin from the baby that the baby doesn't need.... He is performing the ceremony to welcome our baby into the Jewish faith. Officially." Rosie, still uneasy, asks whether this will hurt. "It will sting a little," says her mother; "But every Jewish boy has it done." Although the baby cries briefly during the surgery, he still appears in the illustrations as calm and contented, "enjoying the wine" dabbed on his lips. Rosie remains perplexed. "Moles have claws," she tells her older boy cousin, "but mo-els have nice long fingers." She extends her hands "like claws" and yells "GRRRRRR!" The story ends with Rosie and her cousin lying on the floor beneath a table heaped with sweets and fruit, working their way through cake and pastry sufficient for several adults.[47]

Whether or not Silverman realized it, the remark that girls are "born completely Jewish" echoes the ancient rabbinic doctrine that male infants require surgery to become "complete" (*tamim*). So the belief in circumcision as correction for male imperfection receives "feminist" confirmation in the notion that girls are born already perfect.

Although these are children's books, their adult authors recognize that removal of the "small bit of skin" from an infant penis, whatever its ostensible effect on the boy, may affect little sisters in ways having nothing to do with Judaism or membership in the Jewish people. The illustrations, particularly in *Rosie and the Mole*—joyful adults, exotic-looking mohel, conflicted little girl, emotionless infant—say more than I can convey in words. As in much popular adult literature, the defining themes are uncertainty and anxiety.

Circumcision in Jewish American Fiction

Circumcision turns up infrequently in fiction, but when it does appear (almost always in works by Jewish authors), the message is nearly always negative. One reads little if anything about "covenant" but much about pain and disturbing memories. Nervous attempts at humor are more revealing than amusing; the dominant style is satire, the dominant mode, irony.

"Baby Boys, Chickens, Turkeys"

For a portrait of circumcision as remembered trauma, first honors go to Max Apple's story "The Eighth Day." The narrator introduces us to his lover, Joan, a young Gentile woman who has experimented with every psychological crutch from psychoanalysis to "primitive religion." Having "re-experienced her own birth in primal therapy," she encouraged him to do the same. But "there was a great stumbling block": he "couldn't get back any earlier than the eighth day." Even when he agreed to submit to the torments imposed by a primal therapist, he "could go back no farther than the hairs beneath the chin of the man with the blade who pulled at and then slit my tiny penis, the man who prayed and drank wine over my foreskin." He "howled" and "gagged" at this memory; but when Joan and the therapist urged him to think of "birth canal," he still could remember only his circumcision: "'The knife,' I screamed, 'the blood, the tube, the pain between my legs.'"[48]

Determined to get a "fresh start" on his problem, the narrator and his girlfriend search out the mohel who had performed the circumcision. When he displays a long jackknife, she is impressed: "All that power just to snip at a tiny penis." "Wrong," he replies; "For the shmekel I got another knife. This one kills chickens.... Chickens are my livelihood. Circumcising is a hobby."[49] They ask him to perform a "recircumcision," and at first he agrees to do the job—on his dining room table, when wife and children are asleep. With the narrator lying naked under a sheet, the old man removes "a small double-edged knife" from "a torn and stained case," and muses on his ancient profession:

> "The babies," he says, "always keep their eyes open. You'd be surprised how alert they are. At eight days they already know when something's happening." ... "With babies," he says, "there's always a crowd around, at least the family. The little fellow wrapped in a blanket looks around or screams. You take off the diaper and one-two it's over.... I've been a mohel thirty-four years and I started slaughtering chickens four years before that. I'm almost ready for Social Security. Just baby boys, chickens, turkeys, occasionally a duck."[50]

But he is uneasy about the prospect of cutting into an adult penis. All he need do, says Joan, is "just relive the thing"—draw "one symbolic drop" of blood. "Down there there's no drops," he replies. "It's close to arteries; the heart wants blood there. It's the way the Almighty wanted it to be." When she observes that he has probably always "had second thoughts" about his "career," he replies: "Yes, I have. God's work, I tell myself, but why does God want me to slit the throats of chickens and slice the foreskins of babies?" And even though the narrator, feeling "a lot like a chicken," urges him to continue, the old man decides that he can't go through with it, "even symbolically." The narrator is immensely relieved: "My penis feels like a blindfolded man standing before the executioner who has been saved at the last second."[51]

This story of enduring trauma is a meditation on the age-old association between ritual slaughter and circumcision. The controlling image is the knife. As I noted earlier, in traditional European Jewish communities, rabbis or other practitioners often combined the roles of mohel and slaughterer (shochet), and for a time this was also the case in small Jewish American communities: Jewish religious functionaries wielded knives. The final metaphors represent helplessness and death. Moreover, the narrator's penis was not "saved," since his foreskin is long gone.

"Here Comes the Dirty Part"

In his most popular novel, *The Apprenticeship of Duddy Kravitz*, Mordecai Richler chronicles the adventures of a snappy young hustler in Montreal. Among Duddy's projects is an outrageously kitschy film featured at the celebration of the bar mitzvah of Bernie Cohen, son of a wealthy dealer in scrap metal. Across the years, intones the pompous narrator, *"the Hebrews, whipped like sand by the cruel winds of oppression, have survived by the word ... the law ..."* The screen shows a close-up of a circumcision. Viewers in the audience respond: "Lock the doors. Here comes the dirty part." "Shame on you." "Awright, Sarah. O.K. You've seen one before. You don't have to pretend you're not looking." The narrator continues: *"... and through the centuries the eight-day-old Hebrew babe has been welcomed into the race with blood."* Then come sound effects—"Tom-Toms beat in background"—and a "montage": "Lightning. African tribal dance. Jungle fire. Stukkas diving. A jitterbug contest speeded up. Slaughtering of a cow. Fireworks against a night sky. More African dancing. Torrents of rain. An advertisement for Maiden-Form bras upsidedown. Blood splashing against glass. A lion roars." Bernie's grandfather grows so faint from the sanguinary display that someone wonders whether he has had "another stroke." The tom-toms beat again, and the audience is treated to another circumcision close-up. "It's not me," shouts Bernie, "Honest, guys." A woman asks: "Do you think this'll have a bad effect on the children?" "Never mind the children," a man replies; "I've got such a pain there now you'd think it was me up there."[52]

Duddy's film calls attention to the seldom-recognized linkage between circumcision as initiation into the world of males and bar mitzvah as initiation into manhood. He also dramatizes, crudely but insightfully, the underlying thematic kinship of Jewish and African ritual circumcisions. And of course readers understand the irony of the question about whether the film will have "a bad effect" on children, the males of whom have already undergone circumcision themselves.

"Out and Not In ... Mine and Not Theirs"

The Counterlife, one of Philip Roth's several novels on "the Jewish question," concludes with the answer to a question that must arise often nowadays: Why would a Jewish agnostic, married to a Gentile wife, insist on his infant son's being circumcised—even though he knows that circumcision is anachronistic and irrational? The narrator is Nathan Zuckerman, Roth's alter-ego novelist, addressing (in his own imagination) his pregnant fourth wife, Maria. She is an agnostic Englishwoman who is ready to give up on the marriage because Nathan seems pointlessly fixated on his Jewish identity.[53]

Nathan imagines Maria's farewell letter. Because her mother is determined to have the child baptized, he'll "counterattack by demanding that the child, if a boy, shall make his covenant with Yahweh through the ritual sacrifice of his foreskin." But even though she thinks circumcision is "a barbaric mutilation" and views him as "an intellectual agnostic" who is "irrationally Jewish," Nathan knows that she'll give in anyway.[54] Sure, performing "delicate surgery" on the penis of "a brand-new boy" may seem "the very cornerstone of human irrationality"; but that just shows what "skepticism is worth up against a tribal taboo." He realizes that the trend nowadays is to make birth and the first days of life as gentle and nonstartling as possible:

> Circumcision is startling, all right, particularly when performed by a garlicked old man upon the glory of a newborn body, but then maybe that's what the Jews had in mind and what makes the act seem quintessentially Jewish and the mark of their reality. Circumcision makes it clear as can be that you are here and not there, that you are out and not in—also that you're mine and not theirs. There is no way around it: you enter history through my history and me.[55]

Note that since the child will be born to a non-Jewish mother—so will not be Jewish according to Orthodox tenets—Nathan, the "intellectual agnostic," sees circumcision as indelible confirmation of his paternal ownership. He says nothing about covenant or the will of a deity; the real point is that the child is to "be mine and not theirs"—that is, his and not hers.

Roth sent a copy of *The Counterlife* to the writer Mary McCarthy, who responded with mixed reactions. She enjoyed the first half of the novel, she wrote, but the part on antisemitism "wearied" her; Roth seemed afflicted with "a severe case of anti-antisemitism." What bothered her especially was "all that circumcision business": "Why so excited about making a child a Jew by taking a knife to him?" If Nathan Zuckerman "*isn't* a believing Jew," she asked, "why is he so hung up on this issue?"[56] Roth replied that McCarthy didn't understand

> how serious this circumcision business is to Jews. I am still hypnotized by uncircumcised men when I see them at my swimming pool locker room. The damn thing never goes unregistered. Most Jewish men I know have similar reactions, and when I was writing the book, I asked several of my equally secular Jewish male friends if they could have an uncircumcised son, and they all said no, sometimes without having to think about it and sometimes after

the nice long pause that any rationalist takes before opting for the irrational. Why is N.Z. hung up on circumcision? I hope that's clearer now.[57]

Nathan Zuckerman, the secular agnostic, never retreats into religious rationale. He turns first to the argument for ethnic continuity ("you are out and not in"). But in his response to McCarthy, Roth admits that the real motive for preserving circumcision is the hypnotizing unease he and his friends feel when they see intact penises. That's why the "circumcision business" is inescapable, and why secular Jewish men are so "hung up" on it.

"That Circumcise Shmuck Stuff"

In Bernard Malamud's novel *The Tenants*, two aspiring writers of questionable promise, one Jewish, the other Black, coexist in a tense relationship in an abandoned tenement building. The Jewish writer declares that "[a]rt is the glory and only a shmuck thinks otherwise." The other man wants nothing to do with that "Jewword"—that is, *shmuck*, the slang Yiddish term that means either "genitals" or "jerk"—which sets him off on what may be the most spectacular attack on circumcision in fiction:

> I know what you talkin about, don't think I don't. I know you tryin to steal my manhood. I don't go for that circumcise shmuck stuff. The Jews got to keep us bloods stayin weak so you can take everything for yourself. Jewgirls are the best whores and are tryin to cut the bloods down by makin us go get circumcise, and the Jewdoctors do the job because they are afraid if they don't we gon take over the whole goddamn country and wipe you out. That's what they afraid. I had a friend of mine once and he got circumcise for his Jewbitch and now he ain't no good in his sex any more, a true fag because he lost his pullin power. He is no good in a woman without his pullin power. He sit in his room afraid of his prick. None of that crap on me, Lesser, you Jewbastard, we tired of you fuckn us over.[58]

Taking off from the Jewish speaker's mention of *shmuck*, his Black counterpart picks up on the word's other (primary) meaning and plunges into a seemingly gratuitous tirade against circumcision. Keeping in mind that the actual creator of this mini-lecture was a Jew, we can read it several ways. The key word is "weak." First, of course, there is the age-old belief that circumcision diminishes men's "pullin power"—weakens them sexually, and perhaps makes them less assertive, more compliant. Then there is the claim that Jewish *women* demand that men surrender their full virility in return for sexual concessions. Finally, the emerging breakdown in the Black-Jewish alliance is disguised as a fantasy of rebellion against Jewish assaults on Black manhood: "we tired of you fuckn us over."

"A Standard Kosher Hot Dog"

For a view from across the gender divide, we have "The Pagan Phallus," by Robin Roger, a Toronto writer who attended, among other institutions, the Jewish Theological Seminary. A young Jewish woman named Terry Steinham is beginning work in the unlikely role of "copywriter" (not further explained) for a Salvation Army office. Deciding that she should get in step with her employers by reading the New Testament, Steinham visits a bookstore and is surprised to learn that there are many Christian denominations, each with its own approved biblical text. She is a sexually adventurous woman, and thinking about Christian diversity leads her to think about varieties of men. Why, she wonders, have all her lovers been Jews? "Married men. Professors. Total strangers in bars. Out-of-town guests at Bar Mitzvahs. Rabbis. Schizophrenics. Not a foreskin among them."

A young man with muscles and "a blinding smile" approaches and strikes up a conversation. He "couldn't help noticing" that she was "looking for the Sword" (i.e., the New Testament). The attraction is mutual and immediate, and soon they're at her apartment, wasting no time on "interfaith dialogue." She reaches for his "sword" and is fascinated by its novel appearance: "There it was, the skin of distinction, topping off his shaft like a pink velvet toque. As if doffing its cap, it bobbed down, then up. She just stared. It looked completely different, this quivering creature, with the skin over its glans like a cover on a canary cage."[59]

Later, the Salvation Army commissioner invites Steinham to the organization's retreat, where she is certain that he intends a seduction. She walks to his cabin in the evening and happens to see him naked, at first from the back. But when he turns around, she nearly cries out: "There was no foreskin. His prick hung like a slack hose suspended from his pubic hair, the naked glans shamelessly exposed. She was completely let down at the sight of this familiar-looking pecker—just a standard kosher hot dog." Soon afterward, when the commissioner tells Terry that he "had something in mind" when he invited her to the retreat, she has already made up her mind: "No foreskin, no foreplay." But it turns out that in fact the poor man was hoping for a more exciting conquest: conversion of a Jew.[60]

It's difficult to decide what Roger intended to say here, since we're told nothing about Steinham's experience with the young swordsman's "quivering creature." Presumably she discovered that foreplay with this toy was more fun. But the story is about familiarity and difference. Although this Jewish woman (named Stein plus ham) has decided (at least for the time being) that the "standard kosher hot dog" no longer suffices, she still sees the intact (i.e., Gentile) penis as an anomaly—"something completely different."

"Like a Martian": Circumcision in the Sitcom Imagination

Circumcision, mentioned in more than thirty television sitcoms, has been the main subject or a major feature in several episodes.[61] Sitcoms often aim for humorous treatment of topics and issues that are not amusing in actual life; that certainly applies to circumcision. The dominant theme in most programs, the source of humor (such as it is), is denigration of the foreskin. Male and female characters portray intact penises as weird and ridiculous in appearance, and so unattractive to women that at times a potential partner balks when she sees the offending organ (though it would be difficult for an inexperienced observer to realize that an erect penis lacked a foreskin). Although there is an occasional hint of possible damage to adult sexuality from loss of the foreskin, more often the message is that circumcision enhances sexual performance and satisfaction.

Though adult circumcision is usually treated as a frightening experience, infant circumcision is portrayed as nearly painless, cosmetically desirable, and beneficial to health. When anyone mentions infant surgery, which happens infrequently, it's a minor affair: a single cut, rapid and safe; moreover, infant circumcision is always presented as a Jewish practice. But "normal" men, Jewish *or* Gentile, are assumed to be circumcised. Conflict, especially between intermarried parents, about whether or not an infant should be circumcised, is a recurrent theme; the Gentile parent resists, but inevitably the circumcision proceeds. Those who object—sometimes portrayed as foolish or uninformed—focus on infant pain; but the wiser characters know that it is parents, not infants, who suffer most. One exception is Kramer, the unconventional character in *Seinfeld*, who speaks for the opposition in the episode called "The Bris," discussed below; it is his reputation for quirkiness that qualifies him to speak out.

But if infant circumcision is portrayed as no great trauma, that's not the case for adult circumcision. The intact men are Gentiles who agree reluctantly to the operation, either because they want marriage or a sexual relationship with a Jewish woman or because women have ridiculed and rejected them. Their fear and apprehension—centering again on pain, not damage to sexuality—provide entertainment for the other actors and the audience. Some men renege at the last moment, realizing that they may not be as ill equipped as they had been led to believe. Others, however, like Mike in the episode of *Sex and the City* (also to be discussed below), choose to be circumcised, convinced that this will enhance their sexual potential.

"I Could Have Been a Kosher Butcher"

Episode 69 of *Seinfeld*, originally aired in October 1993, is called "The Bris."[62] In addition to the featured Jewish character, Jerry Seinfeld, the principals are a Jewish couple, Myra and Stan, whose newborn infant is to be circumcised; Kramer, known as a somewhat unstable character given to erratic behavior; George, portrayed as both inept and cynical; and Elaine, a rather hard-boiled realist. Myra and Stan ask Jerry and Elaine to serve as "godparents"—Jerry to play the role of sandek, here called "godfather." Seinfeld does an imitation of the stereotypical Mafia godfather. When Elaine asks what they'll be expected to do, Stan replies that the "most important thing is to help with the *bris*." Jerry and Elaine are puzzled, but Kramer understands: "You mean snip-snip?...I would advise against that." (Audience laughter.)[63]

In the next scene, Jerry tells Elaine to locate a mohel, pronounced to rhyme with foil. (Ordinarily parents, not "godparents," choose the mohel; this is the first of several departures from usual Jewish practice.) Elaine is still puzzled: "What the hell is a mohel?" When Jerry explains, she searches a telephone directory: "How do you find a mohel? Motels, models ..." That's "a piece of cake," says Jerry; he has the "tough job: I have to hold the baby while they do it." Now comes an emblematic exchange on a recurrent theme in sitcoms: women find the intact penis unattractive.

ELAINE   Hey, Jerry: Have you ever seen one?

JERRY   You mean that wasn't...?

ELAINE   Yeah.

JERRY   No...have you?

ELAINE   (recalling an unpleasant experience) Yeah. (Laughter.)

JERRY   What'd you think?

ELAINE   (shaking her head) No.

JERRY   Not good?

ELAINE   No—had no face, no personality, very dull. (Laughter and applause.) It was like a Martian. (Laughter.)

Later, Kramer, George, and Jerry discuss circumcision, with George playing tentative advocate, Seinfeld functioning as uninformed straight man, and Kramer demonstrating that his opposition is rooted in knowledge (but directing his argument to Elaine rather than the parents):

KRAMER   You should call this off, Elaine. It's a barbaric ritual.

GEORGE   But, Kramer, isn't it a question of hygiene?

KRAMER   Oh, that's a myth. Besides, you know, it [i.e., the foreskin] makes sex more pleasurable.

GEORGE   Yeah. So how does that help me?

JERRY   Hey, George, have you ever seen one?

GEORGE   Yeah, my roommate in college.

JERRY   So what'd you think?

GEORGE   I got used to it.

George, who is circumcised (but not Jewish), doesn't want to hear anything further about foreskins and sexual pleasure. He has the final word here, though, confirming that an intact penis is an unpleasant sight.[64]

The circumcision is about to begin in the home of Myra and Stan, but the mohel (chosen by Elaine) has not yet arrived. When Jerry, anxious to be done with his own role, complains that the mohel is late, Elaine replies, "Relax. You'd think *you* were getting whacked." Myra, the infant's mother, is sobbing. Kramer, still the lone contrary voice, sits with her and delivers an indictment of circumcision strikingly unlike the jocular tone of the remainder of the program:

Don't believe them when they tell you it doesn't hurt. It hurts bad. It hurts really bad. Imagine, this will be his first memory—of someone yanking the hat off his little man. I know you love your baby, but what kind of perverts would stand idly by while a stranger rips the cover off his 9-iron, and then serve a catered lunch?

The combination of exceptionally vivid language ("hurts really bad," "perverts") with weakly humorous images is presumably intended to soften the message, and perhaps to encourage the audience to laugh even during serious condemnation of a Jewish ritual practice. But although the hat, "little man," and golf club metaphors may add a lighter touch, the verbs "yanking" and "rips" evoke images of mutilation.[65] Kramer's message is obviously in keeping with Myra's own feelings at this point; still sobbing, she runs off.

The mohel arrives and turns out to be a jittery, loud-mouthed neurotic who becomes inordinately upset at the sound of a pan dropping, then reacts ridiculously when he hears the infant crying:

Is the baby gonna cry like that? Is that how the baby cries—with that loud, sustained, squealing cry? 'Cause that could pose a problem. Do you have any control over your child? 'Cause this is the time to exercise it, when the baby is crying in that high-pitched squealing tone that can drive you insane!

This scene recalls the objections of nineteenth-century German-Jewish physicians to incompetent mohels with trembling hands—a point that will become even more evident shortly. The reference to the infant's "high-pitched squealing" suggests that the writers may have known that infants undergoing circumcision scream in a distinctive high-pitched manner.[66] The next exchange confirms the impression that this mohel is not the kind of person one would choose for surgery on anyone, least of all a baby. Seeing a glass standing near a table edge, he lectures Elaine on the danger of broken glass: "You think you got it all, and two years later, you're walkin' barefoot and step on a piece of broken glass, and you kill yourself." Elaine mumbles to Myra (now back in the room), "He's very highly recommended"; but to Jerry she whispers, "The mohel is twitching."

The circumcision is about to begin. Now the focus shifts to Jerry's apprehension about his own role as "godfather" (i.e., sandek, on whose lap the baby lies during the operation). While the mohel shouts, "Who's holding the baby? I need the baby!" Elaine pushes the reluctant Jerry forward. This is accompanied by more audience laughter. Kramer runs into the bedroom and returns with the baby, but suddenly decides to stand by his principles: "I can't let you do this!" Others rush toward him, demanding that he hand over the baby, but he refuses. A farcical struggle follows; Kramer, shouting "No, no, I won't!" topples backward. Someone grabs the infant. The mohel shouts over the din: "People, compose yourselves! This is a *bris!* We are performing a *bris* here, not a burlesque show.... This is not a baggy-pants farce! This is a *bris*— an ancient, sacred ceremony, symbolizing the covenant between God and Abraham ... or something." The supposedly religious ceremony has indeed become a farce, conducted by an ignoramus.

The mohel opens his surgical bag; his instruments fall out, and he mutters "Damn!" As others move to pick them up, he delivers another monologue: "I could have been a kosher butcher like my brother. The money's good; there's a union, with benefits. And cows don't have families. You make a mistake with a cow, you move on with your life."

The audience sees neither surgery (of course) nor religious rite—no prayers or recitations, in Hebrew or English. I quote the screen script: "He holds up the 'instrument.' He twitches. His hand trembles. We pan the extremely anxious crowd. We angle on a very bug-eyed nervous Jerry as the mohel raises the instrument. Angle back on mohel, as he brings the instrument down. Sound effects: Crowd screaming." In even the most "modernized" of ritual circumcisions the mohel would recite standard blessings. Here the entire event has been reduced to a meaningless performance by a clownishly inept neurotic. Screaming witnesses drown out what the audience might hear at an actual circumcision: infant wailing.

The next scene finds Jerry, George, Elaine, and Kramer in an automobile, on the way to a hospital for repairs to Jerry's finger, "circumcised" by the mohel. Elaine and Jerry argue over whether Jerry "flinched." George confirms that Jerry had indeed flinched, but he himself had fainted ("blacked out") right after that. While Jerry whines that his "phone finger" is still bleeding, Kramer asks, "What about the baby?" He's "fine," says Jerry. "They're just taking him to the hospital as a precautionary measure. I'm the one who's hurt. Look at me!"

ELAINE   Will you stop it? You'll just need a few stitches.

JERRY   Stitches? I've never had stitches. I'll be deformed.
I can't live with that. It goes against my whole personality. It's not me!

Since an infant rests on the lap of the sandek, whose hands are nowhere near the surgical site, only a colossally incompetent mohel could cut the man's finger. But Jerry's injured finger obviously suggests that the baby has also been "deformed." Moreover, no one would take an infant to a hospital as a "precautionary measure" unless he had been seriously injured or was bleeding uncontrollably. Despite the claim that the baby is "fine," this sequel develops further the episode's dominant themes: danger, mishap.

The penultimate scene takes place in the hospital. Jerry is still complaining ("I'm getting faint. I'm losing consciousness") when, suddenly and inexplicably, the mohel reappears. The two argue angrily over whether Jerry "flinched." Jerry, referring to his antagonist as "Shakey," tells Elaine that she "picked a helluva mohel!"

MOHEL   One more peep out of you, and I'll slice you up like a smoked sturgeon!

JERRY   Don't threaten me, Butcher Boy!

They struggle clumsily.

ELAINE   Jerry, be careful—the mohel's got a knife!

Stan appears and stops the fight. After further assurance that the baby is "fine," the mohel turns to Jerry with a threat: "I'll get you for this. This is my business, this is my life. No one ruins this for me—no one!"

In the closing scene, Elaine and Jerry are about to fondle the baby, when Myra says, "Don't touch him." Jerry asks, "What's wrong?" Stan replies: "You're out, Jerry. You're out as Godfather. You too, Elaine. You're both out.... We want Kramer." Kramer replies (in stereotypical Mafia style) that he'd be "honored." Jerry and Elaine watch in disbelief as Myra and Stan embrace Kramer, calling *him* "Godfather"—his reward for concern about their baby's welfare. With the circumcision behind them, the parents' sole appreciation goes to the one person who tried to prevent it.

The inescapable message of this entire performance is that circumcision is perilous. The mohel blames Seinfeld for flinching, but the audience knows that the next time it may be he himself who flinches at the wrong moment. This time it was Jerry's finger; but what might it be another time? Nevertheless, the audience learns that despite the danger and anxiety, Jewish foreskins must be—and will be—removed.[67]

"I'm from Connecticut!"

In an August 1999 episode of *Sex and the City*, titled "Old Dogs, New Dicks," the subject is adult circumcision, and there is no mention of Jewish concerns.[68] Here, even more plainly than in dramas about infant circumcision, the dominant theme is vilification of the foreskin. In contrast to *Seinfeld*, the language is explicit.[69]

Charlotte and Mike are about to have intercourse for the first time. The unseen omniscient narrator explains: "But just when Charlotte had become comfortable with the penis, she got a very unexpected surprise."

CHARLOTTE   Oh! You're...it's...

MIKE   Uncircumcised. Is that okay?

CHARLOTTE   No! Sure...of course it is.

But it was "*not* okay," adds the narrator: "The only uncut version of anything Charlotte had ever seen was the original *Gone with the Wind*."

In the next scene, Charlotte and her three friends (all central characters in the series) discuss her experience. "There was so much skin!" Charlotte reports; "It was like a Shar-Pei!" (a peculiar-looking breed of dog with thick folds of skin). "You've never seen an uncircumcised one?" asks one friend (the narrator). No, says Charlotte, "I'm from Connecticut!...Aesthetics are important to me."

THIRD WOMAN   It's not what it looks like, it's what they can do with it.

CHARLOTTE   Well, I don't need one that can make its own carrying case! (Others laugh.)

THIRD WOMAN   Personally, I *love* an uncircumcised dick. It's like a tootsie-pop: hard on the outside, with a delicious surprise inside.

SECOND WOMAN   I don't like surprises. I like it all out there where I can see it.

CHARLOTTE   Same here. I'm sorry, it is not normal.

SECOND WOMAN   Well, actually it is. Something like 85 percent of men aren't circumcised.[70]

CHARLOTTE   Great! Now they're taking over the world!...He's a nice WASPy guy. What went wrong?

FIRST WOMAN   Well, maybe his parents were hippies and just didn't believe in it.

SECOND WOMAN   I am *so* circumcising my kids.... I don't ever want to know there's a woman out there calling my son a Shar-Pei.

THIRD WOMAN   All I'm saying is uncut men are the best; they try harder. I should know; I've slept with five of them.

The last comment goes unexplained but seems to suggest that intact men have to "try harder" to perform satisfactorily—probably opposite to the actual case.

On their next evening together, when Mike asks whether he may come up to her apartment, Charlotte replies that she has to be up early and her place is "a mess." Mike understands: "What happened the other night—you're not the first woman to react that way. I've gotten that most of my life.... and I've decided to do something about it. I've been uncomfortable for too long—so I'm getting circumcised." He knows it will be painful and will take "a long time to heal," but he wants to "feel good about making love." Charlotte gushes with delight: "But that is so...sweet!"

The evening following his circumcision, Charlotte takes Mike out "for a postoperative Scotch." He walks with her, seeming comfortable and content. Charlotte asks whether "it hurt."

MIKE   On a scale of one to five, I'd give it seventy-two.

CHARLOTTE   Oh, you poor thing!

When Mike assures her that he'll be fine in "another week or so," she replies that she "can't wait!" They kiss, but Mike cries out in pain. Bent over, holding his crotch and groaning, he waves her away; she walks off, smiling with love.

"A week later," reports the narrator (clearly no better informed than Mike on healing time), "Charlotte finally got her chance to break in the new merchandise." Charlotte opens his zipper and gasps with pleasure: "It's perfect!"

MIKE   You realize, this makes me a virgin?

CHARLOTTE (smiling and coy)   I'll be gentle.

They have intercourse; Charlotte burbles that it was "really wonderful," and Mike agrees. Immediately thereafter, though, when Charlotte (clearly with marriage on her mind) suggests what they might do on Saturday night, Mike balks: "Charlotte, listen: I don't think I'm ready for this to be, y'know, like a big thing.... I just feel like I can't be tied down right now. There's a whole new me...I feel like I should get out there and share it."

CHARLOTTE (dismayed)   You wanna share your *penis?*

MIKE   Well, yeah. I mean, I feel like I owe it to myself to take the doggie out for a walk around the block, y'know?

Charlotte turns away in despair, and the narrator concludes: "Charlotte never saw Mike again. She realized you could take the Shar-Pei out of the penis, but you could never take the dog out of the man."

In keeping with the central concern of the characters, these sequences portray the foreskin as an impediment to sexual fulfillment (even though the woman who plays the most sexually knowledgeable character has defended the intact organ). However men may feel about their own genitals, foreskins must be removed because women say no to the intact penis. Women expect "nice WASPy guys" like Mike to be circumcised; only socially marginal "hippies" would reject such cosmetic tailoring. Mike is an exemplary "before and after" character. In the pre-circumcision scenes he appears wistful and forlorn; but at the end, shorn of his troublesome foreskin and no longer uncertain about himself, he is eager to enjoy his improved equipment with new partners.[71]

"Cut Glass from the Bronx": Circumcision in Popular Humor

Circumcision humor, none truly amusing, almost always plays on the theme of cutting or "clipping," and always focuses on the Jewish version. More noteworthy than the jokes themselves is the very existence of feeble humor about a supposedly sacred religious practice. An occasional joke depends on identification of the excised foreskin with the entire penis. I know of no joke touching on belief in Abraham's covenant, and it goes without saying that there are none about female genital cutting. Here, as in the sitcoms, barely disguised beneath the banal humor, is the sense of anxiety that pervades so much of the discourse on circumcision. It seems that no amount of joking and banter obscures the simple fact that circumcision means cutting away part of the penis. Some jokes touch on the circumcision-equals-castration fantasy, implying that more than foreskin is removed. I'll cite a number of examples—but don't expect to laugh.[72]

A number of jokes identify a rabbi as mohel. The simplest version is, "Why does the rabbi have such a good income? Because he gets all the tips." In his book on sexual humor, Gershon Legman describes "little anti-Semitic novelty cards showing 'Abie Getting His First 10 percent Cut' at the hands of a hook-nosed rabbi wielding a large shears."[73] A joke I heard and told as a youth makes light of mohel incompetence: When a man in a public toilet urinates on the man standing next to him, the latter asks, "Aren't you from Cleveland?" The answer to the obvious question is that Cleveland's "Rabbi Bernstein" "circumcises on the bias."[74] I don't know how often the joke is told precisely this way, but note the punning suggestion of bris in "bias," and perhaps even the vague reminder of cleaver in Cleveland. I heard this joke about a "Rabbi Lefkowitz," with the apparent implication that he cuts (the penis) on the slant because he is left-handed.

Cutting and "clipping" appear also in the greeting from the Southern rabbi to his New England colleague: "Hello, Yankee clipper!" Another joke, now ancient, required that one recognize the name of a prominent senator, Carter Glass (d. 1946). A young Jewish man, asked his name by the hostess at an elegant party, replies "Glass, Ma'am." She makes the impossible mistake of thinking he might be the senator: "Carter Glass of Virginia?" "No, Ma'am," he replies, "cut Glass from the Bronx."[75] (This is one of a larger category of jokes featuring inept attempts by semiacculturated Jews to "mix" or "pass" in upper-class Gentile social environments.) Finally, we have the following (vaguely antisemitic) tale: When the local priest receives a gift of a Buick from his parishioners, the rabbi counters by persuading his congregation to buy him a Cadillac. The priest baptizes his car with holy water, upon which the rabbi shears off several inches of his car's exhaust pipe.[76]

Reluctant as I am to end with such material, I hope it will help confirm the central thesis of this chapter: that whatever significance circumcision may still retain for some Jewish Americans, the dominant themes in the contemporary consciousness are surely not covenant, "survival," or anything of the kind. Overriding all other considerations is bare reality: Circumcision means excising part of a child's penis. The more people try to make light of that, the more clearly they reveal their perplexity and discomfort.[77]

Epilogue

The seemingly endless argument about circumcision comes down to
two fundamental questions. First, there is the question of whether
it is an effective medical procedure, with potential benefits out-
weighing possible harmful effects. Second is the question of whether
parents have the right to make this kind of decision for a child. The
published research on both questions is so vast that I can do little
more here than cite some of the most noteworthy literature, but my
notes and bibliography make it possible to explore issues in more
depth.

Is Circumcision Beneficial or Harmful?

We've seen that a number of nineteenth-century British and American physicians advanced claims for circumcision as a *therapeutic*
procedure—assuring one another that it was a near-miraculous
cure for everything from paralysis to epilepsy. Then, when that approach turned out to be a false start, they shifted to claims that it was
prophylactic—that it prevented disease and illness. When they
observed (accurately) that removal of the foreskin made masturbation
more difficult, this became a "moral" argument. But as each claim—
for prevention of syphilis, cancer of the penis, cancer of the prostate,
cancer of the cervix, and so on—proved illusory, invariably another
appeared. In short, for more than a century, circumcision has been a
treatment in search of something to treat. But no one has ever
claimed that large numbers of intact boys or men would ever develop

any problem simply because they retained normal genitals. The claim has always been that mass circumcision would protect a few individuals in later life. Thus, even if circumcision might eventually protect someone from a particular illness, we should ask whether that justifies circumcising millions of others who stand to gain nothing. Some urologists and pediatricians focus on cases coming to their specialized attention, arguing that they see pathology that could have been prevented by circumcision. This may be correct for a few (not all) cases; but of course these physicians see a highly selected cohort, a very small minority of the male population, not the far larger number of boys and men who remain completely healthy with or without circumcision. So the question is not whether *anyone* might eventually benefit from circumcision; the question is whether anticipated benefits to a very few justify submitting *millions* of newborns to a procedure that will never benefit them—but, as I shall argue, in fact causes them harm.

Assessing the Latest Claims

Consider the most popular recent justification for circumcision: that it prevents HIV infection—presumably because the toughened glans might be more resistant to viral invasion. I noted in chapter 7 that this was first proposed as a possibility—without any research evidence—in 1986 by Aaron J. Fink. Despite obvious contradictory evidence from the American experience, the claim has gained support among some epidemiologists focusing on the HIV-AIDS epidemic in Africa. On the American side, the proposal was clearly misplaced, since the evidence points in precisely the opposite direction: the United States has the largest number of circumcised adult males *and* one of the highest HIV infection rates in the developed world.[1]

The literature on HIV infection and AIDS in Africa is much too extensive for more than a brief overview here, but I can outline the dimensions of this complex problem. First, while HIV infection and AIDS in the United States have been especially prevalent among homosexual men and drug users, the great majority of infected Africans are heterosexual men and women. Second, major confounding elements connected with sexual practices have been either overlooked or accorded insufficient consideration, particularly in Africa. For example, circumcised African men are disproportionately Muslim; and since Muslims are supposed to avoid alcohol, these men are less likely to frequent bars where they might come in contact with infected prostitutes. Sexual promiscuity of any kind obviously exposes men and women to danger from infection of all sorts. A widely publicized study of long-distance truck drivers in Kenya argued that their high rate of HIV infection was attributable to their having foreskins. But these men, living on the road and traveling from one truck-stop to another, frequently encounter HIV-infected prostitutes. In contrast, a study in Uganda of HIV transmission in monogamous, heterosexual couples in which only one partner was already infected, found that the circumcision status of the male partner was not a significant factor.[2] Still another consideration is a misguided practice called "dry sex": use of powders, sand, or other agents, ostensibly to heighten sexual sensation by removing normal vaginal lubrication. This is an obvious potential cause of genital abrasions and lacerations that may promote infection with sexually transmitted pathogens in both men and women. Finally, evidence is accumulating that use of nonsterile injection needles by medical personnel and use of contaminated instruments by ritual circumcisers are major causes of HIV infection in Africa—possibly the most important of all.[3]

A 1999 article by two of the most dedicated advocates for mass circumcision in Africa concluded with a sensible "caution":

> Offering male-circumcision services as a way to prevent HIV transmission will be counterproductive if men opt for the procedure believing it will fully protect them from AIDS.... Male circumcision interventions must not be perceived by individuals or communities as a substitute for other HIV and STD prevention strategies.[4]

Now that the value of circumcision as a possible preventive strategy has come to be seen as highly questionable, this warning takes on added cogency.

Returning to the American scene, I've already mentioned the latest medical justification here: that circumcision prevents urinary tract infection (UTI) in infants and young children. As has been the case with each new medical claim, a large literature emerged, and in a familiar pattern: one or two dedicated advocates publish widely and steadily, a few physicians support them, others question or reject their arguments. In this case, as I've shown, the leading claimant has been Thomas E. Wiswell, seconded by that most tireless contemporary advocate for circumcision, Edgar J. Schoen.[5] The first point to note is that although girls are far more likely than boys to develop a UTI, no one proposes "corrective" surgery to protect them. But that matter aside, advocates themselves acknowledge that only about 2.2 percent of *intact* boys will develop a UTI in the crucial first year of life, while a smaller number of circumcised boys will also have the problem. In other words, of every 1,000 circumcised infants, about 980 receive no preventive benefit. Moreover, very few of the other twenty are in serious trouble; most UTIs are readily treatable with antibiotics and, in boys as well as girls, usually resolve within a few days without complications. Most of the few boys who go on to develop more serious urinary tract disease have prior deformities or were inadequately treated in the initial phase of the illness.[6] Some physicians have also proposed that a number of confounding elements—for example, previous maternal infection, premature birth, parental education and hygiene—may influence UTI rates more than circumcision advocates have recognized.[7]

Balanced assessment of the substantial evidence on sexually transmitted diseases has shown no significant differences between circumcised and intact men; if anything, circumcised men may be slightly more susceptible to some infections.[8] In short, by any reasonable standard for cost-benefit analysis, arguments for circumcision as a medical preventive fail; there is no justification for circumcising millions of infants in hopes of preventing a few cases of illness. Finally, we should always keep in mind that, with the single exception of Israel, the United States is the *only* country in the world where nearly 60 percent of male infants are still being circumcised. Comparative studies consistently demonstrate that boys and men in other countries have no medical problems primarily attributable to possession of intact genitals.

Claims that a circumcised penis is "neater," more attractive, and so forth—trivial when measured against evidence for harm—being purely subjective, are impossible to counter with factual arguments. But there is certainly no evidence that European, Latin American, or Asian men—nearly all intact—experience rejection on that account. In fact, women from these continents sometimes express surprise and dismay when they encounter circumcised American men. In the West, acceptance of circumcision as the norm is a cultural phenomenon limited to the United States and Israel.[9]

"Parents Should Determine"

I've shown that, in the absence of convincing arguments for medical benefits—but without fully acknowledging costs to the infant—many physicians have abdicated responsibility for deciding whether to perform circumcisions. By acceding to parental wishes, rather than relying first and foremost on their own medical judgment, they have accepted the fact that circumcision has become a *custom* without medical justification. The remarkable "Circumcision Policy Statement" of 1999 by the American Academy of Pediatrics bears repeated notice here:

> In the case of circumcision, in which there are potential benefits and risks, yet the procedure is not essential to the child's current well-being, parents should determine what is in the best interest of the child. . . . It is legitimate for parents to take into account cultural, religious, and ethnic traditions, in addition to the medical factors, when making this decision.

Just before this comes the statement that although there is evidence for "potential medical benefits," the data "are not sufficient to recommend routine neonatal circumcision."[10] So we're left with an inescapable conclusion: although physicians find insufficient grounds for recommending circumcision, they are willing to have *parents* decide what is in a child's "best interest"—not for medical but for "cultural, religious, and ethnic" reasons. To the best of my knowledge, this extraordinary statement is the only instance of physicians explicitly delegating responsibility for irreversible surgery to persons with no medical credentials.

The phrasing suggests that physicians hope to satisfy two constituencies: first, parents who believe that circumcision produces a cleaner, more attractive penis (hence the word "cultural"); second, Jewish parents who view hospital circumcision as fulfillment of their religious or ethnic obligations. It seems fair to conclude that in this case an ambiguously phrased "policy" statement provides convenient justification for a practice serving admittedly nonmedical purposes.

Is Circumcision Harmful?

If circumcision were an insignificant operation—if the reductive surgery had no adverse consequences—perhaps there might at least be a claim for no harm. To say the least, this is no minor consideration; after all, the fundamental principle of medical practice is, first, do no harm.[11] So I turn now to another side of my first question: Is circumcision harmful? I'll discuss two closely related topics: effects of infant pain during and after the surgery; and longer-term adverse effects, including such immediate "complications" as hemorrhage, injury to the glans, well-documented physiological and behavioral disorders afterward, and—an especially ominous prospect—possible long-term neurological damage that researchers are just beginning to understand.

First, pain: *Infants feel pain*—at least as acutely as we do, probably more.[12] Isn't that self-evident? I've never been able to understand how anyone could believe that infants feel pain less than we do, certainly not after seeing a baby's response to vaccination, or even to a pinprick on the heel. In light of present knowledge, it seems gratuitously cruel to maintain that circumcision is a painless procedure, hence that even local anesthesia is unnecessary. Above all, it is simply unforgivable to argue that early exposure to pain provides a "gainful" experience.[13] A growing list of publications attest to what any witness to a circumcision well knows: that the surgery is exceedingly painful, and that anesthesia—necessarily local—is only partly effective.[14] One of the most striking revelations is that infants undergoing circumcision cry—more accurately, scream—in a distinctive manner.[15] Concluding a survey of the literature on anesthesia for circumcision, pediatrician Robert S. Van Howe warned that "parents need to be told that the currently available pain relief techniques may blunt the pain, but even with these techniques neonatal circumcision is extremely painful and stressful, and produces long-term alterations in neurological response to painful stimuli."[16]

Moreover, pain lingers for days after the surgery, and this affects infant physiology and behavior. Here the evidence continues to accumulate, and some of the most recent research—admittedly into matters not yet fully understood—is deeply unsettling. A number of studies have shown that circumcision adversely affects such basic indicators as blood pressure, pulse, plasma cortisol levels (a measurement of stress), sleep patterns, breast-feeding, early mother-infant bonding, general irritability, and sensitivity to later pain stimuli. Some of these effects are transient, lasting only hours or days; others are more tenacious.[17]

Even more disturbing are recent research reports showing that trauma and injury to the infant body may cause *permanent* neurological damage. Reporting on their research on the effects of pain and trauma on the infant nervous system, Maria Fitzgerald and K. J. S. Anand say that response to injury in a neonate may result in "structural and functional reorganization of the nervous system," altering "the final adult pattern of connections." The effects of damage to "even a small peripheral nerve during development are far-reaching, going beyond the death of its own cell bodies." Adverse changes occur in the spinal cord and probably in the brain as well, producing permanent alteration of normal sensory capacity.[18] In a section on circumcision the authors comment that "painful experiences in neonates could possibly lead to psychological sequelae, based on the fact that several workers have shown that newborns may have a much greater capacity for memory storage than previously thought."[19] Even if it be granted that this research is still in its experimental stage, are we justified in continuing a nontherapeutic practice that may be causing *permanent damage* to the infant central nervous system?

How about complications of the surgery itself? Opponents of circumcision maintain that circumcision is by its nature a "complication," since it removes vital tissue from a healthy person. But setting that argument aside, the medical literature testifies abundantly to dangers ranging from hemorrhage and infection—both more common than is generally recognized—to such horrors as gangrene and accidental amputation of the glans. (A later effect, seldom mentioned, is removal of so much foreskin tissue that some adult men have painful or distorted erections.) Precise numbers and percentages are impossible to come by, since the definition of "complications" is somewhat arbitrary, and, in any event, many hospitals do not publish specific records. But the consensus seems to be that between two and five percent of infants experience some form of serious complication. Occasionally a child dies; and even though that *percentage* is very low, the actual *number* of American infant deaths attributable to circumcision appears to be above two hundred annually. What number of damaged and dead infants constitutes an acceptable price for an optional procedure of disputable worth?[20]

What Good Are Foreskins?

Do foreskins have a specific function, or they are just "extra skin"? The answer is that foreskins are not ordinary skin and they are certainly not extra;

they are highly sensitive tissue, the most sensitive part of male genitals. Like all other parts of our bodies, foreskins evolved during millions of years of human evolution; nature provided them with abundant nerves and blood supply for good reason. In infancy and childhood the foreskin adheres firmly to the glans, providing a protective sheath that guards against contaminating matter. The adhering membrane retracts only gradually during physical maturation. Foreskin removal leads to keratinization (hardening and thickening) of the glans surface, further reducing the relatively modest sensitivity of the glans.[21]

The normal adult foreskin is substantial; it is doubled back on itself in the flaccid state, but when stretched by erection it measures about twelve or more square inches of tissue, richly endowed with specialized nerves. Since this tissue is the principal site of sexual sensation in the normal intact male, circumcised men have lost more capacity for optimal pleasure than they will ever know.[22] The foreskin plays a vital role in foreplay and intercourse, providing a flexible lubricating sheath in which the penis glides smoothly and gently. In its absence intercourse can be traumatic for both partners, particularly those who are older.[23] The most deplorable effect of "routine" circumcisions is loss of maximal sexual fulfillment for both men and women. Some circumcision advocates, while acknowledging the loss of sexual pleasure, maintain that this is socially desirable. I leave that argument for you to judge.

The Ultimate Question

Which leads us to the bottom line in the circumcision debate: Does *anyone* ever have the right to request or perform irreversible alteration of the body of a nonconsenting person for any reason other than absolute medical necessity? In short, is circumcision a human rights violation?

Nearly everyone in this country agrees that parents do not have the right to reject urgent medical treatment for a child. But in such cases we're talking about fairly unusual situations—for example, parents in religious sects who try to refuse blood transfusions or antibiotics for a dangerously ill child. Similarly, very few Americans approve of female genital alteration (if they think about it at all), because such practices seem utterly alien to mainstream American culture. In fact, female children in America are already legally protected: Congressional legislation criminalizing female genital alteration was signed into law by President Clinton in 1996.[24]

But male infant circumcision in America is another story. Here we have widespread agreement that parents have the right to decide on an unnecessary surgical procedure for an infant. The practice has become so embedded in our culture, so taken for granted as the normal and proper thing to do, that objections are likely to raise eyebrows. Why object to a minor operation that

will make the boy healthier and more attractive? And if Jewish or fundamentalist Christian parents want this done for religious reasons, why should
anyone interfere? The simplest solution, for physicians along with everyone
else, has been to leave the decision to the child's parents—to let "cultural,
religious, and ethnic" considerations prevail.

No one can deny that a man may later realize that he would never have
agreed to removal of part of his penis. Moreover, no medical ethicist or legal
scholar would deny that from the very moment of birth we are all persons
with full human and civil rights—including, of course, the right to decide
what happens to our bodies. It follows from this that in our society, a child's
body is *not* the property of his parents; his right to physical integrity should
not be subject to the beliefs or wishes of parents or anyone else—no matter
how well-intentioned they may be.[25] Parental desire does not override the
fundamental principle that any and all medical or surgical intervention must
be unambiguously in a child's best interests. Everyone understands, of course,
that parental consent for surgery must suffice when a young child is in obvious immediate danger from serious disease, injury, or deformity. But removal of healthy genital tissue from a normal body—even when it is claimed
that this *may* be beneficial at some hypothetical future time—is not in any
child's best interests.

Culture, Custom, and Religion versus Individual Rights

The most challenging ethical issue, for advocates and opponents alike, arises
when parents insist that, all medical claims aside, their religion *requires* them
to have their infant sons circumcised. The problem is rooted in the gap between ancient beliefs about absolute paternal authority and modern principles
of individual autonomy, and in how the latter shape our beliefs about the
rights of parents and children. We recognize the right of parents to raise their
children in accord with their own cultural and religious standards. But they
may not harm them physically, nor may they deny essential medical treatment
in the name of cultural or religious traditions. In the final analysis, the
question becomes whether the right to raise a child in a culturally prescribed
manner includes the right to impose nonessential, irreversible surgery on him
before he is able to decide for himself that he wants his genitals permanently
altered. Since no court in this country could or would accept a parental right to
require even minimal genital surgery for a daughter, no matter what the
cultural or religious justification, it must be asked why we sanction genital
surgery for sons. Logic dictates that the fundamental right of female *and* male
children to physical integrity must trump parental beliefs or desires.[26]

Most Jewish Americans have long since abandoned nearly all traditional
practices—everything from regular synagogue attendance to dietary regulations.

Practices mandated or sanctioned in the Hebrew Scriptures—animal sacrifice, slavery, polygamy, rites of purification—are utterly distant from Jewish American culture. Why then has circumcision proved so resistant to change? Is this one custom—in the final analysis a rite of sacrificial bloodshed—appropriate for a modern community? The answer one most often hears—offered without explanation, to be accepted wholly on faith—is that circumcision is an indispensable sign of Jewish identity; that, to quote Anita Diamant once again, if Jews discontinue ritual circumcisions they will "stop being Jews."[27]

Is this correct? Note that Diamant referred not to *surgical* circumcision but to the *ritual* practice. Are ritually circumcised Jewish men somehow endowed with special memory making them singularly likely to be committed to participation in Jewish American life? Does the sight of their own genitals perhaps encourage commitment greater than that of men circumcised in hospitals?

The fact is that the great majority of Jewish Americans have already decided against *ritual* circumcision. No one has assembled firm data on this question, but it is common knowledge that most Jewish boys are circumcised in hospitals, in thoroughly secular "all-American" fashion. A "bris" is supposed to provide a religious or spiritual experience—not for the wailing infant, of course, but for his parents and other witnesses. (Whether that ordinarily happens is a question I addressed earlier.) But nowadays most Jewish American parents, knowing little or nothing about the meaning and intent of ritual circumcision, believe that it's the *surgery* that confirms a boy's Jewish identity. As for genitally intact Jewish boys and men—a silent but real minority—I know of no sociological information on their self-identification.

Tens of thousands of Jewish men, most surely circumcised, seldom appear in a synagogue or participate in any specifically Jewish activities; and many are intermarrying in large numbers. Have they then stopped "being Jews?" I think it can be reasonably argued that they have not—that modern Jewish American identity is far more complex than this would imply, and that these men know very well what being Jewish means in their lives.[28] If some men, or their sons or grandsons, eventually wander away entirely from Jewish identification, they will take their circumcised genitals with them. This is not the place for extended reflection on Jewish American identity; but surely it is self-evident that the vitality of Jewish life and culture in America will never be ensured by removal of infant foreskins.

I've tried to summarize in these few pages the wealth of information that convinced me that male infant circumcision is medically unnecessary, harmful to normal sexuality, and ethically unjustifiable. When all is said and done, I believe we face a single inescapable question: Are we now prepared to accept the principle that, from the moment of birth, every child has all the human rights of any other person—including the inviolable right to freedom from nonconsensual, nontherapeutic bodily alteration?

Notes

The following abbreviations are used in the notes:

JPS   *JPS Hebrew-English Tanakh: The Traditional Hebrew Text and the New JPS Translation.* Philadelphia: Jewish Publication Society, 1999.

RSV   *The Holy Bible with the Apocrypha. Revised Standard Version.* New York: Oxford University Press, 2002.

PROLOGUE

    1. Milos, "Infant Circumcision."

    2. Marilyn F. Milos, personal communication, February 14, 2004.

    3. Aldeeb Abu-Sahlieh, *Male and Female*, chap. 3: "Circumcision among Muslims." Although the Muslim code of religious law (*shariah*) recommends performance of circumcision at the age of seven days, this is seldom followed. Genesis 17 says that Abraham circumcised Ishmael, the putative ancestor of Arab peoples, at age thirteen, and this age is generally taken as the latest acceptable date. Morgenstern, *Rites*, cites nineteenth- and early twentieth-century sources indicating that most Muslims circumcised young boys, with considerable age variation. He says, 50, that "in modern Moslem practice the rite is performed generally between the ages of two and seven years," and very occasionally "as late as the thirteenth year." He cites one author who reported that "the Moslems of Palestine generally circumcise a child upon the eighth day after birth," but another who said that "in Palestine the circumcision of boys is regularly performed between the second and sixth years." He also cites a report on "Arab tribes of Yemen" stating that "children are invariably circumcised upon the seventh day after birth," and another saying that in "Abyssinia circumcision regularly takes place upon the eighth day after

birth" (53–54). But throughout his chapter on circumcision (48–66) he cites many more instances of circumcision of boys at every age prior to puberty. More recent reports by ethnographers also cite various ages. Mehta, "Circumcision," 82, says that Muslims in Uttar Pradesh, India, circumcise boys at ages "two to six years." Peletz, *Reason*, 240, says that among Muslims in Negeri Sembilan, West Malaysia, boys "are usually circumcised when they are about twelve years old." Crapanzano, "Rite," is a perceptive description of a circumcision ceremony in Morocco; he describes the child only as a "boy."

4. On the Ehing of Senegal, see Schloss, *Hatchet's*; on the Gisu of Uganda: Heald, *Controlling*, 57–74; and on the Merina of Madagascar: Bloch, *From Blessing*. Two other noteworthy studies are Beidelman, *Cool Knife*, 131–80, on the Kaguru of Tanzania, and Turner, "*Mukanda*," on the Ndembu of Zambia.

5. Practices obviously vary. Schloss, *Hatchet's*, 76–77, says that among the Ehing, the "major idea of the ritual is to spill sexual blood, and with the very young just the tip of the skin is considered sufficient for them to have entered the initiation." But he adds that children whose wounds closed too completely were subjected to repeat operations—and the "second cutting was much more extensive." Heald, *Controlling*, 60, says that only Gisu youths aged eighteen to twenty-four are eligible for circumcision, which is perceived as a crucial test of masculine bravery and endurance: The youth "must stand absolutely still while first his foreskin is cut and then stripped from around the *glans penis*. He is required to display total fortitude under the knife, betraying no signs of fear," not even involuntary twitching or blinking. The Gisu describe the pain as "fierce, bitter, and terrifying."

6. On local justifications for female genital cutting, see Gruenbaum, *Female Circumcision*; Shell-Duncan and Hernlund, *Female "Circumcision"*; and Boddy, *Wombs*, 49–75.

7. Subincision has generated a large literature. See, e.g., Gould, *Yiwara*, and Róheim, *Eternal Ones*.

8. Shaye Cohen, "Brief History," 32, defines *peri'ah* as "revealing" or "laying bare."

9. Brown and Brown, "Circumcision Decision"; note table 4, p. 218, comparing their survey with others. Brodbar-Nemzer et al., "American Circumcision," studied a group of educated Boston parents who favored natural childbirth. Of those with sons, 62 percent chose circumcision; their foremost reason was wanting the boy "to resemble other males" (276). Circumcised husbands who favored the procedure were highly influential.

The *Circumstitions* website, created by Hugh Young, lists several hundred reasons offered by various people for accepting or favoring circumcision. Among them are the following: "Because it only seems natural." "Because it is a sin not to." "Because all nice families are having it done." "Because Jewish men should be able to feel the pain of others more easily." "Because I don't want him to look like he has a dog dick." "To symbolize humanity's unique essence as more than animal." "Because the decision was made for me, so I'll make the decision for my sons." "To prevent another Holocaust." "To offer our children to a higher spiritual life." "Because we're Episcopalian." "Because [a sister's] doctor said having his glans exposed would help him calm down a little." "Because it reduces a boy's excessive

fascination with his penis." Available online at: http://www.circumstitions.com/
stitions&refs (February 28, 2003). On physician attitudes and beliefs, see Fletcher,
"Circumcision."

10. In *Operating Instructions*, 24–25, the novelist Anne Lamott offered a litany
of misconceptions in explaining why she had her newborn son circumcised: "I had
read that penile cancer occurs almost exclusively in uncircumcised males, that
uncircumcised men have much more frequent urinary tract infections, and that
their female lovers have a much higher rate of cervical cancer . . . but there was also
the matter of keeping the damn thing clean—you would have to cleanse the foreskin
daily. . . . Who's got the time? . . . Then there was the matter of aesthetics. . . . I certainly don't mean to imply that all uncut males look like they're from Enid, Okla-
homa, but I've got to say that I prefer the look of the circumcised unit. The
uncircumcised ones look sort of marsupial, or like little rodents stuck in garden
hoses. And the feel of the uncut ones is a little disconcerting, with all that skin to
peel back and then the worry that it won't stay . . . as my friend Donna put it, 'It
pretty much restores one's faith in Judaism, doesn't it?' " So "with a trembling
bottom lip," Lamott "handed him over" to the physician. Foreskins in young boys
should never be forcefully retracted or manually "cleaned." The comment on
Judaism shows that Americans still think of circumcision as a Jewish procedure.

11. On custom and peer pressure as motivators for acceptance of circumcision,
see Waldeck, "Social" and "Using."

12. Diamant, *Jewish*, 18. Many Jewish Americans, says Diamant, 107, "approach *brit milah* with more confusion and fear than happiness."

13. Mention of grandparents raises other questions, though, since an increasingly large number of Jewish Americans are intermarrying. My impression is that
intermarried couples may experience conflict over circumcision, either between
themselves, or when Jewish relatives insist on it or Gentile relatives object—a topic
calling for sociological research.

14. Snowman, "Circumcision," 575; no reference cited.

15. As an example of this mindset, see Abramson and Hannon, "Depicting,"
113, which cites two websites maintained by right-wing antisemites but says nothing
about those of mainstream organizations reporting on serious research by physicians, nurses, attorneys, and others. True, the authors acknowledge, some opposition to circumcision is based on "valid support from a variety of sources" (which go
unidentified), but they suggest that often opposition serves "as a veneer for a more
fundamental antisemitic bias."

16. Gilmore, *Manhood*, is a cross-cultural study of the belief that boys must be
made into men.

17. See Gollaher, *Circumcision*, chap. 4: "From Ritual to Science"; Hodges,
"Short History"; and Wallerstein, *Circumcision*, chap. 4: "Why Only in the United
States?"

18. The June 16, 2003, issue of *Newsweek*, 64, featured a section on "Men's
Health: Controversies and Clear Thinking" that included a discussion of male
infant circumcision by Dr. Harvey B. Simon. The article was illustrated by a color
photograph of an obviously Orthodox Jewish circumcision being performed by a
bearded man, while the child is held by another bearded man wearing a prayer

shawl (*tallit*). A third man stares intently from the background, eyes fixed on the surgery being performed on the crying infant, whose face is contorted with pain. A truly representative picture of most American circumcisions would have shown a hospital physician operating on an infant strapped to a restraining board.

CHAPTER I

1. *Birkat ha-mazon* (Blessings after Meals), in Harlow, *Siddur*, 758–59. The Hebrew word *basar*, "flesh" (or "meat"), also denotes the penis.

2. Genesis 17:1–2. *JPS*, 28. El Shaddai may have been a local fertility goddess. Biale, *Eros*, 26, suggests that the name meant "something like the 'God (El) with breasts' or the 'God who suckles.'" The Hebrew term *shadayim* means "breasts." Jeremy Cohen, *Be Fertile*, 55, notes that five of the six references to El Shaddai in Genesis are associated with fertility blessings.

3. Genesis 17:4-8; *JPS*, 28. Abram means "Exalted Father." The added letter equivalent to *h* (Hebrew ה) signified that Abram would experience a change in status. A note to the Jewish Publication Society translation says that the new name is "understood" as "father of a multitude." *JPS*, 28–29.

4. Genesis 17:10–27; *JPS*, 29–30. Later, in Exodus 6:2–3 (*JPS*, 122) God says to Moses, "I am the Lord. I appeared to Abraham, Isaac, and Jacob as El Shaddai, but I did not make Myself known to them by My name יהוה" (Yahweh).

5. For the discussion following I am indebted to Hoffman, *Covenant*, chap. 2. Dates for biblical texts are estimates. See Richard Friedman, *Who Wrote*; on uncertainty about dating, see Hoffman, *Covenant*, 28–30. On recent conclusions about biblical composition and dating, see also Finkelstein and Silberman, *Bible*, 28–47, and Lane Fox, *Unauthorized*, 175–84.

6. The first people to practice some form of genital surgery on boys and young men lived somewhere in the region extending from northern Africa and the northeastern shore of the Mediterranean to the eastern shore of the Black Sea. The practice, which was thought of as particularly Egyptian, appears to have reached that people by 3000 BCE, but employed for many centuries principally as a badge of initiation into the priestly caste. The operation probably consisted of a simple longitudinal cut into the upper surface of the foreskin, creating an apron-like opening. There is no evidence of more radical surgery resembling our own version, and nothing to suggest that anyone ever performed genital surgery on infants. See Sasson, "Circumcision"; Nunn, "Ancient," 169–71; Ann M. Roth, "Egyptian," 62–75; Hodges, "Ideal Prepuce," 401–2. Circumcision is now so closely associated with Jews because, while many Middle Eastern peoples, including the ancient Hebrews, genitally altered some boys or youths as a *custom*, it was not until around 500 BCE that the Judeans defined circumcision as an *obligatory* ritual practice for *all* male *infants*. In pre-Yahwist times, circumcising a son (not necessarily an infant) was probably a personal offering to the gods in support of a request for a special favor or forgiveness. In Ezekiel 32 (a sixth-century text) the prophet reviles slain Egyptians, Assyrians, and others who have gone to their graves uncircumcised; but this says nothing about infant circumcision or covenant.

7. *JPS*, 25–27.

8. On infant circumcision as demonstration of father's loyalty to "fraternal interest group," see Paige and Paige, *Politics*, 147–57.

9. Delaney, *Abraham*, 31.

10. Eilberg-Schwartz, *Savage*, chap. 6: "The Fruitful Cut."

11. Eilberg-Schwartz, *Savage*, 149–50.

12. Eilberg-Schwartz, *Savage*, 149. The Hebrew term for "foreskin" is *orlah* (ערלה); the word for "uncircumcised," *arel* (ערל), has the same root. The translators of the Jewish Publication Society text use a circumlocution, e.g., 252: "When you enter the land and plant any tree for food, you shall regard its fruit as forbidden." But they add in a footnote that their "forbidden" is usually translated as "to be uncircumcised." Hertz, *Pentateuch*, 503, also translates *orlah* as "forbidden." His footnote says, "The fruit tree in its first three years is to be regarded as unconsecrated."

13. Eilberg-Schwartz, *Savage*, 152.

14. Isaac, "Circumcision," 453; also Isaac, "Enigma."

15. Hoffman, *Covenant*, 35–36; his emphasis.

16. Leviticus 12:2–5; *JPS*, 231–32. In the English translation, verse 3, on circumcision, is set off with dashes.

17. Leviticus 17:11; *JPS*, 248.

18. Exodus 29:20–21; *JPS*, 177; my brackets.

19. Archer, "Bound." In "In Thy Blood," 35, Archer says: "The belief was that to ritually and voluntarily—and I stress the word 'voluntarily'—shed one's own blood was to recommend oneself to and establish a link with the Creator of the Universe, and this is precisely what happened with circumcision. . . . [T]he individual entered the covenant and joined with his fellow 'circumcisees,' who together formed a community or brotherhood of blood, bound to each other and God by special duties and mutual obligations."

20. See, e.g., Buckley and Gottlieb, *Blood Magic* (but with countering evidence from some societies).

21. Eilberg-Schwartz, *Savage*, 186–89 and Hoffman, *Covenant*, 136–54, are essential sources. Nansi S. Glick pointed out that the blood shed by a virginal bride at marital consummation is the only contact with female genital blood permitted for a Jewish man's circumcised penis.

22. Hoffman, *Covenant*, 96. Hoffman notes that a child born without a foreskin must still have a token drop of blood drawn, as must a convert who had been circumcised earlier. This is called *hatafat dam brit*, "shedding blood of the covenant." Shaye Cohen, "Brief History," argues that, contrary to Hoffman, rabbinic writings on circumcision prior to the eighth century focus entirely on the act of cutting and show no concern with bloodshed. He suggests that the new emphasis on blood after that time was connected with "the idea that circumcision is sacrifice," and "circumcision blood is sacrificial blood." As for why the change occurred then and not earlier, Cohen says this is a difficult question that he will address sometime in the future.

23. Archer, "Bound," 53. In "The Father," 31, Eilberg-Schwartz makes a similar point: "The performance of circumcision occurs at precisely the moment when the boy leaves the state of severe impurity caused during childbirth by the blood of

his mother.... Circumcision is thus a postpartum ritual associated with the separation of the male child from the impurity of his mother.... His blood is clean, unifying and symbolic of God's covenant. His mother's is filthy, socially disruptive and contaminating."

24. *JPS*, 161–62.

25. Levenson, *Death*, pt. 1, esp. 48–52.

26. Levenson, *Death*, 13.

27. Levenson, *Death*, chap. 2. Day, *Molech*, chap. 2 and 83–84. Biblical references: Leviticus 18:21; Leviticus 20:2–5; Jeremiah 32:35; 2 Kings 23:10. Day rejects others that have been proposed. See also Jeremiah 7:31 and 19.5. Day, *Molech*, 85, argues that we cannot "equate the human sacrifices offered to Molech with the first-born offered to Yahweh," because children of both sexes were offered to Molech and there is no mention of first-born children as particular sacrifices; see also 65–71. Levenson, *Death*, 18, agrees that "the two cannot be simply equated," but "both involve child sacrifice, and both seem to have had some frequency in ancient Israel."

28. Levenson, *Death*, 48–52.

29. Exod. 4:24–26; *JPS*, 120. The passage is probably a J text. Levenson, *Death*, 50. Eilberg-Schwartz, *God's Phallus*, 158–60, translates "touched his feet" but notes that this may be a euphemism for genitals.

30. I am indebted to Nansi S. Glick for this convincing interpretation. Robinson, "Zipporah," assesses various interpretations and concludes that Zipporah touched Moses's feet (or genitals, *raglayim*) with their son's bloody foreskin to avert Yahweh's anger at her husband's reluctance to confront Pharaoh.

31. Levenson, *Death*, 50–52.

32. Jeremiah 7:30–31; *JPS*, 1026. A parallel passage appears in Jeremiah 19: 4–5; see also Jeremiah 32:34–35.

33. Genesis 34; *JPS*, 70–72. The Hivites were a Canaanite people; Shechem was a town.

34. Genesis 34:3, 9–16, 25–29.

35. Eilberg-Schwartz, *God's Phallus*, 157.

36. 1 Sam. 18:20–29; *JPS*, 613–14.

37. Eilberg-Schwartz, *God's Phallus*, 158–61.

38. Eilberg-Schwartz, *God's Phallus*, 160.

39. Joshua 5:2–9; *JPS*, 464–65.

40. Jay, *Throughout*, 8–9; first ellipsis in original; her emphasis.

41. Bickerman, *Greek Age*, 33, 6, 26–28.

42. Bickerman, "Historical Foundations," 93–95.

43. 1 Maccabees 1:48, 60–61; 2 Maccabees 6:10; *RSV*, 141–42, 181.

44. Bickerman, *Greek Age*, 37.

45. Barclay, *Mediterranean Diaspora*, 4, 10–11; Smallwood, *Under Roman*, 120–22.

46. Barclay, *Mediterranean Diaspora*, 88, defines Hellenism as "the common urban culture in the eastern Mediterranean, founded on the Greek language... typically expressed in certain political and educational institutions, and largely maintained by the social élite."

47. Barclay, *Mediterranean Diaspora*, 411–12. The quotation from Philo is in *Questions and Answers on Genesis* 3.61. The concept "Jews" came into use in the second century BCE. Someone living in Judea was a Judean; Jews were those who followed the tenets of Judaism. Shaye Cohen, *Beginnings*, chap. 3.

48. Smallwood, *Under Roman*, 123–24; several commas added and Gentiles capitalized.

49. Smallwood, *Under Roman*, 124, comments that "Judaism with its high moral code and non-subversive character fulfilled the criteria for permitted survival, and received toleration on an *ad hoc* basis . . . in the form of exemption from specific Roman requirements which caused religious embarrassment," and later "positive protection under the charter of Jewish religious liberty formulated by Julius Caesar and reiterated by Augustus."

50. Shaye Cohen, *From Maccabees*, 55. Collins, *Between Athens*, 270, says that "beyond reasonable doubt" there were in the Roman Diaspora "adherents [to Judaism] who stopped short of circumcision." They consituted "a broad range of degrees of attachment, not a class with specific requirements or with a clearly defined status in the synagogue."

51. Whittaker, *Jews and Christians*, 80, comments that the practice caused "some instinctive revulsion." Material cited in this discussion is available in Whittaker and in Menahem Stern, *Greek and Latin*.

52. Strabo, *Geographica* 16.2.37; Whittaker, *Jews and Christians*, 51–52. See Menahem Stern, *Greek and Latin*, 1:300. Strabo was a Greek living in Rome; by "excisions" he probably meant female genital cutting—an error, since this was not a Judaic practice.

53. Tacitus, *Histories* 5.1. Menahem Stern, *Greek and Latin*, 2:19, 26, translates this as "base and abominable." Whittaker, *Jews and Christians*, 22, has "evil and disgusting."

54. Martial, *Epigrams* 7.82 and 11.94. Menahem Stern, *Greek and Latin*, 1:526–28; Whittaker, *Jews and Christians*, 82 (latter epigram only); Schäfer, *Judeophobia*, 101–2. Shaye Cohen, *Beginnings*, 41, notes that *verpus* refers to a penis with an exposed glans "either because of erection or because of circumcision," and that the term "often is used in connection with aggressive homosexual love."

55. Petronius, *Satyricon* 68.8. Menahem Stern, *Greek and Latin*, 1:442–43; Whittaker, *Jews and Christians*, 81. Stern, 1:443, remarks that Petronius considered circumcision to be "the most characteristic feature of the Jews." Thus, "circumcision implies Judaism."

56. Hodges, "Ideal Prepuce," 376: The "well-proportioned prepuce was the longer prepuce, with its distinctive taper."

57. Hall, "Circumcision," 1029; Hall, "Epispasm," 36. See also Shaye Cohen, *Beginnings*, 47–48.

58. 1 Maccabees 1:14–15; *RSV*, 140.

59. Charles, *Jubilees* 15.33–34.

60. See, e.g., Feldman, *Jew and Gentile*, 153–58; Schäfer, *Judeophobia*, chap. 5: "Circumcision"; and Barclay, *Mediterranean Diaspora*, 438–39. Schiffman, *Who Was*, 24, says that "the manifold references to this aspect of Judaism show that it was seen by the non-Jew as the distinguishing feature of the Jew. References to it

continue unabated throughout the Hellenistic and Roman periods and relate to both Palestinian and Diaspora Jews of both Hebrew and Greek speech and manners."

61. Barclay, *Mediterranean Diaspora*, 158–80.

62. Philo, *Special Laws* 1.1–7, 103–5 (including Greek text).

63. Philo, *Special Laws*, 1.8–12, 104–7.

64. Philo, *Questions and Answers* 3.47, 241–42; alternative translation "superfluous" based on editor's note.

CHAPTER 2

1. Philippians 3:2–3; *RSV*, 215.

2. Friedlander, *Rabbi Eliezer*, 205.

3. Acts 15:20; *RSV*, 146. See Segal, *Paul*, 187–223; Boyarin, *Radical Jew*, 111–17.

4. Galatians 3:1–3, 13–14; *RSV*, 204–5.

5. Galatians 5:2–4, 6; *RSV*, 206.

6. Galatians 6:15–17; *RSV*, 207. Here "uncircumcision" means absence of circumcision—i.e., intact genitals, not foreskin-stretching.

7. Romans 2:25–29; *RSV*, 166. In another letter he made the point this way: "Was any one at the time of his call already circumcised? Let him not seek to remove the marks of circumcision. Was any one at the time of his call uncircumcised? Let him not seek circumcision. For neither circumcision counts for anything nor uncircumcision, but keeping the commandments of God" (1 Corinthians 7:18–19; *RSV*, 183). Here God's commandments obviously do not include circumcision!

8. Deuteronomy 10:16; *RSV*, 184. This translation follows the Hebrew text (*umaltem et arlat l'vavkhem*), as does the Orthodox Jewish translation in Hertz, *Pentateuch*, 789. The Jewish Publication Society translation alters the imagery: "Cut away, therefore, the thickening about your hearts and stiffen your necks no more" (*JPS*, 398)—presumably to avoid association with the Christian interpretation of "the true circumcision." The phrase appears again in Deuteronomy 30:6 with the same difference in translations; there the *JPS* translation, 441, has "open up your heart" but with a note acknowledging "circumcise" as an alternative.

9. Jeremiah 4:4; *RSV*, 735. The *JPS* translation, 1013, says "Open your hearts to the Lord, Remove the thickening (*arlot*) about your hearts," indicating in a note that the word they translate as "open" (*himolu*, same root as *milah*) is literally "circumcise."

10. Jeremiah 9:25–26; *RSV*, 743. The *JPS* translation, 1033, uses circumcised heart imagery for apparently the only time, and alters the interpretation to single out the Israelites, declaring that other peoples are "circumcised in the foreskin" (i.e., but not in the heart), "but all the House of Israel are uncircumcised of heart" (here verses 24–25). The more accurate translation is "and all," indicating that the Israelites are no better than others who have only foreskin circumcision, because what matters is circumcision of the heart.

11. Boyarin, *Carnal*, 5–7, points out that rabbinic Jews defined the human being as a body "animated" by a soul, while for Hellenistic Jews, including Paul, "the essence of a human being" was "a soul housed in a body." For the former, there

could be no soul without an encasing body; therefore, Jewish identity was not just a "spiritual" matter. The "rite of circumcision," says Boyarin, "became the most contested site of this contention." See also Boyarin, *Radical Jew*, chap. 5: "Circumcision and Revelation." On rabbinic thought about "the body as a signifier... of belonging to a particular kin-group," see Boyarin, "This We Know," 490, and Sacha Stern, *Jewish Identity*.

12. Justin, *Dialogue*, 208–9. See also Glick, *Abraham's Heirs*, 18–23.

13. Justin, *Dialogue*, 175–76. I have changed the translator's Noe and Henoch to Noah and Enoch. Enoch, the father of Methusaleh, is mentioned in Genesis 5; he "walked with God" for 365 years; then "God took him."

14. John Chrysostom, *Discourses*. The translator's title, though not precise (the Greek title is *Logoi kata Ioudaīon*), is historically correct (and presumably less controversial for a contemporary publication) in that John was warning Christians against "Judaizing"–i.e., following Jewish customs.

15. John Chrysostom, *Homilies*, 384; translation slightly modified.

16. John Chrysostom, *Homilies*, 384–86, 388.

17. Feldman, *Jew and Gentile*, 386, remarks that "the questions of conversion and of attraction of Gentiles to Judaism were by far the single most important issues pertaining to the Jews on which the emperors legislated." Smallwood, *Roman Rule*, 541, notes that, despite widespread contempt for Jews and their religious practices, "conversion of gentiles to Judaism was a regular and persistent feature of the Roman world, even if the actual numbers involved were never high."

18. Feldman, *Jew and Gentile*, 385.

19. Linder, *Roman Imperial*, 100. The edict is recorded in the *Digest* of the early third-century jurist Modestin. Cordier, "Les Romains," notes that until the second century CE, the Romans viewed the exposed glans as a sign of lechery, hence a target for humor. But when they equated unauthorized circumcision with castration, it was punished as a mutilation.

20. Linder, *Roman Imperial*, 118.

21. Theodosian Code 16.9.1; translated in Pharr, *Theodosian*, 471, and Linder, *Roman Imperial*, 140.

22. Theodosian Code 16.9.2; translated in Pharr, *Theodosian*, 471, and Linder, *Roman Imperial*, 147–48.

23. Theodosian Code 3.1.5; translated in Pharr, *Theodosian*, 64, and Linder, *Roman Imperial*, 176.

24. Theodosian Code 16.8.22; translated in Pharr, *Theodosian*, 470, and Linder, *Roman Imperial*, 269–70. Pharr's translation, except for the phrase "Jewish mark" (*Iudaica nota*), which he translates "Jewish stigma." Latin original in Linder, 269.

25. Theodosian Code 16.9.4; translated in Pharr, *Theodosian*, 472, and Linder, *Roman Imperial*, 278. The Latin phrase might be literally translated as "mix them with the filth [*caenum*] of his own sect."

26. See, e.g., Linder, *Legal Sources*, 264, 485, 488.

27. Neusner, *Introduction*, xxii, points out that the authors of the Mishnah pay no attention to Christianity, but the two Talmuds and other later rabbinic texts reveal definite awareness of the Christian critique of Judaism. On specific response to the Christian critique of circumcision, see Hoffman, *Covenant*, chap. 7.

28. Rubin, *"Brit Milah,"* argues that rabbis provided sanction for the new ruling by interpreting biblical passages to mean that *peri'ah* was already mandated to Abraham.

29. See introduction to Neusner, *Mishnah*, and Neusner, *Invitation*, chap. 2.

30. Neusner, *Mishnah*, 201–2; his brackets. Neusner marks each line A, B, etc.; I omit these.

31. Neusner, *Mishnah*, 202; his numbers and brackets. Cumin (or cummin) is a plant with aromatic seeds, apparently employed here for soaking the poultice.

32. Shab. 19.6; Neusner, *Mishnah*, 203.

33. On the Orthodox Jewish perspective on *metsitsah*, see Shields, "Making of Metzitzah." Romberg, *Bris Milah*, 111, says that a mohel who omits this step "should be dismissed from his responsibilities."

34. Partial quotation from Ned. 3.11; Neusner, *Mishnah*, 411–12; his italics.

35. Two Talmuds arose, in fact, one in Jerusalem, completed around 400 CE, the other in Babylonia, completed about two centuries later. The Babylonian Talmud, the more thorough of the two, gained foremost recognition, so that unspecified references are assumed to mean Babylonian Talmud.

36. B. Ned. 3.11, 31b–32a. Epstein, *Babylonian Talmud: Nedarim*, 94–96.

37. B. Shab. 5.1., 134a. Neusner, *Talmud, vol. 2E: Shabbat*, 47.

38. B. Yeb. 3.3., 64b. Neusner, *Talmud, vol. 13B: Yebamot*, 150.

39. Genesis R. 46.1–3. Freedman and Simon, *Midrash Rabbah: Genesis*, vol. 1, 389–90. Neusner, *Genesis Rabbah*, vol. 2, 157–59.

40. Genesis R. 46.4. Freedman and Simon, *Midrash Rabbah: Genesis*, vol. 1, 391. Neusner, *Genesis Rabbah*, vol. 2, 159.

41. Genesis R. 46.12. Freedman and Simon, *Midrash Rabbah: Genesis*, vol. 1, 396–97. Neusner, *Genesis Rabbah*, vol. 2, 165–66.

42. Genesis R. 47.7. Freedman and Simon, *Midrash Rabbah: Genesis*, vol. 1, 403. Neusner, *Genesis Rabbah*, vol. 2, 173–74.

43. Ex. R. 19.4. Freedman and Simon, *Midrash Rabbah: Exodus*, 234–35.

44. On images of the divine genitals in the Hebrew Scriptures, see Eilberg-Schwartz, *God's Phallus*.

45. The *JPS* translation describes Job as "blameless."

46. Judah Goldin, *Fathers*, 23.

47. Friedlander, *Rabbi Eliezer*, 203, 205, 209. The reference to Esau recalls Genesis 25:31–34, when Esau relinquished his elder birthright to Jacob in return for bread and lentil stew.

48. Friedlander, *Rabbi Eliezer*, 208–9; parentheses in text. An editor's note says that in an earlier edition the phrase "as though he were eating the flesh of abomination" reads "as though he were eating with a dog. Just as the dog is not circumcised, so the uncircumcised person is not circumcised." A midrashic commentary on the story of Ruth, *Ruth Rabbah* 2.20 (Freedman and Simon, *Midrash Rabbah: Ruth*, 38–39), says that when her sister Orpah left Naomi to return to her own home, she was raped that night by a hundred "foreskins" (i.e., non-Israelite men) and one dog.

49. In an analysis of talmudic regulations pertaining to men with damaged or incomplete genitals (called *tumtum*), Kraemer, *Reading*, 123, shows that, in the

minds of the rabbis, "the uncircumcised male, like the *tumtum*, is a person of ambiguous sexual identity. . . . One who is uncircumcised is not only not fully *Jewish* but also not fully *male*. . . . the uncircumcised Jewish male is not only barely a Jew— he is also, from the Jewish perspective, barely a male" (his emphasis). The talmudic passage is Yebamot 70a–72a, commenting on Mishnah Yeb. 8.1, which equates "uncircumcised" with "unclean." See also Sacha Stern, *Jewish Identity*, 63–67.

50. Hoffman, *Covenant*, 96–97. According to one midrashic text, "angels, being fully spiritual," cannot appreciate circumcision, "which they regard as filthy, bloody, abominable and repulsive," but God regards "the blood of circumcision" as more pleasant "than myrrh and frankincense." Sacha Stern, *Jewish Identity*, 40, n. 279, citing *Tanhuma Vayerra* 2. Apparently the rabbi assumed that angels, like Christians, thought only in "fully spiritual" terms.

51. Yom Kippur is described in Leviticus 16 and 23—P texts, composed some thirteen hundred years after Abraham's supposed lifetime.

52. Friedlander, *Rabbi Eliezer*, 204. See also Hoffman, *Covenant*, 100–3.

53. Friedlander, *Rabbi Eliezer*, p. 210; parentheses in original; my bracketed phrase substituted for original "twofold blood." Hoffman, *Covenant*, 101, says that the passage from Ezekiel should be translated "*By* your blood, live," to make the rabbis' point more explicit: "that Israel lives *by virtue of its blood that is shed in covenant*" (his emphasis).

CHAPTER 3

1. Wolfson, "Circumcision, Vision," 35. Author's restating of a passage from the *Zohar*, not a statement of personal belief.

2. Maimonides, *Mishneh Torah*, "Laws of Circumcision" 3:8, cited in Josef Stern, "Maimonides," 151.

3. Nachman of Bratslav, quoted in Biale, *Eros*, 135.

4. Glick, *Abraham's Heirs*.

5. Hoffman, *Covenant*, esp. chaps. 4–6.

6. Hoffman, *Covenant*, 80; I draw on 64–110. Hoffman's account is based on Birnbaum, *Daily Prayer*, 741–44, and Hyman Goldin, *Hamadrikh*, 33–37; I've consulted both, and Krohn, *Bris Milah*, an ultra-Orthodox text. This section is based on my article "Something Less than Joyful."

7. Numbers 25:10–12; *JPS*, 343.

8. Translations differ in details; mine are based on Hoffman, *Covenant*, 71, and other sources cited in note 6.

9. Hoffman, *Covenant*, 72; Krohn, *Bris Milah*, 137. My wording.

10. Numbers 25; *JPS*, 343–44. A midrash, *Numbers Rabbah* 20.25, adds to the story: "He pierced them both, as one lay on top of the other, through the unclean place of both of them." The Lord assisted Phinehas with twelve miracles, e.g.: The angel "shut their mouths so that they should not cry out." It "lengthened the iron so that it might pierce them both," and it "turned them over at the top of the spear . . . to display their disgraceful conduct to all." Freedman and Simon, *Midrash Rabbah: Numbers*, vol. 2, 824–25.

11. Cahn, *Circumcision*, 14–15; Krohn, *Bris Milah*, 118.

12. Sacha Stern, *Jewish Identity*, 165: intercourse with a non-Jewish woman is "repulsive" and "may be equivalent to bestiality."

13. Hoffman, *Covenant*, 199–207.

14. Hoffman, *Covenant*, 206–7.

15. Hoffman, *Covenant*, 248, n. 35; Friedlander, *Rabbi Eliezer*, 214.

16. I Kings 19; *JPS*, 761–63. Schachter, "Reflections."

17. Hoffman, *Covenant*, 112–21; quotations, 120, 121. Krohn, *Bris Milah*, 127, translates the key phrase as "rescue the beloved . . . from destruction"—less exact but to the point. The Hebrew term, *shachat*, means "pit."

18. Ezekiel 16:3–8; *JPS*, 1181; brackets in original.

19. Hoffman, *Covenant*, 90–91; his emphasis. Some Orthodox mohels take a sip of wine into their mouths before sucking on the bleeding penis.

20. Celebrating a circumcision with a party immediately following dates back to the early rabbinic period.

21. This section draws mainly on Hoffman, *Covenant*, chap. 11.

22. Hoffman, *Covenant*, 196–97. Archer, "In Thy Blood," 39 and 49, n. 55, points out that once infant circumcision was introduced in the immediate postexilic period, only a circumcised male was permitted to perform the operation. Under no circumstances could this be done by a woman, even the child's mother. So although women were for a time accepted as marginal participants, their complete exclusion was not unprecedented.

23. Baumgarten, "Circumcision," 121. She suggests that men may have limited women's participation in circumcisions to offset increased influence of women's families in marriage arrangements.

24. Horowitz, "Eve." Gitlitz, *Secrecy*, 207–9, describes the same custom among Sephardic Jews in Spain and elsewhere.

25. Shaye Cohen, "Brief History," 39–40. Gross, "Blood Libel," suggests that the custom of displaying the bloodstained cloth across the synagogue entrance was abandoned around the thirteenth century to avoid arousing ritual murder accusations.

26. Kirshenblatt-Gimblett, "Cut."

27. Gerber, *Jews of Spain*, chap. 3; quotation, 79.

28. Gerber, *Jews of Spain*, 87.

29. Maimonides, *Guide*, 3.49 (118a), 609. The remark on intercourse with an uncircumcised man is in *Genesis Rabbah* 80.11. (See Freedman and Simon, *Midrash Rabbah: Genesis*, vol. 2, 743.) Biale, *Eros*, 91, quoting part of this passage, comments: "The foreskin, Maimonides seemed to believe, is highly innervated and therefore generates intense sexual pleasure." Maimonides was of course correct.

30. Josef Stern, "Maimonides," shows that the philosopher viewed all "natural things" as perfect creations, beyond improvement—in effect, a refutation of rabbinic statements denigrating the foreskin. Nevertheless, he argued that the "natural perfection of the uncircumcised male organ is also the very condition for its moral imperfection" (133)—and that was the problem circumcision served to rectify. Maimonides' "ideal," says Stern, 135, was "complete denial, or elimination, of bodily impulses," particularly the desire for sexual gratification; but since that was virtually impossible to achieve, he viewed circumcision as "the best that can be done."

31. Maimonides, *Guide*, 3.49 (118b), 610.

32. Josef Stern, "Maimonides," 142, points out that acccording to Maimonides' metaphysics, "relations hold only among members of the same species"; hence the covenant is "an entirely natural, human relation." Stern concludes, 146–48, that Maimonides believed that, although circumcision imposes "moderate sexual restraint," its fundamental purpose is to create a community of men united by belief in the unity of God, signified by the mark imposed on their genitals.

33. Maimonides, *Guide*, 3.49 (118b–119a), 610.

34. Levi ben Gershom (1288–1344), called Gersonides, agreed that circumcision "is designed to help bring perfection in the moral realm by weakening the male sexual organ and quelling sexual desire." He thought that the command to circumcise had been given to Abraham and his descendants "to safeguard them from the licentious practices of their Canaanite neighbors." Eisen, *Gersonides*, 96, 174.

35. Saperstein, *Decoding*, 89.

36. Saperstein, *Decoding*, 97.

37. Saperstein, *Decoding*, 97–98; "sinew of iron [*sic*]"; "circumcized" changed to circumcised. See also his comments, 98–101. This passage is quoted and discussed in Biale, *Eros*, 94–95. Biale remarks (in something of an understatement) that "Isaac's sexual fantasies demonstrate that the problem of Jewish sexuality in a Christian world has a long history."

38. Saperstein, *Decoding*, 99.

39. Scholem, *Major Trends*, 37.

40. Fine, "Kabbalistic," 318–19.

41. Fine, "Kabbalistic," 319–24; 321, illus. The term "phallus" designates the penis in its symbolic aspect.

42. Job 19:25–27; *JPS*, 1686; my brackets. The word translated as "my Vindicator" is more precisely rendered as the familiar "my Redeemer"—presumably avoided here to discourage Christian interpretations. Job says that he wants to "behold God" while he is still alive, but kabbalists sensed the "deeper" meaning.

43. Wolfson, "Circumcision, Vision," 34–35.

44. Wolfson, "Circumcision, Vision," 35.

45. *Zohar* 1:91b, 299. Wolfson, "Circumcision, Vision," 40.

46. Wolfson, "Circumcision, Vision," 40; my brackets.

47. Wolfson, *Through a Speculum*, 396–97; punctuation slightly altered.

48. Wolfson, "Divine Name," 77–78, 85; his brackets.

49. *Zohar* 2:36a; Wolfson, "Circumcision, Vision," 41.

50. Psalm 25:14; *JPS*, 1439 (*sod* translated as "counsel" with a footnote saying "Or secret"). Wolfson, "Circumcision, Vision," 45; I have omitted the Hebrew for "sign of the holy covenant."

51. Wolfson, "Circumcision, Vision," 45.

52. Wolfson, *Abraham Abulafia*, 217, 93, 220; my emphasis; two commas added.

53. Wolfson, "Erasing," 59, quoting a text by a fourteenth-century kabbalist. Wolfson, 63, goes on to discuss early kabbalistic texts describing a *yod* within the brain corresponding to the phallic *yod*.

54. Wolfson, "Divine Name," 102–3, n. 78; brackets in original. Here "lie" means betray. Wolfson's phrase for the forbidden zone is "the demonic Other Side." *Zohar* 2:87b and 3:13b.

55. Wolfson, "Divine Name," 103, n. 79; his brackets. *Zohar* 2:90a.

56. Wolfson, "Occultation," 128.

57. Wolfson, "Re/membering," 216–17.

58. Wolfson, "Re/membering," 221–24. Whether this and similar kabbalistic doctrine evolved in reaction to Christian polemics on Jewish "legalism" and Christian "spirituality" is an open question. Considering, though, that the Zohar was written just when Christians had again become dominant in Spain (after the long Muslim interval), kabbalists had to be aware of their status as heirs to a despised religion.

59. Wolfson, "Re/membering," 223; my brackets for [but]; other brackets in original. The biblical texts are Song of Songs 2:12, Genesis 3:17, and Genesis 18:1.

60. Wolfson, "Re/membering," 223–24.

61. Wolfson, "Re/membering," 224–25. *Sefer ha-Bahir*, sec. 182, translated by Wolfson, 242, n. 90; brackets in original. *Zohar* 2:92b.

62. Wolfson, "Re/membering," 226–27.

63. Lewis, *Jews of Islam*, chap. 2; Gerber, *Jews of Spain*, chaps. 2 and 3.

64. Gerber, *Jews of Spain*, 113–17. Gerber remarks that, in addition to the "religious fervor" of the mobs, they resented "the size, wealth, and prominence" of the Jewish community.

65. Other essentially synonymous terms applied to Conversos include Marranos (the most familiar, but with the insulting connotation of "swine") and New Christians. Yerushalmi, *From Spanish Court*, xv, restricts the term Marranos to individuals who "Judaized," i.e., practiced "crypto-Judaism." Gerber, *Jews of Spain*, 121, follows this usage. I will refer to converts and their descendants as Conversos; those secretly maintaining some Jewish practices will be called Crypto-Jews; and those reidentifying as Jews after emigrating will be clearly described.

66. The most vigorous arguments for the position that by the fifteenth century nearly all Conversos had become sincere Catholics, and that the Inquisition was motivated not by religious considerations but by political and economic jealousy and resentment, have been advanced in Netanyahu, *Origins*. Supporting the view that there were a significant number of Crypto-Jews are Yerushalmi, "Re-education," and Beinart, *Conversos*. Gerber, *Jews of Spain*, 121, says that Crypto-Jews ("Marranos") "may have constituted a significant if pathetic minority" among the converts.

67. Gerber, *Jews of Spain*, 286. I am indebted to Frederick M. Hodges for calling my attention to this passage.

68. Gitlitz, *Secrecy*, 204, says that circumcision "was such blatant evidence of Judaizing that it was not widely practiced among Judaizers." There are only occasional examples from throughout the Iberian peninsula, he says, during the sixteenth to eighteenth centuries.

69. Gitlitz, *Secrecy*, 203–4. They did not blend entirely, though, and not without determination on the "Old Christian" side to remember the difference. Admission to political office required that a candidate demonstrate "purity of blood"

(*limpieza de sangre*), meaning absence of any trace of Jewish or "Moorish" ancestry. See Kamen, *Spanish Inquisition*, chap. 11.

70. Yerushalmi, "Re-education," 3–4. Bodian, *Hebrews*, 189, n. 6, remarks that in this patriarchal society women's identity was a less crucial question but wonders "how women responded to the absence for them of such a differentiating act." I know of no account of Jewish life anywhere, at any time, suggesting that women regretted having been ineligible for infant genital surgery.

71. Yerushalmi, "Re-education," 4–5.

72. Bodian, *Hebrews*, 97.

73. Bodian, *Hebrews*, 112–13; 192, n. 70.

74. Gitlitz, *Secrecy*, 235; two commas added. Bodian, *Hebrews*, 189, n. 8, says that the testimony is "fascinating" but "of doubtful reliability," since there is no evidence that de Fonseca "was pressured into being circumcised in Amsterdam."

75. Bodian, *Hebrews*, 112–13.

76. Steven B. Smith, *Spinoza*.

77. Nadler, *Spinoza*, chap. 6. The text of the *cherem* ("excommunication") spoke of the philosopher's "evil opinions and acts," and the "abominable heresies which he practiced and taught": Nadler, 120.

78. Steven B. Smith, *Spinoza*, 87.

79. Spinoza, *Political Works*, 58–63; quotations, 58 (*aeternam*), 59, 61, 63. I have Americanized the translator's spelling.

80. Spinoza, *Political Works*, 62–63. The term *religiosus* refers to scrupulousness in religious observance but may also imply superstitious adherence to dogma.

81. The key phrase here is *animos effeminarent*, "feminize their minds (or souls)": *Political Works*, 62; editor has *effoeminarent*. Although there is nothing specific to indicate that Spinoza connected circumcision with feminization, his use of the term here is suggestive. Perhaps he meant emphasis on study of religious texts as a highly regarded male occupation.

82. Spinoza, *Political Works*, 63, 65 (64 is facing Latin text).

83. See, e. g., Snowman, "Circumcision," col. 575: "Spinoza declared that the practice of this rite was alone sufficient to ensure the survival of the Jewish people"; and Levenson, "New Enemies," 29: "no lesser a critic of Jewish traditionalism than Baruch Spinoza could see in circumcision the key to Jewish survival."

84. Steven B. Smith, *Spinoza*, 16, 89, 201. See also Yovel, *Spinoza*, chap. 7, on the philosopher as "the first secular Jew."

85. Steven B. Smith, *Spinoza*, 204.

86. Liebman, *New Spain*, 42.

87. Gitlitz, *Secrecy*, 204. Note that he supposedly described only the first stage of a ritual circumcision, not the more extensive *peri'ah*. As usual, we should remember that accounts of this kind were almost certainly obtained from men who had been tortured or threatened with torture.

88. Liebman, *New Spain*, 76. On crypto-Judaism, see Gitlitz, *Secrecy*, 55–58.

89. Martin Cohen, *Martyr*, 102. De Carvajal seems to have realized that he had diminished his sexual sensitivity.

90. Martin Cohen, *Martyr*, 132.

91. Martin Cohen, *Martyr*, 249.

CHAPTER 4

1. Johann Brenz (1499–1570), Lutheran reformer, quoted in J. L. Thompson, "So Ridiculous," 237.

2. Abelard, *Dialogue*.

3. Damage to the penis had profound significance for Abelard. Heloise's guardian uncle, a cleric, furious because the young woman had become pregnant, hired thugs who mutilated Abelard's genitals. Depressed and in despair, he entered a monastery and urged that Heloise take vows and enter a convent; she obeyed and became a distinguished abbess, but her early letters to him express painful sexual and emotional frustration.

4. Abelard, *Dialogue*, 34; translator's "and it does so" altered to "and does so."

5. Abelard, *Dialogue*, 36–38. Abelard was not the first to come up with the argument that Abraham was "justified by faith" alone, which poses Genesis 15 (an earlier J text) against Genesis 17 (a P text). In the former (which, as I've explained, resembles chapter 17 but does not mention circumcision) God promises Abraham many descendants solely because he "put his trust in the Lord." Alexander, "Genesis 22," argues that the covenant promised in Genesis 17 was ratified in Genesis 22, the story of the near-sacrifice of Isaac (another time when Abraham placed his trust in the Lord).

6. Abelard, *Dialogue*, 41–42.

7. Abelard, *Dialogue*, 45–47.

8. Abelard, *Dialogue*, 48–49.

9. Abelard, *Dialogue*, 50. The reference to wild grapes comes from Isaiah 5:2; that to women's punishment is from Genesis 3:16: "in pain shall you bear children."

10. Peter Riga, author of *Aurora*, a popular late twelfth-century verse translation of the Bible, with added commentary, imagined a positive role for circumcision: it marked Jews as people who must not be killed! "The Hebrew has a sign so that he cannot be killed. In truth, that he lives on earth in the midst of his enemies is rather amazing. No king, no duke, no powerful person kills him. His foreskin has been cut back as a sign to all (Pro signo cunctis est resecata cutis). The Hebrew lives among Christians and pagans; Neither the one hand nor the other slays him" (Mellinkoff, *Mark*, 96). Following Shaye Cohen, *Beginnings*, 39, I have altered Mellinkoff's translation of the foreskin line, which she translates "His skin has been cut as a sign to everyone."

11. Jeremy Cohen, *Living Letters*, 364–89.

12. Thomas Aquinas, *Summa Theologiae*, 3a, question 70, "Circumcision," in vol. 57, *Baptism and Confirmation*, 154–71; pages alternate, Latin and English translation.

13. Luther, *Luther's Works*, vol. 45, *Christian in Society II*, 229.

14. Luther, *Luther's Works*, vol. 3, *Lectures*, 133, 136, 144.

15. Luther, *Luther's Works*, vol. 47, *Christian in Society IV*, 149–50, 158.

16. Luther, *Luther's Works*, vol. 47, *Christian in Society IV*, 151–53. Although Luther's argument regarding Ishmael and the others rested on acceptance of myth as history, he was of course correct in recognizing that circumcision is a widespread practice in the Middle East.

17. Luther, *Luther's Works*, vol. 47, *Christian in Society IV*, 155.

18. Luke 2:21; *RSV*, 63. This brief passage gave rise to many artistic portrayals of the Circumcision, some recognizing the Jewish nature of the rite. See, e.g., Schreckenberg, *Jews*, 144–46, and Greenstein, *Mantegna*. The chancel screen at Chartres Cathedral includes a sixteenth-century sculpture portraying the Circumcision.

19. In Mark's account of the Last Supper (14:24; *RSV*, 55), Jesus blesses a cup of wine and asks his disciples to drink from it: "This is my blood of the covenant, which is poured out for many." For Jews of that time, "blood of the covenant" would have signified the blood shed at circumcision. The passage links Jesus's circumcision and crucifixion. Since the wine consumed in the Eucharist (which derives from the Last Supper narrative) is believed to transform into Jesus's blood, participants in this rite might be viewed as consuming the blood of circumcision—as do some mohels.

20. Ragusa and Green, *Meditations*, 42–44; Steinberg, *Sexuality*, 56–57. The "feast" refers to the Feast of the Circumcision, formerly celebrated on January 1. The editors note that the phrase "by His mother" is not in the Latin text; they added it because an illustration accompanying the text shows Mary as the operator and is inscribed "Here [*sic*] how our Lady circumcised the infant Jesus" (394, n. 21; 42, fig. 34; 411, note to fig. 34). Presumably Mary had to perform the circumcision because no ordinary mortal was qualified to undertake such surgery. The "stone knife" recalls the circumcisions conducted by Joshua at the "Hill of Foreskins." Following the Second Vatican Council (1965), the Roman Catholic missal replaced remembrance of the circumcision (*Circumcisio Domini*) with a reading celebrating Mary, and the passage from Luke was no longer included. Steinberg argues that in Renaissance paintings the principal evidence for Jesus's humanity is his penis exhibited as an organ with normal sexual capacity, not as site of the pain of circumcision—even though he recognizes that many paintings link the Crucifixion with the Circumcision by showing blood flowing from the lance wound in Jesus's side down into his groin: *Sexuality*, figs. 63–65, 96, 102, 231, 257, etc. See the "reply" by Bynum, "Body of Christ," 86, 91–92, and Steinberg's response, *Sexuality*, 364–89.

21. Fabre-Vassas, *Singular Beast*, 187–88, citing Damase Arbaud, *Chants populaires de la Provence* (1862).

22. Steinberg, *Sexuality*, 63.

23. Milton's poem "Upon the Circumcision" (1634) emphasizes the infant's suffering: "He who with all Heaven's heraldry whilere / Entered the world, now bleeds to give us ease. / Alas! How soon our sin / Sore doth begin / His infancy to seize!" *Whilere* (erewhile) means some time ago.

24. For examples of how Christian artists portrayed the circumcision of Jesus, see Greenstein, *Mantegna*; Abramson and Hannon, "Depicting," 101–10; Schreckenberg, *Jews*, 144–46; and Blumenkranz, *Le juif*, 81–82. Blumenkranz points out that all three illustrations in his volume convey resistance: two—figs. 86 and 88— show the infant turning away in a gesture of refusal; and fig. 87 shows Mary extending her hands as though she wants to protect the child.

25. Steinberg, *Sexuality*, 51, 163–65.

26. Steinberg, *Sexuality*, 61.

27. Steinberg, *Sexuality*, 61–62; capitalization in original.

28. Sumption, *Pilgrimage*, 46; he does not cite a source.

29. My account of relics is based on Sumption, *Pilgrimage*, 46, 215, 223; and Bentley, *Restless*, 138–42. Bentley provides a bibliography but no reference notes.

30. Bynum, *Holy Feast*, 174–75; 376–77, n. 135.

31. Gollaher, *Circumcision*, 37, citing P. Dinzelbacher and R. Vogeler, trans. & eds., *Leben und Offenbarungen der Wiener Begine Agnes Blannbekin*; I have not seen this source.

32. Müller, *"Die hochheilige Vorhaut Christi,"* 46–52.

33. Bentley, *Restless*, 141–42.

34. On pork avoidance and imagery connecting Jews with pigs, see Fabre-Vassas, *Singular Beast*. By the eighteenth and nineteenth centuries, kosher slaughter, *shechitah* (also *shehitah*), had attracted considerable opposition; see Judd, "German Jewish Rituals," and Gilman, *Franz Kafka*, 134–50.

35. Langmuir, *Toward*, 264; Trachtenberg, *Devil*, 148.

36. Trachtenberg, *Devil*, 149–50; Hsia, *Myth*, 21.

37. Hsia, *Trent*; Fabre-Vassas, *Singular Beast*, 132.

38. Hsia, *Trent*, 41, 47.

39. Hsia, *Trent*, 57; Hsia, *Myth*, 49; Gollaher, *Circumcision*, 39. See also Hsia, *Trent*, 128—not as dramatically bloody but also focusing on the boy's penis. Perhaps some boys were actually murdered by sexual perverts.

40. Fabre-Vassas, *Singular Beast*, illus. 11 and 12a, following 94.

41. Fabre-Vassas, *Singular Beast*, 138–43. I have drawn heavily on chaps. 5 and 6 of this book.

42. Biale, "Blood Libels," 75, suggests that "the blood libel may have originated, at least in part, in a very distorted Christian interpretation of Jewish circumcision rites." It may be more precise to say that essentially accurate knowledge about circumcision combined with belief about deicide to create fantasies about ritual murder.

43. Montaigne, *Complete Works*, 944–46. Montaigne noted with particular interest the practice of *metsitsah*: "As soon as this glans is thus uncovered, they hastily offer some wine to the minister, who puts a little in his mouth and then goes and sucks the glans of this child, all bloody, and spits out the blood he has drawn from it, and immediately takes as much wine again, up to three times. [Description of concluding phase of the ritual.] He meanwhile still has his mouth all bloody." Fynes Moryson, an English traveler, described a circumcision he witnessed in Prague in 1592: "Then the Childes linnen clothes being opened, the Rabby cutt off his prepuce, and . . . did with his mouth sucke the blood of his privy part, and after drawing and spitting out of much blood, sprinckled a red powder upon the wounde. The prepuce he had at the first cutting cast into a guilt sylver bowle full of wyne, whereof the Rabby the Father and the Godfather did drincke, sprinkling some drops into the Chyldes mouth. Then the prepuce or foreskinne was taken out, and putt into a box of salt to be buryed after in the Churchyearde": Frojmovic, "Christian Travelers," 134–35 (spelling and punctuation as in original; she spells the traveler's surname Morrison). The early seventeenth-century traveler Thomas Coryate also remarked on *metsitsah* when describing a circumcision he had witnessed: Having removed the foreskin, he reported, the circumciser, "after a very strange manner, unused (I believe) of the ancient Hebrews, did put his mouth to the child's

yard, and sucked up the blood": Shapiro, *Shakespeare*, 116. Coryate's comment about ancient Hebrew practice was correct.

44. Fabre-Vassas, *Singular Beast*, 113–14. Boiteux, "Les juifs," 759–60; she says that circumcision was a favorite theme for comic interludes and bantering.

45. Fabre-Vassas, *Singular Beast*, 138–43.

46. Shapiro, *Shakespeare*, 88, 111; his emphasis. Although Shapiro provides ample documentation on the English side, the difference between England and the Continent may be an artifact of less available evidence or perhaps incomplete research on this topic by Continental scholars. The illustrations of the supposed martyrdom of Simon of Trent certainly represent beliefs about an assault on the child's penis.

47. Shapiro, *Shakespeare*, 259, n. 81. The notion that such "surgery" could have been performed without obvious evidence was of course completely in error.

48. The name Jurnepin does not appear in the Bible or in Jewish encyclope-dias. Lipman, *Medieval Norwich*, 95, says that a prominent twelfth-century Norwich Jew named Jurnet had a brother named Benedict.

49. Lipman, *Medieval Norwich*, 59–64; quotation, 62. I am indebted to Fre-derick M. Hodges for calling my attention to Lipman's account.

50. Henry III taxed Jews heavily and imprisoned entire families when they could not meet his demands. In *Abraham's Heirs*, 226, I remarked that after 1227, when he reached his majority, "the Jewish community experienced a decline from which it would never recover." A trial held before that king could not have turned out well for Jewish defendants.

51. Donne, *Sermons*, 6:187, 190–92; spelling, punctuation, and italics as in original. Shapiro, *Shakespeare*, 119–20.

52. Shapiro, *Shakespeare*, 127, 130.

53. Pope, *Prose Works*, 1:317–22; spelling, capitals, and italics as in original. See also Felsenstein, *Anti-Semitic*, 143–45.

54. Pope, *Prose Works*, 1:319–22; italics in original.

55. Pope, *Prose Works*, 1:322; italics in original.

56. David Katz, *Jews*, 240–42, 245; capitals and italics in original.

57. Wolper, "Circumcision," 28.

58. David Katz, *Jews*, 246.

59. Wolper, "Circumcision," 29. Another historian, Dresser, "Minority," 73, 75, comments that "of all the negative motifs associated with the Jew...one of the most commonly recurring" was that "he was *circumcised*." Circumcision, she continues, appears to have been "a source of horrified fascination to non-Jewish men....Certainly, the very act of circumcision was seen as an assault upon *male* integrity, both literally and symbolically" (her emphasis).

60. Shapiro, *Shakespeare*, 209. In an article on the role of one newspaper in the opposition to the bill, Cranfield, *"London Evening-Post,"* remarks, 24, that emphasis on circumcision was "perhaps the dominant feature" of the newspaper's satire. He assesses the newspaper's propaganda campaign as "undoubtedly one of the most remarkable" in English history (29).

61. Wolper, "Circumcision," 30; capitals and italics in original. Amri is an-other form of Omri, the name of an Israelite king, but I see nothing in the story of his reign to suggest a connection.

62. Cranfield, *"London Evening-Post,"* 24; brackets and capitals in original.

63. Copy of original text in Wolper, *Pieces*; spelling and italics in original. It will be recalled that the "Shechemites" accepted circumcision in order to marry Israelite women but were massacred while disabled. Felsenstein, *Anti-Semitic*, 119, cites a 1753 London newspaper narrative about Jews as lecherous murderers, who first seduced young women, then circumcised the men; and "whilst their Private Parts were sore ... took up their Swords, and slew every Male of the Britons."

64. Felsenstein, *Anti-Semitic*, 143; on British attitudes to circumcision, see 137–47.

65. Shapiro, *Shakespeare*, 207, 210; spelling in original. Some Jews had clipped coins and engaged in other petty crimes in Edward's time; but they were expelled because, having been reduced to poverty by relentless taxation and extortion, they had become worthless to the monarchy. A popular eighteenth-century joke-book, *Joe Miller's Jests*, included an anecdote about an "impenitent" Christian man condemned to death for coin-clipping. When he pleads that his crime was too trivial for such severe punishment, the judge, unmoved, replies: "Ay, but hark you my friend! ... [W]hat is it to clip a thing but pare it round? And what is paring round called in scripture, but circumcision? And who, under the evangelical dispensation, dares practise circumcision, but one that has actually renounced the Christian-Religion, and is a Jew, a most obstinate and perverse Jew in his heart?" Felsenstein, *Anti-Semitic*, 140. An antisemitic periodical in early twentieth-century Vienna published a cartoon portraying a grinning, grossly ugly Jewish man holding a large pair of scissors and a clipped coin; the title is *Die Beschneidung*, "The Circumcision": Fuchs, *Die Juden*, 194; reproduced also in Shell, "Holy Foreskin," 353.

66. Wolper, "Circumcision," 29. Another version: Cranfield, *"London Evening-Post,"* 23.

67. Wolper, "Circumcision," 32–33.

68. On beliefs about the "indelibility" of circumcision, see Gilman, *Freud, Race*, 49–56.

69. Wolper, "Circumcision," 31.

70. Wolper, *Pieces*: "News for One Hundred Years hence," second page (no pagination); spelling and italics in original.

71. Shapiro, *Shakespeare*, 220.

72. Wolper, "Circumcision," 29.

73. Felsenstein, *Anti-Semitic*, 145.

74. Felsenstein, *Anti-Semitic*, 146. Roth, *Essays*, 212, calls this pamphlet "the earliest (though a highly irresponsible) plea for the reform of the synagogue service and ritual to be published in English," suggesting that the author was a disaffected Jew. The terms "superfluous" and "perfection" do suggest that the author was familiar with the favorite rabbinic rationale for circumcision. Felsenstein, *Anti-Semitic*, 295, thinks it unlikely that a Jewish author would use the term "priest."

75. Felsenstein, *Anti-Semitic*, 147.

76. Sterne, *Tristram Shandy*, vol. 5, chap. 17, 310; spelling, punctuation, italics, etc. in original. "Run," as in "run my country," means flee.

77. Sterne, *Tristram Shandy*, vol. 5, chap. 27, 317–18; spelling, punctuation, italics, etc. in original. In addition to Maimonides, Walter read the section entitled *On the*

foundation or subject of circumcision in John Spencer, *On the Ritual Laws of the Hebrews* (1685); editors' note, 621. Darby, "Oblique," shows conclusively that the injury to Tristram's penis was not (could not have been) circumcision but severe bruising. As Darby points out, Dr. Slop, replying to a question from Tristram's Uncle Toby about the boy's condition, replies, "Twill end in a *phimosis*" (vol. 5, chap. 39, 330)—i.e., tightening due to scarring—and correctly advises conservative treatment.

CHAPTER 5

1. Gilman, *Freud, Race*, 182, explaining the view of Sigmund Freud.
2. Mendes-Flohr and Reinharz, *Jew in Modern World*, 115.
3. Glick, *Abraham's Heirs*, 64–67.
4. On German Jewish enlightenment, see Sorkin, *Transformation*, and Mosse, "Jewish."
5. Gilman, *Freud, Race*, 49; see also chap. 2, "The Construction of the Male Jew."
6. Gilman, "Indelibility," 806, and *Freud, Race*, 49.
7. Gilman, "Indelibility," 809–10 ("major sign," 807); *Freud, Race*, 51–52.
8. Philipson, *Reform*, 107–39; Michael Meyer, "Alienated"; Liberles, *Religious*, 43–61. All three authors maintain their distance from the radical ideology of the Reformfreunde.
9. W. Gunther Plaut, *Rise*, 51.
10. Michael Meyer, "Alienated," 62; Philipson, *Reform*, 118.
11. Philipson, *Reform*, 131. A member of the Reformfreunde wrote to Gabriel Riesser, a leading Jewish advocate for civil rights, asking for his support. Riesser endorsed the original platform but rejected the published version as cowardly retreat from principle, particularly regarding circumcision: "This repugnant ceremony, insofar as it is to be considered as religious, must thoroughly disgust every cultured sensibility, as much as Talmud and messiah put together." Uneasy, however, about delivering ammunition to anti-Jewish ideologues, he proposed simply asserting the right of every individual to complete religious freedom: Michael Meyer, "Alienated," 76–79.
12. Bar Amithai, *Ueber die Beschneidung*, 18–19.
13. Philipson, *Reform*, 131; Liberles, *Religious*, 52–53.
14. Liberles, *Religious*, 53.
15. W. Gunther Plaut, *Rise*, 207. Trier quotes his own letter in *Rabbinische Gutachten*, xi–xii. He obviously took for granted that only the status of male children as "Israelite citizens" was in question.
16. Trier, *Rabbinische Gutachten*; Philipson, *Reform*, 132–33; Liberles, *Religious*, 59–60. Jacob Katz, "Struggle," 327–36, provides a detailed analysis of the responses to Trier's query, showing that a key question for many respondents was whether one should ask non-Jewish authorities to force compliance; most thought not.
17. S. D. Luzzatto, in Trier, *Rabbinische Gutachten*, 75; W. Gunther Plaut, *Rise*, 208–9.
18. Solomon Rapoport, in Trier, *Rabbinische Gutachten*, 140–42; W. Gunther Plaut, *Rise*, 52–53.

19. Zunz, "Gutachten," 199.

20. Geiger, *Nachgelassene Schriften*, 5:181–82. See also Wiener, *Abraham Geiger*, 113–14. Geiger later remarked that he would prefer seeing circumcision replaced by a blessing ceremony similar to those for girls: Heschel, *Abraham Geiger*, 38.

21. Michael Meyer, *Response*, 80–81. Philipson, *Samuel Holdheim*, 6, called him "the keenest and most incisive thinker among the early leaders of the Jewish reform movement." In a recent reassessment of Holdheim's career, Michael Meyer, "'Most'," 2, quotes Abraham Geiger's comment after Holdheim's early death: "Seldom was a man regarded with so much suspicion and animosity, defamed and treated with such forced disregard.... His whole life was a continuous struggle because his steadfast working toward the future was an eternal protest against the decadence of beatifying the past." Holdheim's "attacks" on circumcision, says Meyer, 7–8, "were so painful because they lashed out mercilessly at one of the most central institutions in Judaism... and unsparingly revealed to the world embarrassing, damaging truths about traditional Judaism." For Holdheim, he continues, circumcision "was objectionable because it set the Jews apart from the rest of humanity." His opponents, however, viewed his position "as an abandonment of Judaism itself."

22. Holdheim, *Ueber die Beschneidung*, 6. Philipson, *Reform*, 136–37.

23. Holdheim, *Ueber die Beschneidung*, 8–11.

24. Holdheim, *Ueber die Beschneidung*, 72, 86.

25. Philipson, *Reform*, 277–80; quotation, 280.

26. Philipson, *Reform*, 154.

27. Philipson, *Reform*, 183. The reference to "sexual diseases" almost certainly meant infections contracted through sucking of the bleeding penis by the mohel.

28. Philipson, *Reform*, 216–17. Jacob Katz, "Struggle," 346, notes that Holdheim's participation on the committee shows that he was not absolutely opposed to circumcision, only to rabbinic attempts to enforce it.

29. Philipson, *Reform*, 303–5; W. Gunther Plaut, *Rise*, 209–11.

30. Philipson, *Reform*, 320.

31. Efron, *Medicine*, 61–63.

32. Gilman, *Freud, Race*, 52–56.

33. Efron, *Medicine*, 117–21, notes that despite images of Jews as weak and frail, the fact was that they were more healthy on average than Christians, and their child survival and adult longevity figures were better than those for comparable Christians. But Jewish men may have lived longer because of occupational and cultural differences. This may also explain differences in male sturdiness and physical strength. As Efron recognizes, 121–25, diet, hygiene, child care practices, etc. also influenced child survival.

34. Jacob Katz, "Struggle," 323.

35. Jacob Katz, "Controversy," 357–59; Gilman, *Freud, Race*, 66–69.

36. Brecher, *Die Beschneidung*, third page of foreword.

37. Hirsch B. Fassel, in Brecher, *Die Beschneidung*, 16.

38. Brecher, *Die Beschneidung*, 48. Gilman, *Freud, Race*, 66, cites this passage and remarks that the "disease that is transmitted from adult Jew to Jewish child is Jewishness, hidden under the disguise of the debate about circumcision and

sexually transmitted diseases." I believe that physicians writing about saving infant lives by eliminating dangerous practices meant exactly that.

39. Jaffé, *Rituelle*, 6–15.

40. Jaffé, *Rituelle*, 32.

41. Mishnah: Shab. 19.2, 202; Talmud: Shab. 133b, 672.

42. Jacob Katz, "Controversy," 359–63.

43. Jacob Katz, "Controversy," 374.

44. Jacob Katz, "Controversy," 375–82; quotation, 381.

45. Jacob Katz, "Controversy," 382. "Custom" (*minhag*) is considered less absolutely binding than "law" (*halakhah*), but Ettlinger insisted that both were inviolable.

46. Jacob Katz, "Struggle," 387.

47. Breuer, *Modernity*, 259; Gilman, *Freud, Race*, 68.

48. Jacob Katz, "Controversy," 394, 399.

49. Levit, *Die Circumcision*. Jacob Katz, "Struggle," 349–50, discusses the case briefly, but with incorrect dating.

50. Levit, *Die Circumcision*, 3–4.

51. Levit, *Die Circumcision*, 6–7.

52. Levit, *Die Circumcision*, 12–13.

53. Levit, *Die Circumcision*, 14–15.

54. Levit, *Die Circumcision*, 16–21.

55. Levit, *Die Circumcision*, 23.

56. M. Rawitzki, in Glassberg, *Die Beschneidung*, v-xxxii.

57. A. Kehlberg and Ludwig Loewe, in Glassberg, *Die Beschneidung*, 9.

58. Glassberg, *Die Beschneidung*, 337–55; quoted phrases, 338, 354–55. Judd, "Circumcision," says that *Die Beschneidungsfrage* and *Die Circumcisionsfrage*, both meaning "the circumcision question," referred to two "overlapping deliberations": the former, to debates on whether uncircumcised boys could be formally registered as Jews; the latter, to medical debates on whether the procedure was harmful or beneficial. Glassberg's book, among others, suggests that sometimes the two questions overlapped in the same publication.

59. Szajkowski, "Religious Observance," 795–96.

60. Berkovitz, *Shaping*, 119–25; Michael Meyer, *Response*, 165–67.

61. Michael Meyer, *Response*, 167, calls him "the French equivalent of Samuel Holdheim." But he notes, 165, that Terquem had intermarried, raised his children as Catholics, and did not attend synagogue services.

62. Berkovitz, *Shaping*, 122.

63. Berkovitz, *Shaping*, 122–23.

64. This is my reading of Albert, *Modernization*, 232–33. Her account is unclear on how well Orthodox elements succeeded in resisting change.

65. Harrowitz, *Antisemitism*, 43–44, 49; Harrowitz, "Weininger," 81; translation modified from her two versions. Italian text in Harrowitz, "Weininger," 281, n. 18. Harrowitz, "Weininger," 81, and *Antisemitism*, 50, objects to Lombroso's arguments for "the total obliteration of difference," which she characterizes as "racist logic." Expecting Jews to abandon such practices as circumcision, she argues, is equivalent to "telling Catholics to give up the concept of the Virgin Mary because such a story is impossible medically or scientifically, and is

based on a primitive story that modern science has proved untenable." Of course belief in the Virgin Mary does not require genital surgery on infants.

66. Harrowitz, *Antisemitism*, 52.

67. Mantegazza, *Sexual*, 98–99. Gilman, *Freud, Race*, 57–58.

68. Diner, *Time*, 124–27; quotation, 127.

69. Michael Meyer, *Response*, 226, remarks that among early nineteenth-century settlers, "disregard for Jewish observance was rampant and mixed marriage not infrequent." Naomi Cohen, *Encounter*, 43, cites a lament in 1857 by Isaac Leeser, following his visits to midwestern and western communities, that "the falling off of observance[,] particularly with respect to the Sabbath[,] was deplorable."

70. Naomi Cohen, *Encounter*, 160: "Before 1850 American rabbis were preaching about defections from religion and the common phenomenon of intermarriage."

71. Berman, "Trend," 41.

72. Berman, "Trend," 31, 33; punctuation in original.

73. Berman, "Trend," 34–35, 40.

74. Levinson, *Gold Rush*, 117–18.

75. Tobias, *New Mexico*, 54, 58.

76. Korn, *New Orleans*, 241–42; spelling and italics in original.

77. Sharfman, *First Rabbi*, 594; Berman, "Trend," 43.

78. Sharfman, *First Rabbi*, 116–18. Fein, *Making*, 56–57, says that by 1849, Rice was in despair over the decline of religious observance in America. "The religious life in this land is on the lowest level," he wrote to a former teacher; "most people eat foul food and desecrate the Sabbath in public.... Thousands marry non-Jewish women." He resigned his synagogue rabbinate, began a small congregation of the faithful (serving without salary), and opened a small grocery.

79. Berman, "Trend," 43.

80. Berman, "Trend," 42–44.

81. Sharfman, *First Rabbi*, 114. Leeser was bypassing the principle that anyone born to a Jewish mother is Jewish; he probably meant that boys or men with intact genitals would be denied full participation in religious services.

82. Anon., "The Frankfort Reform Society."

83. T.J.M. and Leeser, "Act of Faith"; punctuation and italics in original.

84. G.L.D. and Wise, Letter and reply; punctuation and italics in original.

CHAPTER 6

1. Hutchinson, "Plea," 15.

2. W. H. Corfield, "Introductory Lecture to a Course of Lectures on Hygiene and Public Health" (1870), 617, cited in Darby, "Where Doctors," 71.

3. Remondino, *History*, 211.

4. Gollaher, "From Ritual," and *Circumcision*, 73–108; Hodges, "Short History." On parallel developments in Australia, see Darby, "Source." I am indebted to Robert Darby for critical commentary and a number of references.

5. I use the term *venereal disease* rather than sexually transmitted disease (STD) because the former was in use until recently.

6. Stengers and Van Neck, *Masturbation*, 39–40. If such unfortunates existed beyond the author's imagination, they may have had tuberculosis, cancer, or a degenerative neurological disease.

7. MacDonald, "Frightful"; Neuman, "Masturbation," 2. On the British reaction to *Onania*, see Roy Porter and Hall, *Facts*, 96–99. Darby, "Masturbation," reviews the scholarly literature, with particular attention to beliefs about circumcision.

8. Shorter, *From Paralysis*, 33–51. Shorter, 38, 45, defines "reflex neurosis" as the theory that "any irritated organ could cause irritation in any other organ in the body, including the brain.... Nervous signals from any irritated organ could travel up and down the spinal cord to any other target organ in the body."

9. Hodges, "Short History," 19; his emphasis.

10. Parsons, "Equal Treatment," discusses beliefs about "excessive sexual activity" and spermatorrhea among American physicians. An entry on "Spermatorrhœa [sic]," by James Cantlie, in Quain's *Dictionary of Medicine*, 1449–50, defined the condition as "discharge of seminal fluid, occurring without voluntary sexual excitement." "The first symptom that alarms the subject," he continued, "is the occurrence of frequent nocturnal emissions" that weaken him, "prey upon his mind," and, if associated with masturbation, cause "extreme mental depression" and inability to tolerate even mention of "sexual matters." Among other treatments Cantlie recommended removal of a "long prepuce" and injections of silver nitrate into the urethra. The dictionary appeared in British and American editions in the 1880s.

11. Hodges, "History of Phimosis," 39–41. In view of the forceful retraction and separation involved in the usual ritual or medical circumcision, it is important to remember that in young boys the normal foreskin is attached to the glans by underlying mucosal tissue. This serves important protective functions. The foreskin gradually retracts and separates from the glans—a process that usually takes a number of years and may not be complete until puberty.

12. Lipman, *Jews in Britain*, 12–18; Lipman, *Social History*, 5–11, 65–71, 85–87, 94–95; Endelman, *Jews of Britain*, 80–82, 92–94. On the superior health of Jewish immigrants, see Gartner, *Jewish Immigrant*, 158–62; he does not mention circumcision. On Jews as alien "other" in Britain, see Cheyette, *Constructions*, and Ragussis, *Figures*.

13. Cooper Forster, "Remarks, 491–92"; comma punctuation altered slightly.

14. Hutchinson, "Influence." At this early date most of his Jewish patients would have come from settled families originating in central and western Europe. According to Hutchinson, 543, his earlier statement appeared in the same periodical, *Medical Times and Gazette*, October 23, 1852, 415, where he had urged removal of the foreskin of infants "born with congenital phimosis"; I have not seen this. On the campaign against syphilis, see Darby, "Where Doctors"; on Hutchinson's 1855 article, see Darby, 58–60. Hutchinson was no medical outsider; he was among the most influential physicians of the century. *Plarr's Lives of the Fellows of the Royal College of Surgeons*, vol. 1 (revised by D'Arcy Power; Bristol, 1930), 588–91, describes him as "one of the great medical geniuses of his time."

15. Robert Darby, personal communication, June 17, 2003.

16. Eve, "Communication," 171.

17. Hutchinson, *Syphilis*, 458–60.

18. Hutchinson, "On Circumcision."

19. Hutchinson, "Advantages," 641–42. This appeared in a review journal, *Medical Review*, as a report on an article published by Hutchinson shortly before in the *Polyclinic*, September 1900. I have not seen the original article. Darby, "Where Doctors," 60–61, characterizes Hutchinson as "a reserved and gloomy Quaker whose watchword was self-denial and who rose early each morning to read the Bible, study his textbooks, and pray."

20. Hyam, *Empire*, 77–78. In Hyam's words: "Hot, humid climates are not good for sensitive foreskins, any more than sandy ones are (as the Jews and Muslims of the Middle East had always known)." Nonetheless, most inhabitants of tropical regions do not practice circumcision. British circumcision rates declined precipitously after World War II. Writing in 1990, Hyam, 75, offered this forecast: "Before another generation has elapsed, no one in Britain will even remember it ever happened or, if they do, will regard it as a quaint post-Victorian fad, on a par with antimacassars and aspidistras." This may prove correct.

21. Edward Dixon, *Treatise*, 158–65; quotation, 158, 160. The determination that a prepuce was "too long" was of course arbitrary. Hodges, "Short History," 19.

22. Edward Dixon, *Treatise*, 161.

23. Edward Dixon, *Treatise*, 163. In 1869, Dr. James Thompson, a former military surgeon, reported that within less than a year he had circumcised some two hundred men, mostly "colored men" with "remarkably long foreskins," but also white men with gonorrhea and "spermatorrhea." Thompson believed that "every person whose foreskin covers the glans ought by all means to be circumcised." He added that a man with a "nozzle-ended penis" was bound to suffer embarrassment and might even be unable to "contract matrimonial alliances." Circumcision, he concluded, "is one of the greatest boons that can be practiced on suffering humanity." The article, which I have not seen, appeared in *Western Journal of Medicine* 4 (1869); quoted in Stone, "Circumcision," 146–47.

24. Dixon, *Treatise*, 164. He believed that syphilis was "produced by a union of foul secretions of both sexes," hence a "shortened prepuce" would facilitate "removal of the secretion that is constantly accumulating about the glans," enabling "dislodgement of the syphilitic poison by immediate ablution."

25. Sayre, "Partial Paralysis," 3–5. I am quoting from an author's reprint; the original publication was in *Transactions of the American Medical Association*, vol. 21, 1870, 205–11. See also Gollaher, "From Ritual," 5–6, and Gollaher, *Circumcision*, 73–76.

26. Sayre, "Partial Paralysis," 7–9; his emphasis.

27. Neither of the two principal historians of American circumcision notes the conservative nature of Sayre's recommendations; discussing his publications they use the term "circumcision" without qualification. Gollaher, "From Ritual," 5–8; Gollaher, *Circumcision*, 73–79; Hodges, "Short History," 22; Hodges, "History of Phimosis," 42.

28. Sayre, "Spinal Anaemia," 257–67.

29. Sayre, "Deleterious Results," 2; his emphasis. I am quoting from an unpaginated author's reprint; the original publication was in *Transactions of the Ninth International Medical Congress*, vol. 3 (1887). Sayre was referring to cases reported in

his earlier papers. Sayre's admonitions were in accord with the anatomical facts: in intact young boys the the foreskin separates from its underlying mucosal lining and retracts from the glans only gradually; forcible separation and retraction (i.e., the contemporary American and Jewish practice) is serious trauma.

30. Sayre, "Deleterious Results." See, e.g., the letters, 3 and 6–7, from Samuel D. Gross (a distinguished Philadelphia surgeon, mistakenly cited by Sayre as S. W. Gross), who spoke of "removing" the prepuce of a two-year-old boy; and J. H. Pooley, a professor of surgery in Columbus, Ohio, who says that he "immediately circumcised" a one-year-old boy to cure him of convulsive movements. However, Sayre appears to have been lax in his own use of the term. An Alabama physician wrote to Sayre, 8, regarding a six-year-old boy with atrophied legs; Sayre "advised him to circumcise the child at once."

31. De Forrest Willard, in Sayre, "Deleterious Results," 13–14 (author's reprint).

32. I. N. Love, in Sayre, "Deleterious Results," 15 (author's reprint).

33. Sayre, "Deleterious Results," 16 (author's reprint).

34. Gollaher, "From Ritual," 9–11; Hodges, "Short History," 18–19, 22. As Gollaher notes, the reflex neurosis theory also led to extensive destructive surgery on women; on this see Moscucci, "Clitoridectomy," and Shorter, *From Paralysis*.

35. Chapman, "Nervous Affections," 314–17; cited in Gollaher, "From Ritual," 10, and Gollaher, *Circumcision*, 84.

36. Gollaher, "From Ritual," 11–13, and Gollaher, *Circumcision*, 86–89. In 1896, a prominent Chicago homeopathic physician named Robert N. Tooker published a book for mothers (not parents) entitled *All About the Baby*. His advice on circumcision, 304: "It is not always necessary, but it is advisable in most cases. It is quite impossible to maintain cleanliness of the parts if the foreskin is incapable of being retracted. . . . The vile habit of masturbation is not infrequently the result of conditions which might have been obviated by this operation. Various reflex nervous troubles are now well known to be caused by a narrow and contracted foreskin." The book is cited briefly in Gollaher, *Circumcision*, 104. (The volume I consulted, from the Princeton University library, was inscribed "To Mrs Grover Cleveland with compliments of the author.")

37. Moses, "Value." Hodges, "Short History," 23, characterizes the article as "exceedingly influential, and widely-cited." I'm indebted to Frederick M. Hodges for sharing summaries of the Moses article appearing in medical periodicals published in Philadelphia, St. Louis, Detroit, and London.

38. Moses, "Value," 368. He did not identify the periodical and I haven't discovered a likely source.

39. Moses, "Value," 368; punctuation in original. His claim that circumcision had received the "tacit sanction of science in almost every age and country" was obviously a gross exaggeration.

40. Moses, "Value," 369. An article on childhood "masturbation and hysteria" published five years later by Abraham Jacobi, a distinguished German-Jewish immigrant pediatrician, described masturbation as a serious problem causing numerous adverse effects and recommended circumcision as the appropriate treatment for the commonest cause, "excessive phimosis": "On Masturbation," 597–602. Kagan, *Jewish Contributions*, 140–43, states that Jacobi was recognized as "the dean of pediatricians in this country" and notes his numerous honors.

41. Moses, "Value," 370. The "tranquil slumber," also described by other circumcision advocates and still sometimes cited in support of the claim that infants feel very little pain, is probably a shock reaction to the sudden intense pain. See the discussion of pain in my epilogue.

42. Moses, "Value," 370. Moses referred to Dr. Simeon Abrahams, who traveled in 1849 to Jerusalem, where he commissioned a scribe to copy his manuscript on circumcision, *Ze Safer Haberit* [sic] (This Is the Book of the Covenant): Sharfman, *First Rabbi*, 507–8.

43. Moses, "Value," 370; his emphasis. Note the operative words "often" and "frequently."

44. Moses, "Value," 370, 372–73.

45. Moses, "Value," 374; his question mark and emphasis.

46. *Medical Record* 13 (May 4, 1878): 358.

47. For a detailed citation, seventeen years after Moses's death, see Stone, "Circumcision," 147–48. By then, the question was whether *all* infants should be circumcised.

48. R. W. Taylor, "On the Question," 582. Note the irony: a procedure that was claimed to *protect* against venereal infection was now suspected of *causing* it.

49. L. H. Cohen, "Rite," 160. Although Taylor noted the dangers of *metsitsah*, he recognized that the practice had become infrequent.

50. L. H. Cohen, "Rite," 161–62.

51. L. H. Cohen, "Rite," 162–63.

52. Arnold, "Circumcision" (1869). A historian of the Baltimore Jewish community, Fein, *Making*, says (but without citation): "Although an extreme Reform Jew (he was even against circumcision), Dr. Arnold enjoyed the respect of Baltimore Jewry, an honor he had earned by his devotion to the community." Fein refers to him as "Abraham," as does Kagan, *Jewish Contributions*, 27 and 487; but two local sources in my possession, including the listing of his name as president of the Maryland Medical and Chirurgical Faculty for 1877–78, record the name as Abram. The medical articles are signed "A. B. Arnold."

53. Arnold, "Circumcision" (1869), 514, 516.

54. Arnold, "Circumcision" (1869), 518.

55. Arnold, "Circumcision" (1869), 520–24.

56. Arnold, "Circumcision" (1886), 173.

57. Arnold, "Circumcision" (1886), 173–74. "Affection" is an older term for infection or medical affliction.

58. Arnold, "Circumcision" (1886), 174.

59. Arnold, "Circumcision" (1886), 174–79; quotation, 174–75.

60. Levien, "Circumcision," 619.

61. Levien, "Circumcision," 620.

62. Levien, "Circumcision," 620.

63. Levien, "Circumcision," 621. I know of no evidence that Levien worked to have a bill introduced.

64. Hochlerner, "Circumcision."

65. See Gollaher, "From Ritual," and Hodges, "Short History," for more on the medical literature.

66. A. U. Williams, "Circumcision." Note that he recommends the procedure specifically for children.

67. Simes, "Circumcision," 376. The periodical volume was issued for 1890–91; my copy of the article has no date.

68. Simes, "Circumcision," 376.

69. Lehman, "Plea." Quotations are from this two-page article. "Scrofula" is an older term referring to enlarged lymph nodes, which might be caused by such conditions as bacterial infections, tuberculosis, or lymphoma.

70. Remondino, *History*, 1. For a fuller (but incomplete) title see my bibliography. Biographical and autobiographical information is available on the website of the San Diego Historical Society, http://sandiegohistory.org/bio/remondino, which describes him as "one of San Diego's most active and well-known physicians during the later nineteenth and early twentieth centuries." I am indebted to Robert Darby for this reference. Remondino was also a creative sex therapist. In a paper published in a urological journal in 1899, he reported that as treatment for a young man suffering from impotence he prescribed three nights in a bed with a "voluptuously developed" and "highly magnetic" young woman, positioned so that her magnetism would flow into him, but with absolutely no physical contact; the patient returned in one day and reported that ten minutes of the magnetic therapy had cured him so completely that had he endured the experience for three nights "he would certainly have exploded from the storing magnetism." Haller and Haller, *Physician*, 233.

71. Remondino, *History*, 206–7.

72. Remondino, *History*, 212–13.

73. Remondino, *History*, 18–19.

74. Remondino, *History*, 2–3. He was of course overlooking more significant variables.

75. Remondino, *History*, 171–72.

76. Remondino, *History*, 173.

77. Remondino, *History*, 174–81.

78. Remondino, "Opponents," 65–66.

79. Remondino, "Opponents," 66–67. Note that these circumcisions were performed on adult men.

80. Remondino, "Opponents," 67–69; second photograph, 73. Here *hydrocele* means accumulation of serous fluid in the scrotum.

81. Remondino, "Opponents," 73. I have omitted statements in the article that would now be rejected as racist and sexist.

82. Newman, "Operation," 1738.

83. Goren, *New York*, 84–85. Reuben, "Ritual," 689–90.

84. Pass, "Should"; spelling in original.

85. The letters appeared in issues of *The Medical World* from July to November, 1915, 270–71, 298, 351–52, 390–91, and 433–35. I am indebted to Frederick M. Hodges for these references.

CHAPTER 7

1. Guttmacher, "Should," 78. Guttmacher (1898–1974), a Johns Hopkins obstetrician, later became president of the Planned Parenthood Federation.

According to *Current Biography Yearbook, 1965,* 181, he was known for his "special ability to mobilize medical and public opinion behind his crusades."

2. Grossman and Posner, "Circumcision Controversy," 192.

3. Gerald N. Weiss, a prominent circumcision *advocate,* noted that circumcision is often "delegated to junior members of the medical staff who have little surgical experience," and that the procedure may be "done at odd hours, often late at night, with minimal supervision, and by careless and inexperienced operators": "Neonatal," 1199. Another leading advocate recently commented as follows: "The current method of performing the procedure is still all too often barbaric. The infant is typically strapped to a restraining board, and the prepuce is usually removed without analgesia. Practitioners would never allow older children or adults to be subjected to such practices, nor would they submit to it themselves": Wiswell, "Circumcision Circumspection," 1245.

4. Gollaher, *Circumcision,* 127, estimated that about four thousand articles on circumcision had appeared in the medical literature between 1870 and 2000; he did not provide a citation. If correct this would amount on average to two or three articles monthly for the 130-year period, which seems credible.

5. For example, in a study reported in 1982, when interviewers asked physicians who recommended against routine circumcision, "if the parents wanted it done, should it be done anyway," 80 percent replied yes: Patel et al., "Factors," 635.

6. Wertz and Wertz, *Lying-In,* 133; Leavitt, *Brought,* 171.

7. Wertz and Wertz, *Lying-In,* chap. 5; Leavitt, *Brought,* chap. 7.

8. The national rate peaked around 1980 at about 85 percent, possibly higher, and has been falling since then. The present rate is estimated at about 58 percent, with substantial regional differences—highest in the Midwest, lowest in the West. Wallerstein, *Circumcision,* 217; Goldman, *Circumcision,* 2; Gollaher, *Circumcision,* 126–27.

9. Charles Weiss, "Worldwide," 36–37. For example, Weiss reported that during the first six months of 1960, of thirty-six Jewish male infants born at Mount Zion Hospital in San Francisco, only twelve were circumcised on the eighth day, either in the hospital or at home, and sixteen had no religious service of any kind.

10. Charles Weiss, "Ritual," 69–71; photographs, 70. Weiss, a distinguished physician and microbiologist who was sharply critical of practices associated with ritual circumcisions, reported, 70, having seen infants carried to and from the operation in elevators with "cans full of trash," and having "watched guests smoking and joking all through the ritual."

11. Bolande, "Ritualistic."

12. In addition to Sydney S. Gellis, Charles Weiss, and Paul M. Fleiss, the first comprehensive critical assessment of the medical evidence was by Edward Wallerstein, a telecommunications engineer and health consumer activist, whose 1980 book, *Circumcision: An American Health Fallacy,* is still authoritative. Jewish physician opposition to circumcision had already appeared in early twentieth-century secular Yiddish publications. The June 15, 1907, issue of *Fraye Arbeter Shtime* (Voice of the Free Worker), an anarchist newspaper, published an article on circumcision by Dr. Ben-Zion Liber (1875–1958), a prominent medical educator with socialist and anarchist leanings. The article was reprinted in the February 1913 issue of

Liber's monthly periodical, *Unzer Gezund* (Our Health), which reached thousands of subscribers (Lederhendler, *Jewish Responses*, 144, 217). Dismissing "modern hypocrites" who claimed religious belief when they had none, Liber urged readers with open minds to "discard all the dirt [*shmutz*] you inherited from earlier generations," and to face life honestly and openly. Rejecting the claim that circumcision makes the penis "cleaner," he declared for soap and water, not foreskin removal. "I won't ask believing Jews what *right* they have to circumcise their children, what right they have to 'make Jews' in this way of their innocent children, who are incapable of deciding about these things. I will, however, ask it of those who consider themselves progressive, yet circumcise their children only because they lack the courage to free themselves entirely of all customs, only because they are afraid of their neighbors. It is an act of brutality and shame" (518, his emphasis). He concluded, 519, that circumcision is "a substitute for human sacrifice." I am indebted to Neil Zagorin for research and translation assistance.

13. Goldman, *Circumcision*, 2.

14. Biographical sketches in Kagan, *Jewish Contributions*, 222; *The Universal Jewish Encyclopedia*, 10:552; and *Who Was Who*, 793. Although Wolbarst appears to have been moderately engaged in Jewish communal affairs, this was a minor concern. He was active in medical and urological organizations, the Euthanasia Society, and several artistic and musical groups, and he obviously kept busy as an author of medical books and articles, inventor of urological instruments, journal editor, translator from French and German, and sculptor (in 1940, he received first prize in sculpture from the American Physicians' Art Association). Aside from his membership in the Jewish Board of Guardians (probably for assistance to orphaned children), I find no evidence of engagement in Jewish organizations or strong commitment to Jewish interests.

15. Wolbarst, "Universal," 92. Holt, "Tuberculosis." (Holt was the author of a widely used text, *The Diseases of Infancy and Childhood*, which first appeared in 1897 and went through numerous revised editions thereafter, eventually under the title *Pediatrics*.) In his article, Holt stated, 99, that inquiries had led him to conclude "that many cases occur which do not find their way into print." He reported, 102, on a three-month-old patient who had been circumcised at eight days by a tuberculous mohel ("a pale, thin, almost emaciated individual") who had performed *metsitsah*. The child died shortly after Holt saw him. Holt summarized forty other cases from the German, English, and American medical literature, including one verbal report from another prominent pediatrician who told him that a child's parents had reported that the mohel "spat on a cloth which was used as a dressing for the wound after operation." Of the forty-one cases Holt knew about, sixteen infants had died and twelve had an unknown outcome. He declared his agreement with a German surgeon who had said that "it is the duty of the physician to raise his protest against the performance of ritualistic circumcision in every case." Wolbarst quoted this last statement as evidence for the condemnation he was arguing against. Holt condemned ritual circumcisions only; in the 1902 edition of his text he advised that any infant with an "adherent prepuce" be circumcised to prevent such afflictions as "priapism, masturbation, insomnia, night terrors" and indeed "most of the functional nervous disease [*sic*] of childhood." Gollaher, "From Ritual," 21.

16. Wolbarst, "Universal," 92.

17. Wolbarst, "Universal," 92.

18. Wolbarst, "Universal," 93.

19. Wolbarst, "Universal," 93–94. This remarkable claim, recorded by Wolbarst without comment, apparently suggested that circumcised men exposed themselves to danger more than others but had about the same rate of infection. More recent sociological research suggests that the claim may have been correct. Possible explanations include social class differences (more circumcision and more sexual experimentation at the upper end of the scale) and the effect of circumcision itself (diminished sexual gratification leading to more intensive efforts to obtain it). See Laumann et al., "Circumcision."

20. Wolbarst, "Universal," 94. Chancroid is a nonsyphilitic genital lesion. The term "epithelioma" refers to basal cell carcinoma, most often occurring on the face.

21. Wolbarst, "Universal," 95.

22. Wolbarst, "Universal," 97.

23. Abr. L. Wolbarst (sic), "Circumcision in Infancy," 23, 26, 29. The abbreviated form of Abraham appears also in his publications cited hereafter.

24. Wolbarst, "Is Circumcision a Prophylactic." The word in the title is penis, not penile.

25. Wolbarst, "Is Circumcision a Prophylactic," 301–2. (The "for" was Wolbarst's contribution to Shakespeare.)

26. Wolbarst, "Is Circumcision a Prophylactic," 303.

27. Wolbarst, "Is Circumcision a Prophylactic," 304.

28. Wolbarst, "Is Circumcision a Prophylactic," 305. Wolbarst had obviously read Remondino's book.

29. Anon. editorial, Lancet (Jan. 1, 1927): 39–40.

30. Wolbarst, "Penile Cancer," 150.

31. Wolbarst, "Penile Cancer," 151–52.

32. Wolbarst, "Penile Cancer," 153.

33. Wolbarst, "Circumcision" (1936), 129, 131. He included claims surprising for this relatively late date: "Circumcision is a prophylactic against masturbation, convulsions in infants, and other reflex irritative phenomena": 130.

34. Charles Weiss, "Routine." Seventy years old when this article appeared, Weiss had been director of clinical research at Mount Zion Hospital in San Francisco: Kagan, Jewish Contributions, 317–18. He should not be confused with Gerald N. Weiss, discussed later.

35. See, e.g., Hardner et al., "Carcinoma," and Leiter and Lefkovits, "Penile Carcinoma."

36. One urologist calculated that a surgeon would have to perform "one circumcision every ten minutes, eight hours a day, and five days a week," for between six and twenty-nine years (depending on estimates in various studies) to prevent a single case of penile cancer: Victor Marshall, "Should", 790.

37. Schoen, "Status," 1309. Schoen's remarkable success in having his articles accepted for publication in major medical and pediatric journals (often without challenge to his claims) contrasts with the experience of opponents of circumcision. See Fleiss, "Analysis," and Van Howe, "Peer-Review."

38. Fleiss and Hodges, "Neonatal," and Frisch et al., "Falling Incidence." (Morten Frisch sic.)

39. Schoen, "Neonatal." Fleiss and Hodges, "Authors' Reply."

40. Schoen et al., "New Policy," 621.

41. Centers for Disease Control and Prevention, "Trends in Circumcisions among Newborns," available online at: www.cdc.gov/nchs/products/pubs/pubd/hestats/circumcisions/circumcisions.htm (Oct. 9, 2004).

42. Vineberg, "Etiology." Other researchers reported similar findings thereafter; see note 60.

43. Ironically, the unpleasant term "smegma" originated in a Greek word meaning a detergent or cleansing agent. It is a normal physiological secretion providing lubrication during intercourse, and requiring no attention other than as part of ordinary bathing.

44. Ravich, "Relationship," 298–99; "carcinogenetic" and "gonorrhoeal" sic.

45. *Newsweek*, June 28, 1943, 110.

46. Ravich, *Preventing*, 10.

47. Ravich and Ravich, "Prophylaxis," 1519.

48. Alfred Plaut and Kohn-Speyer, "Carcinogenic."

49. Ravich and Ravich, "Prophylaxis," 1520.

50. Ravich also tried to export his theory to eastern Europe. In an article published in the *National Jewish Monthly* in 1966 ("Circumcision," his second in that periodical on the subject of circumcision and cancer), he reported on a trip to Poland and the Soviet Union. He had enjoyed a favorable reception in Poland but found prospects bleak in the Soviet Union.

51. Ravich, *Preventing*, 129–30, 157; he doesn't name the journals.

52. Ravich, *Preventing*, 104.

53. Ravich, *Preventing*, 87, 89, 94, 95, 100.

54. Ravich, *Preventing*, 9–10.

55. Human papillomavirus, found in genital warts, has been implicated as a cause of penile and cervical cancer, but the warts occur in both circumcised and intact men. Cook et al., "Clinical," reported a higher infection rate among circumcised men.

56. For example, three survey articles on circumcision published in the past two decades do not mention cancer of the prostate: Grossman and Posner, "Circumcision Controversy"; Poland, "Question"; Denniston, "Tyranny."

57. George W. Kaplan and O'Conor, "Incidence," 804; George W. Kaplan, "Circumcision," 10. A carefully conducted British study showed that Jews do *not* have a lower incidence of prostatic cancer than Gentiles, and that infant circumcision does not decrease the incidence: Gibson, "Carcinoma."

58. Vineberg, "Etiology," 417–18.

59. Vineberg, "Etiology," 419.

60. In 1931, a Jewish physician in Britain, Maurice Sorsby, published a book entitled *Cancer and Race*—the "race" being Jews, whose medical records in a number of European cities he reviewed. He concluded that "the low incidence of cancer of the uterus" among Jewish women was explainable not by "racial immunity" but by "the Mosaic code with its insistence on sexual hygiene" (84, 88). He did

not mention circumcision of husbands. In 1941, a New York gynecologist, Frank R. Smith, published an article concluding that although there was "no adequate explanation" as yet for the "low Jewish incidence," the "most plausible explanations" centered on "circumcision and other racial customs": "Nationality," 429. The "racial customs" were endogamy and readiness to seek prompt medical attention.

61. Wynder, Cornfield, et al., "Study," 1016.

62. Wynder, Cornfield, et al., "Study," 1017–19, 1045–46. Wynder's name was listed in this article as Ernest; in his later article it was Ernst.

63. *Time*, April 5, 1954, 96 and 98.

64. Wynder, Mantel, et al., "Statistical," 1029–30. *Time* favored circumcision because it contributed to "personal cleanliness." Wynder's group favored it because it promoted "personal hygiene." Wolbarst had called attention to its "sanitary" qualities, and Ravich discovered that Moses had taught "cleanliness" and "hygiene" to the Israelites. "Cleanliness" and "personal hygiene" were (and are) major American concerns, and contemporary circumcision advocates often use the same language: Gollaher, *Circumcision*, 86–90. See also Sivulka, *Stronger*, 18: "Cleanliness became an indicator that some individuals were morally superior, of better character, or more civilized than others."

65. Jones et al., "Study," 8, 10; similar conclusions were reported by Terris and Oalmann, "Carcinoma." In their 1960 article, Wynder and colleagues cited the Jones article among several that, in their judgment, "would, independent of circumcision, account for the difference in incidence of cervical cancer among Jews and non-Jews as well as among Hindus and Moslems" (1026). See also Terris et al., "Relation," which concluded, 1056, that "[n]o significant differences were found in the circumcision status" of the husbands of patients with and without cervical cancer; the authors acknowledged, 1064, that they had not investigated the status of "extra-marital partners."

66. See, e.g., Schoen, "Status," 1309–10, and Friedman Ross, "Advantages." Human papillomavirus (HPV) has been linked with cervical and penile cancers. Among the latest claims is that intact men are more likely to carry the virus, but several studies have shown the virus to be equally or even more common in circumcised men: Van Howe, "Does Circumcision," 57.

67. Proctor, *Cancer Wars*, on the politics of cancer research; Patterson, *Dread Disease*, on cancer research and claims in the United States. James S. Olson, *The History of Cancer: An Annotated Bibliography* (New York: Greenwood, 1989), has no entries for circumcision or for any of the publications discussed here.

68. Biographical information in Wan, "GOMCO," 791–92.

69. Yellen, "Bloodless," 146.

70. For descriptions of circumcision with a Gomco clamp see Grossman, *Circumcision*, 18–19, and Gelbaum, "Circumcision."

71. Wan, "GOMCO," 790. "GOMCO" is the company's spelling.

72. Lefkovits, *Analytical*, 7. The pamphlet seems to have been largely ignored, although it is mentioned by Charles Weiss, "Worldwide," 36, n. 30.

73. Food and Drug Administration, "Potential for Injury from Circumcision Clamps," available online at: www.fda.gov/cdrh/safety/circumcision.html (June 28,

2003). The reports on the Gomco included use of damaged or mismatched parts, leading to breakage, slipping, falling off, or tearing tissue. Boston surgeons: Patel et al., "Genitourinary."

74. Wan, "GOMCO," 794. Other testimonials to the clamp's continuing popularity: Gelbaum, "Circumcision" (by a midwife-mohel); Kunin, "Case" (by a urologist-mohel). Kunin describes a number of frightful circumcision injuries seen in his medical practice. The Gomco clamp is now marketed by Allied Healthcare Products Inc., St. Louis, Missouri.

75. R. D. Reynolds, "Mogen Clamp"; Kaweblum et al., "Circumcision"; Schlosberg, "Thirty Years." The clamp is illustrated in Grossman, *Circumcision*, 33, and in the Reynolds and Kaweblum articles.

76. Kaweblum et al., "Circumcision," 682.

77. For the FDA report, see note 73; Patel et al., "Genitourinary." The Mogen clamp is marketed by the Mogen Instrument Company, Brooklyn. The only other instrument in frequent use for circumcisions is the Hollister Plastibell, a disposable plastic bell that is fitted over the glans and beneath the foreskin; a cord is then tied tightly around the device, ending blood flow to the forward tissue. This remains in place for about five to ten days, until the tissue necrotizes and drops off.

78. Morgan, "Rape," 123. Judging from his Welsh surname, three personal names, classical education, and graduation from Sheffield University Medical School, I assume that Morgan was British, hence viewed circumcision from the perspective of someone whose home country had largely rejected the procedure. For his education see his "final rejoinder" to letters, *Journal of the American Medical Association* 194 (1965): 311.

79. Morgan, "Rape," 224.

80. Morgan, "Rape," 224. Muslims do not circumcise infants; they usually circumcise prepubertal boys. Although the Koran says nothing about genital circumcision, this has been a Muslim tradition since about the ninth century. See Aldeeb Abu-Sahlieh, *Male and Female*, chap. 3.

81. The exchange appeared in *American Journal of Diseases of Children* 111 (April 1966): 448–49.

82. Preston, "Whither," 1854, 1858, 1857.

83. Letters from C. J. Falliers, L. D. Freedman, R. S. Nadel, and M. C. Daley, *Journal of the American Medical Association* 214 (1970): 2194–95; emphasis in Falliers letter.

84. The first comment followed the letters cited in the preceding note; the second appeared in *Journal of the American Medical Association* 218 (1971): 1051.

85. Gellis, "Circumcision," 1169. Letters opposing and supporting Gellis, with his reply, appeared in the same periodical, *American Journal of Diseases of Children* 133 (1979): 1079–80.

86. Weiss practiced surgery in Louisiana until 1979, served as an Air Force surgeon from 1979 to 1984, then moved to Little Rock, Arkansas. He retired in 1996 and moved to Fort Collins, Colorado.

87. Gerald N. Weiss, "Jews [sic] Contribution," 797–98. There are no references or citations for the quoted phrases.

88. Gerald N. Weiss, "Jews Contribution," 802.

89. Gerald N. Weiss, "Neonatal," 1198–2000.

90. Gerald N. Weiss and Elaine B. Weiss, "Perspective," 726.

91. Cited in George L. Williams, "Significance," 33. Williams, an Australian pediatrician opposed to circumcision, conducted a two-year study and concluded that, in contrast to Weiss's contention, the foreskin is heavily innervated with Langerhans cells, which serve "a highly protective and necessary function for survival" (34).

92. Gerald N. Weiss and Elaine B. Weiss, "Perspective," 728. Paul did not characterize circumcision as mutilation or castration; as I explained earlier, he argued that circumcision was spiritually worthless, hence its presence or absence were irrelevant for those following the new dispensation.

93. Gerald N. Weiss and Elaine B. Weiss, "Perspective," 729. A recent article by Levenson, "New Enemies," to be discussed later, is another paean to control of sexuality.

94. Letters from P. M. Fleiss, W. L. M. Robson, and A. K. C. Leung, and R. S. Van Howe, *Clinical Pediatrics* 34 (July 1995): 395–98.

95. G. N. Weiss and E. B. Weiss, "Reply," *Clinical Pediatrics* 34 (July 1995): 398–400; quotation, 399. Chlamydia is a virus-like organism that may cause urethritis.

96. P. M. Fleiss, "More on Circumcision"; G. N. Weiss and E. B. Weiss, "Reply," *Clinical Pediatrics* 34 (1995): 623–24.

97. Gerald N. Weiss, "Prophylactic," 727–29.

98. Gerald N. Weiss, "Prophylactic," 729–30.

99. Gerald N. Weiss, "Prophylactic," 730. Cercaria are the larval form of the flatworm. As I stated in note 91, Weiss's claim that the foreskin is "immunodeficient" has been contradicted by George L. Williams.

100. Gerald N. Weiss, "Prophylactic," 731.

101. Gerald N. Weiss, "Prophylactic," 731. Aside from the fact that the normal intact adult penis is readily cleaned by rolling back the foreskin, the "secretions" are physiological and play an important role in intercourse.

102. Gerald N. Weiss, "Prophylactic," 733. In fact, neonatal circumcision is very rare in non-Western countries.

103. The publisher is listed as "Wiser Publications" (perhaps a pun on Weiss) in Fort Collins, Colorado, Weiss's home town at that time. The name is not among those of 1,170 publishers listed in the 1999 edition of Kristen C. Holm, ed., *Writer's Market* (Cincinnati, Ohio: Writer's Digest Books, 1998).

104. Gerald N. Weiss and Harter, *Circumcision*, 60–62; capitalization and punctuation as in original.

105. Gerald N. Weiss and Harter, *Circumcision*, 38–40.

106. In an internet article entitled "Neonatal Circumcision *Is* Necessary," entered in 1997, Weiss describes the foreskin as "a functionless vestigial tissue," now "redundant and obsolete." Adults with intact foreskins, he says, may find it "necessary to clean the area several times a day, which leads to excessive penile attention and manipulation. Ease of cleanliness can make life smoother for the mother and the circumcised child." www.users.dircon.co.uk/~vernon/G_Weiss/necessary.html (June 26, 2003).

107. Fink, *Circumcision*, xiii.

108. Wallerstein, "Circumcision: Information," 507; he presents a systematic critique of Fink, 507–12.

109. Fink, "Possible Explanation." Fink seems to have ignored the fact that, in sharp contrast to the United States, European countries have very low circumcision rates and relatively low rates of HIV infection. He had no research evidence; he *suspected* that circumcised American men were resistant to AIDS. World Health Organization (WHO) statistical data for 1995 indicated these HIV rates per 100,000: Congo: 58.4; Kenya: 24.8; United States: 16.0; Italy: 8.9; Denmark: 4.4; Germany: 2.2; Poland: 0.2. None of the European countries practices routine infant circumcision. Fleiss, "Analysis," 393–94.

110. Statement on "nothing I can prove": Van Howe, "Neonatal," 118. Most of the literature on HIV-AIDS has focused on heterosexual transmission in Africa. For references and opposing views, see Halperin and Bailey, "Male," and Van Howe, "Neonatal." For a general assessment, see Siegfried et al., "Male." See also Fleiss and Hodges, *What Your Doctor*, 159–67. As they note (166), the American Academy of Pediatrics 1999 Task Force on Circumcision stated that "[b]ehavioral factors appear to be far more important risk factors in the acquisition of HIV infection than circumcision status." The American Medical Association Council on Scientific Affairs concurred. See also note 121 and my discussion of the AIDS claims in the epilogue.

111. The publisher is listed as "Kavanah Publishing Company," Mountain View, California. As with the publisher of Gerald Weiss's book, the name is not listed in the *Writer's Market* cited in note 103. Fink's home was in Mountain View. *Kavvanah* is a Hebrew word meaning complete concentration during prayer and devotion to spiritual fulfillment; the term is especially favored by adherents of Hasidism.

112. Fink, *Circumcision*, 1. Diabetics are especially vulnerable to infectious diseases.

113. Fink, *Circumcision*, 3.

114. Aaron Fink, California Medical Association, Resolution 712–87, March 7–11, 1987; Joan B. Hodgman and Joseph B. Hart, "Report to the Scientific Board" (undated, March 1987?).

115. Aaron J. Fink, California Medical Association, Resolution 305–88, March 5–9, 1988; Fink, *Circumcision*, 63–65. I am indebted to Marilyn F. Milos for copies of documents and additional information regarding the 1987 and 1988 resolutions.

116. Hardebeck, "Newborn"; Snyder, "Testimony." See also Snyder, "Problem."

117. Marilyn Milos, personal communication, July 27, 2001. The core proceedings of the symposium were published in the *Truth Seeker* 1, 3 (July-August 1989).

118. Denniston and Milos, *Sexual*; Denniston et al., *Male*; Denniston et al., *Understanding*; Denniston et al., *Flesh*.

119. Fink, "Newborn." The replies, by M. A. Waugh and R. D. Spicer, appeared in the same periodical, *Journal of the Royal Society of Medicine* 83 (April 1990): 278.

120. Fink, "Circumcision and Sand."

121. In February 2003, several medical reports suggested that the alarming prevalence of HIV infection in Africa may be attributable in large measure to use of

contaminated instruments in medical procedures, including circumcisions—and also in ritual circumcisions performed on young boys and youths. See articles by D. Gisselquist and J. J. Potterat, and by D. D. Brewer, both in *International Journal of Sexually Transmitted Diseases and AIDS* 14 (2003): 144–73.

122. Ginsburg and McCracken, "Urinary."

123. Enzenauer et al., "Decreased." The study was conducted in 1982–83.

124. Wiswell, F. R. Smith, and Bass, "Decreased."

125. Wiswell and Roscelli, "Corroborative." In addition to articles I cite, see, e.g., Wiswell, "Circumcision—An Update," and Wiswell, "Circumcision Circumspection."

126. Wiswell and Geschke, "Risks," 1014. Note the unusual term "ablation"—accurate but seemingly more weighted than, say, "removal" or "excision."

127. Wiswell, "Prepuce." The letters from Van Howe and others, and Wiswell's reply, are in "Circumcision: Again," *Pediatrics* 108 (August 2001): 522–24.

128. Gollaher, *Circumcision*, 168.

129. H. C. Thompson et al., "Report."

130. For more information on Schoen, see his personal website, entitled "Circumcision: A Lifetime of Personal Benefits." Among his many publications on circumcision, see "Status," "Urologists," and "Highly Protective."

131. Schoen, Anderson, et al., "Report," 390.

132. Lannon et al., "Circumcision Policy," 691.

133. Schoen, Wiswell, and Moses, "New Policy," 623.

134. Lannon et al., "Circumcision Debate," 641.

135. Schoen, Wiswell, and Moses, "Reply," 211.

136. *Pediatrics* 105, 3 (March 2000), 681–85.

137. Schoen, "It's Wise."

138. Activists opposing circumcision often use the term "mutilation" for female and male genital alteration, and their conferences regularly include speakers and discussion on both genders. See, for example, articles in Denniston et al., *Understanding*, and Denniston et al., *Flesh*.

139. Why the rate declined so sharply for a time, then leveled off, is not entirely clear. One possible explanation is the increasingly prominent presence of Hispanic and Asian immigrants, many with large numbers of children but perhaps more likely to reject circumcision. Rates in the West are the lowest in the nation by a clear margin. In 1997, with a nationwide rate of about 63 percent, the rate in the West was about 38 percent, while the rate in the Midwest was over 81 percent. Statistics are available online at the website maintained by NOCIRC, "United States Circumcision Incidence": http://www/cirp.org/library/statistics/USA (October 21, 2004).

140. J. R. Taylor et al., "Prepuce." Mucosa is mucous tissue, such as occurs on the inner surface of the mouth, as contrasted with the outer cheek skin. See also Cold and Taylor, "Prepuce." On implications for women partners, see K. O'Hara and J. O'Hara, "Effect."

141. The idea that circumcision is akin to castration (or, more accurately, emasculation) has found most explicit expression in the work of psychoanalysts. Psychoanalytic interpretations of circumcision began with Freud's claim that our

unconscious psychic life was shaped by events in prehistoric human experience. In the earliest times, he hypothesized, fathers castrated their sons as punishment for acting out the Oedipal conflict: that is, for rebelliousness, disobedience, and challenges to paternal access to women. As civilization progressed, traumatic memories were repressed by transformation into ritual practices that symbolically repeated or re-created the original actions or situations. Eventually the threat of castration became tempered and disguised in rites of circumcision (Gilman, *Freud, Race*, 75–77). Psychoanalysts and psychoanalytically oriented authors all agree that circumcision is motivated by largely subconscious beliefs and intentions. Some show how initiation rites promote collective solidarity, gender segregation, and male dominance, all with subconscious intent. See, e.g., Reik, "Puberty," and Roheim, *Eternal*. Psychoanalytically oriented authors writing on Jewish circumcision also focus on the unconscious meaning of the rite—for adults, of course. For example, Zimmermann, "Origin," 109–10, offered an interpretation reminiscent of El Shaddai's promises to Abraham, arguing that ritual circumcision symbolically created a potent penis that would someday generate sons. While in an intact penis the glans is exposed only during erection, he noted, in a circumcised penis the glans is always visible—as though one had a permanent erection. The ancient Hebrews, he suggested, "unconsciously thought as follows, 'May the penis of this infant now circumcised be always sexually potent and fertile, and ready to fertilize as if in perpetual erection.'" Remarkably, Freud himself seldom mentioned Jewish circumcision. In an often-quoted footnote to "Analysis," his study of a phobia in a five-year-old boy called "Little Hans," he commented that juvenile fantasies about circumcision might connect with antisemitism: "The castration complex is the deepest unconscious root of anti-semitism; for even in the nursery little boys hear that a Jew has something cut off his penis—a piece of his penis, they think—and this gives them the right to despise Jews" (36). Later, in *Moses and Monotheism*, 144, he hypothesized that Gentiles resented the way in which Jews "marked off their aloof position," particularly through circumcision "which reminds them of the dreaded castration idea." Geller, "Paleontological," applies gender theory to interpret Freud's views on circumcision.

CHAPTER 8

1. Zborowski and Herzog, *Life*, 319. A *shtetl* was a small-town Jewish community in eastern Europe. The book was a publication of the "culture at a distance" project conducted during the 1940s and 1950s by Margaret Mead and Ruth Benedict. The authors interviewed immigrants on their memories of life in eastern Europe and constructed an impressionistic composite portrait.

2. Aaron Jesin, physician-mohel, Downsview, Ontario, letter to Toronto *Globe and Mail*, December 9, 2000.

3. Material in this chapter appeared in somewhat different form in Glick, "Something Less."

4. A study conducted in 1995–96 among affiliated respondents yielded these percentages; the first number refers to members of congregations, the second to nonmembers: Orthodox: 6, 2; Conservative: 18, 15; Reform: 16, 22; Other: 2, 19.

Note that these figures do not include the large numbers of nonaffiliated individuals. Steven M. Cohen, "Assessing," 16.

5. "The most important aspect of recent American Jewish history has been the transformation of American Jews into Jewish Americans": Edward Shapiro, *Time*, 254.

6. A major recent study of a large sample of moderately engaged, middle-aged Jews revealed their most striking characteristic to be that they are intensely individualistic and self-directed. They present themselves as "universalist, liberal, and personalist." They declare that they will decide "which rituals they will observe and how they will observe them ... which beliefs they will hold, which loyalties they will acknowledge." They do not believe "in special divine commandments to the Jews, or special divine providence watching over Jews." Steven M. Cohen and Eisen, *Jew Within*, 7, 11. Unfortunately, these researchers did not include even a single question about circumcision. I wrote to Arnold Eisen, asking about the omission. In a letter of June 19, 2001, he acknowledged that neither he nor Steven Cohen could explain their failure to ask about circumcision, other than that they "simply forgot to do so." Assuming (as I do) that this was a frank and honest answer, it is mystifying. These experienced scholars asked about such matters as membership in Jewish organizations, participation in Jewish study groups, candle lighting, and Christmas trees but asked nothing about a universally recognized Jewish practice that has been controversial for more than a century. Although professional Jewish studies scholars are understandably cautious when discussing circumcision, asking one or two questions among dozens would have implied nothing about personal beliefs. Is circumcision taken so completely for granted that even those studying Jewish belief and practice never think to ask about it?

7. My categories have inevitably simplified the complex, changing character of the Jewish population. I've omitted specific consideration of the Conservative movement, even though large numbers still identify with it, because Conservative Judaism is self-defined as "centrist" and because it seems to be losing ground to other groups, particularly Reform. On denominations and trends, see Wertheimer, *People*, and Heilman, *Portrait*, as well as the Cohen and Eisen study, *Jew Within*, cited above.

8. Nosson Scherman, "An Overview," in Krohn, *Bris Milah*, 22–25.

9. Scherman, "Overview," 26.

10. Scherman, "Overview," 28–30.

11. Krohn, *Bris Milah*, 35–51.

12. Krohn, *Bris Milah*, 52–53.

13. Krohn, *Bris Milah*, 54–56.

14. Krohn, *Bris Milah*, 69.

15. In an anthology of short sermons for delivery at circumcisions, distributed by the ultra-Orthodox publisher of the Krohn volume, there are repeated references to "completing" or "perfecting" the male body by removing the foreskin, and "harnessing" the physical, or "natural," body in preparation for an elevated spiritual life: Ganchrow, *Entering*, xiii, 24–26, 50, 54, 65–66, etc. As noted earlier, this imagery derives from interpretations of the word *tamim* in the first verse of Genesis 17. These authors portray the foreskin as both source and symbol of the male sexual drive; in fact, it has no influence on libido one way or another, although it does have a major role in sexual intercourse.

16. Aryeh Kaplan, *Innerspace*. The woman had decided, after some hesitation, to have her son ritually circumcised. In a letter to me she said that the experience taught her "the importance of always making an effort to curb harmful behaviors, those actions which would infringe on another person's health or well-being. . . . The act of severing the most primitive and harmful aspects of our selves (represented in the foreskin) is a physical effort to uproot these emotions so that they they do not affect our actions." She went on to say that since it is men who are "responsible for most forms of inhumanity towards their brothers," circumcision may "in its own way" be "an effort to overcome these behaviors." In any event, she concluded, "this is the way one Jewish mother has come to understand the power of this ritual." (I assume that her husband, who is not Jewish, did not try to interfere, but we didn't discuss that.)

17. Aryeh Kaplan, *Innerspace*, 171; his emphasis. In everyday parlance the term *mitzvah*, literally "commandment," refers to a good deed, such as visiting the sick or assisting a needy person.

18. Aryeh Kaplan, *Innerspace*, 172.

19. Aryeh Kaplan, *Innerspace*, 175–76.

20. The website of Aish (Hebrew for "fire," here perhaps connoting flame), an ultra-Orthodox Jerusalem-based organization, founded by an American rabbi and dedicated to combatting "alarming assimilation rates," includes several articles on circumcision. All extol the practice as the ultimate expression of Jewish faith. Rabbi Moshe Schapiro says that Abraham "vowed that he would teach his descendants to serve God with perfect devotion," and in return, God assured him that "there would always be Jews." The rite of circumcision, he continues, "reminds us that Jewish survival is not a natural phenomenon, but a supernatural one. Jewish survival defies the laws of nature. This explains why the mark of circumcision is made on the reproductive organ—it symbolizes the idea that the Jewish People's seed will never be destroyed." The article is in the "Jewish Literacy" section of the website, http://www.aish.com/literacy/lifecycle (April 26, 2003). Schapiro's explanation recalls the ancient belief, expressed repeatedly in Genesis, that it is men alone who "beget" children by depositing "seed" (Hebrew *zera*, "seed" or "sperm") into women. This explains why the female "reproductive organ" does not require ritual marking. In the same section Rabbi Daniel Frank, a practicing mohel in the New York area, declares that Hitler waged World War II "against the Jewish inventions of circumcision and ethics," and "we are still at war." Jewish parents "stand at the frontlines of this battle, armed with the decision whether to choose Bris or not."

21. Malka, "Mazel Tov," 1.

22. Malka, "Mazel Tov," 2–4; his emphasis.

23. Naomi Cohen, *Encounter*, 160–63; Philipson, *Reform*, 377.

24. The complete text is in Michael Meyer, *Response*, 387–88, and in Philipson, *Reform*, 355–57. Philipson, 357, describes the platform as "the utterance most expressive of the teachings of Reform Judaism."

25. Chap. 10 of Michael Meyer, *Response*, is entitled "The New American Reform Judaism." On the connection between Israel, Holocaust memory, and conservative political trends among Jewish Americans, see Novick, *Holocaust*.

26. Berit Mila Board of Reform Judaism, Berit Mila Program, Fact Sheet, available online at the website of Union of American Hebrew Congregations: www.uahc.org/congs/ot/ot005/facts97.html, 1–2 (May 31, 2001).

27. A Reform physician-mohel whom I asked about *metsitsah* seemed astonished and puzzled; he appeared not to have heard of the practice. He responded similarly to my question about Phinehas.

28. Barth, *Berit Mila*, xvii; their spelling of what is more often called *brit milah*.

29. Barth, *Berit Mila*, xix.

30. Ragins, "Berit Mila," 128, 139.

31. Chyet and Mirsky, "Reflections," 59, 61, 63. The term "salvationary" is apparently their neologism. The mention of wine refers to the practice of placing a few drops of wine on the infant's lips—probably symbolic of blood replacement.

32. Meisel, "Neonatal," 6. I've substituted "unkindest" where the text has "unkindness." This citation, and those by Greenbaum and the Marders to follow, were taken from internet copies of the newsletters, available online at: http://www.uahc.org/congs/ot (May 31, 2001) and http://www.rj.org/beritmila/bmnews (August 29, 2002). Page references are to the internet copies.

33. Greenbaum, "In Pursuit," 2–3. Here, as so often in the religious literature on circumcision, we find the notion that *man*, but not woman, requires "perfecting." Ironically, a rite that originated to affirm patriarchy is now explained with reference to imagined male imperfection.

34. Greenbaum, "In Pursuit," 3–5.

35. Janet Marder, "Judaism," 6–8. Here again we see the notion that circumcision is a form of symbolic "repair."

36. Sheldon Marder, "Flexibility," 8.

37. Hoffman, *Covenant*, 218.

38. Herzbrun, "Circumcision," 1; his emphasis. Note that although the article is a call for relieving *infant* pain, the title ("Circumcision: The Pain of the Fathers") suggests self-concern.

39. Herzbrun, "Circumcision," 2, 8–11.

40. Hoffman, *Covenant*, 250, n. 20, notes that the journal published replies (which I haven't seen). One rabbi argued that pain is sometimes a "virtue."

41. All information on Kogen, including quotations, comes from his personal website, www.briss.com. The film *L.A. Mohel*, featuring Kogen, Ilene Gelbaum (a nurse-midwife also certified as a circumciser by the Berit Mila Board), and an Orthodox mohel, is available from Filmakers Library (*sic*), New York. A set of photographs of a circumcision at which Kogen officiated is available at the personal website of Skylar Tevya Winig, the child who was circumcised. No surgical details are visible. In several photographs the father appears singularly ill at ease.

42. "Goals and Philosophy," www.briss.com/coreinfo (August 29, 2002).

43. "The Mohel of the Moment," *New York Times*, December 1996 (no day cited); available online at: www.beritmila.com/moment (August 29, 2002).

44. "Thoughts About Newborn Circumcision" and "Set-Up Instructions," available online at: www.briss.com/details.

45. Jay Pawlowski, "Magazine's Series Finds Real L.A.," *Rocky Mountain News*, January 3, 2003. Among Kogen's other claims to fame is the tale of his performance of a ritual circumcision on the child of a Jewish biker in the Mojave Desert of Nevada. See "Press" section of www.briss.com.

46. Jacob, *Responsa*, 236–37.

47. Jacob, *Responsa*, 238.

48. "Reform Rabbis' Vote Reflects Expanding Interest in Rituals," *New York Times*, June 28, 2001, A16. The terms *mohelim* and *mohalim* are alternative spellings, the latter now preferred. See also Rachel Zoll, "Reform Jews to Advise on Tradition," Associated Press, June 26, 2001, available online at: www.ccarnet.org.

49. Wine, "Circumcision," 4.

50. Wine, "Circumcision," 5–6; "Yahveh" [*sic*].

51. Wine, "Circumcision," 5, 7–8.

52. Karsenty, "Mother," 14. The other contribution is a gently worded letter to the author's parents explaining her decision not to circumcise her child. "We wrote rather than telephoned," she remarks, "because we were afraid of the reaction." Bivas, "Letter," 11.

53. Karsenty, "Mother," 15–21.

54. Diamant, *Jewish*, 18–19.

55. Diamant, *Jewish*, 105, 107–8.

56. Diamant, *Jewish*, 111; Diamant reduces the passage to "I saw you wallowing in your blood." Her description of a representative rite is on 124–27. The passage reappears in another version (136), in a section entitled "New Liturgies."

57. Diamant, *Jewish*, 111–13. One might wonder why nature provided such an ample supply of blood (and nerves) to "superfluous" tissue.

58. Diamant, *Jewish*, 113. In 1993, Jewish Lights, a Vermont publisher of spiritual and inspirational literature, issued a revised version of Diamant's book as *The New Jewish Baby Book*. The section on circumcision is an abridged version of the original text. This time, presumably to be in keeping with the publisher's orientation, Diamant tells readers that at its "heart" the ceremony "is not about the circumcision; it is about the flesh and blood miracle of our lives as human beings" (95). As so often happens in contemporary texts, Abraham's covenant has disappeared. The section concludes with four suggested sets of readings; none mention blood or Phinehas. The first opens with statements by the parents as they hold the child. The mother says, "My son, my child, you have been as dear to me as my own breath. May I hold you gently now with the love to keep you close and with the strength to let you grow." The father then takes the child and says, "My son, my child, a piece of my life is you. You have grown to life apart from me, but now I hold you close to my heart and cradle you in my arms with my love." Following additional statements of this sort, the circumcision "is performed" (117–18).

59. Diamant, *Jewish*, 114–16.

60. Neusner, *Enchantments*, 5–6.

61. Neusner, *Enchantments*, 43–44.

62. Neusner, *Enchantments*, 45.

63. Neusner, *Enchantments*, 46.

64. Neusner, *Enchantments*, 46–47, 50.

65. Neusner, *Enchantments*, 50–51. Although the word "cut" seems to be an unfortunate choice here, it recalls the biblical term "to cut a covenant," discussed earlier. As I noted, Hoffman, *Covenant*, 112–21, explains the origins and meaning of this prayer.

66. Neusner, *Enchantments*, 52. We encountered the word "dazed" also in Anita Diamant's opening statement.

67. Gordis, *Becoming*, 295–96.

68. Gordis, *Becoming*, 296–99; his emphasis.

69. Finally in this regard, a photographic volume entitled *Witness to the Covenant of Circumcision*, by Dale Lieberman, portrays parental anxiety more memorably than words can. Commenting on feminine "sensibility," preceding a picture of an apprehensive mother, mouth open wide as she witnesses the surgery, the photographer remarks, 92, that most mothers avoid watching "for a variety of reasons—psychological, social, religious, and anthropological." He doesn't elaborate on this cryptic statement, but the photograph says enough. He also remarks, 94, that family members comfort one another "at a time that is often more difficult for the parents than it is for the infant"—that notion based on his belief that circumcision is almost painless, owing to the mohel's speedy technique, local anesthesia, "or the immaturity of nerve endings in the extra skin." Nevertheless, he continues, 98, the event produces "anxiety and stress" that are "relieved only by its conclusion." The photograph of the parents as the surgery ends, 99, suggests that their anxiety indeed requires relief.

CHAPTER 9

1. Sukenick, *Mosaic*, 60. The Yiddish term *shiksa* means "Gentile woman."

2. J. Boyarin and D. Boyarin, "Self-Exposure," 36: "We hasten to assure the reader that neither of us was so gauche as to film our sons' circumcision [*sic*]. A distant relative was kind enough to do that for one of us, however, and so we were able to witness the star of that video, by now aged three or four, calling out just before the scene of the fateful cut: 'Don't do it!' In a sense that is hardly literal yet still more than allegorical, a simulacrum of one's own circumcision now can be experienced. This suggests a potential heightening of reflection as an integral aspect of self-fashioning." Apparently the authors did not think to ask the boy whether he experienced heightening of reflection as an integral aspect of his self-fashioning. More to the point, a child of that age would have believed that his protest could still avert the "fateful cut."

3. Braver Moss, "Painful," 70–71.

4. Braver Moss, "Painful," 72.

5. Landes and Robbin, "Gainful," 74; their emphasis. In apparent ignorance of readily available information, they assert that newborn infants feel little pain because "neural connections are not well developed," hence that "bodily perception of pain is therefore minimal and is not worth even the slight risk of complications that could result from the dorsal penile block."

6. Landes and Robbin, "Gainful," 72.

7. Landes and Robbin, "Gainful," 73. The Hebrew word *tikkun* means "repair." The journal title refers to "repair" of social injustice and inequality, not bodily improvement.

8. Landes and Robbin, "Gainful," 74.

9. Braver Moss, "Circumcision," 20–22.

10. Braver Moss, "Circumcision," 23.

11. Raul-Friedman, "Rebuttal," 31–33.

12. One of the five, by Robert G. Hall on epispasm, was mentioned in chapter 3, but since it stands apart from the implicit debate in the other articles, I will not discuss it here.

13. Eilberg-Schwartz, "Why Not," 28–29.

14. Eilberg-Schwartz, "Why Not," 29–30.

15. Eilberg-Schwartz, "Why Not," 31.

16. Eilberg-Schwartz, "Why Not," 32–33.

17. Eilberg-Schwartz taught religion at leading universities for a time but it appears that he is no longer in academia.

18. Singer, "Pain," 39–40. A photograph on the first page of this article (38) shows adults, presumably parents and guests at a circumcision, who do not appear to be experiencing pleasure. Singer reassures readers: "In a moment the anxiety reflected in their faces will turn to unbounded joy" (39). She offers no prediction on the infant's emotions.

19. Joel Roth, "Meaning," 41–44.

20. David J. Meyer, "Doing It."

21. Schoen, "Circumcision Decision." The suggestion that the foreskin protected prehistoric men against abrasion from brambles and the like is predicated on the assumption that the foreskin is simply hard outer skin with very limited sensitivity, and that its primary purpose is to protect the glans. In fact, the foreskin is much more richly innervated than the glans and contributes substantially more to sexual sensitivity. Even if the assumption were correct, it might be questioned how removal of a protective cover could benefit the glans even now.

22. Kimmel, "Kindest," 44, 45, 47, 48.

23. Zaslow, "Circumcision," 49. Schachter-Shalomi founded a group called B'nai Or [Sons of Light] Religious Fellowship. A sociologist describes him as the "spiritual guru" of Jews practicing a "nonorthodox brand of hasidic spiritualism," aimed at bringing about a mystically based "Jewish Renewal" (Waxman, *Jewish*, 136). Jewish "baby boomers," as defined by Waxman, would have been between ages thirty-seven and fifty-five in 2001. In a contribution to an edited volume on "Jewish masculinity," Schachter-Shalomi, "How to Deal," 82–83, muses on his son's circumcision: "Foreskin (*orlah*), a stopped-up dullness, is removed, leaving a penis sharply exposed, vulnerable yet intimate when caressed, standing erect, full of consciousness." He performed the operation himself: "it is I, Zalman as *mohel*, who am about to do this unspeakable thing to my child." But he strengthened his resolve with thoughts of what it all meant: "As God exists in relation to humans in his AM-NESS … so in some smaller way do I stand in relationship to my son. In the am-ness of being as father, I sired him with sperm from my body," and so on.

24. Zaslow, "Circumcision," 49. Writing the divine name as G-d is a common Jewish practice.

25. Zaslow, "Circumcision," 50.

26. Zaslow, "Circumcision," 50.

27. Ollivier, "Circumcision." Quotations are from pt. 1 of this article, dated October 26, 1998.

28. Ollivier, "Circumcision." The three myths and the concluding comments are in the second part of the article, dated October 27.

29. Levenson, "New Enemies," 36, 35.

30. Levenson, "New Enemies," 29. An uncertain number of American men, Gentile and Jewish, are following in the footsteps of the Hellenized Jews I described earlier. No one can restore lost innervation, of course, but men practicing restoration report definite benefits. See, e.g., the section on "Foreskin Restoration" in Denniston et al., *Male and Female*.

31. Levenson, "New Enemies," 34.

32. Gollaher, letter to the editor, *Commentary* 109 (June 2000): 3; response by Levenson, 7. This issue contains ten other letters in response to Levenson's article, most opposed to circumcision. Eugene J. Cohen, a rabbi-mohel, wrote in support, 6, commenting that "no pain registers in the child's brain," that he cries when being circumcised because of "removal of his diaper." Levenson, 10, thanked Cohen but wisely disagreed on why infants cry during circumcision.

33. Levenson, "New Enemies," 34.

34. Levenson, "New Enemies," 35.

35. Levenson, "New Enemies," 36.

36. Levenson, *Death*, 51.

37. *New York*, May 21, 2001, 17, and June 11, 2001, 10.

38. Witchel, "Bagels." Barney Greengrass is a New York "appetizing store."

39. Shaye J. D. Cohen, "Why Aren't," 572–73.

40. Plaskow, *Standing*, xx.

41. Plaskow, *Standing*, 82–83; her emphasis.

42. Plaskow, *Standing*, 58–59. The hymenotomy proposal came from Mary Gendler, in "Sarah's Seed—A New Ritual for Women," which appeared in *Response* 24 (winter 1974–75); *Response*, now defunct, featured perspectives on Jewish issues contributed mainly by young authors. Not surprisingly, this suggestion has not gained support. However, Fishman, *Breath*, 283–84, notes that a 1978 novel by E. M. Broner, *A Weave of Women*, describes a ceremony involving infant hymenotomy in an Israeli women's commune.

43. Fishman, *Breath*, 122–23.

44. Fishman, *Breath*, 123–25. Fishman cites a secondary source for Julie Cohen's statement.

45. In *ReVisions: Seeing Torah Through a Feminist Lens* (Woodstock, Vt.: Jewish Lights, 1998), Rabbi Elyse Goldstein characterized circumcision as a "ceremony of male bonding through some form of violence" and commented that feminists had not yet contributed "in full power" to the discourse on the subject. Whenever they speak critically, she noted, "they are often accused of being traitors for merely questioning the centrality of circumcision." Cited in Mark, "Crossing," xvii–xviii. I have not seen Goldstein's book. Only one essay in Peskowitz and Levitt, *Judaism*, mentions circumcision—and that is by a male author writing about a woman. In an essay on the nineteenth-century "salon Jewess" Rahel Levin Varnhagen, Geller, "Circumcision," 183, observes that in describing her own conflicted feelings about her Jewish identity, she "resorted repeatedly to the figure for male Jewish identity: circumcision." No other author in this collection of twenty-five feminist essays on gender issues in Judaism says anything about circumcision.

46. Wilkowski, *Baby's Bris*.

47. Silverman, *Rosie*. An appendix, 37–47, by Philip L. Sherman, a prominent New York mohel, lists popular names for Jewish boys and girls with suggested Hebrew equivalents. Among the boys' names are Blake, Brandon, and Brett (Hebrew: Baruch), Sawyer (Simcha), and Tyler (Tevye). Girls' names include Ashley (Aviva), Bailey (Basya), Jade (Yocheved), Kelly (Kayla), and Schuyler (Sarah). Apparently Sherman has been circumcising little Brandon Bernsteins, Sawyer Shapiros, and Tyler Teitelbaums.

48. Apple, "Eighth Day," 44–45. The "tube" is a reference to *metsitsah.*

49. Apple, "Eighth Day," 47, 49. *Shmekel* is the slang diminutive for *shmuck*— hence a small penis.

50. Apple, "Eighth Day," 51.

51. Apple, "Eighth Day," 52–53.

52. Richler, *Apprenticeship*, 153–55; ellipsis in original. Readers may want to rent the video of the film version to see the scene of blood splashing on the camera lens.

53. Philip Roth, *Counterlife*, 305.

54. Philip Roth, *Counterlife*, 314–15.

55. Philip Roth, *Counterlife*, 323.

56. McCarthy and Philip Roth, "Exchange," 98; her emphasis.

57. McCarthy and Philip Roth, "Exchange," 99. Note that Roth's friends (and Roth?) believe that parents have the right to decide on genital surgery for their male (but presumably not female) children—for nonmedical, non-"religious," purely *personal* reasons.

58. Malamud, *The Tenants*, 50–51. Dictionaries give *schmuck* (the German spelling), but I follow the author.

59. Roger, "Pagan," 240–41. Note that Roger labels the Christian man's intact penis "pagan."

60. Roger, "Pagan," 243–44.

61. The most complete coverage is on www.circumstitions.com/TvSitcoms.html (May 6, 2003), a website created by Hugh Young, in the section entitled "Treatment of Circumcision on TV." The texts correctly represent the essential content of shows but are not necessarily exact on script details. This excellent site includes critical commentary and additional documentation on films and other television shows.

62. Episode credits: created by Larry David and Jerry Seinfeld, written by Larry Charles, directed by Tom Cherones. I am indebted to the Museum of Television and Radio, New York, for access to a videotape of this episode. I quote from the text available online at: www.seinfeldscripts.com/TheBris.htm (NewsGuy Seinfeld Lists, August 6, 2003). This differs in minor details from the version I viewed and transcribed at the Museum of Television and Radio. I've made occasional very minor changes to the printed script—e.g., added commas or sentence breaks. Occasionally I add a word or two from the viewing that does not appear in the script. I'll note differences of possible interest, but none influences the message of the episode.

63. I heard Kramer say: "You mean circumcision?"

64. In an earlier *Seinfeld* episode, no. 38, Elaine tells George that she skipped her boss's son's circumcision to attend a baseball game. George expresses amused

surprise that she refused the invitation. Elaine replies with a shrug: "Yeah. . . . What makes you think anyone would want to go to a circumcision?" George has no such illusions: "I'd rather go to a hanging."

65. Here the script differs most sharply from what I heard. I did not hear the sentence beginning "It hurts bad" or much of what follows. Here is what I heard: "We're not talking about a manicure. Imagine, this is going to be his first memory—of his parents just standing there, while some stranger (uch) cuts off a piece of his manhood—and then serves a catered lunch!"

66. Fran Lang Porter et al., "Neonatal." See also Goldman, *Circumcision*, 20–24.

67. *The Outside Chance of Maximilian Glick*, a film produced by the Canadian Film Board, portrays a love affair in a conservative small town between two gifted young pianists, a Jewish Canadian boy and a Polish Canadian girl. The front cover of the videocasette case says: "When Max was born they cut off his . . . It's 13 years later, 1960, his Bar Mitzvah, and they're still at it" (ellipsis in original). The boy's parents and grandparents try to end the relationship. The film opens with a brief, exotic-looking circumcision scene in a synagogue; soon after, the adolescent Max muses to himself: "A Jewish boy's life starts with them cutting off his tip; then they spend the rest of his life trying to cut off the rest." Here circumcision (symbolizing repression) is again the definitive Jewish male experience, and the comment on cutting equates physical and behavioral emasculation.

68. Series 2, episode 9, August 1, 1999. Available on videotape, in *Sex and the City*, season 2, vol. 3. The Charlotte-Mike narrative occupies only about a quarter of the full episode, which follows the on-again, off-again "love lives" of two other women as well. Parenthetical descriptions of characters' emotions and behavior are my additions.

69. Readers may know that the program aired on HBO—hence the free language.

70. She means that 85 percent of males in the world, not those in the United States, are intact. This is a generally accepted figure, but impossible to document precisely. A reasonable estimate for American men aged thirty-five would be 30 percent intact.

71. Circumcision has appeared as a theme in a number of other sitcom episodes, with essentially the same messages each time. See the summaries and partial texts at www.circumstitions.com/TVSitcoms.html. Note in particular the episodes in *Cheers*, *Judging Amy*, and *7th Heaven*. In the *South Park* episode entitled "Ike's Wee-Wee," or "Ike's Briss" [sic], there are repeated references to chopping—e.g., "They're going to chop off his wee-wee!" and "wee-wee chopping parents." One character refers to the physician-mohel as a "sick-ass weirdo." Nevertheless, two characters are so favorably impressed that they intend to be circumcised the next day. Available online at: http://www.members.tripod.com/~Stephen_Williamson/brissscript.html (August 20, 2003).

72. A few of these jokes are common currency. I depend mainly on Legman, *No Laughing*, 2:528–53. The Jewish author is opposed to circumcision.

73. Legman, *No Laughing*, 2:538; punctuation slightly altered.

74. Legman, *No Laughing*, 2:539.

75. Legman, *No Laughing*, 2:541; somewhat modified.

76. Legman, *No Laughing*, 2:541–42; somewhat modified. This theme reappeared in a cartoon in the January 17, 2000, issue of the *New Yorker*, showing paired drawings labeled "Boat Christening" and "Boat Bris." In the former a man wearing a nautical cap is about to break a bottle over the protruding bow; in the latter, a bearded man in clerical garb is sawing away the front portion of the bow. An interview with David Gollaher, author of *Circumcision*, on the National Public Radio program *Fresh Air*, February 14, 2001, was followed by an interview with a mohel (granting the last word to the status quo). Then one Larry Josephson told circumcision jokes. Since anyone reading Gollaher's book with reasonable care would have understood that his research led him to oppose the practice, it seems very unlikely that he approved of a conclusion in such poor taste. Would jokes have followed a program on female genital cutting?

77. The August 30, 2004, issue of the *New Yorker*, 64–65, offered a satirical chart titled "What Government Best Suits You?" by Jon Stewart and the writers of his television program, "The Daily Show." One column was titled "What's Your Take on Genital Mutilation?" Under the heading "Democracy" the answer was "Foreskin is gross/hilarious. Off with it." Under "Theocracy" the answer was "Why stop at genitals?"

EPILOGUE

1. For example, 1995 data from the World Health Organization showed these AIDS rates per 100,000 for that year: United States: 16.0; Canada: 3.8; France: 3.5; Germany: 2.2; Norway: 1.6. This information is available as part of the extensive literature review at the NOCIRC website, http://www.cirp.org/library/disease/HIV (February 12, 2004), where articles cited here and many others are available.

2. Bwayo et al., "Human"; Gray et al., "Probability." See also Malamba et al., "Risk Factors."

3. Baleta, "Concern"; Brody et al., "Evidence."

4. Halperin and Bailey, "Male," 1815. For overall evaluation of the African research data, see Van Howe, "Does Circumcision"; Van Howe, "Circumcision and HIV"; and Siegfried et al., "Male Circumcision." A recent study in India—Steven Reynolds et al. "Male Circumcision"—concluded once again that circumcision is protective against HIV infection; however, the authors aggregated statistically nonsignificant results in two distinct and noncomparable populations: Hindus and Muslims. I am indebted to Hugh O'Donnell for a personal communication (April 4, 2004) analyzing this article.

5. See, e.g., Schoen, Colby, and Ray, "Newborn"; Wiswell, "Prepuce" (including references to five of his other publications on UTI).

6. For a sampling of recent opinion pro and con, see "Newborn Circumcision and Urinary Tract Infections," letters in *Pediatrics* 107 (January 2001): 210–14; and "Circumcisions: Again," letters in *Pediatrics* 108 (August 2001): 522–24, all in response to Schoen, Colby, and Ray, "Newborn." The first set of letters includes a reply by Schoen; the second set, a reply by Wiswell.

7. See the references cited in the letter from Christopher J. Cold and Michelle R. Storms, one of the first set of response letters cited in note 6.

8. Van Howe, "Does Circumcision"; Cook et al., "Circumcision and Sexually."

9. Waldeck, "Social," and Waldeck, "Using." See also Van Howe, "Why," and Miller, "Circumcision."

10. Lannon et al., "Circumcision," 691.

11. Denniston, "Circumcision."

12. The most comprehensive source is the CIRP site maintained by NOCIRC: http://www.cirp.org/library/pain (September 19, 2003); see there the bibliographic essay "Pain of Circumcision and Pain Control." Here as elsewhere I am indebted to the CIRP bibliographer, George Hill. See also Chamberlain, "Babies"; Goldman, *Circumcision*, 19–24; and Gollaher, *Circumcision*, 135–39. In 2000 the International Evidence-Based Group for Neonatal Pain issued the following statement: "Compared to older children and adults, neonates are more sensitive to pain and vulnerable to its long-term effects": Anand and International Evidence-Based Group for Neonatal Pain, "Consensus," 173. In September 2001, the American Academy of Pediatrics and the American Pain Society stated, "Despite the magnitude of effects that acute pain can have on a child, it is often inadequately assessed and treated. Numerous myths, insufficient knowledge among caregivers, and inadequate application of knowledge contribute to the lack of effective management": "The Assessment and Management of Acute Pain in Infants, Children, and Adolescents," *Pediatrics* 108, 3 (September 2001): 793–97; the quoted passage is from the abstract. On inadequate physician training for relief of circumcision pain, see Howard et al., "Neonatal."

13. See Landes and Robbin, "Gainful Pain." I mentioned this singularly outrageous argument before, but it bears repeated notice. Landes, a rabbi, holds the University Chair in Jewish Ethics and Values at Yeshiva University of Los Angeles. "The point" of a ritual circumcision, we are informed by this professor of ethics and values, and his coauthor, a specialist in "human development," is "to have the infant *there* as a participant in the event, without being numbed by anesthesia, either general or local" (74; their emphasis). Note that the article appeared in *Tikkun*, generally recognized as the leading *progressive* Jewish periodical. In a letter to the June 2000 issue of *Commentary*, a friendly reply to Levenson's article, "New Enemies," Eugene J. Cohen, a rabbi-mohel, remarked that he and his colleagues had been "assured" by neurologists that "since an infant's nervous system is still undeveloped at eight days, no pain registers in the child's brain. When an infant cries, it is not during the procedure itself but rather at the removal of his diaper" (6). (So infant brains register diaper removal but not foreskin removal!) Levenson distanced himself—guardedly and partially—from Cohen's anachronistic argument: "The use of anesthetics during the *brit* is sufficiently controversial in Jewish law [rather than medical ethics] that I decided not to discuss it in my article. The weight of scientific research does not, however, support Rabbi Cohen's claim that 'no pain registers in the child's brain'"(10). For the view that needlessly inflicting pain on children is unethical, see Walco et al., "Pain."

14. In addition to the references cited in note 12, see the pioneering 1987 article by Anand and Hickey, "Pain." Their conclusion: "Physiologic responses to painful stimuli have been well documented in neonates of various gestational ages and are reflected in hormonal, metabolic, and cardiorespiratory changes similar to

but greater than those observed in adult subjects. Other responses in newborn infants are suggestive of integrated emotional and behavioral responses to pain and are retained in memory long enough to modify subsequent behavior patterns" (1326, my emphasis). Their article is followed by 201 references, and of course far more research information has accumulated since then. Fitzgerald, "Birth," reports on extremely important research revealing that the spinal sensory nerve cells of infants are more excitable than those of adults, hence that their responses to harmful stimuli are greater and more prolonged. She discusses the possibility that painful trauma in infancy may have serious long-term neurological consequences. See also Anand, Stevens, and McGrath, *Pain in Neonates.* An important article in this volume by Grunau, "Long-Term," focuses on low birthweight infants but pays surprisingly little attention to circumcision. In the same volume, Plotsky et al., "Behavioral," describes research on animal subjects and also cites research on human infants. The authors point out that noteworthy similarities in pain physiology between newborn animals and human infants indicate that animal research has implications for our understanding of human responses to pain.

15. Fran Lang Porter et al., "Neonatal."

16. Van Howe, "Anaesthesia."

17. See http://www.cirp.org/library, section entitled "Circumcision, Breast-feeding, and Maternal Bonding." There note especially Anders and Chalemian, "Effects"; Gunnar et al., "Coping"; Taddio et al., "Effect"; Richard E. Marshall, Stratton, et al., "Circumcision I"; Richard E. Marshall, F. L. Porter, et al., "Circumcision: II"; S. Dixon et al., "Behavioral"; and Richards et al., "Early."

18. Fitzgerald and Anand, "Developmental," 15. For obvious reasons, the research was conducted on infant rats, but the authors say that their findings "have important implications in human premature and full-term infants who undergo painful experiences." See also Anand and Scalzo, "Can Adverse."

19. Fitzgerald and Anand, "Developmental," 20. Another entry in http://www.cirp.org/library, "Psychological Impacts of Male Circumcision," cites more than fifty references. See also Goldman, "Psychological," and Boyle et al., "Male," both with extensive references. However, I do not accept the argument that circumcised men are more prone than others to violence and vicious behavior.

20. Again, the best source on the medical literature is the CIRP library site; see http://www.cirp.org/library/complications. See also Fleiss and Hodges, *What Your Doctor,* chap. 4. It seems certain that manageable complications are underreported, since these occur too frequently to rate publication in medical journals; obviously, only the more serious problems are reported in published form. Moreover, mohels—the only nonmedical persons legally permitted to perform surgery—are not required to report to anyone. Here is a small sample of the medical literature: N. Williams and Kapila, "Complications"; George W. Kaplan, "Circumcision," 16–30 (with photographs); Amukele et al., "20-Year"; Bliss et al., "Necrotizing" ("necrotizing fasciitis" is gangrene); Cleary and Kohl, "Overwhelming"; Gluckman et al., "Newborn"; Sherman et al., "Circumcision" (seven infants, six circumcised and amputated by mohels). On deaths following circumcision, including a list of a few children known by name, see http://www.cirp.org/library/death.

21. Gollaher, *Circumcision*, chap. 5; Cold and Taylor, "Prepuce"; J. R. Taylor et al., "Prepuce"; Winkelmann, "Cutaneous"; McGrath, "Frenular"; Scott, "Anatomy"; George L. Williams, "Significance."

22. Ritter and Denniston, *Doctors*, 18–1.

23. Milos and Macris, "Circumcision: Male"; Kristen O'Hara and Jeffrey O'Hara, "Effect."

24. Chessler, "Justifying," 592–93; see also Svoboda, "Attaining," 455–59. In 1996 physicians and nurses at a Seattle hospital located in a neighborhood with a population of Somali immigrants were taken aback when Somali women requested circumcision for both male and female infants. They soon realized that if they did not perform a hospital operation, the girls would either be subjected to surgery by a local Somali operator or would be returned to Somalia for equally destructive operations. The physicians decided to offer a compromise solution: a very modest nick on the clitoral prepuce, followed by culturally appropriate festivities. But when news of their proposal reached the media, the public outcry against *any* surgery on girls was so overwhelming that the physicians quickly withdrew the offer—knowing that they were condemning young girls to genital mutilation far more damaging than what they intended. The episode is described in Davis, "Male and Female," a thorough analysis of whether differentiation between male and female can be legally justified.

25. See the comprehensive review of this issue in Dwyer, "Parents' Religion."

26. Here again I recommend the CIRP sites: http://www.cirp.org/library/ ethics and http://www.cirp.org/library/legal. Somerville, *Ethical*, chap. 8, is by a leading medical ethicist; Svoboda et al., "Informed," is indispensable. Two related statements, by the same authors with others, are Van Howe et al., "Involuntary," and Hodges et al., "Prophylactic." Other important articles on legal and ethical issues are Milos and Macris, "Circumcision: A Medical"; Price, "Male"; Chessler, "Justifying"; Miller, "Circumcision"; all are documented by extensive bibliographies. Michael Benatar and David Benatar, "Between," defends parents' right to decide on circumcision; it highlights medical claims, wanders into an academic discussion of the meaning of "mutilation," and glosses over ethical issues. The article was followed by much commentary, mostly negative, and a response by the authors. Some responses follow the Benatar article in the same journal issue; others and the Benatar reply are available online from the *American Journal of Bioethics* website at: http://www.bioethics.net/journal/correspondence (August 5, 2003).

27. Diamant, *New Jewish*, 95.

28. For reflections on Jewish identity in America, see Biale et al., *Insider/ Outsider*; Seltzer and Cohen, *Americanization*; Sorin, *Tradition*, chap. 14; Heilman, *Portrait*, chap. 3; and Goldscheider and Zuckerman, *Transformation*, 172–88. Jewish readers will also find much food for thought in Goldman, *Questioning*.

Bibliography

Abelard, Peter. *Dialogue of a Philosopher with a Jew and a Christian*. Trans. Pierre J. Payer. Toronto: Pontifical Institute of Mediaeval Studies, 1979.

Abramson, Henry, and Carrie Hannon. "Depicting the Ambiguous Wound: Circumcision in Medieval Art." In *The Covenant of Circumcision*, ed. Elizabeth Wyner Mark. Hanover, N.H.: Brandeis University Press/University Press of New England, 2003.

Albert, Phyllis Cohen. *The Modernization of French Jewry: Consistory and Community in the Nineteenth Century*. Hanover, N.H.: Brandeis University Press/University Press of New England, 1977.

Aldeeb Abu-Sahlieh, Sami A. *Male and Female Circumcision: Among Jews, Christians, and Muslims*. Warren Center, Pa.: Shangri-La, 2001.

Alexander, T. Desmond. "Genesis 22 and the Covenant of Circumcision." *Journal for the Study of the Old Testament* 25 (1983): 17–22.

Amukele, S. A., G. W. Lee, et al. "20-Year Experience with Iatrogenic Penile Injury." *Journal of Urology* 170, 4 (October 2003): 1691–94.

Anand, K. J. S., and P. R. Hickey. "Pain and Its Effects in the Human Neonate and Fetus." *New England Journal of Medicine* 317, 21 (1987): 1321–29.

Anand, K. J. S., and the International Evidence-Based Group for Neonatal Pain. "Consensus Statement for the Prevention and Management of Pain in the Newborn." *Archives of Pediatrics and Adolescent Medicine* 155 (2001): 173–80.

Anand, K. J. S., and Frank M. Scalzo. "Can Adverse Neonatal Experiences Alter Brain Development and Subsequent Behavior?" *Biology of the Neonate* 77, 2 (2000): 69–82.

Anand, K. J. S., B. J. Stevens, and P. J. McGrath, ed. *Pain in Neonates*, 2nd rev. and enl. ed. Amsterdam: Elsevier, 2000.

Anders, Thomas F., and Robert J. Chalemian. "The Effects of Circumcision on
Sleep-Wake States in Human Neonates." *Psychosomatic Medicine* 36, 2 (March–
April 1974): 174–79.

Anon. [Isaac Leeser?]. "The Frankfort Reform Society." *Occident and American
Jewish Advocate* 2, 6 (September 1844). Available online at: http://www
.jewish-history.com/Occident/volume2/Sep1844/frankfort.html (Jewish-
American History Documentation Foundation, Inc.; June 5, 2001).

Apple, Max. "The Eighth Day." In *Free Agents*. New York: Harper and Row, 1984.

Archer, Léonie J. "Bound by Blood: Circumcision and Menstrual Taboo in Post-
Exilic Judaism." In *After Eve*, ed. Janet M. Soskice. London: Collins Marshall
Pickering, 1990.

———. " 'In Thy Blood Live': Gender and Ritual in the Judaeo-Christian Tradition."
In *Through the Devil's Gateway: Women, Religion, and Taboo*, ed. Alison
Joseph. London: SPCK, 1990.

Arnold, Abram B. "Circumcision." *New York Medical Journal* 9 (1869): 514–24.

———. "Circumcision." *New York Medical Journal* 39 (February 1886): 173–79.

Baleta, A. "Concern Voiced over 'Dry Sex' Practices in South Africa." *Lancet* 352
(October 1998): 1292.

Bar Amithai [Joseph Johlson]. *Ueber die Beschneidung in historischer und dogmatischer
Hinsicht*. Frankfurt: I. C. Hermann, 1843.

Barclay, John M. G. *Jews in the Mediterranean Diaspora: From Alexander to Trajan
(323 BCE–117 CE)*. Berkeley: University of California Press, 1996.

Barth, Lewis M., ed. *Berit Mila in the Reform Context*. Los Angeles: Berit Mila Board
of Reform Judaism, 1990.

Baumgarten, Elisheva. "Circumcision and Baptism: The Development of a Jewish
Ritual in Christian Europe." In *The Covenant of Circumcision*, ed. Elizabeth
Wyner Mark. Hanover, N.H.: Brandeis University Press/University Press of
New England, 2003.

Beidelman, T. O. *The Cool Knife: Imagery of Gender, Sexuality, and Moral Education
in Kaguru Initiation Ritual*. Washington, D.C.: Smithsonian Institution Press, 1997.

Beinart, Haim. *Conversos on Trial: The Inquisition in Ciudad Real*. Jerusalem:
Magnes, 1981.

Benatar, Michael, and David Benatar. "Between Prophylaxis and Child Abuse:
The Ethics of Neonatal Male Circumcision." *American Journal of Bioethics* 3, 2
(spring 2003): 35–48.

Bentley, James. *Restless Bones: The Story of Relics*. London: Constable, 1985.

Berkovitz, Jay R. *The Shaping of Jewish Identity in Nineteenth-century France*. Detroit:
Wayne State University Press, 1989.

Berman, Jeremiah J. "Trend in Jewish Religious Observance in Mid-nineteenth Century
America." *Publications of the American Jewish Historical Society* 37 (1947): 31–53.

Biale, David. "Blood Libels and Blood Vengeance." *Tikkun* 9, 4 (1994): 39–40, 75.

———. *Eros and the Jews: From Biblical Israel to Contemporary America*. New York:
Basic Books, 1992.

Biale, David, Michael Galchinsky, and Susannah Heschel, eds. *Insider/Outsider:
American Jews and Multiculturalism*. Berkeley: University of California Press,
1998.

Bickerman, Elias J. "The Historical Foundations of Postbiblical Judaism." In *The Jews: Their History*, 4th ed., ed. Louis Finkelstein. New York: Schocken, 1970.
——. *The Jews in the Greek Age*. Cambridge, Mass.: Harvard University Press, 1988.
Birnbaum, Philip, trans. and ed. *Daily Prayer Book: Ha-Siddur Ha-Shalem*. Rev. ed. New York: Hebrew Publishing, 1977.
Bivas, Natalie Krauss. "Letter to Our Son's Grandparents: Why We Decided Against Circumcision." *Humanistic Judaism* 16, 3 (1988): 11–13.
Bliss, David P., Jr., Patrick J. Healey, and John H. T. Waldhausen. "Necrotizing Fasciitis after Plastibell Circumcision." *Journal of Pediatrics* 31 (September 1997): 459–62.
Bloch, Maurice. *From Blessing to Violence: History and Ideology in the Circumcision Ritual of the Merina of Madagascar*. Cambridge: Cambridge University Press, 1986.
Blumenkranz, Bernhard. *Le Juif medieval au miroir de l'art chrétien*. Paris: Études Augustiennes, 1966.
Boddy, Janice. *Wombs and Alien Spirits: Women, Men, and the Zār Cult in Northern Sudan*. Madison: University of Wisconsin Press, 1989.
Bodian, Miriam. *Hebrews of the Portuguese Nation: Conversos and Community in Early Modern Amsterdam*. Bloomington: Indiana University Press, 1997.
Boiteux, Martine. "Les juifs dans le carnaval de la Rome moderne, XVe–XVIIIe siècle." *Mélanges de l'Ecole française de Rome* 88 (1976): 745–87.
Bolande, Robert P. "Ritualistic Surgery—Circumcision and Tonsillectomy." *New England Journal of Medicine* 280, 11 (March 13, 1969): 591–96.
Boyarin, Daniel. *Carnal Israel: Reading Sex in Talmudic Culture*. Berkeley: University of California Press, 1993.
——. *A Radical Jew: Paul and the Politics of Identity*. Berkeley: University of California Press, 1994.
——. " 'This We Know to Be the Carnal Israel': Circumcision and the Erotic Life of God and Israel." *Critical Inquiry* 18 (1992): 474–505.
Boyarin, Jonathan, and Daniel B. Boyarin. "Self-Exposure as Theory: The Double Mark of the Male Jew." In *Rhetorics of Self-Making*, ed. Debbora Battaglia. Berkeley: University of California Press, 1995.
Boyle, Gregory J., Ronald Goldman, J. Steven Svoboda, and Ephrem Fernandez. "Male Circumcision: Pain, Trauma, and Psychosexual Sequelae." *Journal of Health Psychology* 7, 3 (May 2002): 329–43.
Braver Moss, Lisa. "Circumcision: A Jewish Inquiry." *Midstream* 38 (January 1992): 20–23.
——. "A Painful Case." *Tikkun* 5, 5 (September-October 1990): 70–72.
Brecher, Gideon. *Die Beschneidung der Israeliten von der historischen, praktisch-operativen, und ritualen Seite*. Vienna: Franz E. Schmid and J. J. Busch, 1845.
Breuer, Mordechai. *Modernity Within Tradition: The Social History of Orthodox Jewry in Imperial Germany*. Trans. Elizabeth Petuchowski. New York: Columbia University Press, 1992.
Brodbar-Nemzer, Jay, Peter Conrad, and Shelly Tenenbaum. "American Circumcision Practices and Social Reality." *Sociology and Social Research* 71 (1987): 275–79.

Brody, Stuart, David Gisselquist, et al. "Evidence of Iatrogenic HIV Transmission in Children in South Africa." *British Journal of Obstetrics and Gynaecology* 110 (May 2003): 450–52.

Brown, Mark S., and Cheryl A. Brown. "Circumcision Decision: Prominence of Social Concerns." *Pediatrics* 80, 2 (August 1987): 215–19.

Buckley, Thomas, and Alma Gottlieb, eds. *Blood Magic: The Anthropology of Menstruation.* Berkeley: University of California Press, 1988.

Bwayo, J., F. Plummer, et al. "Human Immunodeficiency Virus Infection in Long-Distance Truck Drivers in East Africa." *Archives of Internal Medicine* 154, 12 (June 1994): 1391–96.

Bynum, Caroline Walker. "The Body of Christ in the Later Middle Ages: A Reply to Leo Steinberg." In *Fragmentation and Redemption: Essays on Gender and the Human Body in Medieval Religion.* New York: Zone, 1991.

———. *Holy Feast and Holy Fast: The Religious Significance of Food to Medieval Women.* Berkeley: University of California Press, 1987.

Cahn, Yehuda. *Circumcision: The Covenant of Abraham.* Baltimore, 1999.

Cantlie, James. "Spermatorrhea." In *A Dictionary of Medicine,* ed. R. Quain, 2 vols. London: Longmans, Green, 1882.

Chamberlain, David B. "Babies Don't Feel Pain: A Century of Denial in Medicine." In *Cyborg Babies: From Techno-Sex to Techno-Tots,* ed. Robbie Davis-Floyd and Joseph Dumit. New York: Routledge, 1998.

Chapman, Norman H. "Some of the Nervous Affections Which Are Liable to Follow Neglected Congenital Phimosis in Children." *Medical News* (Philadelphia) 41 (1882): 314–17.

Charles, R. H., trans. and ed. *The Book of Jubilees or The Little Genesis.* London: Adam and Charles Black, 1902.

Chessler, Abbie J. "Justifying the Unjustifiable: Rite v. Wrong." *Buffalo Law Review* 45 (1997): 555–613.

Cheyette, Bryan. *Constructions of "the Jew" in English Literature and Society: Racial Representations, 1875–1945.* Cambridge: Cambridge University Press, 1993.

Chyet, Stanley F., and Norman B. Mirsky. "Reflections on Circumcision as Sacrifice." In *Berit Mila in the Reform Context,* ed. Lewis M. Barth. Los Angeles: Berit Mila Board of Reform Judaism, 1990.

Cleary, Thomas G., and Steve Kohl. "Overwhelming Infection with Group B β-Hemolytic *Streptococcus* Associated with Circumcision." *Pediatrics* 64, 3 (September 1979): 301–3.

Cohen, Jeremy. *"Be Fertile and Increase, Fill the Earth and Master It": The Ancient and Medieval Career of a Biblical Text.* Ithaca, N.Y.: Cornell University Press, 1989.

———. *Living Letters of the Law: Ideas of the Jew in Medieval Christianity.* Berkeley: University of California Press, 1999.

Cohen, L. H. "The Rite of Circumcision; Why Is It Sometimes Followed by Disease and Considered Dangerous?" *New York Medical Journal* 19 (1874): 160–63.

Cohen, Martin A. *The Martyr: The Story of a Secret Jew and the Mexican Inquisition in the Sixteenth Century.* Philadelphia: Jewish Publication Society, 1973.

Cohen, Naomi W. *Encounter with Emancipation: The German Jews in the United States, 1830–1914.* Philadelphia: Jewish Publication Society, 1984.

Cohen, Shaye J. D. *The Beginnings of Jewishness: Boundaries, Varieties, Uncertainties.* Berkeley: University of California Press, 1999.

———. "A Brief History of Jewish Circumcision Blood." In *The Covenant of Circumcision*, ed. Elizabeth Wyner Mark. Hanover, N.H.: Brandeis University Press/University Press of New England, 2003.

———. *From the Maccabees to the Mishnah: A Profile of Judaism.* Philadelphia: Westminster, 1987.

———. "Why Aren't Jewish Women Circumcised?" *Gender and History* 9 (1997): 560–78.

Cohen, Steven M. "Assessing the Vitality of Conservative Judaism in North America: Evidence from a Survey of Synagogue Members." In *Jews in the Center: Conservative Synagogues and Their Members*, ed. Jack Wertheimer. New Brunswick, N.J.: Rutgers University Press, 2000.

Cohen, Steven M., and Arnold M. Eisen. *The Jew Within: Self, Family, and Community in America.* Bloomington: Indiana University Press, 2000.

Cold, C. J., and J. R. Taylor. "The Prepuce." *BJU International* 83, suppl. 1 (January 1999): 34–44.

Collins, John J. *Between Athens and Jerusalem: Jewish Identity in the Hellenistic Diaspora.* 2nd ed. Grand Rapids, Mich.: Eerdmans, 2000.

Cook, Linda S., Laura A. Koutsky, and King K. Holmes. "Circumcision and Sexually Transmitted Diseases." *American Journal of Public Health* 84, 2 (1994): 197–201.

Cook, L. S., L. A. Koutsky, and K. K. Holmes. "Clinical Presentation of Genital Warts among Circumcised and Uncircumcised Heterosexual Men Attending an Urban STD Clinic." *Genitourinary Medicine* 69, 4 (1993): 262–64.

Cooper Forster, J. "A Few Remarks on the Surgical Diseases of Children. Part 1: Congenital Phymosis." *Medical Times and Gazette*, November 17, 1855, 491–92.

Cordier, Pierre. "Les Romains et la circoncision." *Revue des études Juives* 160 (2001): 337–55.

Cranfield, G. A. "The *London Evening-Post* and the Jew Bill of 1753." *Historical Journal* 8 (1965): 16–30.

Crapanzano, Vincent. "Rite of Return: Circumcision in Morocco." In *Hermes' Dilemma and Hamlet's Desire: On the Epistemology of Interpretation.* Cambridge, Mass.: Harvard University Press, 1992.

Darby, Robert. "The Masturbation Taboo and the Rise of Routine Male Circumcision: A Review of the Historiography." *Journal of Social History* 36 (spring 2003): 737–57.

———. "'An Oblique and Slovenly Initiation': The Circumcision Episode in *Tristram Shandy*." *Eighteenth-Century Life* 27, 1 (March 2003): 72–84.

———. "'A Source of Serious Mischief': The Demonization of the Foreskin and the Rise of Preventive Circumcision in Australia." In *Understanding Circumcision*, ed. George C. Denniston, Frederick Mansfield Hodges, and Marilyn Fayre Milos. New York: Kluwer Academic/Plenum, 2001.

———. "'Where Doctors Differ': The Debate on Circumcision as a Protection Against Syphilis." *Journal of the Social History of Medicine* 16, 1 (2003): 57–78.

Davis, Dena S. "Male and Female Genital Alteration: A Collision Course with the Law?" *Health Matrix: Journal of Law-Medicine* 11 (summer 2001): 487–570.

Day, John. *Molech: A God of Human Sacrifice in the Old Testament*. Cambridge: Cambridge University Press, 1989.

Delaney, Carol. *Abraham on Trial: The Social Legacy of Biblical Myth*. Princeton, N.J.: Princeton University Press, 1998.

Denniston, George C. "Circumcision and the Code of Ethics." *Humane Health Care International* 12, 2 (April 1996): 78–80.

———. "Tyranny of the Victims: An Analysis of Circumcision Advocacy." In *Male and Female Circumcision*, ed. George C. Denniston, Frederick Mansfield Hodges, and Marilyn Fayre Milos. New York: Kluwer Academic/Plenum, 1999.

Denniston, George C., Frederick Mansfield Hodges, and Marilyn Fayre Milos, eds. *Flesh and Blood: Perspectives on the Problem of Circumcision in Contemporary Society*. New York: Kluwer Academic/Plenum, 2004.

———. *Male and Female Circumcision: Medical, Legal, and Ethical Considerations in Pediatric Practice*. New York: Kluwer Academic/Plenum, 1999.

———. *Understanding Circumcision: A Multi-Disciplinary Approach to a Multi-Dimensional Problem*. New York: Kluwer Academic/Plenum, 2001.

Denniston, George C., and Marilyn Fayre Milos, eds. *Sexual Mutilations: A Human Tragedy*. New York: Plenum, 1997.

Diamant, Anita. *The Jewish Baby Book*. New York: Summit, 1988.

———. *The New Jewish Baby Book: A Guide for Today's Families*. Woodstock, Vt.: Jewish Lights, 1993.

Diner, Hasia R. *A Time for Gathering: The Second Migration, 1820–1880*. Baltimore: Johns Hopkins University Press, 1992.

Dixon, Edward H. *A Treatise on Diseases of the Sexual Organs*. New York: Burgess, Stringer, 1845.

Dixon, Suzanne, Joel Snyder, et al. "Behavioral Effects of Circumcision with and Without Anesthesia." *Journal of Developmental and Behavioral Pediatrics* 5, 5 (1984): 246–50.

Donne, John. *The Sermons of John Donne*. Vol. 6. Ed. Evelyn M. Simpson and George R. Potter. Berkeley: University of California Press, 1953.

Dresser, Madge. "Minority Rites: The Strange History of Circumcision in English Thought." *Jewish Culture and History* 1, 1 (1998): 72–87.

Dwyer, James G. "Parents' Religion and Children's Rights: Debunking the Doctrine of Parents' Rights." *California Law Review* 82, 6 (December 1994): 1371–1447.

Efron, John M. *Medicine and the German Jews: A History*. New Haven: Yale University Press, 2001.

Eilberg-Schwartz, Howard. "The Father, the Phallus, and the Seminal Word: Dilemmas of Patrilineality in Ancient Judaism." In *Gender, Kinship, Power: A Comparative and Interdisciplinary History*, ed. Mary Jo Maynes, Ann Waltner, et al. New York: Routledge, 1996.

———. *God's Phallus, and Other Problems for Men and Monotheism*. Boston: Beacon, 1994.

———. *The Savage in Judaism: An Anthropology of Israelite Religion and Ancient Judaism*. Bloomington: Indiana University Press, 1990.

———. "Why Not the Earlobe?" *Moment* 17 (February 1992): 28–33.

Eisen, Robert. *Gersonides on Providence, Covenant, and the Chosen People*. Albany: State University of New York Press, 1995.

Endelman, Todd M. *The Jews of Britain, 1656–2000*. Berkeley: University of California Press, 2002.

Enzenauer, Robert W., John M. Powell, Thomas E. Wiswell, and James W. Bass. "Decreased Circumcision Rate with Videotape Counseling." *Southern Medical Journal* 79 (1986): 717–20.

Epstein, Isidore, ed. *The Babylonian Talmud*. London: Soncino, 1938.

Eve, F. S. "Communication of Tuberculosis by Ritual Circumcision." *Lancet* (January 28, 1888): 170–71.

Fabre-Vassas, Claudine. *The Singular Beast: Jews, Christians, and the Pig*. Trans. Carol Volk. New York: Columbia University Press, 1997.

Fein, Isaac M. *The Making of an American Jewish Community: The History of Baltimore Jewry from 1773 to 1920*. Philadelphia: Jewish Publication Society, 1971.

Feldman, Louis H. *Jew and Gentile in the Ancient World*. Princeton, N.J.: Princeton University Press, 1993.

Felsenstein, Frank. *Anti-Semitic Stereotypes: A Paradigm of Otherness in English Popular Culture, 1660–1830*. Baltimore: Johns Hopkins University Press, 1995.

Fine, Lawrence. "Kabbalistic Texts." In *Back to the Sources: Reading the Classic Jewish Texts*, ed. Barry W. Holtz. New York: Summit, 1984.

Fink, Aaron J. "Circumcision and Sand." *Journal of the Royal Society of Medicine* 84 (November 1991): 696.

———. *Circumcision: A Parent's Decision for Life*. Mountain View, Calif.: Kavanah, 1988.

———. "Newborn Circumcision: A Long-term Strategy for AIDS Prevention" (letter). *Journal of the Royal Medical Society* 82 (1989): 695.

———. "A Possible Explanation for Heterosexual Male Infection with AIDS." *New England Journal of Medicine* 315, 18 (1986): 1167.

Finkelstein, Israel, and Neil Asher Silberman. *The Bible Unearthed: Archaeology's New Vision of Ancient Israel and the Origin of Its Sacred Texts*. New York: Free Press, 2001.

Fishman, Sylvia Barack. *A Breath of Life: Feminism in the American Jewish Community*. New York: Free Press, 1993.

Fitzgerald, Maria. "The Birth of Pain." *MRC News* (London, summer 1998): 20–23.

Fitzgerald, Maria, and K. J. S. Anand. "Developmental Neuroanatomy and Neurophysiology of Pain." In *Pain Management in Infants, Children, and Adolescents*, ed. Neil L. Schechter, Charles B. Berde, and Myron Yaster. Baltimore: Williams and Wilkins, 1993.

Fleiss, Paul M. "An Analysis of Bias Regarding Circumcision in American Medical Literature." In *Male and Female Circumcision*, ed. George C. Denniston, Frederick Mansfield Hodges, and Marilyn Fayre Milos. New York: Kluwer Academic/Plenum, 1999.

Fleiss, Paul M., and Frederick M. Hodges. "Authors' Reply." *British Medical Journal* 313 (July 1996): 47.

————. "Neonatal Circumcision Does Not Protect Against Penile Cancer." *British Medical Journal* 312 (March 1996): 779–80.

————. *What Your Doctor May Not Tell You About Circumcision.* New York: Warner, 2002.

Fletcher, Christopher R. "Circumcision in America in 1998: Attitudes, Beliefs, and Charges of American Physicians." In *Male and Female Circumcision*, ed. George C. Denniston, Frederick Mansfield Hodges, and Marilyn Fayre Milos. New York: Kluwer Academic/Plenum, 1999.

Freedman, H., and Maurice Simon, eds. *Midrash Rabbah: Exodus.* Trans. S. M. Lehrman. London: Soncino, 1939.

————. *Midrash Rabbah: Numbers.* Trans. Judah J. Slotki. 2 vols. London: Soncino, 1939.

————. *Midrash Rabbah: Ruth.* Trans. L. Rabinowitz. London: Soncino, 1939.

Freedman, H., and Maurice Simon, trans. and eds. *Midrash Rabbah: Genesis.* 2 vols. London: Soncino, 1939.

Freud, Sigmund. "Analysis of a Phobia in a Five-Year-Old Boy." In *The Standard Edition of the Complete Works of Sigmund Freud*, ed. James Strachey, vol. 10 (1909). London: Hogarth Press, 1955.

————. *Moses and Monotheism.* Trans. Katherine Jones. New York: Knopf, 1939.

Friedlander, Gerald, trans. and ed. *Pirkê de Rabbi Eliezer.* London, 1916; reprint, New York: Benjamin Blom, 1971.

Friedman, Richard Elliott. *Who Wrote the Bible?* New York: Summit, 1987.

Friedman Ross, Lainie. "Advantages and Disadvantages of Neonatal Circumcision" (letter). *Journal of the American Medical Association* 278 (July 1997): 201.

Frisch, Morten, Søren Friis, et al. "Falling Incidence of Penis Cancer in an Uncircumcised Population." *British Medical Journal* 311 (December 1995): 1471.

Frojmovic, Eva. "Christian Travelers to the Circumcision: Early Modern Representations." In *Covenant of Circumcision*, ed. Elizabeth Wyner Mark. Hanover, N.H.: Brandeis University Press/University Press of New England, 2003.

Fuchs, Eduard. *Die Juden in der Karikatur.* Munich: Langen, 1921.

Ganchrow, Mandell I. *Entering the Covenant: An Anthology of Divrei Torah for Bris Milah and Pidyon Haben.* New York: Mesorah, 2001.

Gartner, Lloyd P. *The Jewish Immigrant in England, 1870–1914.* 2nd ed. London: Simon, 1973.

Geiger, Abraham. *Abraham Geigers Nachgelassene Schriften.* Ed. Ludwig Geiger. Vol. 5. Berlin: Louis Gerschel, 1878.

Gelbaum, Ilene. "Circumcision: Refining a Traditional Surgical Technique." *Journal of Nurse-Midwifery* 38, 2 (suppl.) (March-April 1993): 18S–30S.

Geller, Jay. "Circumcision and Jewish Women's Identity: Rahel Levin Varnhagen's Failed Assimilation." In *Judaism Since Gender*, ed. Miriam Peskowitz and Laura Levitt. New York: Routledge, 1997.

————. "A Paleontological View of Freud's Study of Religion: Unearthing the *Leitfossil* Circumcision." *Modern Judaism* 13 (1993): 49–70.

Gellis, Sydney S. "Circumcision." *American Journal of Diseases of Children* 132 (1978): 1168–69.

Gerber, Jane S. *The Jews of Spain: A History of the Sephardic Experience.* New York: Free Press, 1992.

Gibson, E. C. "Carcinoma of the Prostate in Jews and Circumcised Gentiles." *British Journal of Urology* 26 (1954): 227–29.

Gilman, Sander L. *Franz Kafka, the Jewish Patient.* New York: Routledge, 1995.

———. *Freud, Race, and Gender.* Princeton, N.J.: Princeton University Press, 1993.

———. "The Indelibility of Circumcision." *Koroth* 9 (1991): 806–17.

Gilmore, David D. *Manhood in the Making: Cultural Concepts of Masculinity.* New Haven: Yale University Press, 1990.

Ginsburg, C. M., and G. H. McCracken, Jr. "Urinary Tract Infections in Young Infants." *Pediatrics* 69 (1982): 409–12.

Gitlitz, David M. *Secrecy and Deceit: The Religion of the Crypto-Jews.* Philadelphia: Jewish Publication Society, 1996.

Glassberg, Abraham, ed. *Die Beschneidung in ihrer geschlichtlichen, ethnographischen, religiösen, und medicinischen Bedeutung.* Berlin: M. Poppelauer, 1896.

G. L. D. and Isaac Mayer Wise. Letter from "Gentile Friend" and reply. *Israelite,* April 8, 1870.

Glick, Leonard B. *Abraham's Heirs: Jews and Christians in Medieval Europe.* Syracuse: Syracuse University Press, 1999.

———. "Jewish Circumcision: An Enigma in Historical Perspective." In *Understanding Circumcision,* ed. George C. Denniston, Frederick Mansfield Hodges, and Marilyn Fayre Milos. New York: Kluwer Academic/Plenum, 2001.

———. "Something Less Than Joyful: Jewish Americans and the Circumcision Dilemma." In *Flesh and Blood,* ed. George C. Denniston, Frederick Mansfield Hodges, and Marilyn Fayre Milos. New York: Kluwer Academic/Plenum, 2004.

Gluckman, Gordon R., Marshall L. Stoller, et al. "Newborn Penile Glans Amputation During Circumcision and Successful Reattachment." *Journal of Urology* 153, 3, pt. 1 (March 1995): 778–79.

Goldin, Hyman E. *Hamadrikh: The Rabbi's Guide.* Rev. ed. New York: Hebrew Publishing, 1956.

Goldin, Judah, trans. and ed. *The Fathers According to Rabbi Nathan.* New Haven: Yale University Press, 1955.

Goldman, Ronald. *Circumcision: The Hidden Trauma.* Boston: Vanguard, 1997.

———. "The Psychological Impact of Circumcision." *BJU International* 83, suppl. 1 (January 1999): 93–102.

———. *Questioning Circumcision: A Jewish Perspective.* Boston: Vanguard, 1998.

Goldscheider, Calvin, and Alan S. Zuckerman. *The Transformation of the Jews.* Chicago: University of Chicago Press, 1984.

Gollaher, David L. *Circumcision: A History of the World's Most Controversial Surgery.* New York: Basic Books, 2000.

———. "From Ritual to Science: The Medical Transformation of Circumcision in America." *Journal of Social History* 28 (1994): 5–36.

Gordis, Daniel. *Becoming a Jewish Parent.* New York: Three Rivers, 1999.

Goren, Arthur A. *New York Jews and the Quest for Community: The Kehillah Experiment, 1908–1922.* New York: Columbia University Press, 1970.

Gould, Richard A. *Yiwara: Foragers of the Australian Desert.* New York: Scribner's, 1969.

Gray, Ronald H., Maria J. Wawer, et al. "Probability of HIV-1 Transmission per Coital Act in Monogamous, Heterosexual, HIV-1 Discordant Couples in Rakai Uganda." *Lancet* 357 (April 2001): 1149–53.

Greenbaum, Dorothy. "In Pursuit of the Painless Bris." *Berit Mila Newsletter* 7, 1 (June 1995). Available online at: http://beritmila.org/bmnews7.html.

Greenstein, Jack M. *Mantegna and Painting as Historical Narrative.* Chicago: University of Chicago Press, 1992.

Gross, Abraham. "The Blood Libel and the Blood of Circumcision: An Ashkenazic Custom That Disappeared in the Middle Ages." *Jewish Quarterly Review* 86 (1995): 171–74.

Grossman, Elliot A. *Circumcision—A Pictorial Atlas of Its History, Instrument Development and Operative Techniques.* Great Neck, N.Y.: Todd and Honeywell, 1982.

Grossman, Elliot A., and Norman A. Posner. "The Circumcision Controversy: An Update." *Obstetrics and Gynecology Annual* 13 (1984): 181–95.

Gruenbaum, Ellen. *The Female Circumcision Controversy: An Anthropological Perspective.* Philadelphia: University of Pennsylvania Press, 2001.

Grunau, Ruth Eckstein. "Long-term Consequences of Pain in Human Neonates." In *Pain in Neonates,* ed. K. J. S. Anand, B. J. Stevens, and P. J. McGrath. 2nd rev. and enl. ed. Amsterdam: Elsevier, 2000.

Gunnar, Megan R., Stephen Malone, et al. "Coping with Aversive Stimulation in the Neonatal Period: Quiet Sleep and Plasma Cortisol Levels During Recovery from Circumcision." *Child Development* 56, 2 (August 1985): 824–34.

Guttmacher, Alan F. "Should the Baby Be Circumcised?" *Parents' Magazine* 16, 9 (1941): 26, 76–78.

Hall, Robert G. "Circumcision." In *The Anchor Bible Dictionary,* vol. 1, ed. David Noel Freedman et al. New York: Doubleday, 1992.

———. "Epispasm: Circumcision in Reverse." *Moment* 17 (February 1992): 34–37, 64.

Haller, John S., Jr., and Robin M. Haller. *The Physician and Sexuality in Victorian America.* Urbana: University of Illinois Press, 1974.

Halperin, Daniel T., and Robert C. Bailey. "Male Circumcision and HIV Infection: 10 Years and Counting." *Lancet* 354 (November 1999): 1813–15.

Hardebeck, John W. "Newborn Circumcision: Medical Necessity or Useless Mutilation?" *Truth Seeker* 1, 3 (July-August 1989): 50.

Hardner, G. J., T. Bhanalaph, et al. "Carcinoma of the Penis: Analysis of Therapy in 100 Consecutive Cases." *Journal of Urology* 108 (1972): 428–30.

Harlow, Jules, ed. and trans. *Siddur Sim Shalom: A Prayerbook for Shabbat, Festivals, and Weekdays.* New York: Rabbinical Assembly, 1985.

Harrowitz, Nancy A. *Antisemitism, Misogyny, and the Logic of Cultural Difference: Cesare Lombroso and Matilde Serao.* Lincoln: University of Nebraska Press, 1994.

———. "Weininger and Lombroso: A Question of Influence." In *Jews and Gender: Responses to Otto Weininger,* ed. Nancy A. Harrowitz and Barbara Hyams. Philadelphia: Temple University Press, 1995.

Heald, Suzette. *Controlling Anger: The Sociology of Gisu Violence.* Manchester: Manchester University Press, 1989.

Heilman, Samuel C. *Portrait of American Jews: The Last Half of the 20th Century.* Seattle: University of Washington Press, 1995.

Hertz, J. H., ed. and trans. *The Pentateuch and Haftorahs.* 2nd ed. London: Soncino, 1960.

Herzbrun, Michael B. "Circumcision: The Pain of the Fathers." *CCAR Journal* 38, 4 (fall 1991): 1–13.

Heschel, Susannah. *Abraham Geiger and the Jewish Jesus.* Chicago: University of Chicago Press, 1998.

Hochlerner, R. "Circumcision—Do We Need Legislation for It?" *Medical Record* (New York) 46 (1894): 702.

Hodges, F. M., J. S. Svoboda, and R. S. Van Howe. "Prophylactic Interventions on Children: Balancing Human Rights with Public Health." *Journal of Medical Ethics* 28 (2002): 10–16.

Hodges, Frederick M. "The History of Phimosis from Antiquity to the Present." In *Male and Female Circumcision,* ed. George C. Denniston, Frederick Mansfield Hodges, and Marilyn Fayre Milos. New York: Kluwer Academic/Plenum, 1999.

———. "The Ideal Prepuce in Ancient Greece and Rome: Male Genital Aesthetics and Their Relation to *Lipodermos,* Circumcision, Foreskin Restoration, and the *Kynodesmē.*" *Bulletin of the History of Medicine* 75 (2001): 375–405.

———. "A Short History of the Institutionalization of Involuntary Sexual Mutilation in the United States." In *Sexual Mutilations,* ed. George C. Denniston and Marilyn Fayre Milos. New York: Plenum, 1997.

Hoffman, Lawrence A. *Covenant of Blood: Circumcision and Gender in Rabbinic Judaism.* Chicago: University of Chicago Press, 1996.

Holdheim, Samuel. *Ueber die Beschneidung zunächst in religiös-dogmatischer Beziehung.* Schwerin: C. Kürschner, 1844.

Holt, L. Emmett. "Tuberculosis Acquired Through Ritual Circumcision." *Journal of the American Medical Association* 61 (July 12, 1913): 99–102.

The Holy Bible with the Apocrypha. Revised Standard Version. New York: Oxford University Press, 2002.

Horowitz, Elliott. "The Eve of the Circumcision: A Chapter in the History of Jewish Nightlife." *Journal of Social History* 23 (1989): 45–69.

Howard, Cynthia R., Fred M. Howard, et al. "Neonatal Circumcision and Pain Relief: Current Training Practices." *Pediatrics* 101, 3 (March 1998): 423–28.

Hsia, R. Po-Chia. *The Myth of Ritual Murder: Jews and Magic in Reformation Germany.* New Haven: Yale University Press, 1988.

———. *Trent 1475: Stories of a Ritual Murder Trial.* New Haven: Yale University Press, 1992.

Hutchinson, Jonathan. "The Advantages of Circumcision." *Medical Review* 3 (1900): 641–42.

———. "On Circumcision." *Archives of Surgery* (London) 4 (1893): 379–80.

———. "On the Influence of Circumcision in Preventing Syphilis." *Medical Times and Gazette,* December 1, 1855, 542–43.

———. "A Plea for Circumcision." *Archives of Surgery* 2 (1890): 15.

———. *Syphilis.* London: Cassell, 1887.

Hyam, Ronald. *Empire and Sexuality: The British Experience.* Manchester: Manchester University Press, 1990.

Isaac, Erich. "Circumcision as a Covenant Rite." *Anthropos* 59 (1964): 444–56.

————. "The Enigma of Circumcision." *Commentary* 43 (January 1967): 51–55.

Jacob, Walter, ed. *American Reform Responsa: Jewish Questions, Rabbinic Answers.* New York: Central Conference of American Rabbis, 1983.

Jacobi, Abraham. "On Masturbation and 'Hysteria' in Young Children." *American Journal of Obstetrics* 8, 4 (1876): 595–606, and 8, 5 (1876): 218–38.

Jaffé, Julius. *Die rituelle Beschneidung im Lichte der antiseptischen Chirurgie mit Berücksichtigung der religiösen Vorschriften.* Leipzig: Gustav Fock, 1886.

Jay, Nancy. *Throughout Your Generations Forever: Sacrifice, Religion, and Paternity.* Chicago: University of Chicago Press, 1992.

John Chrysostom, Saint. *Discourses Against Judaizing Christians.* Trans. Paul W. Harkins. Washington, D.C.: Catholic University of America Press, 1979.

————. *Homilies on Genesis 18–45.* Trans. Robert C. Hill. Washington, D.C.: Catholic University of America Press, 1990.

Jones, Edward G., Ian Macdonald, and Lester Breslow. "A Study of Epidemiologic Factors in Carcinoma of the Uterine Cervix." *American Journal of Obstetrics and Gynecology* 76 (1958): 1–10.

JPS Hebrew-English Tanakh: The Traditional Hebrew Text and the New JPS Translation. 2nd ed. Philadelphia: Jewish Publication Society, 1999.

Judd, Robin E. "Circumcision and Modern Jewish Life: A German Case Study, 1843–1914." In *The Covenant of Circumcision,* ed. Elizabeth Wyner Mark. Hanover, N.H.: Brandeis University Press/University Press of New England, 2003.

————. "German Jewish Rituals, Bodies, and Citizenship." Ph.D. diss., University of Michigan, 2000.

Justin Martyr, Saint. "Dialogue with Trypho." In *Writings of Saint Justin Martyr,* trans. and ed. Thomas B. Falls. Washington, D.C.: Catholic University Press, 1948.

Kagan, Solomon R. *Jewish Contributions to Medicine in America.* Boston: Boston Medical, 1934.

Kamen, Henry. *The Spanish Inquisition: A Historical Revision.* New Haven: Yale University Press, 1998.

Kaplan, Aryeh. *Innerspace: Introduction to Kabbalah, Meditation, and Prophecy.* Brooklyn: Moznaim, 1990.

Kaplan, George W. "Circumcision—An Overview." *Current Problems in Pediatrics* 7 (1977): 3–33.

Kaplan, George W., and Vincent J. O'Conor, Jr. "The Incidence of Carcinoma of the Prostate in Jews and Gentiles." *Journal of the American Medical Association* 196 (May 30, 1966): 803–4.

Karsenty, Nelly. "A Mother Questions *Brit Milla.*" *Humanistic Judaism* 16, 3 (1988): 14–21.

Katz, David S. *The Jews in the History of England, 1485–1850.* Oxford: Clarendon Press, 1994.

Katz, Jacob. "The Controversy over the *Mezizah*: The Unrestricted Execution of the Rite of Circumcision." In *Divine Law in Human Hands: Case Studies in Halakhic Flexibility.* Jerusalem: Magnes, 1998.

———. "The Struggle over Preserving the Rite of Circumcision in the First Part of the Nineteenth Century." In *Divine Law in Human Hands: Case Studies in Halakhic Flexibility.* Jerusalem: Magnes, 1998.

Kaweblum, Yosef Aaron, Shirley Press, et al. "Circumcision Using the Mogen Clamp." *Clinical Pediatrics* 23 (December 1984): 679–82.

Kimmel, Michael S. "The Kindest Un-cut: Feminism, Judaism, and My Son's Foreskin." *Tikkun* 16, 3 (May-June 2001): 43–48.

Kirshenblatt-Gimblett, Barbara. "The Cut That Binds: The Western Ashkenazic Torah Binder as Nexus Between Circumcision and Torah." In *Celebration: Studies in Festivity and Ritual,* ed. Victor Turner. Washington, D.C.: Smithsonian Institution Press, 1982.

Korn, Bertram W. *The Early Jews of New Orleans.* Waltham, Mass.: American Jewish Historical Society, 1969.

Kraemer, David. *Reading the Rabbis: The Talmud as Literature.* New York: Oxford University Press, 1996.

Krohn, Paysach J. *Bris Milah: Circumcision—The Covenant of Abraham.* Brooklyn: Mesorah, 1985.

Kunin, Samuel. "A Case for the Gomco Clamp." *Berit Mila Newsletter* 7 (1995): 13–15. Available online at: http://beritmila.org/bmnews7.html.

Lamott, Anne. *Operating Instructions: A Journal of My Son's First Year.* New York: Fawcett Columbine, 1993.

Landes, Daniel, and Sheryl Robbin. "Gainful Pain." *Tikkun* 5, 5 (September-October 1990): 72–74.

Lane Fox, Robin. *The Unauthorized Version: Truth and Fiction in the Bible.* New York: Knopf, 1992.

Langmuir, Gavin I. *Toward a Definition of Antisemitism.* Berkeley: University of California Press, 1990.

Lannon, Carole M., Ann G. D. Bailey, et al. "Circumcision Debate." *Pediatrics* 105, 3 (March 2000): 641–42.

———. "Circumcision Policy Statement." *Pediatrics* 103, 3 (March 1999): 686–92.

Laumann, Edward O., Christopher M. Masi, and Ezra W. Zuckerman. "Circumcision in the United States: Prevalence, Prophylactic Effects, and Sexual Practice." In *Sex, Love, and Health in America,* ed. Edward O. Laumann and Robert T. Michael. Chicago: University of Chicago Press, 2001.

Leavitt, Judith W. *Brought to Bed: Childbearing in America, 1750–1950.* New York: Oxford University Press, 1986.

Lederhendler, Eli. *Jewish Responses to Modernity: New Voices in America and Eastern Europe.* New York: New York University Press, 1994.

Lefkovits, Isaac B. *An Analytical Discussion Regarding the Gumco Clamp [sic].* New York, 1953.

Legman, G. [Gershon]. *No Laughing Matter: An Analysis of Sexual Humor,* 2 vols. Bloomington: Indiana University Press, 1982.

Lehman, Mark J. "A Plea for Circumcision." *Medical Review* 28 (1893): 64–65.

Leiter, Elliot, and Albert M. Lefkovits. "Circumcision and Penile Carcinoma." *New York State Journal of Medicine* 75 (1975): 1520–22.

Levenson, Jon D. *The Death and Resurrection of the Beloved Son: The Transformation of Child Sacrifice in Judaism and Christianity*. New Haven: Yale University Press, 1993.
——. "The New Enemies of Circumcision." *Commentary* 109, 3 (March 2000): 29–36.
Levien, Harry. "Circumcision—Dangers of Unclean Surgery." *Medical Record* (New York) 46 (1894): 619–21.
Levinson, Robert E. *Jews in the California Gold Rush*. New York: Ktav, 1978.
Levit, Eugen. *Die Circumcision der Israeliten beleuchtet vom ärtzlichen und humanen Standpunkte von einem altern Artze*. Vienna: Carl Gerold's Sohn, 1874.
Lewis, Bernard. *The Jews of Islam*. Princeton, N.J.: Princeton University Press, 1984.
Liberles, Robert. *Religious Conflict in Social Context: The Resurgence of Orthodox Judaism in Frankfurt am Main, 1838–1877*. Westport, Conn.: Greenwood Press, 1985.
Lieberman, Dale. *Witness to the Covenant of Circumcision: Bris Milah*. Northvale, N.J.: Aronson, 1997.
Liebman, Seymour B. *The Jews in New Spain: Faith, Flame, and the Inquisition*. Coral Gables. Fla.: University of Miami Press, 1970.
Linder, Amnon, trans. and ed. *The Jews in the Legal Sources of the Early Middle Ages*. Detroit: Wayne State University Press, 1997.
——. *The Jews in Roman Imperial Legislation*. Detroit: Wayne State University Press, 1987.
Lipman, V. D. *A History of the Jews in Britain Since 1858*. New York: Holmes and Meier, 1990.
——. *The Jews of Medieval Norwich*. London: Jewish Historical Society of England, 1967.
——. *Social History of the Jews in England, 1850–1950*. London: Watts, 1954.
Luther, Martin. "The Christian in Society, II." In *Luther's Works*, vol. 45, trans. and ed. Walther I. Brandt. Philadelphia: Muhlenberg, 1962.
——. "The Christian in Society, IV." In *Luther's Works*, vol. 47, ed. Franklin Sherman, trans. Martin H. Bertram. Philadelphia: Fortress, 1971.
——. "Lectures on Genesis, Chapters 15–20." In *Luther's Works*, vol. 3, ed. Jaroslav Pelikan, trans. George V. Schick. St. Louis, Mo.: Concordia, 1961.
MacDonald, Robert. "The Frightful Consequences of Onanism: Notes on the History of a Delusion." *Journal of the History of Ideas* 28 (1967): 423–31.
Maimonides, Moses. *The Guide of the Perplexed*. Trans. and ed. Shlomo Pines. Chicago: University of Chicago Press, 1963.
Malamba, S. S., H. U. Wagner, et al. "Risk Factors for HIV-1 Infection in Adults in a Rural Ugandan Community: A Case-Control Study." *AIDS* 8, 2 (February 1994): 253–57.
Malamud, Bernard. *The Tenants*. New York: Farrar, Straus and Giroux, 1971.
Malka, Raphael. "Rabbi Malka's Brit Milah Page—Mazel Tov." Available online at: http://look.net/ForYou/malka (October 24, 1998).
Mantegazza, Paolo. *The Sexual Relations of Mankind*. Trans. Samuel Putnam. New York: Eugenics, 1938.
Marder, Janet. "Judaism in the '90s: All the News That's Fit to Print." *Berit Mila Newsletter* 5, 1 (December 1992). Available online at: http://beritmila.org/bmnews5.html.

Marder, Sheldon. "Flexibility, Rigidity, and Ethical Issues in Berit Mila." *Berit Mila Newsletter* 5, 1 (December 1992). Available online at: http://beritmila.org/bmnews5.html.

Mark, Elizabeth Wyner, ed. *The Covenant of Circumcision: New Perspectives on an Ancient Jewish Rite.* Hanover, N.H.: Brandeis University Press/University Press of New England, 2003.

———. "Crossing the Gender Divide: Public Ceremonies, Private Parts, Mixed Feelings." In *The Covenant of Circumcision,* ed. Elizabeth Wyner Mark. Hanover, N.H.: Brandeis University Press/University Press of New England, 2003.

Marshall, Richard E., Fran L. Porter, et al. "Circumcision: II. Effects upon Mother-Infant Interaction." *Early Human Development* 7 (1982): 367–74.

Marshall, Richard E., William C. Stratton, et al., "Circumcision I: Effects upon Newborn Behavior." *Infant Behavior and Development* 3 (1980): 1–14.

Marshall, Victor F. "Should Circumcision of Infant Males Be Routine?" *Medical Record and Annals* 48 (February 1954): 790–92.

McCarthy, Mary, and Philip Roth. "An Exchange." *New Yorker,* December 28, 1998/January 4, 1999, 98–99.

McGrath, Ken. "The Frenular Delta: A New Preputial Structure." In *Understanding Circumcision,* ed. George C. Denniston, Frederick Mansfield Hodges, and Marilyn Fayre Milos. New York: Kluwer Academic/Plenum, 2001.

Mehta, Depak. "Circumcision, Body, Masculinity." In *Violence and Subjectivity,* ed. Veena Das, Arthur Kleinman, et al. Berkeley: University of California Press, 2000.

Meisel, Barry. "Neonatal Circumcision and Dorsal Penile Nerve Block." *Berit Mila Newsletter* 2, 1 (October 1989). Available online at http://beritmila.org/bmnews2.html.

Mellinkoff, Ruth. *The Mark of Cain.* Berkeley: University of California Press, 1981.

Mendes-Flohr, Paul, and Jehuda Reinharz, eds. *The Jew in the Modern World: A Documentary History.* 2nd ed. New York: Oxford University Press, 1995.

Meyer, David J. "Doing It Myself." *Moment* 17 (February 1992): 45.

Meyer, Michael A. "Alienated Intellectuals in the Camp of Religious Reform: The Frankfurt Reformfreunde, 1842–1845." *AJS Review* 6 (1981): 61–86.

———. "'Most of My Brethren Find Me Unacceptable': The Controversial Career of Rabbi Samuel Holdheim." *Jewish Social Studies,* 9, 3 (2003): 1–19.

———. *Response to Modernity: A History of the Reform Movement in Judaism.* New York: Oxford University Press, 1988.

Miller, Geoffrey P. "Circumcision: Cultural-Legal Analysis." *Virginia Journal of Social Policy and the Law* 9 (2002): 497–585.

Milos, Marilyn Fayre. "Infant Circumcision: What I Wish I Had Known." *Truth Seeker* 1, 3 (July–August 1989): 3.

Milos, Marilyn Fayre, and Donna R. Macris. "Circumcision: Male—Effects upon Human Sexuality." In *Human Sexuality: An Encyclopedia,* ed. Vern L. Bullough and Bonnie Bullough. New York: Garland, 1994.

———. "Circumcision: A Medical or a Human Rights Issue?" *Journal of Nurse-Midwifery* 37, 2 (suppl.) (March-April 1992): 87S-96S.

Montaigne, Michel Eyquem de. *The Complete Works of Montaigne.* Trans. Donald M. Frame. Stanford: Stanford University Press, 1958.

Morgan, William K. C. "The Rape of the Phallus." *Journal of the American Medical Association* 193 (July 19, 1965): 223–24.

Morgenstern, Julian. *Rites of Birth, Marriage, Death and Kindred Occasions among the Semites*. Chicago: Quadrangle Books, 1966.

Moscucci, Ornella. "Clitoridectomy, Circumcision, and the Politics of Sexual Pleasure in Mid-Victorian Britain." In *Sexualities in Victorian Britain*, ed. Andrew H. Miller and James Eli Adams. Bloomington: Indiana University Press, 1996.

Moses, M. J. "The Value of Circumcision as a Hygienic and Therapeutic Measure." *New York Medical Journal* 14, 4 (October 1871): 368–74.

Mosse, George L. "Jewish Emancipation: Between *Bildung* and Respectability." In *The Jewish Response to German Culture*, ed. Jehuda Reinharz and Walter Schatzberg. Hanover, N.H.: University Press of New England, 1985.

Müller, Alphons Victor. *Die "hochheilige Vorhaut Christi" im Kult und in der Theologie der Papstkirche*. Berlin: C. A. Schwetschke, 1907.

Nadler, Steven. *Spinoza: A Life*. Cambridge: Cambridge University Press, 1999.

Netanyahu, B. *The Origins of the Inquisition in Fifteenth Century Spain*. New York: Random House, 1995.

Neuman, R. P. "Masturbation, Madness, and the Modern Concepts of Childhood and Adolescence." *Journal of Social History* 8 (spring 1975): 1–27.

Neusner, Jacob. *The Enchantments of Judaism: Rites of Transformation from Birth Through Death*. New York: Basic Books, 1987.

———. *Introduction to Rabbinic Literature*. New York: Doubleday, 1994.

———. *Invitation to the Talmud*. Rev. ed. New York: Harper and Row, 1984.

———. *The Mishnah: A New Translation*. New Haven: Yale University Press, 1988.

———, trans. *The Talmud of Babylonia: An American Translation*. No. 251, vol. 13B: *Yebamot*, chaps. 4–6. Atlanta: Scholars, 1992.

———, trans. *The Talmud of Babylonia: An American Translation*. No. 275, vol. 2E: *Shabbat*, chaps. 18–24. Atlanta: Scholars, 1993.

———, trans. and ed. *Genesis Rabbah: The Judaic Commentary to the Book of Genesis. A New American Translation*. 3 vols. Atlanta: Scholars, 1985.

Newman, Samuel E. "A Circumcision Operation for the Young." *Journal of the American Medical Association* 53 (1909): 1737–38.

Novick, Peter. *The Holocaust in American Life*. Boston: Houghton Mifflin, 1999.

Nunn, John F. *Ancient Egyptian Medicine*. London: British Museum Press, 1996.

O'Hara, K., and J. O'Hara. "The Effect of Male Circumcision on the Sexual Enjoyment of the Female Partner." *BJU International* 83, suppl. 1 (January 1999): 79–84.

Ollivier, Debra S. "Circumcision in America." *Salon*, pts. 1 and 2, October 26 and 27, 1998. Available online at: http://www.salon.com/mwt/feature/1998/10/26feature.html.

Paige, Karen Ericksen, and Jeffery M. Paige. *The Politics of Reproductive Ritual*. Berkeley: University of California Press, 1981.

Parsons, Gail Pat. "Equal Treatment for All: American Medical Remedies for Male Sexual Problems, 1850–1900." *Journal of the History of Medicine* 32 (1977): 55–71.

Pass, M. D. "Should Circumcision Be Abolished?" *Medical World* 33, 6 (June 1915): 227.

Patel, Daksha A., Emalee G. Flaherty, and Judith Dunn. "Factors Affecting the Practice of Circumcision." *American Journal of Diseases of Children* 136 (1982): 634–36.

Patel, H. I., K. P. Moriarty, et al. "Genitourinary Injuries in the Newborn." *Journal of Pediatric Surgery* 36 (January 2001): 235–39.

Patterson, James T. *The Dread Disease: Cancer and Modern American Culture.* Cambridge, Mass.: Harvard University Press, 1987.

Peletz, Michael G. *Reason and Passion: Representations of Gender in a Malay Society.* Berkeley: University of California Press, 1996.

Peskowitz, Miriam, and Laura Levitt, eds. *Judaism Since Gender.* New York: Routledge, 1997.

Pharr, Clyde, trans. and ed. *The Theodosian Code and Novels and the Sirmondian Constitution.* Princeton, N.J.: Princeton University Press, 1952.

Philipson, David. *The Reform Movement in Judaism.* Rev. ed. New York: Macmillan, 1931.

———. *Samuel Holdheim, Jewish Reformer 1806–1860.* Paper presented at the annual meeting of the Central Conference of American Rabbis, Indianapolis, July 4, 1906.

Philo. *Questions and Answers on Genesis.* Suppl. 1. Trans. Ralph Marcus. Cambridge, Mass.: Harvard University Press, 1953.

———. "The Special Laws." In *Philo,* vol. 7, trans. F. H. Colson. Cambridge, Mass.: Harvard University Press, 1937.

Plaskow, Judith. *Standing Again at Sinai: Judaism from a Feminist Perspective.* New York: HarperCollins, 1990.

Plaut, Alfred, and Alice C. Kohn-Speyer. "The Carcinogenic Action of Smegma." *Science* 105 (1947): 391–92.

Plaut, W. Gunther. *The Rise of Reform Judaism.* New York: World Union for Progressive Judaism, 1963.

Plotsky, P. M., C. C. Bradley, and K. J. S. Anand. "Behavioral and Neurological Consequences of Neonatal Stress." In *Pain in Neonates,* ed. K. J. S. Anand, B. J. Stevens, and P. J. McGrath. 2nd rev. and enl. ed. Amsterdam: Elsevier, 2000.

Poland, Ronald L. "The Question of Routine Neonatal Circumcision." *New England Journal of Medicine* 322 (1990): 1312–15.

Pope, Alexander. *The Prose Works of Alexander Pope.* Vol. 1. Ed. Norman Ault. Oxford: Blackwell, 1936.

Porter, Fran Lang, Richard H. Miller, and Richard E. Marshall. "Neonatal Pain Cries: Effect of Circumcision on Acoustic Features and Perceived Urgency." *Child Development* 57 (1986): 790–802.

Porter, Roy, and Lesley Hall. *The Facts of Life: The Creation of Sexual Knowledge in Britain, 1650–1950.* New Haven: Yale University Press, 1995.

Preston, E. Noel. "Whither the Foreskin? A Consideration of Routine Neonatal Circumcision." *Journal of the American Medical Association* 213 (September 14, 1970): 1853–58.

Price, Christopher. "Male Non-Therapeutic Circumcision." In *Male and Female Circumcision*, ed. George C. Denniston, Frederick Mansfield Hodges, and Marilyn Fayre Milos. New York: Kluwer Academic/Plenum, 1999.

Proctor, Robert N. *Cancer Wars: How Politics Shapes What We Know and Don't Know About Cancer*. New York: Basic Books, 1995.

Ragins, Sanford. "*Berit Mila* and the Origins of Reform Judaism." In *Berit Mila in the Reform Context*, ed. Lewis M. Barth. Los Angeles: Berit Mila Board of Reform Judaism, 1990.

Ragusa, Isa, and Rosalie B. Green, eds. *Meditations on the Life of Christ*. Trans. Isa Ragusa. Princeton, N.J.: Princeton University Press, 1961.

Ragussis, Michael. *Figures of Conversion: "The Jewish Question" & English National Identity*. Durham, N.C.: Duke University Press, 1995.

Raul-Friedman, Esther. "A Rebuttal—Circumcision: A Jewish Legacy." *Midstream* 38 (May 1992): 31–33.

Ravich, Abraham. "Circumcision as a Cancer Preventive." *National Jewish Monthly* (December 1966): 14, 43–46.

———. *Preventing V.D. and Cancer by Circumcision*. New York: Philosophical Library, 1973.

———. "The Relationship of Circumcision to Cancer of the Prostate." *Journal of Urology* 48 (September 1942): 298–99.

Ravich, Abraham, and R. A. Ravich. "Prophylaxis of Cancer of the Prostate, Penis, and Cervix by Circumcision." *New York State Journal of Medicine* 51 (1951): 519–20.

Reik, Theodor. "The Puberty Rites of Savages." In *Ritual: Psycho-Analytic Studies*. New York: Farrar, Straus, 1946.

Remondino, Peter C. "Circumcision and Its Opponents." *American Journal of Dermatology and Genito-Urinary Diseases* 6 (March 1902): 65–73.

———. *History of Circumcision from the Earliest Times to the Present. Moral and Physical Reasons for Its Performance*. Philadelphia: F. A. Davis, 1891.

Reuben, Mark S. "Ritual Circumcision." *New York Medical Journal* 105 (April 14, 1917): 688–90.

Reynolds, R. D. "Use of the Mogen Clamp for Neonatal Circumcision." *American Family Physician* 54 (1996): 177–82.

Reynolds, Steven J., Mary E. Shepherd, et al. "Male Circumcision and Risk of HIV-1 and Other Sexually Transmitted Infections in India." *Lancet* 363 (2004): 1039–40.

Richards, M. P. M., J. F. Bernal, and Yvonne Brackbill. "Early Behavioral Differences: Gender or Circumcision?" *Developmental Psychobiology* 9, 1 (January 1976): 89–95.

Richler, Mordecai. *The Apprenticeship of Duddy Kravitz*. London: Valentine, Mitchell, 1972.

Ritter, Thomas J., and George C. Denniston. *Doctors Re-examine Circumcision*. Seattle: Third Millenium, 2002.

Robinson, Bernard P. "Zipporah to the Rescue: A Contextual Study of Exodus IV 24–6." *Vetus Testamentum* 36, 4 (1986): 447–61.

Roger, Robin. "The Pagan Phallus." In *Writing Our Way Home: Contemporary Stories by American Jewish Writers*, ed. Ted Solotaroff and Nessa Rapoport. New York: Schocken, 1992.

Róheim, Géza. *The Eternal Ones of the Dream: A Psychoanalytic Interpretation of Australian Myth and Ritual*. New York: International Universities Press, 1945.

Romberg, Henry C. *Bris Milah: A Book About the Jewish Ritual of Circumcision*. New York: Feldheim, 1982.

Roth, Ann Macy. *Egyptian Phyles in the Old Kingdom: The Evolution of a System of Social Organization*. Chicago: Oriental Institute, University of Chicago, 1991.

Roth, Cecil. *Essays and Portraits in Anglo-Jewish History*. Philadelphia: Jewish Publication Society, 1962.

Roth, Joel. "The Meaning for Today." *Moment* 17 (February 1992): 41–44.

Roth, Philip. *The Counterlife*. New York: Farrar, Straus and Giroux, 1987.

Rubin, Nissan. "*Brit Milah*: A Study of Change in Custom." In *Covenant of Circumcision*, ed. Elizabeth Wyner Mark. Hanover, N.H.: Brandeis University Press/University Press of New England, 2003.

Saperstein, Marc. *Decoding the Rabbis: A Thirteenth-Century Commentary on the Aggadah*. Cambridge, Mass.: Harvard University Press, 1980.

Sasson, Jack M. "Circumcision in the Ancient Near East." *Journal of Biblical Literature* 85 (1966): 473–76.

Sayre, Lewis A. "On the Deleterious Results of a Narrow Prepuce and Preputial Adhesions." Reprinted from *Transactions of the Ninth International Medical Congress*, vol. 3 (1887). Philadelphia: Wm. F. Fell, 1888.

———. "Partial Paralysis from Reflex Irritation, Caused by Congenital Phimosis and Adherent Prepuce." Extracted from *Transactions of the American Medical Association* 21 (1870): 205–11. Philadelphia: Collins, 1870.

———. "Spinal Anaemia with Partial Paralysis and Want of Coordination, from Irritation of the Genital Organs." *Transactions of the American Medical Association* 26 (1875): 255–74.

Schachter, Lifsa. "Reflections on the Brit Mila Ceremony." *Conservative Judaism* 38 (summer 1986): 38–41.

Schachter-Shalomi, Zalman. "How to Deal with a Jewish Issue: Circumcision." In *A Mensch Among Men: Explorations in Jewish Masculinity*, ed. Harry Brod. Freedom, Calif.: Crossing, 1988.

Schäfer, Peter. *Judeophobia: Attitudes Toward the Jews in the Ancient World*. Cambridge, Mass.: Harvard University Press, 1997.

Schiffman, Lawrence H. *Who Was a Jew? Rabbinic and Halakhic Perspectives on the Jewish-Christian Schism*. Hoboken, N.J.: Ktav, 1985.

Schlosberg, Charles. "Thirty Years of Ritual Circumcision." *Clinical Pediatrics* 10, 4 (April 1971): 205–9.

Schloss, Marc R. *The Hatchet's Blood: Separation, Power, and Gender in Ehing Social Life*. Tucson: University of Arizona Press, 1988.

Schoen, Edgar J. "The Circumcision Decision: On the Cutting Edge." *Moment* 22 (October 1997): 44–46, 68–69.

————. "It's Wise to Circumcise: Time to Change Policy." *Pediatrics* 111, 6 (June 2003): 1490–91.

————. "Neonatal Circumcision and Penile Cancer." *British Medical Journal* 313 (July 6, 1996): 46.

————. "The Status of Circumcision of Newborns." *New England Journal of Medicine* 322 (1990): 1308–12.

————. "Urologists and Circumcision of Newborns." *Urology* 40 (1992): 99–101.

Schoen, Edgar J., Glen Anderson, et al. "Report of the Task Force on Circumcision." *Pediatrics* 84, 4 (August 1989): 388–91.

Schoen, Edgar J., Christopher J. Colby, and G. Thomas Ray. "Newborn Circumcision Decreases Incidence and Costs of Urinary Tract Infections During the First Year of Life." *Pediatrics* 105, 4 (April 2000): 789–93.

Schoen, Edgar J., Michael Oehrli, et al. "The Highly Protective Effect of Newborn Circumcision Against Invasive Penile Cancer." *Pediatrics* 105, 3 (March 2000): Abstract e36, 627–28.

Schoen, Edgar J., Thomas E. Wiswell, and Stephen Moses. "New Policy on Circumcision—Cause for Concern." *Pediatrics* 105, 3 (March 2000): 620–23.

————. "Reply to Carole M. Lannon and the Task Force on Circumcision." *Pediatrics* 108, 1 (July 2001): 211.

Scholem, Gershom G. *Major Trends in Jewish Mysticism.* 3rd ed. New York: Schocken, 1954.

Schreckenberg, Heinz. *The Jews in Christian Art: An Illustrated History.* New York: Continuum, 1996.

Scott, Steve. "The Anatomy and Physiology of the Human Prepuce." In *Male and Female Circumcision*, ed. George C. Denniston, Frederick Mansfield Hodges, and Marilyn Fayre Milos. New York: Kluwer Academic/Plenum, 1999.

Segal, Alan F. *Paul the Convert: The Apostolate and Apostasy of Saul the Pharisee.* New Haven: Yale University Press, 1990.

Seltzer, Robert M., and Norman J. Cohen. *The Americanization of the Jews.* New York: New York University Press, 1995.

Shapiro, Edward S. *A Time for Healing: American Jewry Since World War II.* Baltimore: Johns Hopkins University Press, 1992.

Shapiro, James. *Shakespeare and the Jews.* New York: Columbia University Press, 1996.

Sharfman, I. Harold. *The First Rabbi: Origins of Conflict Between Orthodox and Reform.* Malibu, Calif.: Joseph Simon/Pangloss, 1988.

Shell, Marc. "The Holy Foreskin; or, Money, Relics, and Judeo-Christianity." In *Jews and Other Differences: The New Jewish Cultural Studies*, ed. Jonathan Boyarin and Daniel Boyarin. Minneapolis: University of Minnesota Press, 1997.

Shell-Duncan, Bettina, and Ylva Hernlund, eds. *Female "Circumcision" in Africa: Culture, Controversy, and Change.* Boulder, Colo.: Lynne Rienner, 2000.

Sherman, J., J. G. Borer, et al. "Circumcision: Successful Glanular Reconstruction and Survival Following Traumatic Amputation." *Journal of Urology* 156, 2, pt. 2 (August 1996): 842–44.

Shields, Yehudi Pesach. "The Making of Metzitzah." *Tradition* 13 (summer 1972): 36–48.

Shorter, Edward. *From Paralysis to Fatigue: A History of Psychosomatic Illness in the Modern Era.* New York: Free Press, 1992.

Siegfried, N., M. Muller, et al. "Male Circumcision for Prevention of Heterosexual Acquisition of HIV in Men." (Cochrane Review.) *Cochrane Library*, iss. 3, July 21, 2003.

Silverman, Judy. *Rosie and the Mole: The Story of a Bris.* Illus. Katherine Janus Kahn. New York: Pitspopany, 1999.

Simes, J. Henry C. "Circumcision." *Annals of Gynaecology and Paediatry* (Philadelphia) 4 (1890–91): 374–83.

Singer, Suzanne F. "The Pain and the Pleasure." *Moment* 17 (February 1992): 38–40.

Sivulka, Juliann. *Stronger Than Dirt: A Cultural History of Advertising Personal Hygiene in America, 1875 to 1940.* Amherst, N.Y.: Humanity, 2001.

Smallwood, E. Mary. *The Jews Under Roman Rule: From Pompey to Diocletian.* 2nd ed. Leiden: Brill, 1981.

Smith, Frank R. "Nationality and Carcinoma of the Cervix." *American Journal of Obstetrics and Gynecology* 41 (1941): 424–29.

Smith, Steven B. *Spinoza, Liberalism, and the Question of Jewish Identity.* New Haven: Yale University Press, 1997.

Snowman, Leonard V. "Circumcision." In *Encyclopaedia Judaica*, vol. 5, cols. 567–76. Jerusalem: Keter, 1971.

Snyder, James L. "The Problem of Circumcision in America." *Truth Seeker* 1, 3 (July-August 1989): 39–42.

———. "Testimony Against Circumcision." (California Medical Association, March 4, 1989.) *Truth Seeker* 1, 3 (July-August 1989): 51.

Somerville, Margaret. *The Ethical Canary: Science, Society, and the Human Spirit.* Toronto: Viking, 2000.

Sorin, Gerald. *Tradition Transformed: The Jewish Experience in America.* Baltimore: Johns Hopkins University Press, 1997.

Sorkin, David. *The Transformation of German Jewry, 1780–1840.* New York: Oxford University Press, 1987.

Sorsby, Maurice. *Cancer and Race: A Study of the Incidence of Cancer Among Jews.* London: J. Bale, Sons & Danielsson, 1931.

Spinoza, Benedict de. *The Political Works.* Trans. and ed. A. G. Wernham. Oxford: Clarendon Press, 1965.

Steinberg, Leo. *The Sexuality of Christ in Renaissance Art and in Modern Oblivion.* 2nd ed. Chicago: University of Chicago Press, 1996.

Stengers, Jean, and Anne Van Neck. *Masturbation: The History of a Great Terror.* Trans. Kathryn A. Hoffmann. New York: Palgrave, 2001.

Stern, Josef. "Maimonides on the Covenant of Circumcision and the Unity of God." In *The Midrashic Imagination: Jewish Exegesis, Thought, and History*, ed. Michael Fishbane. Albany: State University of New York Press, 1993.

Stern, Menahem. *Greek and Latin Authors on Jews and Judaism.* 3 vols. Jerusalem: Israel Academy of Sciences, 1974–84.

Stern, Sacha. *Jewish Identity in Early Rabbinic Writings.* Leiden: Brill, 1994.

Sterne, Laurence. *The Life and Opinions of Tristram Shandy, Gentleman.* Ed. Melvyn New and Joan New. London: Penguin Books, 1997.

Stone, T. Ritchie. "Circumcision." *Maryland Medical Journal* 34, 9 (1895): 145–54.

Sukenick, Ronald. *Mosaic Man.* Normal, Ill.: FC2, 1999.

Sumption, Jonathan. *Pilgrimage: An Image of Mediaeval Religion.* London: Faber and Faber, 1975.

Svoboda, J. Steven. "Attaining International Acknowledgment of Male Genital Mutilation as a Human Rights Violation." In *Male and Female Circumcision*, ed. George C. Denniston, Frederick Mansfield Hodges, and Marilyn Fayre Milos. New York: Kluwer Academic/Plenum, 1999.

Svoboda, J. Steven, Robert S. Van Howe, and James G. Dwyer. "Informed Consent for Neonatal Circumcision: An Ethical and Legal Conundrum." *Journal of Contemporary Health Law and Policy* 17 (2000): 61–133.

Szajkowski, Zosa. "Jewish Religious Observance During the French Revolution of 1789." In *Jews and the French Revolutions of 1789, 1830, and 1848.* New York: Ktav, 1970.

Taddio, Anna, Joel Katz, et al. "Effect of Neonatal Circumcision on Pain Response during Subsequent Routine Vaccination." *Lancet* 349 (1997): 599–603.

Taylor, J. R., A. P. Lockwood, and A. J. Taylor. "The Prepuce: Specialized Mucosa of the Penis and Its Loss to Circumcision." *British Journal of Urology* 77 (1996): 291–95.

Taylor, R. W. "On the Question of the Transmission of Syphilitic Contagion in the Rite of Circumcision." *New York Medical Journal* 18 (December 1873): 561–82.

Terris, Milton, and Margaret C. Oalmann. "Carcinoma of the Cervix." *Journal of the American Medical Association* 174 (1960): 1847–51.

Terris, Milton, Fitzpatrick Wilson, and James Nelson, Jr. "Relation of Circumcision to Cancer of the Cervix." *American Journal of Obstetrics and Gynecology* 117, 8 (1973): 1056–66.

Thomas Aquinas, Saint. *Summa Theologiae.* Vol. 57, *Baptism and Confirmation.* Trans. James J. Cunningham. London: Blackfriars, 1975.

Thompson, H. C., L. R. King, et al. "Report of the Ad Hoc Task Force on Circumcision." *Pediatrics* 56, 4 (October 1975): 610–11.

Thompson, J. L. "So Ridiculous a Sign: Men, Women, and the Lessons of Circumcision in Sixteenth-Century Exegesis." *Archiv für Reformationsgeschichte* 86 (1995): 236–56.

T. J. M. and Isaac Leeser. "An Act of Faith, at Augusta, Georgia." *Occident and American Jewish Advocate* 5, 7 (October 1847). Available online at: www.jewish-history.com/Occident/volume5/Oct1847/augusta.html.

Tobias, Henry J. *A History of the Jews in New Mexico.* Albuquerque: University of New Mexico Press, 1990.

Tooker, Robert N. *All About the Baby and Preparations for Its Advent: A Book for Mothers.* Chicago: Rand, McNally, 1896.

Trachtenberg, Joshua. *The Devil and the Jews.* New Haven: Yale University Press, 1943.

Trier, Salomon Abraham, ed. *Rabbinische Gutachten über die Beschneidung*. Frankfurt: Bach, 1844.

Turner, Victor. "*Mukanda*: The Rite of Circumcision." In *The Forest of Symbols: Aspects of Ndembu Ritual*. Ithaca: Cornell University Press, 1967.

Van Howe, Robert S. "Anaesthesia for Circumcision: A Review of the Literature." In *Male and Female Circumcision*, ed. George C. Denniston, Frederick Mansfield Hodges, and Marilyn Fayre Milos. New York: Kluwer Academic/Plenum, 1999.

———. "Circumcision and HIV Infection: Review of the Literature and Meta-Analysis." *International Journal of STD and AIDS* 10 (January 1999): 8–16.

———. "Does Circumcision Influence Sexually Transmitted Diseases?: A Literature Review." *BJU International* 83, suppl. 1 (January 1999): 52–62.

———. "Neonatal Circumcision and HIV Infection." In *Male and Female Circumcision*, ed. George C. Denniston, Frederick Mansfield Hodges, and Marilyn Fayre Milos. New York: Kluwer Academic/Plenum, 1999.

———. "Peer-Review Bias Regarding Circumcision in American Medical Publishing: Subverting the Dominant Paradigm." In *Male and Female Circumcision*, ed. George C. Denniston, Frederick Mansfield Hodges, and Marilyn Fayre Milos. New York: Kluwer Academic/Plenum, 1999.

———. "Why Does Neonatal Circumcision Persist in the United States?" In *Sexual Mutilations*, ed. George C. Denniston and Marilyn Fayre Milos. New York: Plenum, 1997.

Van Howe, R. S., J. S. Svoboda, J. G. Dwyer, and C. P. Price. "Involuntary Circumcision: The Legal Issues." *BJU International* 83, suppl. 1 (January 1999): 63–73.

Vineberg, Hiram M. "Etiology of Cancer of the Pelvic Organs." *American Journal of Obstetrics and Gynecology* 53 (1906): 410–19.

Walco, Gary A., Robert C. Cassidy, and Neil L. Schechter. "Pain, Hurt, and Harm: The Ethics of Pain Control in Infants and Children." *New England Journal of Medicine* 331, 8 (August 1994): 541–44.

Waldeck, Sarah E. "Social Norm Theory and Male Circumcision: Why Parents Circumcise." *American Journal of Bioethics* 3, 2 (spring 2003): 56–57.

———. "Using Male Circumcision to Understand Social Norms as Multipliers." *University of Cincinnati Law Review* 72, 2 (winter 2003): 455–526.

Wallerstein, Edward. *Circumcision: An American Health Fallacy*. New York: Springer, 1980.

———. "Circumcision: Information, Misinformation, Disinformation." In *Male and Female Circumcision*, ed. George C. Denniston, Frederick Mansfield Hodges, and Marilyn Fayre Milos. New York: Kluwer Academic/Plenum, 1999.

Wan, Julian. "GOMCO Circumcision Clamp: An Enduring and Unexpected Success." *Urology* 59 (May 2002): 790–94.

Waxman, Chaim I. *Jewish Baby Boomers: A Communal Perspective*. Albany: State University of New York Press, 2001.

Weiss, Charles. "Ritual Circumcision: Comments on Current Practices in American Hospitals." *Clinical Pediatrics* 1 (October 1962): 65–72.

———. "Routine Non-Ritual Circumcision in Infancy: A New Look at an Old Operation." *Clinical Pediatrics* 3 (September 1964): 560–63.

————. "A Worldwide Survey of the Current Practice of Milah (Ritual Circumcision)." *Jewish Social Studies* 24 (January 1962): 30–48.

Weiss, Gerald N. "The Jews Contribution to Medicine [*sic*]." *Medical Times* 96 (August 1968): 797–802.

————. "Neonatal Circumcision." *Southern Medical Journal* 78 (1985): 1198–2000.

————. "Prophylactic Neonatal Surgery and Infectious Diseases." *Pediatric Infectious Disease Journal* 16 (1997): 727–34.

Weiss, Gerald N., and Andrea W. Harter. *Circumcision: Frankly Speaking*. Fort Collins, Colo.: Wiser, 1998.

Weiss, Gerald N., and Elaine B. Weiss. "A Perspective on Controversies over Neonatal Circumcision." *Clinical Pediatrics* 33, 12 (December 1994): 726–30.

Wertheimer, Jack. *A People Divided: Judaism in Contemporary America*. New York: HarperCollins, 1993.

Wertz, Richard W., and Dorothy C. Wertz. *Lying-In: A History of Childbirth in America*. 2nd ed. New Haven: Yale University Press, 1989.

Whittaker, Molly. *Jews and Christians: Graeco-Roman Views*. Cambridge: Cambridge University Press, 1984.

Wiener, Max, ed. *Abraham Geiger and Liberal Judaism*. Trans. E. J. Schlochauer. Philadelphia: Jewish Publication Society, 1962.

Wilkowski, Susan. *Baby's Bris*. Illus. Judith Friedman. Rockville, Md.: Kar-Ben, 1999.

Williams, A. U. "Circumcision." *Medical Standard* (Chicago) 6 (1889): 138–39.

Williams, George L. "Significance and Function of Preputial Langerhans Cells." In *Male and Female Circumcision*, ed. George C. Denniston, Frederick Mansfield Hodges, and Marilyn Fayre Milos. New York: Kluwer Academic/Plenum, 1999.

Williams, N., and L. Kapila. "Complications of Circumcision." *British Journal of Surgery* 80 (October 1993): 1231–36.

Wine, Sherwin. "Circumcision." *Humanistic Judaism* 16 (summer 1988): 4–8.

Winkelmann, R. K. "The Cutaneous Innervation of Human Newborn Prepuce." *Journal of Investigative Dermatology* 26 (1956): 53–67.

Wiswell, Thomas E. "Circumcision Circumspection." *New England Journal of Medicine* 336 (1997): 1244–45.

————. "Circumcision—An Update." *Current Problems in Pediatrics* 22 (1992): 424–31.

————. "The Prepuce, Urinary Tract Infections, and the Consequences." *Pediatrics* 105, 4 (April 2000): 860–62.

Wiswell, Thomas E., and Dietrich W. Geschke. "Risks from Circumcision during the First Month of Life Compared with Those for Uncircumcised Boys." *Pediatrics* 83, 6 (June, 1989): 1011–15.

Wiswell, Thomas E., and John D. Roscelli. "Corroborative Evidence for the Decreased Incidence of Urinary Tract Infections in Circumcised Male Infants." *Pediatrics* 78, 1 (July 1986): 96–99.

Wiswell, Thomas E., Franklin R. Smith, and James W. Bass. "Decreased Incidence of Urinary Tract Infections in Circumcised Male Infants." *Pediatrics* 75, 5 (May, 1985): 901–3.

Witchel, Alex. "Bagels, Lox, Lollipops and Smelling Salts." *New York Times*, March 3, 2004, F1–2.

Wolbarst, Abraham L. "Circumcision." In *Encyclopaedia Sexualis*, ed. Victor Robinson. New York: Dingwall-Rock, 1936.

———. "Circumcision and Penile Cancer." *Lancet* 1 (January 16, 1932): 150–53.

———. "Circumcision in Infancy: A Prophylactic and Sanitary Measure." *American Medicine* 32 (1926): 23–29.

———. "Is Circumcision a Prophylactic Against Penis Cancer?" *Cancer* 3 (1925–26): 301–10.

———. "Universal Circumcision as a Sanitary Measure." *Journal of the American Medical Association* 62 (January 10, 1914): 92–97.

Wolfson, Elliot R. *Abraham Abulafia—Kabbalist and Prophet: Hermeneutics, Theosophy, and Theurgy*. Los Angeles: Cherub, 2000.

———. "Circumcision and the Divine Name: A Study in the Transmission of Esoteric Doctrine." *Jewish Quarterly Review* 78 (1987): 77–112.

———. "Circumcision, Vision of God, and Textual Interpretation: From Midrashic Trope to Mystical Symbol." In *Circle in the Square: Studies in the Use of Gender in Kabbalistic Symbolism*. Albany: State University of New York Press, 1995.

———. "Erasing the Erasure/Gender and the Writing of God's Body in Kabbalistic Symbolism." In *Circle in the Square: Studies in the Use of Gender in Kabbalistic Symbolism*. Albany: State University of New York Press, 1995.

———. "Occultation of the Feminine and the Body of Secrecy in Medieval Kabbalah." In *Rending the Veil: Concealment and Secrecy in the History of Religions*, ed. Elliot R. Wolfson. New York: Seven Bridges, 1999.

———. "Re/membering the Covenant: Memory, Forgetfulness, and the Construction of History in the *Zohar*." In *Jewish History and Jewish Memory*, ed. Elisheva Carlebach, John M. Efron, and David N. Myers. Hanover, N.H.: Brandeis University Press/University Press of New England, 1998.

———. *Through a Speculum That Shines: Vision and Imagination in Medieval Jewish Mysticism*. Princeton, N.J.: Princeton University Press, 1994.

Wolper, Roy S. "Circumcision as Polemic in the Jew Bill of 1753: The Cutter Cut?" *Eighteenth-Century Life* 7, 3 (1982): 28–36.

———, ed. *Pieces on the "Jew Bill" (1753)*. Augustan Reprint Society publication no. 217. Los Angeles: William Andrews Clark Memorial Library, 1983.

Wynder, Ernest L., Jerome Cornfield, et al. "A Study of Environmental Factors in Carcinoma of the Cervix." *American Journal of Obstetrics and Gynecology* 68 (1954): 1016–52.

Wynder, Ernst L., Nathan Mantel, and Samuel D. Licklider. "Statistical Considerations on Circumcision and Cervical Cancer." *American Journal of Obstetrics and Gynecology* 79 (1960): 1026–30.

Yellen, H. S. "Bloodless Circumcision of the Newborn." *American Journal of Obstetrics and Gynecology* 30 (1935): 146–47.

Yerushalmi, Yosef Hayim. *From Spanish Court to Italian Ghetto: Isaac Cardoso: A Study in Seventeenth-Century Marranism and Apologetics*. New York: Columbia University Press, 1971.

———. *The Re-education of Marranos in the Seventeenth Century*. Cincinnati: University of Cincinnati Judaic Studies Program, March 26, 1980.

Yovel, Yirmiyahu. *Spinoza and Other Heretics: The Marrano of Reason*. Princeton, N.J.: Princeton University Press, 1989.

Zaslow, David. "Circumcision and *Brit*: They're Not the Same Thing." *Tikkun* 16, 3 (May-June 2001): 49–50.

Zborowski, Mark, and Elizabeth Herzog. *Life Is with People: The Culture of the Shtetl*. New York: Schocken, 1962.

Zimmermann, Frank. "Origin and Significance of the Jewish Rite of Circumcision." *Psychoanalytic Review* 38 (April 1951): 103–12.

The Zohar. Trans. Harry Sperling and Maurice Simon. 2nd ed. 5 vols. London: Soncino, 1984.

Zunz, Leopold. "Gutachten über die Beschneidung" (1844). In *Gesammelte Schriften von Dr. Zunz*, vol. 2. Berlin: Louis Gerschel, 1876.

Index

criticized, 234, 312 nn.3,10
origin of, in USA, 180–81
human papillomavirus (HPV), 315 n.55,
316 n.66
Humanistic Judaism, 231–33
Hutchinson, Jonathan, 154–56, 307 n.14,
308 n.19
Hyam, Ronald, 157, 308 n.20
hymenotomy, proposed, 255

India
British in, 156–57
HIV in, 331 n.4
studies of cervical cancer incidence
in, 194
Isaac, 14, 22, 298 n.5
Isaac ben Yedaiah, 67–69
Isaac, Erich, 19
Ishmael, 14, 245

Jacob, Walter, 231
Jacobi, Abraham, 309 n.40
Jaffé, Julius, 128–29
Jay, Nancy, 27
Jesus, circumcision of, 299 n.20
in late-medieval Christian theology,
93–98
sermons on, 94–95, 103–04
Jesus's foreskin as sacred relic, 96–98
Jewish Americans
attitude of, to circumcision, 8,
215–17, 281
attitude of, to religious ritual,
322 n.6
contemporary, characterized, 216–18
in nineteenth century, 140–47
Jewish Enlightenment (haskalah),
116–18, 125–26
Jewish periodicals, discussion of
circumcision in, 241–49, 250–53
Jewish ritual circumcision (bris/brit)
adult anxiety about, 7–8, 227–28, 232,
233–38, 246, 285 n.12, 326 n.69, 327
n.18
bloodshed required in, 215, 234,
287 n.22
characterized as beneficial medical
procedure, 157–58, 164–68,
184–86
children's books on, 257–58

as commemoration of Abraham's
covenant, 9
compared to circumcision in African
societies, 245, 260
contemporary American versions of,
229–30, 254, 325 n.58
criticized by German-Jewish
physicians, 125–29, 132–34
defended as essential for ethnic survival, 234, 246, 250–51, 261–62
defended by German rabbis, 129–32
defended as medical practice,
134–36, 184–86, 192–93, 247
explanations of, in popular literature,
233–39
in hospitals, 181, 312 n.10
male-centered nature of, 229, 245,
247–48, 254–55
mystical interpretations of, 220–21,
248–49. See also kabbalah
naming of child during, 57–58, 219,
329 n.47
nineteenth-century, described,
170–71
opposed by Jewish American
physicians, 168–70, 178, 312 n.10
origins of, 15–17, 286 n.6
pain of, attitudes toward, 226,
227–28, 232, 242–43
parties accompanying, 230, 254,
294 n.20
photographic volume on, 326 n.69
portrayed in fiction, 258–60
procedure described, 6
as prototype for American medical
practice, 6, 11, 173
religious meaning of, 9, 17–23
rite explained, 56–62
Sabbath regulations for, 46–47
sandek in, 57, 59
Jewish ritual slaughter (shechitah), 98,
102, 259–60, 300 n.34
Job, 70
John Chrysostom, 41
Jones, Edward G., 195
Joshua, 26–27
Jubilees, Book of, 31–32
Judaism, circumcision in. See Jewish
ritual circumcision
Judd, Robin E., 305 n.58

CPSIA information can be obtained
at www.ICGtesting.com
Printed in the USA
FSHW010821271018
53292FS